T0377281

"*Digital Government* provides a comprehensive synthesis of multidisciplinary research on how the Internet, social media, mobile, and big data are reshaping how and what governments do and what differences it makes. Professor Miriam Lips provides an ideal text for courses on government, public administration, or public management."

Professor William H. Dutton,
University of Southern California and Oxford University

"Professor Lips has been at the leading edge of academic and practical understanding of digital change in Government for more than 20 years. Her academic work in Europe on digital identities and on personalised services was ground-breaking. She is a committed educator too as this new book reveals."

Professor John A. Taylor, *Professor Emeritus of Government and Information Management, Caledonian Business School, Glasgow; Honorary Professor, University of Nottingham*

"This book brings clarity to the development of digital government as a cross-disciplinary field. It helps newcomers to the field, but also junior and senior researchers to understand this complex research area. For us as digital government teachers it is what was needed for a long time! A must read."

Dr Ines Mergel, *Professor of Public Administration, University of Konstanz*

"This important book tackles the key topics of digital government and highlights the direct relation between technology and social change. It is a must read for managers in the public sector since every process is being influenced by technology."

Professor Albert Meijer, *Professor of Public Innovation, Utrecht University*

Digital Government

Digital Government: Managing Public Sector Reform in the Digital Era presents a public management perspective on digital government and technology-enabled change in the public sector. It incorporates theoretical and empirical insights to provide students with a broader and deeper understanding of the complex and multidisciplinary nature of digital government initiatives, impacts and implications.

The rise of digital government and its increasingly integral role in many government processes and activities, including overseeing fundamental changes at various levels across government, means that it is no longer perceived as just a technology issue. In this book Miriam Lips provides students with practical approaches and perspectives to better understand digital government. The text also explores emerging issues and barriers as well as strategies to more effectively manage digital government and technology-enabled change in the public sector.

Digital Government is the ideal book for postgraduate students on courses in public administration, public management, public policy, political science and international relations, and e-government. It is also suitable for public service managers who are experiencing the impact of digital technology and data in the public sector.

Miriam Lips is Professor of Digital Government and Programme Director of the new e-Government Master's programme at Victoria University of Wellington's School of Government, New Zealand.

Routledge Masters in Public Management
Edited by Stephen P. Osborne

Routledge Masters in Public Management series is an integrated set of texts. It is intended to form the backbone for the holistic study of the theory and practice of public management – as part of:

- a taught Masters, MBA or MPA course at a university or college,
- a work-based, in-service programme of education and training, or
- a programme of self-guided study.

Each volume stands alone in its treatment of its topic, whether it be strategic management, marketing or procurement and is co-authored by leading specialists in their field. However, all volumes in the series share both a common pedagogy and a common approach to the structure of the text. Key features of all volumes in the series include:

- a critical approach to combining theory with practice which educates its reader, rather than solely teaching him/her a set of skills,
- clear learning objectives for each chapter,
- the use of figures, tables and boxes to highlight key ideas, concepts and skills,
- an annotated bibliography, guiding students in their further reading, and
- a dedicated case study in the topic of each volume, to serve as a focus for discussion and learning.

Marketing Management and Communications in the Public Sector
Martial Pasquier and Jean-Patrick Villeneuve

Contracting for Public Services
Carsten Greve

Managing Change and Innovation in Public Service Organizations
Stephen P. Osborne and Kerry Brown

Digital Government
Managing Public Sector Reform in the Digital Era
Miriam Lips

Digital Government
Managing Public Sector Reform
in the Digital Era

Miriam Lips

LONDON AND NEW YORK

First published 2020
by Routledge
2 Park Square, Milton Park, Abingdon, Oxon OX14 4RN

and by Routledge
52 Vanderbilt Avenue, New York, NY 10017

Routledge is an imprint of the Taylor & Francis Group, an informa business

© 2020 Miriam Lips

The right of Miriam Lips to be identified as author of this work has been asserted by her in accordance with sections 77 and 78 of the Copyright, Designs and Patents Act 1988.

All rights reserved. No part of this book may be reprinted or reproduced or utilised in any form or by any electronic, mechanical, or other means, now known or hereafter invented, including photocopying and recording, or in any information storage or retrieval system, without permission in writing from the publishers.

Trademark notice: Product or corporate names may be trademarks or registered trademarks, and are used only for identification and explanation without intent to infringe.

British Library Cataloguing-in-Publication Data
A catalogue record for this book is available from the British Library

Library of Congress Cataloging-in-Publication Data
Names: Lips, Miriam, 1967– author.
Title: Digital government : managing public sector reform in the digital era / Miriam Lips.
Description: Abingdon, Oxon ; New York, NY : Routledge, 2019. | Series: Routledge masters in public management | Includes bibliographical references and index.
Identifiers: LCCN 2019008071 | ISBN 9781138655645 (hardback) | ISBN 9781138655652 (pbk.) | ISBN 9781315622408 (ebook)
Subjects: LCSH: Internet in public administration. | Electronic government information. | Public administration—Data processing.
Classification: LCC JF1525.A8 L57 2019 | DDC 352.3/80285—dc23
LC record available at https://lccn.loc.gov/2019008071

Typeset in Bembo
by Apex CoVantage, LLC

Printed in the United Kingdom
by Henry Ling Limited

Contents

List of illustrations	ix
Acknowledgements	xi
List of abbreviations	xii

PART I
Introduction   1

1 Introducing and positioning digital government   3

PART II
Theory   21

2 The contribution of digital technologies and data to societal change   23

3 Different theories and perspectives on digital government   41

PART III
Areas of public sector reform   75

4 The service state   77

5 Open and transparent government   106

6 Smart government   132

7 Participatory democracy and public engagement   168

PART IV
Emerging issues   195

8 Citizen identity, privacy, ethics and security   197

viii *Contents*

9 Digital citizenship 222

10 Digital government strategy, leadership and governance 248

PART V
Conclusions 269

11 Conclusions: Managing institutional innovation and digital
governance 271

Index 283

Illustrations

Boxes

1.1	UN e-government surveys	10
1.2	The OECD'S Going Digital Project	10
2.1	A centralised database with integrated data on every child in the UK	26
2.2	Castells' information technology paradigm	31
2.3	Exercise 2.1	34
2.4	Examples of lying with statistics	35
2.5	Exercise 2.2	36
3.1	The information polity	49
3.2	Digital-Era Governance: which perspectives?	61
3.3	Exercise 3.1	65
4.1	The GOV.UK portal	87
4.2	Citizen-centric service provision around the birth of a child in New Zealand	91
4.3	FixMyStreet website and FIXiT app	92
4.4	Exercise 4.1	101
5.1	Data.gov	115
5.2	Open data case studies from New Zealand	117
5.3	Find and compare schools in England	118
5.4	Exercise 5.1	127
6.1	UN Global Pulse	134
6.2	Smart city: Songdo, South Korea	147
6.3	Smart government initiatives in the USA	151
6.4	Smart government strategy in Singapore	152
6.5	Exercise 6.1	154
6.6	Exercise 6.2	163
7.1	Better Reykjavik website in Iceland	172
7.2	Participatory lawmaking in Taiwan	173
7.3	Crowdsourcing flood reports from Twitter in Jakarta	178
7.4	Wheelmap.org	181
7.5	Street Bump in the city of Boston	183
7.6	Health patients sharing their data	183

x *Illustrations*

7.7	Exercise 7.1	190
8.1	Digital driver's licence in Australia	200
8.2	Social behaviour credit system in China	201
8.3	Case study: Online provisional driver's licence application in the UK	212
8.4	Blockchain use in Estonia	214
8.5	Exercise 8.1	217
9.1	Exercise 9.1	244
10.1	Integration of the vertical, horizontal and socio-technical construct dimensions	258
10.2	Exercise 10.1	264

Figures

| 2.1 | The knowledge pyramid | 35 |

Tables

3.1	Revolutionary public sector reform visions vs. evolutionary public sector reform visions	50
4.1	Emerging managerial principles vs. traditional managerial principles	82
8.1	Surveillance state vs. fair state perspective	209
9.1	Exclusion of population groups in digital government	240
10.1	Core elements of the NPG, in contrast to PA and the NPM	259

Acknowledgements

The section in Chapter 3 about an alternative perspective of complex public management is largely based on the PhD thesis of Dr Elizabeth A. Eppel (2010), a joint contribution of Eppel, Turner and Wolf (2011) and a joint contribution of Eppel and Lips (2016). The author would like to acknowledge Dr Eppel's invaluable contribution in constructing a new lens for "seeing" complex public management

Abbreviations

ADP	Automatic Data Processing
AI	Artificial Intelligence
ANPR	Automatic Number Plate Recognition
API	Application Programming Interface
BAU	Business as Usual
BOLD	Big Open and Linked Data
BPR	Business Process Reengineering
CCTV	Closed-Circuit Television
CE	Chief Executive
CIO	Chief Information Officer
CT	Communication Technology
D9	Nine digital government leaders
ENIAC	Electronic Numerical Integrator and Computer
ESRC	Economic and Social Research Council
EU	European Union
GDPR	General Data Protection Regulation
HRM	Human Resources Management
ICT	Information and Communication Technology
IPR	Intellectual Property Rights
IS	Information Systems
IT	Information Technology
IoT	Internet of Things
MSD	Ministry of Social Development
NGO	Non-Governmental Organization
NPM	New Public Management
NPG	New Public Governance
OECD	Organization for Economic Co-operation and Development
PA	Public Administration
PC	Personal Computer
R&D	Research and Development
SMS	Short Message Service
SSC	State Services Commission
UK	United Kingdom
UN	United Nations
US	United States
WWW	World Wide Web

Part I

Introduction

1 Introducing and positioning digital government

Learning objectives

By the end of this chapter you should:

- Be clear about the approach and scope of this book;
- Understand the important emphasis on digital government as an integrated, socio-technical phenomenon in the broader context of government; and
- Have developed clear objectives for your own learning.

Key points of this chapter

- The unique nature of government, which influences the context and outcomes of digital government and its relationships with citizens;
- The highly complex socio-technical phenomenon of digital government and its influence on and overlap with the digital economy and digital society;
- Digital government developments started before governments' adoption of the Internet;
- Digital government is an evolving and dynamic concept, which likely will be just "government" in the future; and
- The importance of understanding both the digital aspects and the government aspects of digital government in a comprehensive, multidisciplinary and empirical way.

Key terms

- *Digital government:* the introduction, application and use of digital technologies and data in government and its external relationships (including citizens, businesses, civil society and international organizations) and the democratic, governmental and managerial implications.
- *Electronic government or e-government:* the term used before "digital government." Although a dynamic and evolving concept, e-government usually refers to the introduction, management and use of information and communication technologies (ICTs), such as the Internet, in government and its external relationships (Lips & Schuppan, 2009).

4 *Introduction*

- *Electronic democracy or e-democracy:* a term that was used for an area of study and experimentation around innovative, Internet-enabled forms of democracy. This e-democracy concept later merged with the concept of e-government to become digital government.
- *Legacy systems:* the operation and use of existing older digital technologies, data and ICT systems in government.

Introduction

Governments around the world are becoming increasingly digital governments. Fast-moving developments in the area of digital technologies, such as the Internet, social media, mobile technologies and devices, smart technologies and, more recently, also robotics and artificial intelligence (AI), offer governments a wide range of innovative opportunities to fundamentally change their core functions, structures, operations, processes, activities and relationships with external stakeholders, including citizens, businesses and civil society. Moreover, another fast-moving technological development enabled by smart technologies and devices in particular is the creation of large volumes of data, which are further adding to the enormous reinvention potential available to governments in the digital age (e.g. Gil-Garcia, Pardo & Nam, 2016; Meijer & Bolivar, 2016; Borgman, 2015; Kitchin, 2014; van Zoonen, 2016).

Governments are seizing these various innovative opportunities in the digital age and, as a result, are changing. Many believe that digital government will be revolutionary, transformational and a completely new type of government compared to its paper-based past: in that respect, some scholars and practitioners refer to a new "government 2.0" or, in Korea for example, even "government 3.0" (e.g. Mergel, 2013; Nam, 2016; O'Reilly, 2010). Such a fundamental reinvention is also what society seems to expect from government: namely, not to lag behind in the digital age. For example, why would government not be able to reap the benefits of the digital age as commercial organizations do, such as in areas like online shopping and banking, booking air flights directly without the need to speak to a travel agent, using integrated data to make better decisions, engaging with citizens and businesses via their preferred social media platforms and using robots for various mechanical tasks? Moreover, a study conducted by McKinsey & Company (Dilmegani, Korkmaz & Lundqvist, 2014) suggests that capturing the full potential of digital government reform could free up to US$1 trillion annually in economic value worldwide, through improved cost and operational performance. Unfortunately, fundamentally changing governments by introducing digital technologies and data is not as easy as it may seem.

In this book, we explore the unique nature and context of digital government, which dominantly shape the outcomes of technology- and data-enabled changes in the public sector and its external relationships. Although governments have important relationships with a variety of external stakeholders, such as private sector organizations, we primarily focus in this book on governments'

Introducing and positioning 5

relationships with citizens. In so doing, we mainly explore the relationships between citizens and the executive parts of government and therefore will not consider in great detail the impact and implications of digital technologies and data in citizens' relationships with political representatives or political parties.

We also need to take into consideration in our discussions that digital government is not completely designed from scratch: in other words, governments haven't stopped their operations and activities in order to undertake a complete "reset" in the digital age. Governments are adopting digital technologies and new forms of data use whilst they are dealing with BAU: business as usual. Moreover, as the costs involved with digital government changes and initiatives are so significant, many governments are reluctant to take on large-scale government technology projects that will have a major impact on their structures, functioning and external relationships. Needless to say, there are substantial risks involved for governments in becoming digital governments, which are not attractive from a political leadership point of view, for example.

These kinds of issues suggest a highly complex environment for governments in which they want to become, or are becoming, digital governments. In this book, we explore various areas where governments are introducing digital technologies and innovative data uses to realise public sector reform, such as in the area of public service provision, around open and transparent government, governments wanting to become "smart" and in promoting new participatory and collaborative forms of public engagement. In looking at each of these areas more in depth, we discuss what governments' reform ambitions are, the types and extent of changes that are happening both in government organizations and in relationships with citizens, what the emerging issues and barriers are for governments in their technology- and data-related reform ambitions and particularly what the social, ethical, democratic and governmental implications are.

In all of this it is vital that we observe these complex changes in the context of digital government and its relationships with citizens comprehensively, empirically and robustly. This is of particular importance because if we are able to look at this complex world of digital government in depth, it will help us to ask the right questions. And if we are able to ask the right questions, it will help us to identify solutions and strategies for managing these complexities in digital government and its relationships with citizens. In Part 2 of this book, we discuss different theoretical and analytical perspectives on the roles of digital technologies and data and the extent to which they are contributing to societal change. Also, we discuss nine dominant perspectives that are often used by both scholars and practitioners to observe or "see" changes in the context of digital government and its relationships with citizens. Each of these nine perspectives helps us not only to understand how changes in the context of digital government are differently observed, but also how the deployment of that perspective leads to narrow and restricted observations, which, of course, have direct consequences for the actions and activities guided by those observations. We also explore an alternative, complex public management perspective that helps us to understand and analyse digital government more comprehensively and empirically.

6 *Introduction*

But before we do so, it is important to get some more insights into the phenomenon we will be further exploring and discussing in this book: digital government. In the next sections, we briefly explore the origins of digital government as a concept, as well as some concepts closely related to digital government, such as e-government and e-democracy. We look at a short historical overview of government computing and information technology (IT) developments in the public sector prior to the adoption of the Internet and propose a working definition for digital government to date. Also, we position digital government in close connection and interaction with two other major societal domains: namely, the digital economy and the digital society.

Furthermore, two dominant focus areas in digital government which are often more or less separated from each other in scholarly work are discussed: i.e. the "digital" aspects of digital government and the "government" aspects of digital government. In this book we use a comprehensive and combined perspective in order to better explore digital government as a socio-technical phenomenon and identify a number of the complexities around digital government. And finally, the need for a multidisciplinary, if not interdisciplinary, approach towards digital government and its relationships with citizens is discussed in order to more fully understand and explain this complex, socio-technical phenomenon.

What is digital government?

A short history of digital government as a concept

Digital government as a concept did not exist until the late 1990s. "Electronic government," a concept that was introduced shortly after the arrival of the public Internet in the early 1990s, preceded it. When the first e-commerce applications were launched on the World Wide Web (WWW), governments, too, became interested in using this new Internet technology in similar ways for e-government. Consequently, in 1993, the US federal government was the first government to present a vision on how the Internet could create the government of the future: this e-government could overcome barriers of time and distance to provide citizens with 24/7 access to public information and services regardless of their location (see also Chapter 2).

As this first vision of the government of the future demonstrates and similar to the first e-commerce applications, e-government initially was associated with a radically different way of providing public services to customers. This early conceptualisation of digital government became popular at the time that new public management (NPM) thinking was influencing governments around the world: many governments saw a strategic alignment to using e-government in order to achieve the NPM objectives of improving customer orientation in government and delivering more efficient and effective public services (Homburg, 2004; Homburg, 2008). As e-government was more narrowly associated with Internet-enabled public

Introducing and positioning 7

service provision at the time, scholars and practitioners saw an additional opportunity to study or experiment with a range of new democratic innovations enabled by the Internet under the term "electronic democracy" or "e-democracy." E-democracy research interests around that time covered topics such as online discussion groups and communities, the Internet as public sphere, electronic city halls, digital cities, technology-enabled support for political representatives, enhanced forms of citizen participation and deliberation, improved voter turnout in elections and new forms of direct democracy (Raab *et al*, 1996; Schalken, 1998; Ward & Vedel, 2006; Norris & Reddick, 2013; Grönlund, 2001).

In 1999, the US National Science Foundation adopted the term "digital government" as a new umbrella concept to cover aspects of both e-government and e-democracy, including the use of digital technologies to provide public services, support public policy, improve government operations, and engage citizens (Dawes, 2008). Since then, scholars have argued that digital government should be understood as a wider concept, covering all government functions and activities as well as relationships with all external stakeholders, including citizens, businesses and civil society (Garson, 2006; Dawes, 2008). Some scholars also use the term "e-governance" to make a clear distinction between the early, more narrow concept of e-government and the acknowledgement of the need for a wider, democratic reform conception (Garson, 2006; Dawes, 2008).

In the last two decades, the digital government concept has further expanded as new digital technology developments, including mobile technologies, smart technologies, AI and robotics, have become of interest to governments for adoption. Moreover, as a result of rapid developments around innovative data use, governments around the world are seizing new public-sector reform opportunities to become open and transparent governments (see Chapter 5) or smart governments (see Chapter 6).

A short history of digital government before the Internet

Although digital government commonly is observed as a development that started with governments' adoption of the Internet, it should not be underestimated that the application of IT in government was not a new phenomenon at the time. Government computing had existed already for many years, with the first computers in government being used to perform simple mathematical calculations (Agar, 2003; Lips, 2017). For example, in 1890, the US Census Bureau used a mechanical tabulator for data processing as part of the census (Lips, 2017). In the early 20th century, government departments started to use punch-card machines in large-volume operational activities, such as the processing of large numbers of forms, which supported the centralisation of administrative processes in government (Daly, 2013). During World War II, government budgets were made available to support R&D in the area of complex wartime calculations (Lips, 2017). Between 1943 and 1945, the first programmable

8   *Introduction*

digital computer, the so-called Electronic Numerical Integrator and Computer (ENIAC), was built and used by the military.

From the 1950s until the 1980s, governments started working with big centralised mainframe computing machines for the execution of large-scale numerical processing tasks (Bellamy & Taylor, 1998; Agar, 2003; Lips, 2017). This particularly concerned government agencies responsible for storing and managing large quantities of data, such as tax authorities, social welfare departments and national census bureaus. But other government agencies also employed mainframe computers for large-scale automatic data processing (ADP), which improved their efficiency. As government agencies used the mainframe computer to process data that had centralised corporate functionality, it had the effect of sustaining and even reinforcing characteristics of large hierarchical bureaucracies (Bellamy & Taylor, 1998). Introduced in government departments in the 1980s, personal computers (PCs) were initially used for word processing, calculation, data processing and programming and became ubiquitous throughout government agencies (Bellamy & Taylor, 1998). With the introduction of server-based networked computing, the PCs of public officials could be connected to the Internet, for example, which led to a shift away from centralised mainframe computing towards decentralised network computing in government.

The influence of these early IT solutions on government should not be underestimated. For example, governments continued to use centralised mainframe-computing systems in parallel with decentralised network computing solutions after their adoption of the Internet. The operation and use of existing older digital technologies and IT systems in government is also referred to as "legacy systems." Legacy systems often have a profound impact on digital government developments, as governments have the costs of operating and maintaining these older operational systems whilst making investment decisions about the adoption of new technology. We will explore several types of legacy systems in this book, including their impact on digital government.

A working definition of digital government

As we can observe from our discussion thus far, digital government is a domain of study that is still evolving. Although there are good reasons to treat this emerging domain as a separate field of study at the moment, over time we likely will see a development where digital government becomes a fully integrated part of government. This is similar to other influential technological developments in history, where the new technology initially required separate scholarly inquiry in order to position it in society: for example, nowadays, we don't consider separating out "telephony-enabled government" or "electricity-enabled government" from the study of government, and yet that is how we are treating digital technologies and data in the context of digital government at the moment.

As the concept of digital government is still evolving, we use the following working definition in this book:

The introduction, application and use of digital technologies and data in government and its external relationships (including citizens, businesses, civil society and other non-governmental organizations (NGOs) and international organizations) and the democratic, governmental and managerial implications.

Digital government, digital economy and digital society

Digital government doesn't operate in a vacuum but is intersecting, overlapping, influencing, intervening and interacting with other parts of society, most notably with the emerging digital economy and the digital society. For example, national digital government programmes and initiatives, such as digital government service provision and open-data initiatives, create new businesses, jobs, innovation and R&D opportunities as part of the digital economy and lead to new start-ups and a growing technology industry in countries around the world. Digital government also influences digital society directly, such as through digital government services in areas like taxation, social services, education, health, transport and the environment, and indirectly via government interventions, such as regulation in areas like privacy, copyright and intellectual property rights (IPR) and government programmes, including the promotion of digital inclusion, cyber security and digital knowledge and skills in school curricula.

Although governments at different administrative levels are, or are becoming, digital governments, such as smart cities, digital government programmes and interventions often are developed and coordinated at the national level. Many countries have dedicated national government programmes to promote digital government but also to build, grow and develop their digital economy and digital society. For example, the Thai national government has set up a Ministry on Digital Economy and Society with the mission to develop and promote Thailand's digital economy and digital society in order to increase the country's competitiveness and enhance the well-being of its people. We will further discuss digital government strategies in Chapter 10.

Besides the development of digital government strategies and action plans at the national or federal, state, regional and local administrative levels of countries, we can also observe the keen digital government policy and programme interest of international organizations like the Organization for Economic Co-operation and Development (OECD), the European Union (EU), the United Nations (UN) and the World Bank. Moreover, international bodies like the EU are intervening in digital government developments via their regulatory powers, such as with the EU's data protection regulation (i.e. the EU's General Data Protection Regulation or GDPR) and regulations around trans-border flows of data and information.

Box 1.1 UN e-government surveys

The United Nations (UN) has developed a benchmarking tool that provides a comparative assessment of the e-government development of UN member states based on the UN global e-readiness reports and the UN e-government surveys. The UN e-government surveys are published every two years and assess the e-government readiness and the extent of e-participation of the UN member states according to a quantitative composite index of e-readiness based on the provision of online services (website assessment), telecommunication connectivity and human capacity. The e-participation index is derived as a supplementary index to the UN e-government survey and extends the dimension of the provision of online services to facilitate provision of information by governments to citizens ("e-information-sharing"), interaction with stakeholders ("e-consultation") and engagement in decision-making processes ("e-decision making"). The latest UN e-government survey can be accessed here: https://publicadministration.un.org/egovkb/en-us/Reports/UN-E-Government-Survey-2018 [accessed 23 January 2019].

Box 1.2 The OECD's Going Digital Project

Some countries and groups are better placed than others to harness the benefits of digital transformation. The essence of the OECD's Going Digital Project (www.oecd.org/going-digital/project) is to build a coherent and comprehensive public policy approach that brings about stronger and more inclusive growth from the digital revolution. In order to do so, the OECD first examines how the digital transformation affects policy-making across a large spectrum of policy areas. The project acknowledges that responding to the digital transformation will require fundamental rethinking of public policies across many different areas. It draws on national experiences and public policy experimentation occurring across the OECD's 35 member countries, its accession countries, key partners and many other economies involved in the OECD's work.

The project was launched in January 2017 and actively engages with governments, stakeholders and independent experts. It builds on three main pillars, each designed to break new ground in our understanding of the digital transformation and its effects on our economies and societies:

- Pillar 1: an integrated policy framework for making the digital transformation work for growth and well-being. This pillar also includes

other activities that are relevant across all policy areas, such as an analysis of how the digital transformation manifests itself across the economy and society and what this implies for policy;
- Pillar 2: analysis of the extent, nature, benefits and challenges of the digital transformation in specific policy areas and in the broader economy; and
- Pillar 3: a set of modules focusing on key cross-cutting issues. This work involves deep dives into some of the major challenges we face in the digital era and that are at the intersection of more than one policy area. Examples are jobs and skills in the digital economy, productivity and making the digital transformation work for society and well-being.

The project draws on the OECD's capacity to provide a whole-of-government perspective on complex policy challenges. It articulates recommendations for pro-active policies that will help to drive greater growth and societal well-being and help address the challenges of slow productivity growth, high unemployment and growing inequality in many countries.

Digital and government

Roughly speaking, two different areas of emphasis can be distinguished in digital government endeavours, both in scholarly work and in digital government practice: one dominant focus area is the "digital" aspects of digital government, and another, less dominant focus area is the "government" aspects of digital government. We briefly discuss both focus areas next.

Digital *government*

Especially in the early days of digital government but also more recently, many scholars and practitioners have been predominantly focused on the "digital" aspects of digital government. Initially, this dominant digital technology focus in digital government initiatives can be explained by the high expectations that surrounded the introduction of the Internet in the early 1990s: for example, the Internet's technological capabilities were expected not only to lead to new innovative forms of government and democracy, but also to reengineer government in a way that would radically streamline bureaucracy, making government more responsive to the individual needs of citizens (Bellamy & Taylor, 1998; Fountain, 2001).

Compared to the centralised computing solutions in government at the time, the adoption of Internet technology was a major technological paradigm shift for governments, especially through the Internet's decentralised architecture, global reach, active user participation and open and informal structures for

12 *Introduction*

technical management (Abbate, 1999). Moreover, the new Internet technology represented a technological convergence of several digital technologies and media that traditionally had been separated, including IT, telecommunications and broadcasting, into new ICTs. This technological convergence which involved the coming together of content, infrastructures, the storage and processing capabilities of computers and consumer electronics, was caused by the following technological trends happening simultaneously (Lips, Frissen & Prins, 1999: 214):

- *Digitisation*: the conversion of analogue data into digital format and the increasing use of digital technology in networks, products and services;
- *Integration*: digitisation makes it possible to integrate networks, products and services, leading to a situation where any kind of carrier is able to transmit any kind of services to any kind of device. As a result, text, audio, images, video and data can all be integrated into the same product or service;
- *Interactivity*: digitisation allows for active user participation, where the output from the interactive service comes from the input from users. As a result, users themselves can decide on the consumption time of the interactive service;
- *Improvement of compression techniques*, which increasingly reduces problems around the scarcity of spectrum or limited network capacity; and
- *Increasing processing power of computers*, creating new innovative opportunities for service provision to consumers.

Since then, further technological convergence has led to strongly improved Internet connection speeds, the introduction of broadband initiatives, and the integration of mobile technologies and devices, such as smartphones and tablets. More recently, the "digital" aspects of digital government also involve the introduction and use of data innovation, smart technologies, the Internet of Things (IoT), blockchain technologies, AI and robotics.

However, several scholars caution that, although the technological potential for revolutionary change in government is there, the actual realisation of this enormous potential remains to be seen; actual achievements in digital government will not be determined by the technology *per se*, but by deep-seated social, institutional, legal, political, economic and cultural processes and structures, leading to fragmented and evolutionary outcomes (e.g. Bellamy & Taylor, 1998; Fountain, 2001; Dutton, 1997; Garnham, 1996).

Digital Government

This then brings us to the unique nature and characteristics of government, which directly influence digital government outcomes: unlike private sector organizations, governments are subject to, and have to manage, multiple complex dimensions, including political, democratic, ethical, legal, social, institutional, economic and cultural dimensions. The unique characteristics of government particularly come to the fore when we consider its political, legal and democratic dimensions: for example, most governments are subject to regular democratic elections and, with that, regular changes in political leadership on the basis of the election outcomes. They have both law-making and law-enforcing powers; and they have equal, democratic responsibilities for all of their citizens, regardless of whether these citizens are "customers" of government service or not. On their mission to become digital governments, governments need to manage an additional dimension: namely, the "digital" dimension of digital technologies and data.

However, digital government developments hardly have received any notice thus far from scholars in government-related academic fields, such as public management, political science and public administration scholars (Meijer, 2007; Fountain, 2001), with a few good exceptions (e.g. Bellamy & Taylor, 1998; Borins et al, 2007; Chadwick & Howard, 2008; Chen & Ahn, 2017; Coleman & Blumler, 2009; Dawes, 2008; Dunleavy et al, 2006; Dutton, 1996; Dutton, 1999; Gil-Garcia, Pardo & Nam, 2016; Homburg, 2008; Lips, Bekkers & Zuurmond, 2004; McLoughlin & Wilson, 2013; Noveck, 2015; Snellen & van de Donk, 1998). Moreover, among those public management and public administration scholars with a keen research interest in digital technologies in government, attention often more narrowly focuses on the government aspects of digital government without opening the "black box" of digital technologies (Lenk, 2007).

In general, scholarly opportunities for an interdisciplinary study of digital technology and government have remained largely ignored by social scientists with relevant backgrounds (Fountain, 2001). And yet, the institutional foundations of government are fundamentally different from those of other organizations in society, including the private sector: public sector reform, including digital government reform, is necessarily different from restructuring in firms and industries, for example (Fountain, 2001).

Furthermore, another problem around the study of digital government has been that scholars with a technological background, such as information systems (IS) scholars or computer scientists, usually do not make a distinction in their work between different types of organizations; with research interests in technological phenomena, their research focus is predominantly on the individual and meso levels of society, not on the macro level, where government's unique position becomes more clear. As scholars with an IS or computer science background usually treat public and private sector organizations as similar organizations with comparable issues, this has caused critical blind spots in much of the scholarly work on digital government (Lips, 2012).

Digital and government: 1 + 1 = 3

Thus far, many scholars and practitioners have been predominantly occupied with the digital aspects of digital government. At the same time, those scholars and practitioners with relevant expertise around public sector reform and

14 *Introduction*

government often have been treating digital government as an issue that is out of scope for them: i.e. a technology issue belonging to a government IT department or to another, technology-focused scholarly discipline.

However, over time, we can observe an increasing awareness amongst both scholars and practitioners that digital government is about 'digital' *and* 'government': that is, digital government in a combined, integrated and more complex way. That digital government is not about a digital dimension driving change in government, but about public sector reform enabled by government. And yet, digital government reform is not a similar affair for governments compared to other types of public sector reform. We could consider it as "government on steroids": public sector reform enabled by digital technologies and data has an additional, highly complex dimension to it. Digital government in its combined, integrated and complex form is about changes in the unique settings, dimensions, institutional arrangements and external relationships of government as a result of the adoption and use of digital technologies and data and how to manage those technology- and data-enabled changes and their democratic, governmental and managerial implications. But it's also about the role and contribution of government in an increasingly digital society, where we need to ask ourselves which democratic, social and ethical norms and values we consider to be of importance in digital government relationships, such as fairness, social justice, privacy, security, openness and transparency, digital inclusion and democratic participation and what government interventions may be needed to promote those important values in these changing relationships. We explore this further in Chapter 6. Moreover, similar to governments' response to the Industrial Revolution, we may want to ask ourselves if there is a need for any new citizens' rights around the current digital technology and data revolution and its impact on government's democratic relationships; if so, what would they be? We discuss this matter of digital citizenship further in Chapter 9.

Digital government is complex

A senior public servant responsible for digital government on behalf of the UK central government and with extensive experience in the private sector, once admitted: "IT in government is as difficult as it gets" (Ian Watmore cited in Institute for Government, 2010: 9). The examples he gave in order to support his admission include the following (Institute for Government, 2010):

- Chronic delays in digital government projects;
- IT suppliers failing to deliver on contractual commitments;
- Not designing with the user in mind;
- Incompatible digital technologies and systems;
- High costs involved;
- "Gold-plating" digital solutions;
- Perceived political risks;
- Failing to re-use existing investments;

Introducing and positioning 15

- Problems around legacy systems; and
- Lack of technical interoperability within and across government organizations.

These kinds of problematic observations around digital government are relatively common for governments all over the world, and the list of problems could be extended even further in that respect. In general, digital government initiatives often take much more time and resources than initially planned or expected, and many of these initiatives fail (Heeks, 1999; Heeks, 2003; Heeks, 2006). As a result, leadership is one of the critical success factors in digital government initiatives (Gil-Garcia & Pardo, 2005; West & Berman, 2001; see Chapter 10).

A further complex issue around digital government becomes apparent when we consider digital government uptake figures. For example, if we take into consideration that, in 2016, 79 percent of people aged 16 to 74 in the EU used the Internet at least once a week, the results for digital government uptake amongst Europeans of the same age group and in that same year are rather disappointing as only 48 percent had used the Internet for digital government purposes (Eurostat, 2016): 42 percent of EU citizens aged 16 to 74 had used the Internet in order to obtain government information 29 percent of Europeans had downloaded forms online and only 28 percent had submitted completed forms online (Eurostat, 2016). With governments around the world becoming digital by default (see Chapter 4), these figures suggest that we need to have a much better understanding of what citizens need from digital government in order to pursue such bold public sector reform ambitions. We discuss this issue further in Chapter 4, where we look at public sector reform in the area of public service provision, and in Chapter 9, where we consider the existence of multiple digital divides amongst different population groups.

An empirical and multidisciplinary understanding of digital government

Based on our discussion thus far, it becomes clear that the complex phenomenon of digital government can't be understood via a single disciplinary lens but requires at least a multidisciplinary, if not an interdisciplinary, approach (e.g. Hardy & Williams, 2011). Moreover, as we are exploring an emerging dynamic phenomenon, we need to use an empirical approach to be able to critically observe and assess the changes happening in digital government and its relationships with citizens. We also need to take into consideration that empirical observations around digital government can't be interpreted free of context; digital government needs to be understood as a complex socio-technical phenomenon within the broader context of government (Lips & Schuppan, 2009; Gil-Garcia, Pardo & Nam, 2016; Meijer & Bolivar, 2016; Kitchin, 2014; van Zoonen, 2016).

In Chapters 2 and 3, we further look into this important matter of how to observe and understand this complex socio-technical phenomenon of digital government and its relationships with citizens, the various dominant lenses and

16 *Introduction*

perspectives that are available to us in the area of digital government and the preference for using an alternative, empirical non-linear perspective of complex public management in order to better understand and explain digital government.

The approach adopted in this book

This book is intended for students of government, public administration and public management (often public managers themselves) and the wider social sciences who want to develop a critical understanding of the emerging socio-technical phenomenon of digital government. It is neither a prescriptive handbook nor a theoretical text, but rather seeks to educate you in the following five ways:

- To provide you with a critical, empirically based understanding of digital government as a socio-technical phenomenon;
- To educate you about the various dominant perspectives that are held by scholars and practitioners about digital government, the contribution of digital technologies and data to societal change and the implications of these perspectives for seeing, understanding and managing digital government as a phenomenon;
- To provide you with a deep understanding of the contextual approach that is needed to consider changes in digital government, its relationships with citizens and the democratic, social, ethical, governmental and managerial implications;
- To provide you with a deep understanding of the emerging issues, barriers and complexities around digital government and possible strategies to manage these; and
- To demonstrate to you the value of taking a complex public management approach to more comprehensively and empirically understand and explain emerging forms of digital government and governance.

Besides the core text, each chapter in this book will include the following:

- Learning objectives for the chapter;
- A short summary of the key points to be covered in the chapter;
- Descriptions of key terms used in the chapter;
- Boxes, tables and figures to present essential and further learning material;
- Discussion questions and/or exercises;
- References; and
- Some suggestions for further reading.

Structure of the book

Chapter 2 explores *different perspectives on the contribution of digital technologies and data to societal change* and identifies which perspectives are most useful in order to understand and explain digital government. Chapter 3 then looks further into the various *different theories and perspectives that are held on digital government* and suggests a more comprehensive and empirical perspective of complex public management.

Chapters 4 through 7 consider *digital government developments in various areas of public sector reform*, including *public service provision to citizens* and governments' reform efforts towards becoming *"a service state"* (Chapter 4); governments' reform ambitions of becoming *open and transparent government* (Chapter 5); governments wanting to become *smart government* or smarter and how they could make use of *a new ethical framework of contextual integrity* to do so (Chapter 6) and governments' reform efforts on the horizontal dimension of digital government in using *more participatory and collaborative forms of digital government and governance in their relationships with citizens*, including in public engagement (Chapter 7).

Chapters 8 through 10 then consider some critically important emerging issues around digital government. Chapter 8 discusses the increasingly important issue of *citizen identity in digital government and governance* and looks at the related *privacy, ethical and security issues and implications*. Chapter 9 considers emerging issues around *digital citizenship*: more specifically, the existence of *multiple digital divides in digital government relationships around digital technologies, data and digital government services* and the necessity for governments to acknowledge and adopt new *citizens' rights in digital government*. And Chapter 10 looks into emerging issues around three critically important areas for digital government, namely *digital government strategy, leadership and governance*.

And finally, in Chapter 11, some *conclusions* to this book will be presented around the implications of digital government and governance for the *institutional innovation of government as a whole* and for *public management of digital governance*.

Discussion questions

1   Find out how your government is using digital technologies and/or data in its relationships with citizens. What has changed in citizen–government relationships from a citizen's perspective?
2   Find out if your government was using any computers or technologies before it started to use the Internet. If so, what are they, and how long have they been used for? Are there, or have there been, any legacy systems in your government? If so, how have they influenced government operations?
3   Look up a large digital government project failure in your country and find out why this project failed. How did the media and the political leader(s) responsible for the project respond? Were there any lessons learned from this digital government project failure? If so, what were they?
4   Which scholarly disciplines are useful for studying digital government phenomena in your country? Motivate your answer.

References

Abbate, J. (1999) *Inventing the Internet*. Cambridge: Massachusetts Institute of Technology Press.

Agar, J. (2003) *The Government Machine: A Revolutionary History of the Computer*. Cambridge, MA: Massachusetts Institute of Technology Press.

Bellamy, C. & Taylor, J.A. (1998) *Governing in the Information Age*. Buckingham: Open University Press.

18   Introduction

Borgman, C.L. (2015) *Big Data, Little Data, No Data: Scholarship in the Networked World*. Cambridge, MA: Massachusetts Institute of Technology Press.

Borins, S., Kernaghan, K., Brown, D., Bontis, N., 6, P. & Thompson, F. (eds.) (2007) *Digital State at the Leading Edge*. Toronto: University of Toronto Press.

Chadwick, A. & Howard, P.N. (eds.) (2008) *The Routledge Handbook of Internet Politics*. Abingdon: Routledge.

Chen, Y. & Ahn, M.J. (eds.) (2017) *Routledge Handbook on Information Technology in Government*. London: Routledge.

Coleman, S. & Blumler, J.G. (2009) *The Internet and Democratic Citizenship: Theory, Practice and Policy*. New York, NY: Cambridge University Press.

Daly, J. (2013) The history of federal data centers. *FedTech Magazine*. Available from: https://fedtechmagazine.com/article/2013/05/history-federal-data-centers-infographic [accessed 19 June 2018].

Dawes, S.S. (2008) The evolution and continuing challenges of e-governance. *Public Administration Review*, 68, 86–102.

Dilmegani, C., Korkmaz, B. & Lundqvist, M. (December 2014) *Public-Sector Digitization: The Trillion-Dollar Challenge*. McKinsey & Company. Available from: https://www.mckinsey.com/business-functions/digital-mckinsey/our-insights/public-sector-digitization-the-trillion-dollar-challenge [accessed 20 June 2018].

Dunleavy, P., Margetts, H., Bastow, S. & Tinkler, J. (2006) *Digital Era Governance: IT Corporations, the State, and E-Government*. Oxford: Oxford University Press.

Dutton, W.H. (ed.) (1996) *Information and Communication Technologies: Visions and Realities*. Oxford: Oxford University Press.

Dutton, W.H. (1997) Multimedia visions and realities. In: Kubicek, H., Dutton, W.H. & Williams, R. (eds.) *The Social Shaping of Information Superhighways: European and American Roads to the Information Society*. Frankfurt: Campus Verlag, pp. 133–155.

Dutton, W.H. (ed.) (1999) *Society on the Line: Information Politics in the Digital Age*. Oxford: Oxford University Press.

Eurostat. (2016) Internet access and use statistics – households and individuals. Available from: http://ec.europa.eu/eurostat/statistics-explained/index.php?title=Archive:Internet_access_and_use_statistics_-_households_and_individuals [accessed 19 June 2018].

Fountain, J.E. (2001) *Building the Virtual State: Information Technology and Institutional Change*. Washington, DC: Brookings Institution Press.

Garnham, N. (1996) Constraints of multimedia convergence. In: Dutton, W.H. (ed.) *Information and Communication Technologies: Visions and Realities*. Oxford: Oxford University Press, pp. 103–120.

Garson, D.G. (2006) *Public Information Technology and E-Governance: Governing the Virtual State*. Raleigh, NC: Jones and Bartlett Publishers.

Gil-Garcia, J.R. & Pardo, T.A. (2005) E-government success factors: Mapping practical tools to theoretical foundations. *Government Information Quarterly*, 22, 187–216.

Gil-Garcia, J.R., Pardo, T.A. & Nam, T. (eds.) (2016) *Smarter as the New Urban Agenda: A Comprehensive View of the 21st Century City*. Public Administration and Information Technology, Vol. 11, Springer International Publishing Switzerland, eBook, DOI: 10.1007/978-3-319-17620-8

Grönlund, A. (2001) Democracy in an IT-framed society. *Communications of the ACM*, 44 (1), 23–26.

Hardy, C.A. & Williams, S.P. (2011) Assembling e-government research designs: A transdisciplinary view and interactive approach. *Public Administration Review*, 71 (3), 405–413.

Introducing and positioning 19

Heeks, R. (ed.) (1999) *Reinventing Government in the Information Age: International Practice in IT-Enabled Public Sector Reform*. London: Routledge.

Heeks, R. (2003) *eGovernment for Development: Success and Failure Rates of eGovernment in Developing/Transitional Countries: Overview*. Available from: https://www.egov4dev.org/success/sfrates.shtml [accessed 19 June 2018].

Heeks, R. (2006) *Implementing and Managing E-Government: An International Text*. London: Sage.

Homburg, V. (2004) *E-Government and NPM: A Perfect Marriage?* Proceedings of the 6th International Conference on Electronic Commerce, ACM, pp. 547–555.

Homburg, V. (2008) *Understanding E-Government: Information Systems in Public Administration*. London: Routledge.

Institute for Government. (2010) *System Error: Fixing the Flaws in Government IT*. London: Institute for Government.

Kitchin, R. (2014) *The Data Revolution: Big Data, Open Data, Data Infrastructures & Their Consequences*. London: Sage.

Lenk, K. (2007) Reconstructing public administration theory from below. *Information Polity*, 12 (4), 207–212.

Lips, A.M.B. (2012) 'E-government is dead: Long live networked governance': Fixing system errors in the New Zealand public management system. In: Ryan, B. & Gill, D. (eds.) *Future State: Directions for Public Management in New Zealand*. Wellington: Victoria University of Wellington, pp. 248–261.

Lips, A.M.B. (2017) Transforming government services over time: Meanings, impacts, and implications for citizen-government relationships. In: Chen, Y. & Ahn, M.J. (eds.) *Routledge Handbook on Information Technology in Government*. London: Routledge, pp. 11–26.

Lips, A.M.B., Bekkers, V.J.J.M. & Zuurmond, A. (eds.) (2004) *ICT en Openbaar Bestuur*. Utrecht: Lemma.

Lips, A.M.B., Frissen, P.H.A. & Prins, C.J. (1999) *Regulatory Review Through New Media in Sweden, the UK, and the USA: Convergence or Divergence of Regulation?* ITeR Series, 17. Deventer: Kluwer, pp. 209–368.

Lips, A.M.B. & Schuppan, T. (2009) Transforming e-government knowledge through public management research. *Public Management Review*, 11 (6), 739–749.

McLoughlin, I. & Wilson, R., with Martin, M. (2013) *Digital Government @Work: A Social Informatics Perspective*. Oxford: Oxford University Press.

Meijer, A.J. (2007) Why don't they listen to us? Reasserting the role of ICT in public administration. *Information Polity*, 12 (4), 233–242.

Meijer, A.J. & Bolivar, M.P.R. (2016) Governing the smart city: A review of the literature on smart urban governance. *International Review of Administrative Sciences*, 82 (2), 392–408.

Mergel, I. (2013) *Social Media in the Public Sector: A Guide to Participation, Collaboration, and Transparency in the Networked World*. San Francisco, CA: Jossey-Bass.

Nam, T. (2016) Government 3.0 in Korea: A country study. *Information Polity*, 21 (4), 1–10.

Norris, D.F. & Reddick, C.G. (2013) E-democracy at the American grassroots: Not now . . . not likely? *Information Polity*, 18, 201–216.

Noveck, B.S. (2015) *Smart Citizens, Smarter State: The Technologies of Expertise and the Future of Governing*. Cambridge, MA: Harvard University Press.

O'Reilly, T. (2010) Government as a platform. In: Lathrop, D. & Ruma, L. (eds.) *Open Government: Collaboration, Transparency, and Participation in Practice*. Sebastopol, CA: O'Reilly, pp. 11–39.

Raab, C.D., Bellamy, C., Taylor, J.A., Dutton, W.H. & Peltu, M. (1996) The information polity: Electronic democracy, privacy, and surveillance. In: Dutton, W.H. (ed.) *Information*

20   *Introduction*

and Communication Technologies: Visions and Realities. Oxford: Oxford University Press, pp. 283–299.

Schalken, C.A.T. (1998) Internet as a new public sphere for democracy? In: Snellen, I.Th.M. & van de Donk, W.B.H.J. (eds.) *Public Administration in an Information Age: A Handbook.* Amsterdam: IOS Press, pp. 159–174.

Snellen, I.Th.M. & van de Donk, W.B.H.J. (eds.) (1998) *Public Administration in an Information Age: A Handbook.* Amsterdam: IOS Press.

Ward, S. & Vedel, T. (2006) Introduction: The potential of the Internet revisited. *Parliamentary Affairs*, 59 (2), 210–225.

West, J.P. & Berman, E.M. (2001) The impact of revitalized management practices on the adoption of information technology: A national survey of local governments. *Public Performance and Management Review*, 24 (3), 233–253.

van Zoonen, L. (2016) Privacy concerns in smart cities. *Government Information Quarterly*, 33, 472–480.

Further reading

Abbate, J. (1999) *Inventing the Internet.* Cambridge, MA: Massachusetts Institute of Technology Press.

Agar, J. (2003) *The Government Machine: A Revolutionary History of the Computer.* Cambridge, MA: Massachusetts Institute of Technology Press.

Bellamy, C. & Taylor, J.A. (1998) *Governing in the Information Age.* Buckingham: Open University Press.

Chadwick, A. & Howard, P.N. (eds.) (2008) *The Routledge Handbook of Internet Politics.* Abingdon: Routledge.

Chen, Y. & Ahn, M.J. (eds.) (2017) *Routledge Handbook on Information Technology in Government.* London: Routledge.

Dutton, W.H. (ed.) (1996) *Information and Communication Technologies: Visions and Realities.* Oxford: Oxford University Press.

Dutton, W.H. (ed.) (1999) *Society on the Line: Information Politics in the Digital Age.* Oxford: Oxford University Press.

Homburg, V. (2008) *Understanding E-government: Information Systems in Public Administration.* London: Routledge.

Snellen, I.Th.M. & van de Donk, W.B.H.J. (eds.) (1998) *Public Administration in an Information Age: A Handbook.* Amsterdam: IOS Press.

Part II

Theory

2 The contribution of digital technologies and data to societal change

Learning objectives

By the end of this chapter you should be able to:

- Recognise a particular perspective on the role and contribution of digital technologies to societal change;
- Identify different kinds of data in the context of the public sector;
- Understand the difference between data, information and knowledge and be able to convert data into information and information into knowledge; and
- Understand issues around data inaccuracies and data biases in government datasets as well as around the presentation and visualisation of data.

Key points of this chapter

- There are three different scholarly perspectives on the role and contribution of digital technologies in societal change: technological determinism, social determinism and mutual shaping. The perspectives of technological determinism and social determinism are both problematic;
- The mutual shaping perspective helps us to understand why the same digital technology may be designed, developed and used differently in different contexts at a particular moment in time, leading to varying outcomes. This perspective also explains why there is often a mismatch between intentions with or expectations around a particular digital technology and the actual experience with this technology;
- Empirical observations and analysis are of critical importance in order to understand the mutual shaping of digital technologies, data and society and their varying impacts and outcomes;
- Although people may consider data as objective, in reality data are social in the sense that they do not exist independently of the people, interpretations, technologies and contexts that produce them;
- How data are produced, processed, managed and used varies between socio-technical assemblages in contexts with different stakeholders involved, technologies, institutions, policies and power (Borgman, 2015);
- Data vary by form, structure, source, producer and type;

24 *Theory*

- Data are not the same as information or knowledge, but need to be seen as a fundamental base layer of a knowledge pyramid; and
- Digital technologies and data are critical parts of socio-technical constructs or assemblages in the context of digital government and its relationships with citizens.

Key terms

- *Technological determinism*: the intrinsic capabilities of digital technologies determine and drive the direction of societal change.
- *Social determinism*: people determine in an instrumental way the outcomes of societal change by using digital technology as a (neutral) tool.
- *Mutual shaping perspective*: digital technology and society influence and shape each other.
- *Data*: entities used as representations of objects, observations or other phenomena. Those representations vary according to the people who are constructing them and the context in which they are constructed and over time.
- *Information*: adds meaning to data through interpretation and processing.
- *Knowledge*: actionable information generated through the processes of analysing and organizing information.

Introduction

Digital technologies have become pervasive in every aspect of people's daily lives, changing profoundly how people communicate, work, play, learn, shop, run their businesses, experience entertainment and interact with government. However, although it is unquestionable that these digital technologies have a major impact on society at large, there are fundamentally different perspectives on what exactly their role in and contribution to societal change are. Understanding these different perspectives is critically important, as they help us understand how scholars and practitioners consider not only the impact digital technologies have on society, but also what their role in and contribution to changes in the context of digital government and its relationships with citizens are.

These differences in scholarly perspectives on the role and contribution of technology to societal change are also referred to as the "technology debate." Roughly, the following three varying perspectives can be observed in the scholarly literature: technological determinism, social determinism, and the mutual shaping of digital technology and society. We discuss each of these perspectives in more detail next.

Similarly, we can observe different perspectives on the role and contribution of data, often with quite some confusion around what data are. Or, as Borgman (2015) reformulates the question: When are data? Is information the same as data? And how then do data relate to knowledge? What exactly are data's role in

Digital technologies and societal change 25

and contribution to societal change? These questions are critically important as they will help us understand how to consider the role and contribution of data, information and knowledge in digital government. We also explore and discuss these matters further in this chapter.

And finally, we point out how digital technologies and data need to be seen as critical parts of socio-technical constructs or assemblages in the context of digital government.

Technology debate: the role of digital technologies in societal change

Technological determinism

According to technological determinists, digital technologies inevitably cause societal change and, consequently, are the governing force in society (Kallinikos, 2011; Henman, 2010). The intrinsic capabilities of digital technologies are what determine the direction of societal change, creating societal effects that are inherent, autonomous and independent (MacKenzie & Wajcman, 1985). Thus, technological determinists perceive digital technologies as pervasive and beyond the control of society; the effects of digital technologies are pre-determined in a linear way through the intrinsic capabilities of these technologies. This acknowledgement leads technological determinists to believe that the evolution of societal and organizational structures is analogous to the evolution of the technology itself (Fleck, Webster & Williams, 1990).

Problems with technological determinism

Two major problems have been identified with this technological determinist perspective (e.g. Woolgar, 2006). Firstly, it is difficult to completely isolate the technology from other factors, actors and elements involved in the process of societal change and establish a direct causal relationship between the intrinsic technological capabilities and a particular societal change outcome. To illustrate this point, Woolgar (2006) wants us to consider whether the introduction of mobile technology has caused a more mobile lifestyle in societies; he wonders if this more mobile lifestyle was going to happen anyway, influenced by a wide range of societal factors and with industry spotting the market opportunity (Woolgar, 2006)? Other examples of technological determinist thinking are the expectation of seeing a productivity gain just from digital technology itself (Fountain, 2001) or the disappearance of jobs as an exclusive result of the introduction of technology.

Secondly, the claim that digital technology determines the direction of societal change requires us to specifically identify the technological capability that is effecting that change (Woolgar, 2006). However, if we take an historical view and consider societal change after the uptake of new technologies, such as after the introduction of the automobile, telephone or mobile phone, we need

26　*Theory*

to come to the conclusion that outcomes are usually quite different from the initial public expectations around these new technologies (Lips, 2011; Dutton, 1995; Woolgar, 2006). For example, with a general expectation that the automobile would be used on farms to replace the carriage with horses, it was only later that people started to use cars for long-distance travel. This, then, unexpectedly made urban planning and design of suburbs a viable option. Similarly, the telephone was not intended for use in interactive communication as we know it today, but only for "one-way broadcasting": namely, listening to opera at a distance. And when the mobile phone was launched, people did not foresee that young people would dominantly use this technology for text messaging instead of making phone calls.

What we can learn from this discussion is that we must firmly resist putting digital technology in the explanatory driver's seat of societal change (Crawford, 2016). Moreover, we should not focus so much on digital technologies or devices *per se*, but more on the socio-technical assemblages where negotiations take place between people, technologies, data, organizations and institutions, which determine societal outcomes (Galloway, 2013). Digital technologies are not driving these socio-technical constructs, but they are a critical part of these human and non-human assemblages operating within a particular context.

Social determinism

A different and more or less opposite perspective of technological determinism is that digital technologies do not cause any effects; they are essentially neutral. According to this so-called social deterministic viewpoint, the direction of societal change only depends on how the technology is used. That is, not technology itself but people determine in an instrumental way the outcomes of societal change by using digital technology as a tool. Social determinist thinking assumes not only that society is the governing force that determines change, but also that users or organizations are free to choose their digital "instruments" to achieve desired outcomes and deploy these technologies as they see fit.

Box 2.1　A centralised database with integrated data on every child in the UK

We can observe the application of social determinist thinking in digital government where technology is used by decision-makers to control the achievement of desirable outcomes. For example, the construction and use of a large centralised database holding integrated data on a particular public policy problem or population group gives public decision-makers the confidence that they have all the knowledge in one place in order to make effective decisions. A practical example can be found in the UK: in response to a 2003 inquiry by Lord Laming into the abuse and death of an eight-year-old child (Victoria Climbie), with various child care agencies involved in her care failing to prevent her death, UK central government officials decided to create a new centralised database with data on every child in England. With that, they wanted to ensure that no other child would slip through the net as had happened to Victoria Climbie. The new ContactPoint system had an estimated set-up cost of GBP £224 million and an operational cost of GBP £41 million per year. With the intention of making it easier to coordinate the work of different child protection agencies by allowing access to at least 330,000 professionals in 150 local authorities, the database held for all 11 million children under 18 years of age their name, address, date of birth, gender, parental or carers' contact information, a unique identifying number, details of the child's school, details of any practitioners or services working with the child and whether the practitioner is the lead professional for that child (BBC, 2007).[1] ContactPoint received heavy criticism from various advocacy groups for privacy, security and child protection reasons. Moreover, research demonstrated that professionals who were supposed to be using ContactPoint were reluctant to do so as the database did not contain any context-relevant information around the data presented, information that is commonly of value to professionals who need to make decisions about children in their local care (Peckover, White & Hall, 2008). ContactPoint was shut down by the new UK coalition government in 2010.

Problems with social determinism

In line with similar objections to linear thinking in the deployment of a technological deterministic perspective, this social deterministic perspective, too, raises doubts about technology users' ability to directly and unambiguously determine the desired societal change outcomes. For instance, many historical examples of unintended outcomes around the use of technology demonstrate that an assumed cause-and-effect relationship between users and digital technology is highly problematic. Another weakness of this social deterministic perspective is the claim that digital technology is neutral and, with that, the assumption that the design and development of digital technology are completely separate from its use and effects. In general, social determinist thinking can easily lead to treating digital technologies as an instrumental panacea to every problem: for instance, if all you have is a hammer, everything looks like a nail (Woolgar, 2006).

28   *Theory*

Mutual shaping of digital technology and society

The perspective of the mutual shaping of technology and society emerged as a critique of the linear cause-and-effect thinking of technological determinists and social determinists. Instead, scholars supporting this mutual shaping perspective insist that technology design and use need to be seen as inherently social processes (Woolgar, 2006; Williams & Edge, 1996; Fleck, Webster & Williams, 1990). Moreover, digital technologies cannot be seen as static, homogeneous artefacts with uniform technical capabilities, but the "black box" of technology must be opened in order to understand the outcomes of technology-enabled change (Williams & Edge, 1996). In other words, a mutual shaping perspective acknowledges that digital technology and society influence and shape each other and, as a result, are mutually constituted rather than being neutral, mutually exclusive and separate.

Proponents of this perspective point out that every stage in the design, development and use of the technology involves social choices between different technical options. These choices are not always conscious decisions; selected options depend on a wide range of technological and social factors, which, in interaction, co-shape the direction and outcomes of the technology itself and the societal change processes it enables (Williams & Edge, 1996).

As an example, based on empirical research into the design and implementation processes of digital technologies in organizations and the impact these digital technologies have on the workplace, Fleck, Webster and Williams (1990) come to the conclusion that it is not the digital technology *per se* which shapes the use of a certain organizational logic or practices in the workplace, but rather the particular dynamics and politics of the workplace in interaction with the digital technology. As these dynamics emerge from managerial decisions about how to organize work, rather than being driven by technological capabilities, digital technology–enabled change is predominantly a socio-political process (Fleck, Webster & Williams, 1990). Empirical findings such as these demonstrate the importance of understanding the social dynamics and processes around the design and implementation of digital technologies in organizations, which bring about particular managerial decisions, and why these lead to the adoption of some configurations of digital technology and patterns of work organization and not others.

In general, what this mutual shaping perspective reveals is a dynamic, complex and incremental working together of digital technology capabilities on the one hand and socio-cultural, economic, political, institutional and organizational factors on the other; put differently, the design, development and use of digital technology can be understood as a social phenomenon: an inextricable part of society (MacKenzie & Wajcman, 1999). As social factors are context dependent and co-evolve with the technology, societal change outcomes of this mutual shaping, too, are contingent and unique due to different social, cultural, institutional and historical circumstances within a particular context.

Dutton (2006) introduces the concept of an "ecology of games" to better understand the mutual shaping eco-system: how digital technology applications are the outcome of an unfolding interaction of various actors pursuing a diverse array of goals and objectives and operating within a broader context of intertwined economic, social, cultural, organizational, technological and legal dimensions. Several scholars emphasise the critical role of users as co-shapers of the digital technology within this mutual shaping eco-system (Oudshoorn & Pinch, 2003; Dutton, 1999; Williams & Edge, 1996).

This mutual shaping perspective, which is also referred to as the social shaping of technology (MacKenzie & Wajcman, 1985), helps us to understand differences in the socio-technical construct of a digital technology within a particular context. Most importantly, it helps us to understand why the same digital technology may be designed, developed and used differently in different contexts at a particular moment in time, leading to varying outcomes. This perspective also explains why there is often a mismatch between intentions for or expectations around a particular technology and the actual experience with this technology: for instance, it provides us with an understanding of why digital technologies often fail to deliver on predicted or desirable outcomes.

Mutual shaping of technology is commonly a process in which there is no single dominant shaping force (MacKenzie & Wajcman, 1999). The often unintended or unexpected outcomes of this process can be more or less successful, and the journey towards these outcomes can be conceptualised as a complex negotiation process between various actors and technological, social and institutional factors in a particular context (Latour, 1986). In accordance with this mutual shaping thinking, the history of technology and technological change is a path-dependent history in the sense that local, short-term events can have lasting effects (MacKenzie & Wajcman, 1999).

The case for an empirical, non-linear perspective

Based on our discussion thus far, we need to come to the following conclusion: as linear extrapolation of the potential effects of digital technologies is not going to provide us with any predictable outcomes, empirical observations and analysis are of critical importance in order to understand the mutual shaping of digital technologies and society and their varying impacts and outcomes (Castells, 1996; Brown & Duguid, 2000; Woolgar, 2002a). A good example of the critical contribution of empirical research to the exploration and assessment of this mutual shaping of digital technologies and society is provided by Woolgar and his research colleagues (2002a). When early ideas about the effects of digital technologies were pointing towards the advent of a new virtual society in which digital activities would replace real-world activities and, with that, facilitate disintermediation and the "death of distance" (Cairncross, 1998), Woolgar identified the following five rules of virtuality based on empirical research findings from a large UK Economic and Social Research Council (ESRC)–sponsored Virtual Society? programme, researching societal transformation as a result of new digital technologies (Woolgar, 2002b: 14–19):

30   *Theory*

Rule 1 – The uptake and use of new digital technologies depend crucially on local social context.

Various projects under this research programme successfully demonstrate the importance of non-technical, social circumstances in order to explain technology-enabled outcomes. For example, although it was widely expected that Internet uptake by individuals and households would only increase, Wyatt, Thomas and Terranova (2002) point towards counter-intuitive evidence of extensive non- and former use of the Internet, which can be explained by various social and contextual factors.

Rule 2 – The fears and risks associated with new digital technologies are unevenly socially distributed.

Several research projects under the Virtual Society? programme show that the result of digital technology narratives – positive or negative – depends on the strength of the actor network through which the new digital technology is enacted (Woolgar, 2002b). The uneven distribution of views about new digital technology becomes particularly exposed in research about the introduction and use of closed-circuit television (CCTV) and other digital surveillance technologies in high-rise housing, which shows that views on these new technologies are continuously being promoted and recanted (Woolgar, 2002b).

Rule 3 – Virtual technologies supplement rather than substitute for "real" activities.

As Brown and Duguid (2000) point out, the rise of the digital age has brought about many predictions of the end of certain things, including the end of the press and television, the end of intermediaries, the end of bureaucratic organizations, the end of politics, the end of the nation- state and, last but not least, the end of paper-based documents in offices. In each case, these endings were expected to be caused by the substitution of digital technology for processes, objects, activities and organizations in the real world. A more recent example of this point is the widespread public expectation that many jobs will disappear as a result of the use of robots (e.g. Elliott, 2018). However, empirical research from the Virtual Society? programme shows that digital technologies tend to supplement rather than substitute for existing practices and activities, creating interesting new relationships between and modifications of the online and offline worlds (Woolgar, 2002b). A good example is empirical research on the prospects for e-learning at tertiary education institutions.

Rule 4 – The more virtual, the more real.

According to empirical research, not only do new virtual activities sit alongside real-world activities, the use of digital technologies can also lead to more of

Digital technologies and societal change 31

the corresponding real-world activity (Woolgar, 2002b). For example, research shows that a rapid growth in the uptake and use of digital communication technologies has gone hand in hand with strong increases in personal air travel and car transport (e.g. Rainie & Wellman, 2012) and that an increase in the numbers of people visiting museums online has led to a larger number of people physically visiting museums (Woolgar, 2002b).

Rule 5 – The more global, the more local.

Although digital technologies facilitate networked communication and activities at a global scale and seem to promise independence from location, empirical research shows that this can only happen through using and managing these digital technologies in a specific local context. For example, new forms of virtual organization are created between teams of workers by incorporating digital technologies within existing local work practices (Woolgar, 2002b: 20).

Box 2.2 Castells' information technology paradigm

Digital technologies are inherently different from earlier technologies in the sense that they shape society through their distinctive capabilities and are being shaped by society: more specifically, by users. Castells (1996) uses the notion of the information technology paradigm to describe and analyse what he sees as the essence of revolutionary mutual shaping developments happening in society. In his view, this new information technology paradigm has the following five core characteristics (Castells, 1996: 61–62):

1) These technologies *act on information*, with information and data flow being the raw material for the new technological paradigm;
2) *The effects of these technologies are pervasive*: because information is an integral part of all human activity, all social processes are shaped by, and are shaping, these technologies;
3) Any system or set of relationships using these technologies has a *networking logic*. As a result, this technology-enabled networking logic can be implemented in all kinds of processes and organizations;
4) The new technological paradigm is based on *flexibility*: these technologies have the ability to reconfigure processes and organizations by rearranging their components; and
5) The growing *convergence of specific technologies into a highly integrated, digitised system*, within which old, separate technological trajectories become indistinguishable.

32   *Theory*

According to Castells (1996), what is different under this new information technology paradigm is that the feedback loop between introducing new technology, using it, and developing it into new innovative application becomes much faster. Moreover, the introduction of new digital technologies is not restricted to a particular society or region, but they have spread throughout the world. In other words, although the mutual shaping of digital technologies and society is happening through a spiral process of learning, both the scale and the rapid speed of this learning process lead to revolutionary change rather than evolutionary development, according to Castells (Castells, 1996).

The contribution of data to societal change

Conceptualising data

Derived from the Latin word *dare* which means "to give," data are raw elements that can be "given by," or abstracted from, phenomena and measured and recorded in various ways (Kitchin, 2014: 2). However, data are not things or natural objects with an essence of their own; they are entities used as representations of objects, observations or other phenomena (Borgman, 2015). Those representations vary according to the people who are constructing them and the context in which they are constructed and over time (Borgman, 2015; Latour, 1986). Consequently, according to Borgman (2015), questions of "What are data?" are better addressed as "When are data?" In other words, as data are always a selection made by people in a particular context and from all the data that could possibly be given at any moment in time, they are inherently partial, selective, social, contextual and representative (Kitchin, 2014; Borgman, 2015).

This suggests that the criteria that have been used to select and represent the data have major consequences for further interpretations and outcomes of data (Kitchin, 2014). Indeed, Levitin (2016) claims that it is easy to lie with graphs and other presentations of data as few people take time to look under the hood and see how the selection, collection, processing, application and use of data works. Consequently, data representations or statistics are not objective facts: they are data selections, collections, interpretations and presentations undertaken by people (Levitin, 2016; Kitchin, 2014).

Data *per se* do not have value; they are a means to an end. Their value lies in their use (Borgman, 2015: 3). As data uses may vary and can happen long after the data were collected or for a different purpose than they were originally collected for, the value of data may not be apparent in first instance. As a result, the value of data varies widely over contexts, people, data uses, social relationships, institutions and time.

Digital technologies and societal change 33

Consequently, data are never simply just data: although people may consider them "objective," "independent" or "raw material" for producing information and knowledge, in reality data do not exist independently of the people, interpretations, technologies and contexts that produce them (Kitchin, 2014). Being a core part of a socio-technical configuration or assemblage, data are social in the sense that they are a product of the people, practices, technologies, institutions, organizations and relationships mutually shaping each other in a particular context (Borgman, 2015; Dutton, 2006; Latour, 1986). Consequently, how data are produced, processed, managed and used varies between socio-technical assemblages in contexts with different stakeholders, technologies, institutions, policies and power involved (Borgman, 2015). This then not only leads to differences in the selection, interpretation, processing, management, impact and outcomes related to data in different contexts, but also has further consequences for how data need to be selected, interpreted, managed and regulated in socio-technical assemblages that are positioned in different contexts.

Different kinds of data

Data vary by form, structure, source, producer and type. Their different characteristics determine how they are processed, analysed, managed and used (Kitchin, 2014: 4–9):

- *Form*: quantitative data and qualitative data. Quantitative data are numeric records and have four different measurement levels (nominal data, ordinal data, interval data and ratio data), which delimit how they can be processed and analysed. In contrast, qualitative data are non-numeric and include texts, pictures, art, video and sounds. Although qualitative data analysis is usually practised on the original materials, significant progress is being made in processing and analysing qualitative data computationally through techniques like machine learning and data mining (Kitchin, 2014: 5);
- *Structure*: structured data, semi-structured data and unstructured data. Structured data can be easily organized, stored and transferred in a defined-data model with a consistent format (e.g. name, address, date of birth), and processed by computers using calculus and algorithms. Semi-structured data are loosely structured data that have no predefined data model, but they do have a reasonably consistent set of fields, and the data are tagged, providing metadata that can help sort, order and structure the data. Unstructured data do not have a defined data model or common structure; instead, each individual element of a dataset may have its own specific structure or format distinct from other data in the dataset;
- *Source*: captured data, exhaust data, transient data and derived data. Data can be captured directly and deliberately through some form of measurement (e.g. in lab experiments, in observation surveys or through sensors or cameras). In contrast, exhaust data are produced by a technical device, programme or system as a by-product (e.g. data on customer purchasing

34 *Theory*

behaviours from goods sold electronically). Exhaust data can be used but can also be transient data if they are never examined or processed and discarded. Where captured data and exhaust data are raw data as they have not been converted or combined with other data, derived data are produced through additional processing or analysis of captured data;

- *Producer*: primary data, secondary data and tertiary data. Primary data are generated by a researcher, whereas secondary data are data made available to others for re-use and analysis. Tertiary data are a form of derived data (i.e. primary data which have been additionally processed or analysed); and
- *Type*: indexical data, attribute data and metadata. Indexical data enable identification and linking and include unique identifiers (e.g. passport numbers, social security numbers, credit card numbers, IP addresses, order numbers, names, postal codes or zip codes, fingerprint, DNA sequence). Attribute data represent aspects of a phenomenon but are not indexical in nature (e.g. age, weight, colour, blood group). Metadata are data about data and can either refer to the data content, including names and descriptions of specific fields and data definitions, or to the whole dataset.

Box 2.3   Exercise 2.1

Try to find a practical example of each of the different kinds of data (form, structure, source, producer and type) in government or the wider public sector. Please elaborate for each practical example in which area of government or the wider public sector you have found the data and for what purpose the data have been used.

Data form the fundamental base layer of a knowledge pyramid

Data is not the same as information or knowledge but need to be seen as a fundamental base layer of a knowledge pyramid where each layer is distinguished by a process of distillation that adds meaning, organization and value (Kitchin, 2014). Information, as the second layer of the knowledge pyramid, is not similar to data but adds meaning to them through interpretation and processing (Floridi, 2010). This then also suggests that, in order to arrive at the right information, having the right data is usually better than having more data (Borgman, 2015).

Knowledge composes the third layer of the knowledge pyramid and is actionable information; through processes of analysing and organizing the information, knowledge provides the basis for understanding and explaining (Kitchin, 2014). In other words, data (i.e. abstracted elements) precedes information (i.e. processed and linked elements), which then precedes knowledge (i.e. analyzed and organized information) (Kitchin, 2014). This knowledge pyramid is visualised in Figure 2.1 (cf Kitchin, 2014).

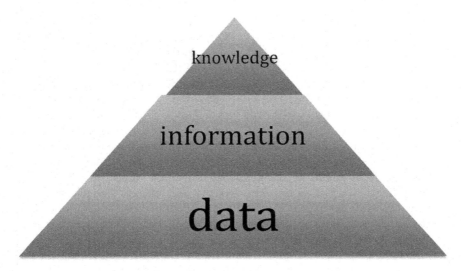

Figure 2.1 The knowledge pyramid
Source: Kitchin (2014).

Data are social constructs

As discussed, data are not objective truths that can be detected in the real world but social constructs produced by people. This creates situations where, if people are not educated and skilled around the selection, collection, interpretation, analysis, organization and use of data, it is relatively easy to have data inaccuracies or biases or any other mistakes made in processing and managing data or datasets. This then can also lead to incorrect information or knowledge. A further issue is around the presentation of data: although data visualisation can help people to process and interpret the data and convert them into information, we should not forget that data visualisations are social constructs themselves as they are interpretations of data made by the people who have put the data visualisation together.

Some good examples of how easy it is to lie with statistics are provided by Levitin (2016). A few of his examples are described in Box 2.4.

Box 2.4 Examples of lying with statistics

Statisticians call it a correlation when two things are related, whether or not one thing causes the other (Levitin, 2016). However, correlation doesn't imply causation. We can come across so-called logical fallacies that

36 *Theory*

arise from thinking that just because one thing (Y) occurs after another (X), that X caused Y (Levitin, 2016: 48–49). For example, people typically brush their teeth before going off to work in the morning, but brushing their teeth doesn't cause them to go to work (Levitin, 2016: 49).

Another logical fallacy arises from thinking that just because two things co-occur, one must have caused the other (Levitin, 2016: 49). Levitin demonstrates this logical fallacy by showing two identical graphs: one graph shows the number of people who drowned by falling into a pool in a particular year, and the other graph presents the number of films Nicolas Cage appeared in in a particular year. You could interpret these identical graphs by thinking that drownings cause the release of new Nicolas Cage films or, vice versa, that the release of Nicolas Cage films causes drownings. Or that a third unidentified factor causes both. However, these findings are simply unrelated, and the correlation is a coincidence (Levitin, 2016: 49).

Manipulating the framing of data can influence public policy outcomes. For example, a survey of recycling yield on various streets in Los Angeles shows that one street in particular recycles 2.2 times as much as any other street (Levitin, 2016: 54). However, framing the data at the street level is only relevant if all streets are identical. What about the possibility that this street has twice as many residents as other streets or is much longer than other streets? Also, how something is defined or categorised can make a big difference in the statistic you end up with (Levitin, 2016: 93). Think about the various ways in which you can define "rainfall," "inflation" or "homelessness."

When you are selecting your sample and you want to lie with statistics, you could for example take the average height of people near a basketball court or ask about income by sampling near the unemployment office (Levitin, 2016). You can also have a bias in your reporting as people sometimes lie when asked about their opinions in a survey: for example, people may want to make a good impression on you and lie about their income or the newspaper they read (Levitin, 2016).

Box 2.5 Exercise 2.2

Identify a government dataset or database and theoretically explore what data inaccuracies and data biases might possibly exist in that particular dataset. Please elaborate what or who might have caused a particular data inaccuracy or bias.

Complex socio-technical assemblages in the context of digital government

Digital technologies and data form critical parts of complex socio-technical assemblages positioned within the context of digital government. Besides digital technologies and data, these socio-technical assemblages in the digital government context are made up of people and communities, users and stakeholders, government organizations and institutions, political leadership, public sector norms and values, democratic and ethical arrangements, legal and regulatory arrangements, budgets, policies, processes and procedures, forms of knowledge and experience and practices and activities. If we want to understand and explain how digital technologies and data are being introduced, managed and used in the context of digital government and its relationship with citizens, we will need to focus on the socio-technical assemblage as a whole and not just on the digital technology and/or the data *per se* (Lips, 2012; Bellamy & Taylor, 1998; Ananny & Crawford, 2018; Kitchin, 2014).

However, we can observe that, in most cases around data use, attention is more narrowly focused on the data *per se* and not so much on the information and knowledge derived from them (Kitchin, 2014). Similarly, based on their study *The Social Life of Information*, Brown and Duguid (2000) argue that focusing too narrowly and in a linear way on digital technologies and data overlooks the particular context and social relationships in which digital technologies and data are being constructed and used. Empirical research in the context of digital government and its external relationships has confirmed that digital technology– and data-related change in government should not be considered a rational, predictable, easy or straightforward process but an extremely challenging, unpredictable, complex and non-linear course of action (Lips, 2012: 240).

Consequently, taking the digital government context of digital technologies and data seriously will help us to better understand and explain the design, management and use of these digital technologies and data as part of particular socio-technical assemblages in digital government and its relationships with citizens (Lips, 2012; Bellamy & Taylor, 1998; Ananny & Crawford, 2018; Brown & Duguid, 2000):

> The way forward [with data and digital technologies in digital government, ML] is paradoxically to look not ahead, but to look around.
> (Brown & Duguid, 2000: 8).

This then critically requires detailed empirical research into these socio-technical assemblages within the digital government context in order to understand and explain changes, impact, outcomes and implications (Lips, 2012).

38   *Theory*

Discussion questions

1   Choose a digital government strategy document and explore which perspective(s) on the role and contribution of digital technologies in societal change can be recognised.
2   Under what conditions would public decision-making be truly evidence based? Motivate your answer.
3   Choose a socio-technical assemblage around a particular digital technology or dataset in the context of digital government and its relationships with citizens and describe the various components of that socio-technical assemblage. Please describe and explain differences in understanding between only looking at the digital technology or data *per se* and considering the socio-technical assemblage as a whole: what do you see differently and understand better about digital government? Motivate your answers.

Note

1   BBC (2007) Child database system postponed. 27 November. Available from: http://news.bbc.co.uk/2/hi/uk_news/education/7115546.stm [accessed 24 January 2019].

References

Ananny, M. & Crawford, K. (2018) Seeing without knowing: Limitations of the transparency ideal and its application to algorithmic accountability. *New Media & Society*, 20 (3), 973–989.

Bellamy, C. & Taylor, J.A. (1998) *Governing in the Information Age*. Buckingham: Open University Press.

Borgman, C.L. (2015) *Big Data, Little Data, No Data: Scholarship in the Networked World*. Cambridge, MA: Massachusetts Institute of Technology Press.

Brown, J.S. & Duguid, P. (2000) *The Social Life of Information*. Boston, MA: Harvard Business School Press.

Cairncross, F. (1998) *The Death of Distance: How the Communications Revolution Will Change Our Lives*. London: Orion Business Books.

Castells, M. (1996) *The Rise of the Network Society: The Information Age: Economy, Society and Culture*. Vol. 1. Oxford: Blackwell Publishers.

Crawford, K. (2016) Can an algorithm be agonistic? Ten scenes from life in calculated publics. *Science, Technology & Human Values*, 41 (1), 77–92.

Dutton, W.H. (1995) Driving into the future of communications? Check the rear view mirror. In: Emmott, S.J. (ed.) *Information Superhighways: Multimedia Users and Futures*. London: Academic Press, pp. 79–102.

Dutton, W.H. (ed.) (1999) *Society on the Line: Information Politics in the Digital Age*. Oxford: Oxford University Press.

Dutton, W.H. (2006) The social informatics of the internet: An ecology of games. In: Berleur, J., Numinen, M.I. & Impagliazzo, J. (eds.) *Social Informatics: An Information Society for All? In Remembrance of Rob Kling*. IFIP International Federation for Information Processing, Vol. 223. Boston, MA: Springer, pp. 243–253.

Elliott, L. (2018) Robots will take our jobs: We'd better plan now, before it's too late. *The Guardian*. Available from: https://www.theguardian.com/commentisfree/2018/feb/01/robots-take-our-jobs-amazon-go-seattle [accessed 3 December 2018].

Fleck, J., Webster, J. & Williams, R. (1990) The dynamics of IT implementation: A reassessment of paradigms and trajectories of development. *Futures*, 22, 618–640.

Floridi, L. (2010) *Information: A Very Short Guide*. Oxford: Oxford University Press.

Fountain, J.E. (2001) *Building the Virtual State: Information Technology and Institutional Change*. Washington, DC: Brookings Institution Press.

Galloway, A.R. (2013) *The Interface Effect*. Cambridge: Polity Press.

Henman, P. (2010) *Governing Electronically: E-Government and the Reconfiguration of Public Administration, Policy and Power*. Basingstoke: Palgrave MacMillan.

Kallinikos, J. (2011) *Governing Through Technology: Information Artefacts and Social Practice: Technology, Work and Globalization*. Basingstoke: Palgrave MacMillan.

Kitchin, R. (2014) *The Data Revolution: Big Data, Open Data, Data Infrastructures & Their Consequences*. London: Sage.

Latour, B. (1986) *Science in Action: How to Follow Scientists and Engineers Through Society*. Cambridge, MA: Harvard University Press.

Levitin, D. (2016) *A Field Guide to Lies and Statistics: A Neuroscientist on How to Make Sense of a Complex World*. London: Viking.

Lips, A.M.B. (2011) 'E-government is dead: Long live networked governance': Fixing system errors in the New Zealand public management system. In: Ryan, B. & Gill, D. (eds.) *Future State: Directions for Public Management in New Zealand*. Wellington: Victoria University of Wellington, pp. 248–261.

Lips, A.M.B. (2012) E-government is dead: Long live public administration 2.0. *Information Polity*, 17 (3–4), 239–250.

MacKenzie, D.A. & Wajcman, J. (1985) *The Social Shaping of Technology: How the Refrigerator Got Its Hum*. Milton Keynes: Open University Press.

MacKenzie, D.A. & Wajcman, J. (eds.) (1999) *The Social Shaping of Technology*. 2nd ed. Buckingham: Open University Press.

Oudshoorn, N. & Pinch, T. (eds.) (2003) *How Users Matter: The Co-Construction of Users and Technology*. Cambridge, MA: Massachusetts Institute of Technology Press.

Peckover, S., White, S. & Hall, C. (2008) Making and managing electronic children: E-assessment in child welfare. *Information, Communication & Society*, 11 (3), 375–394.

Rainie, L. & Wellman, B. (2012) *Networked: The New Social Operating System*. Cambridge, MA: Massachusetts Institute of Technology Press.

Williams, R. & Edge, D. (1996) The social shaping of technology. In: Dutton, W.H. (ed.) *Information and Communication Technologies: Visions and Realities*. Oxford: Oxford University Press, pp. 53–67.

Woolgar, S. (ed.) (2002a) *Virtual Society? Technology, Cyberbole, Reality*. Oxford: Oxford University Press.

Woolgar, S. (2002b) Five rules of virtuality. In: Woolgar, S. (ed.) *Virtual Society? Technology, Cyberbole, Reality*. Oxford: Oxford University Press, pp. 1–22.

Woolgar, S. (2006) Perspectives on technology and society. In: Restivo, S. (ed.) *Science, Technology and Society: An Encyclopedia*. Oxford: Oxford University Press, online publication, eISBN 9780199891269

Wyatt, S., Thomas, G. & Terranova, T. (2002) They came, they surfed, they went back to the beach: Conceptualizing use and non-use of the internet. In: Woolgar, S. (ed.) *Virtual Society? Technology, Cyberbole, Reality*. Oxford: Oxford University Press, pp. 23–40.

Further reading

Borgman, C.L. (2015) *Big Data, Little Data, No Data: Scholarship in the Networked World*. Cambridge, MA: Massachusetts Institute of Technology Press.

40 *Theory*

Brown, J.S. & Duguid, P. (2000) *The Social Life of Information.* Boston, MA: Harvard Business School Press.

Castells, M. (1996) *The Rise of the Network Society: The Information Age: Economy, Society and Culture.* Vol. 1. Oxford: Blackwell Publishers.

Fountain, J.E. (2001) *Building the Virtual State: Information Technology and Institutional Change.* Washington, DC: Brookings Institution Press.

Henman, P. (2010) *Governing Electronically: E-Government and the Reconfiguration of Public Administration, Policy and Power.* Basingstoke: Palgrave MacMillan.

Kitchin, R. (2014) *The Data Revolution: Big Data, Open Data, Data Infrastructures & Their Consequences.* London: Sage.

Levitin, D. (2016) *A Field Guide to Lies and Statistics: A Neuroscientist on How to Make Sense of a Complex World.* London: Viking.

MacKenzie, D.A. & Wajcman, J. (eds.) (1999) *The Social Shaping of Technology.* 2nd ed. Buckingham: Open University Press.

Woolgar, S. (ed.) (2002a) *Virtual Society? Technology, Cyberbole, Reality.* Oxford: Oxford University Press.

3 Different theories and perspectives on digital government

Learning objectives

By the end of this chapter you should be able to:

- Understand the various theories and perspectives on digital government;
- Identify the limitations of different digital government perspectives; and
- Apply the complex public management perspective to empirical digital government case studies.

Key points of this chapter

- Each perspective on digital government provides us with a different way of "seeing" and understanding digital government. At the same time, each perspective narrows our view on digital government by not accounting for other aspects of the same socio-technical phenomenon;
- Understanding which perspective is used in scholarly or practitioners' debates on digital government helps us to understand what changes and outcomes are expected of digital government, what decisions will be made and what processes will be followed; and
- None of the nine perspectives is sufficient to observe the full breadth and depth of a particular socio-technical assemblage in the context of digital government. However, an alternative complex public management perspective helps us to empirically and comprehensively observe digital government as an adaptive complex socio-technical phenomenon.

Key terms

- *Technology perspective*: a belief that digital technology drives changes in digital government and its relationships with citizens and autonomously and independently determines digital government outcomes.
- *Data and information perspective*: data (or information) drive and determine digital government changes and outcomes.
- *Revolutionary vs. evolutionary perspective*: people believe in either rapid, radical and fundamental change in digital government or a digital government change process of gradual evolution.

42 Theory

- *Private sector perspective*: this private sector perspective is applied to digital government, regardless of digital government's unique characteristics and context.
- *Transformational perspective*: although the meaning of "transformation" is usually ambiguous and ill defined, a transformational perspective is often used as a public sector reform ambition or as a key concept to explore changes in and "maturity" of digital government.
- *Institutional perspective*: the institutional nature of government is considered to be the determining, shaping force in technology- and data-enabled public sector reform.
- *Reinforcement thesis*: digital technologies and data are used in ways that reinforce existing political, governmental and managerial structures and arrangements in government.
- *Networked governance perspective*: this perspective acknowledges that digital government is not just about government or government organizations and focuses on the wider network of actors involved in digital government processes and activities, such as citizens, private sector organizations and civil society.
- *Surveillance state perspective*: a belief that the introduction and use of digital technologies and data will lead to increased surveillance of citizens and, with that, to erosion of public trust, potential violation of human rights and substantial information imbalances in citizen-government relationships.
- *Good governance perspective*: the use of digital technologies and data by governments in order to standardise government processes and activities to reduce corruption, increase government transparency and improve government accountability and effectiveness.
- *Complex public management perspective*: this perspective helps us to both empirically and comprehensively explore, understand and explain digital government as dynamically reflexive interactions of people, technology and public management institutions and processes: a complex socio-technical phenomenon.

Introduction

In 1998, a substantial scholarly handbook was published, titled *Public Administration in an Information Age* (Snellen & van de Donk, 1998). It was the consolidated effort of a group of leading European and American scholars who, for many years, had been involved in empirical research initiatives in order to reflect on, understand and explain the introduction and use of digital technologies across the public sector and the implications for government, democracy and the multidisciplinary scholarly field of public administration. At the time, the following summarizing empirical research statements were derived from the various book contributions (Snellen & van de Donk, 1998: 14–18):

1) The nation-state is losing its territorial basis. Digital technology developments, such as the Internet, facilitate this deterritorialisation and lead to a

Different theories and perspectives 43

certain degree of "virtualization" of the state. The nation-state exists only insofar as it succeeds in maintaining and controlling a physical or technological link with individuals and groups in society;

2) The system of checks and balances in democratic government, which traditionally has served as protection against an over-powering government and a warranty for civil liberties, is eroding;

3) The scales of the delicate balance between the public and the private spheres are tilting in the direction of the public sphere. Surveillance technologies deployed by government agencies are seductive as they promise public safety in public spaces though reducing the private sphere at the same time;

4) Territorial and functional jurisdictions of government are gradually being replaced by *ad hoc* collaborative arrangements between government agencies from different administrative levels, private sector organizations and NGOs;

5) Digital technologies are eroding the checks and balances traditionally built into Weberian bureaucratic models in government and, with that, transforming bureaucratic structures and processes in government organizations;

6) Digitised information and knowledge systems are taking over the professional and administrative discretion of the street-level bureaucrat. This development requires a review of the professional and ethical foundations of public service;

7) New foundations of trust need to be found between government and society, due to eroding democratic checks and balances and a blurring of the public and private spheres;

8) Foundations of democracy tend to be weakened, rather than strengthened, by the application of digital technologies in the public sector. Digital technology applications tend to reinforce existing organization structures and powerful positions of politicians and senior public managers;

9) The Weberian bureaucratic structure of government organizations is being replaced by a digitised information and communication infrastructure which provides public officials with increasing (automated) control over government business operations and activities, leading to strengthening hierarchical power imbalances within public sector organizations and between government and society; and

10) Drastically increased digital capabilities to collect, store, aggregate, analyse and present data enable a rationalization of public policy-making, which potentially may harm the democratic quality of the policy process.

In 1998, the editors of this handbook admitted that it was still too early to fully understand the impact of digital technologies on government and democracy, reflecting the empirical ambiguities and uncertainties around the development of digital government, in both practice and theory, in many of the handbook contributions at the time. However, what these empirical research statements demonstrate to us as scholars is that *when* we look at socio-technical assemblages

44   *Theory*

in the context of digital government and *how* we look at these socio-technical constructs, such as the theoretical lenses, perspectives and heuristic frameworks we use and the research methods we deploy, are vitally important for how we understand and explain changes and outcomes related to digital government.

In this chapter, we explore and discuss nine different theoretical and analytical perspectives that are commonly used as ways of "seeing" digital government. Each of these lenses is putting different emphasis on what can be seen and, therefore, commonly narrowing our views on digital government as a socio-technical phenomenon by not accounting for other aspects of that same phenomenon. A good example of how these different perspectives work is Graham Allison's famous study *Essence of Decision: Explaining the Cuban Missile Crisis* (Allison, 1971) on the Cuba crisis in the 1960s. Allison's study shows us that using three completely different lenses will lead us to see three different sets of processes, activities and outcomes, which then lead to different follow-up actions and decisions. Consequently, understanding which perspective is used in scholarly and practitioners' debates on digital government will help us to understand what changes and outcomes are expected of digital government, what decisions will be made and what processes will be followed.

The following nine theoretical and analytical perspectives on digital government are discussed in this chapter:

1)   A technology perspective;
2)   A data and information perspective;
3)   A revolutionary change vs. evolutionary change perspective;
4)   A private sector perspective;
5)   A transformational perspective;
6)   An institutional perspective;
7)   A networked governance perspective;
8)   A surveillance state perspective; and
9)   A good governance perspective

Some of these perspectives are normative; others have empirical foundations. However, none of them is sufficient to observe the full breadth and depth of socio-technical assemblages in the context of digital government. Consequently, we propose an alternative complex public management perspective which helps us to more comprehensively and empirically observe the socio-technical phenomenon of digital government.

Nine dominant perspectives on digital government

1. A technology perspective

As we discussed in Chapter 2, people who use a narrow technology perspective on digital government believe that inherent technological capabilities drive changes in digital government and its relationships with citizens.

Consequently, digital technology capabilities would autonomously and independently determine the outcomes of digital government (Lips, 2012; Snellen, 2005; Frissen, 1998; Henman, 2010). As an example, inherent technological capabilities of the Internet, including its "informating" and information processing capabilities, decentralised and diffused networking capabilities and virtual reality capabilities, would drive the following changes in the public sector (Frissen, 1998):

- *Horizontalisation*: the vertical and hierarchical bureaucratic organization of the public sector is being replaced by a networked configuration of independent organizations inside and outside the public sector. This leads to an increasing importance of horizontal relationships, collaboration on a contractual basis, co-production of public policy and service provision and participatory democracy;
- *Deterritorialisation*: as a result of 24/7 Internet access from anywhere in the world, public service provision, public policy and public decision-making are organized without any restrictions of time or location; and
- *Virtualisation*: the potential of having virtual meetings at long distance and the digital simulation of reality, such as through 3-D urban planning maps, leads to new innovative forms of public consultation and other forms of democratic participation. Also, the physical borders of government organizations become more fluid, and physical organizations are replaced by virtual organizations.

Similarly, with the arrival of Web 2.0, which is a more interactive and collaborative conception of the World Wide Web, several scholars theorised about this digital technology's driving force towards a new form of interactive and collaborative government: government 2.0 (Mergel, 2013; O'Reilly, 2010) (see also Chapter 7).

Other scholars, too, point to the determining role of digital technologies in different areas of the public sector, such as the structure and restructuring of government organizations (Zuurmond, 1998; Snellen, 2005; Kallinikos, 2011), computer code driving the execution of legislation (Bovens & Zouridis, 2002; Schokker, 1996) and automated public decision-making based on algorithms (Zouridis, 1999; Zuurmond, 1998). For example, Bovens and Zouridis (2002) theorise that the application of digital technologies in the public sector would rapidly change the structure of government agencies: digital technologies would shift traditional machine bureaucracies in which street-level public officials exercise administrative discretion in providing services to individual clients to become system-level bureaucracies in which system analysts and software designers are the key public decision-makers through their conversion of legislation into software code embedded in decision-making systems. As a result, the new technology-driven public decision-making systems would dictate public service outcomes and, with that, limit the discretionary power of those providing public services.

46 *Theory*

Technological deterministic thinking can also be found in digital government practice, such as in digital government strategy and public policy documents. For example, in 1996, the UK central government proposed a strategy for a radically new way of public service provision across the UK called Government.direct. Founded on capabilities offered by new digital technologies at the time, such as the Internet, the strategy was expected to fundamentally change the way in which public services had been provided in the UK for the past 150 years: for instance, public services would be more accessible, more convenient, easier to use, quicker in response, less costly to the taxpayer and, last but not least, delivered electronically (UK Office of Public Service, 1996). Using a three-step process, digital technologies would offer the unique opportunity of horizontally integrating the vertical independent "silos" of government organizations in the UK (UK Office of Public Service, 1996):

- Step 1: paper flows between the UK government and the public would be replaced with transmission and reception of information via electronic terminals;
- Step 2: although government organizations would still retain their separate identities, a new privately-owned digital technology infrastructure would be placed on top of all vertical silos. This digital infrastructure would provide the link or interconnection between government organizations for specific public services and the individual customer;
- Step 3: a variety of shared cross-government digital networks and services would be established, such as a government-wide email system, shared databases containing customer names and addresses, and other functional digital networks through shared governmental areas with heavy data and information flows (e.g. criminal justice). This then would achieve not only increased efficiency and duplication reduction from a customer perspective, but also new opportunities to reach several public servants in different government organizations simultaneously and, with that, speed up the policy process and eventually a cultural change in government towards integrated public service provision.

As the UK government acknowledged the existence of legal restrictions to the sharing of citizens' personal data between government organizations, they would consider whether legislation would be necessary or appropriate to allow for such data sharing (UK Office of Public Service, 1996: 17).

According to Woolgar (2002b), objectifying the potential of digital technology and, with that, assuming a causal progression from the digital technology to societal change often happens around the introduction of new and unfamiliar technologies, such as the Internet in the 1990s, when there are no or very limited experiences with the new digital technology and, with that, no empirical references to the actual circumstances. This scholarly observation reconfirms our discussion thus far about the critical need for scholars to undertake empirical research, preferably at various moments in time, into actual uses of digital

Different theories and perspectives 47

technologies and data as part of socio-technical assemblages in order to understand and explain digital government changes and outcomes.

2. A data and information perspective

Recent smart technology developments around data and datafication processes in society have led to a narrow perspective that data drive and determine digital government changes and outcomes (see also Chapter 6; Kitchin, 2014). In other words, data are being objectified and separated from the socio-technical assemblages in which they are used. Moreover, critical social processes to interpret data in order to generate information and the processing of this information into actionable information or knowledge are not taken into consideration (Brown & Duguid, 2000). This narrow data-driven perspective then leads to restricted observations around changes and outcomes as a result of data use in digital government.

In earlier research efforts, especially around the informating capabilities of digital technologies (Zuboff, 1988), we can witness a similar objectifying approach towards information in the context of digital government. For example, based on research into social welfare service provision in the Netherlands, Zuurmond (1998) observes a radically different set of information-based operational processes in order to provide a service to a social welfare client. He describes these new information-based processes, which are enabled by a likely to happen future opportunity of data matching across various government databases in the social welfare sector, in the following seven subsequent steps (Zuurmond, 1998: 262–263):

- Step 1: the client identifies herself to the social welfare agency (e.g. by using a smart card), provides minimal personal information on a digital intake form at the agency's service counter and makes another appointment. This digital intake form is sent to the electronic document interchange (EDI) connection point of the social welfare agency;
- Step 2: an EDI message with the client's information is sent to the central verification office of all government agencies operating in the social security sector and connected to the digital network;
- Step 3: the central verification office collects relevant information on behalf of the client from various government agencies across the EDI network, including the citizens' registration office (home address of the client, any other people living at the same address), inland revenue (client's last income), the vehicle registration office (estimated value of the client's car), the employment agency (client's job seeking history), the unemployment benefits agency (any benefits the client receives), public health insurance (has the client enrolled?) and other social security agencies (is the client known by any other agency?);
- Step 4: the central verification office uses an EDI application to send the collected information on the client to the social welfare agency, where the

48 *Theory*

client's digital intake form is automatically populated with the collected data;

- Step 5: the client comes back for her meeting appointment and learns about the various pieces of information collected by the central verification office through the network. The frontline staff member who meets the client writes a report and prepares a draft application for the client, based on information gathered through the network;
- Step 6: staff members of the social security agency perform a minor legal check on the client's application to see if there are any legal objections to the client's request for a benefit allowance. This legal check is minor as the information gathered through the network has already been legally validated by the various host organizations;
- Step 7: the client receives her monthly benefit payment. However, the central verification office has placed "flags" on the client's information in the databases of most government organizations that were contacted through the EDI network; as soon as the client's personal circumstances change and, with that, her flagged personal information in the various government databases, a copy of the new information is sent to the social security agency, and the client's benefit payment is adjusted.

In this new information-based service delivery process, the social security agency staff providing the service to the client rely heavily on information provided through the EDI network to construct the client's profile objectively, rather than on information provided by the client or their own administrative discretion (Zuurmond, 1998). As a result, organizational control of public service provision is not managed in traditional bureaucratic ways through hierarchy and rules, but rather through new "infocratic" ways of "informational control" (Zuurmond, 1998).

This research focused dominantly on the new informating capabilities that would become available to social security agency staff through an EDI network that was still under construction at the time of the research. These information-driven research findings remind us of the importance not only to undertake empirical research across socio-technical assemblages in the digital government context at various moments in time, but also to focus on the context-relative social construction of data, information and knowledge, rather than considering potential scenarios in order to better understand and explain digital government outcomes.

For instance, Taylor (1998) points at the opportunity of a scholarly "x-raying" vision on government and its external relationships by conducting empirical research focused on the actual use of digital technology–enabled data and information flows as part of socio-technical assemblages in the context of digital government and its relationships with citizens; in so doing, we are able to develop a much deeper understanding of the changes happening to and within the public sector and their outcomes, compared to other scholarly approaches to the study of government (Lips, 2011).

Box 3.1 The information polity

Taylor's concept of the information polity can be used as an empirical heuristic for exploring and analysing information flows in the public sector. In so doing, it will reveal information-related changes and outcomes in and around government, including information- and ICT-based innovations and their relationships to changing public sector structures, processes and values. For a more in-depth understanding of this concept of the information polity and its value as an empirical heuristic for the public sector, read Taylor (2012) and Taylor and Williams (1991).

3. A revolutionary change vs. evolutionary change perspective

New technologies are often regarded as enablers of radical and fundamental change in society, including in government. Many people seem to have a modernist conception of a future government transformed by new technology: the idea that new technologies will enable something that is not only new and different, but also better than what we had before (Woolgar, 2002b). These ideas also surfaced around the introduction of the Internet in the early 1990s, such as the Internet enabling new innovative forms of direct democracy and enhanced citizen empowerment. However, as with the introduction of other new technologies in society, an important question became whether we are witnessing revolutionary change in government and its external relationships as a result of digital technologies or only small evolutionary step changes. To some, the rapid uptake and spread of digital technologies in society are evidence of revolutionary change in government as well (e.g. Castells, 1996); to others, technology-enabled change in government needs to be seen as a process of gradual evolution (e.g. Fountain, 2008; Lips & Schuppan, 2009; Homburg, 2008). What is beyond dispute, though, is that the pace of technological change in society has quickened and has continued to accelerate in recent decades and also that the scale of technological change is widespread in society and has become global (Webster, 2004).

A person's perspective in this debate usually matches with his or her position in the technology debate we discussed in Chapter 2. For instance, technological determinists support the view that the transformative capabilities of digital technologies drive revolutionary change in government. However, social determinists and those supporting a mutual shaping perspective are more inclined to believe in evolutionary change in government: social determinists, as they perceive technology as a neutral instrument in the hands of decision-makers who are able to control and resist change in government and advocates of the mutual shaping perspective, as they perceive technology-enabled change outcomes in government not as a linear development, but as a spiral process of learning

50   *Theory*

(Williams & Edge, 1996). As examples of how revolutionary, technology-driven change perspectives on digital government can be different from evolutionary change perspectives where digital technologies are seen as enablers of change in digital government, we can look at various public sector reform visions that can be found in digital government strategies around the world from different moments in time (see Table 3.1 for an overview (Lips, 2014: 181)).

In supporting the mutual shaping perspective, MacKenzie and Wajcman (1999) consider two different types of learning to be critically important in evolutionary change processes in both society and government: first of all, "learning by using" (i.e. the feedback from experience of use) and secondly, "learning by doing" (i.e. the making of new innovative things). They come to the conclusion that individual small changes may add up eventually to considerable change outcomes in any particular social context, including in the context of digital government (MacKenzie & Wajcman, 1999). Similarly, Castells (1996) points out that new technology used in the 1970s and 1980s have gone through the following three distinctive stages: 1) the automation of tasks; 2) experimentation of uses; and 3) the reconfiguration of applications. In the first two stages, technology-enabled change happened through the process of learning by using; in the third stage, the technology users learned by doing and ended up reconfiguring and developing new innovative applications (Castells, 1996). According to Castells (1996), what is different around the societal introduction and use of new digital technologies since the 1990s is that societal feedback loops between introducing new technology, using it and developing it into new innovative applications have become much faster.

However, if we consider the impact of digital technologies and data on the public sector to date, we need to come to the conclusion that revolutionary change hasn't happened in governments around the world. Similarly, after analysing 49 academic journal articles with empirical research findings around the impact of digital technologies on the public sector, Danziger and Andersen (2002) come to the conclusion that revolutionary change manifested in a rapidly 'transformed' government has not occurred between 1987 and 2000. However, their study does point towards substantial impacts of digital technologies on government, with many significant changes within government organizations, for example, which could point to a more gradual evolutionary process over time (Danziger & Andersen, 2002).

Table 3.1 Revolutionary public sector reform visions vs. evolutionary public sector reform visions

Revolutionary visions based on digital technology as driver of change	*Evolutionary visions based on digital technology as enabler of change*
• Virtual government	• Customer-focused public services
• Direct democracy	• Citizen-centric government
• Surveillance state	• Open government

Different theories and perspectives 51

4. A private sector perspective

Both scholarly work and practice in the field of digital government are often inspired by what is happening in the private sector with the uptake of digital technologies and data. In digital government practice, the idea is often that the government is lagging behind people's online commercial experience, for example. Consequently, the thinking is that government should try to do similar things in its own digital government context, with a comparable outcome experience for digital government customers (Lips, 2012).

An example of where scholars have applied a private sector or "e-commerce" perspective to digital government can be found amongst many digital government maturity models. These digital government maturity models reflect the evolving linear pathway from the introduction of digital technologies in individual government organizations to the final destination of mature technology-enabled transformation in the public sector (see also the transformational perspective described next). For instance, according to a widely adopted digital government maturity model developed by the Gartner Group, government organizations should go through the following four stages in order to achieve fully mature digital government (Baum & Di Maio, 2000):

- Stage 1: Web presence: having a static website through which basic information is provided to citizens;
- Stage 2: Interaction: providing online interaction tools and features in relationships with citizens;
- Stage 3: Transaction: citizens can complete a government transaction online; and
- Stage 4: Transformation: not further defined by the Gartner Group.

However, Borins (2007) warns against a commonly made mistake in scholarly literature that the maturity pathway for introducing and applying digital technologies in the private sector would be exactly the same maturity pathway for digital government. He points out that government has a unique mandate to publish democratic information and create public records that are accessible to all members of the general public. This democratic obligation of information provision could be considered not only as the end-stage of a digital government maturity pathway in itself but also of much greater significance in the context of digital government compared to other stages identified in the digital government maturity model, such as transaction (Borins, 2007). Moreover, in comparison to digital commercial transactions, government transactions, such as getting a social benefit, renewing a passport or arranging vehicle registration, are usually much more complex and, with that, much more difficult to achieve in the context of digital government (Borins, 2007).

More in general, as we discussed in Chapter 1, many scholarly works in the broad field of digital government do not take into account the unique characteristics and context of government. A common reason for this is that scholars

52 *Theory*

deploy disciplinary perspectives which usually do not distinguish between different types of organizations, such as between government and commercial organizations; however, they do make distinctions between applications and use of different technologies and data within those organizations: distinctions around "digital," so to speak. The information systems discipline, for instance, does not embrace any public management or public administration theory. It mainly focuses on the physical or engineering aspects of digital technologies, including data and information systems, with the objective of designing methodologies, finding solutions to problems and exploring what works in an organization, given the functional requirements of digital technologies and systems as well as organizational constraints in terms of time and budget (Homburg, 2008).

And yet, we need to be aware that a lot of work published under the umbrella of digital government comes from IS scholars. This has led to the application of a narrow, private sector organization perspective, with blind spots around the unique characteristics and context of government and its external relationships in much of the scholarly work on digital government (Lips, 2011; Lips, 2012; Homburg, 2008).

5. A transformational perspective

In the last few decades, the transformational potential of applying digital technologies and data in government has strongly captured the interest of both scholars and practitioners (Taylor & Lips, 2008). Typically, some form of radical transformation in the public sector is seen as an inevitable and often desirable outcome of the rapid technological developments that are happening in society at the same time (Lips, 2014; Taylor & Lips, 2008). Nonetheless, as we discussed earlier, the transformational potential embedded in digital technologies should not be considered as a given; instead, digital government outcomes depend on the actual use of digital technologies and data as part of a particular socio-technical assemblage (Lips, 2012). Moreover, although many scholars have used "transformation" as a key concept to explore changes in the context of digital government, the meaning of this concept is usually ambiguous, ill defined, or not defined at all (Lips, 2017; O'Neill, 2009).

The ambiguous meaning of transformation becomes clear when we consider various existing digital government maturity models, all indicating a linear development towards better, mature and transformed digital government (Andersen & Henriksen, 2006; Klievink & Janssen, 2009). For example, besides the digital government maturity model developed by the Gartner Group as mentioned earlier, the following scholarly digital government models provide us with some insight into what this linear evolution towards transformed digital government may look like.

For example, Layne and Lee (2001) developed a four-stage digital government maturity model with the first stage, "catalogue," representing the presence of a government organization on the Internet; the second stage, "transaction,"

Different theories and perspectives 53

referring to the maturity milestone that citizens can do transactions online with the government; the third stage of "vertical integration," involving the integration of a functional area across either one hierarchical government organization or different administrative levels; and the fourth and final stage of "horizontal integration" pointing to the integration of processes and activities within and across different public sector organizations.

Another example is the digital government maturity model developed by Klievink and Janssen (2009), which has the following five stages towards transformation (Klievink & Janssen, 2009: 278):

1 *Stovepipes*: few applications, public services or products are interconnected, and data are not shared between government organizations;
2 *Integrated government organizations*: public service delivery and digital technologies within government organizations are integrated to create a one-stop shop at the organizational level;
3 *Nationwide portal*: a nationwide government portal is introduced to provide access to existing government products and services, including a digital vault personalised for each individual citizen. The digital vault can be used to provide government organizations with access to citizens' personal data when their public services and products are being requested;
4 *Inter-organizational integration*: clearly defined and standardised cross-agency services are bundled and integrated and can be delivered as virtually one service via the portal; and
5 *Demand-driven, joined-up government*: instead of citizens having to find and apply for government services, the portal will search for the relevant public services and make recommendations.

A further example of a digital government maturity model that leads to transformation is the open government maturity model developed by Lee and Kwak (2012). This open government maturity model consists of the following five stages towards transformed open government (Lee & Kwak, 2012: 496–499):

1 *Initial conditions*: no or few open government capabilities exist, and social media are hardly used. The focus is on presenting and broadcasting information to the general public;
2 *Data transparency*: high-value, high-impact government data are published online and shared with members of the public. Data quality is assured in terms of accuracy, consistency and timeliness;
3 *Open participation*: interactive communications with members of the general public are established around open government data, including participatory opportunities for public feedback, conversation, voting and crowd-sourcing;
4 *Open collaboration*: inter-agency collaboration and open collaboration with members of the general public around open government data are established. The focus is on co-creating value-added government services; and

54 *Theory*

5 *Ubiquitous engagement*: public engagement around open government data becomes easier for members of the general public and universally accessible through mobile and ubiquitous computing devices and applications. Also, open government data, public engagement methods, social media tools and government services are seamlessly integrated within and across government agencies so that the public can easily navigate and engage in various open government activities.

These examples of digital government maturity models clearly demonstrate not only the variety of meanings attached to fully transformed digital government, but also how to get there in different, subsequent stages. Moreover, they seem to suggest that a fully transformed digital government is in fact an ideal type, rather than a realistic, achievable output of digital technology and data use in the public sector.

A further scholarly reflection on the meaning of transformation is offered by O'Neill (2009). She points out that transformation in fact has two separate and quite different meanings (O'Neill, 2009):

1 *Instrumental transformation*: a radical change in the existing administration, information management and service delivery practices of government agencies that may also have a consequential impact on organizational structures and/or management practices. This application of transformation often results in less disruptive changes to operational and management practices that deliver benefits of increased speed, better quality of government service and lower transaction costs and can be described as "doing the same things differently"; and

2 *Systemic transformation*: a radical, disruptive change in existing governance arrangements in the public sector, including constitutional responsibilities and accountabilities, fiscal management, legislation, regulation and decision-making rights over public resources. From this perspective, transformation is also about a disruptive, fundamental change in key institutional and democratic relationships, such as between government and citizens, within a broader systemic order. Therefore, systemic transformation is about "doing different things" (O'Neil, 2009).

Nevertheless, although this further specification of transformation might be useful in considering the type of changes happening in the public sector as a result of the use of digital technologies and data, the actual meaning of this phenomenon has not become much clearer, other than that this transformation concept could be replaced by the concept of radical change. However, how we as researchers are able to empirically observe transformation as a sociotechnical phenomenon has not been demonstrated in research findings thus far (e.g. Andersen & Henriksen, 2005; Grönlund, 2005; Heeks & Bailur, 2007).

At the same time, though, a convincing case for the benefits of digital government transformation is made not only through many linear digital government

Different theories and perspectives 55

maturity models, such as the ones we have discussed thus far, but also in an economical sense. For example, based on research data from 28 digital government projects in one of the OECD member states, Foley and Alfonso (2009) found that the net benefits of digital government substantially increase when digital government projects are moving from the transaction stage into the transformation stage.

In general, since empirical research findings on the impact of digital technologies and data on governments have been available, many scholars have come to the conclusion that high expectations around digitally enabled transformed government have not been met (e.g. Fountain, 2001; Fountain, 2008; Lips, 2014; Lips, 2017; Taylor & Lips, 2008). Moreover, research shows that digital government transformation has different meanings to different people for varying socio-technical assemblages in the context of digital government in different countries and usually is very difficult and complex to achieve (Lips, 2017). For example, West (2005) concludes on the basis of empirical research on over 17,000 government websites in the USA that, although digital technologies may offer the potential for transformational change in government, social, political and economic forces very much constrain the scope of such change.

6. An institutional perspective

Several scholars argue that the institutional nature of government needs to be considered as the determining, shaping force in public sector reform enabled by digital technologies (e.g. Fountain, 2001; Fountain, 2008; Kraemer & King, 2006; Snellen, 2005). In their view, digital government outcomes depend on the actual use of digital technologies in a particular institutional context (Fountain, 2001; Fountain, 2008; Lips, 2011; Ananny & Crawford, 2018; Brown & Duguid, 2000). For instance, Fountain (2001) distinguishes between "objective technology" and the "raw" technological capabilities before any design choices are made and "enacted technology" or objective technology in use. Enacted technology, then, consists of user perceptions as well as the design and use of digital technologies in particular institutional settings in government (Fountain, 2001). These institutional arrangements mediate and shape technology enactment in the public sector and vice versa. Moreover, when institutional settings and digital technology affect one another, they do so as a consequence of the actions and decisions of political actors (Fountain, 2001: 15). Together, this leads to a refined mutual shaping perspective on digital government change and outcomes, with a strong focus on the interplay and interdependence between individual actions by politicians and public servants, institutional structure and practice and digital technology enactment (Fountain, 2001).

Consequently, in accordance with the mutual shaping perspective discussed in Chapter 2, digital government outcomes of this interplay between digital technology and governmental institutions are contextual and vary depending on institutional, political, social, cultural, technological, economic and organizational logic and behaviours. This then not only implies that government,

56 *Theory*

through its unique institutional characteristics, will use digital technology differently compared to the private sector, but also that, within and across government organizations, outcomes of the same technology may vary. Furthermore, the institutional nature of the public sector also explains not only why rapid and radical transformation as a result of digital technologies is very difficult if not impossible to achieve in the public sector, but also why both successes and failures of evolutionary, technology-enabled change can be observed in digital government over longer periods of time (Fountain, 2008).

Through Fountain's institutional lens of technology enactment in government, we can further analyse the strategic role of digital technologies in the public sector in the following three ways (Fountain, 2001: 195–196):

1   Enacted digital technologies are tools of politicians, public decision-makers and public managers. These tools can be used or misused;
2   Enacted digital technologies become a vital digital infrastructure in governments. Once adopted, designed and constructed, these digital technologies become part of the institutional settings of government organizations. Important influencing factors here are the high sunk costs of large digital government projects and the legislative arrangements that have been put in place to legally embed these digital technologies in the fabrics of government. This situation then not only influences future actions in government organizations, but also creates a tendency to persist with this digital infrastructure even when technology changes rapidly, as institutionally embedded digital technologies are difficult to change; and
3   Enacted digital technologies serve not only as enablers of change across government but even more so as strong catalysts for change within individual government organizations as they promise dramatic efficiency gains, productivity improvements and more control. This strategic alignment between digital technologies and the interests of government organizations makes it difficult for public managers to resist using these technologies to produce such organizational promises; the institutional design of the bureaucratic state overwhelmingly structures behaviour within government agencies rather than between agencies (Fountain, 2001: 196).

However, although digital technologies are often expected to enable change in the public sector and regularly do so, Fountain (2001) observes that in many cases in government, public officials use digital technologies in order to sustain or strengthen what she calls "deep institutions," i.e. the history and culture encoded in the existing norms and values of a government organization. This phenomenon, which is also referred to as the "reinforcement thesis," acknowledges technology enactment by public sector decision-makers in ways that leave institutional structures and processes undisturbed or even reinforce and strengthen the institutional status quo (Kraemer & King, 2006; Fountain, 2001).

Based on empirical research findings around public sector changes in the USA from the 1980s through the early 2000s, Kraemer and King (2006) introduced

Different theories and perspectives 57

their reinforcement thesis as an alternative perspective on the role and impact of digital technologies on public sector reform. Interestingly, although public officials had embraced the ideology of digital technology as a tool for public sector reform in theory, in reality digital technologies had been used largely in ways that reinforced existing political, governmental and managerial structures and arrangements in the public sector (Kraemer & King, 2006). In summary, Kraemer and King (2006) come to the following four conclusions on the basis of their US-based empirical research:

1   Digital technologies do not *cause* reform (other factors do);
2   Digital technologies reinforce existing organization structures in the public sector;
3   Senior public officials are the primary beneficiaries; and
4   Senior public managers use digital technologies in their own interests.

Consequently, Kraemer and King's (2006) reinforcement thesis also suggests a reinforcement of the status quo of government's relationships with citizens as a result of using digital technologies. This then might imply either a reinforcement of existing power relationships between government and citizens or even increased power imbalances in government's relationships with citizens as a result of the interests and behaviours of senior public officials.

7.   *A networked governance perspective*

A networked governance perspective acknowledges the fact that digital government is not just about government or government organizations *per se*, but should focus on the wider network of actors involved in digital government processes and activities, such as citizens, local communities, private sector organizations, NGOs, other administrative layers of government and international organizations (Lips, 2011; Dutton, 2009; Dutton, 2010; Bellamy & Taylor, 1998; Castells, 1996; Benkler, 2006; Rainie & Wellman, 2012). In order to reflect this broader actor involvement in digital government, some scholars deliberately use the term "governance" instead of "government" in conceptualisations of digital government (e.g. Garson, 2006).

Networked governance can have many disguises, as we further explore and discuss in Chapter 7 in particular. Commonly, digital technologies, such as the Internet or social media, form the enabling platform of networked governance processes, activities and outcomes, but increasingly innovative forms of data generation and use, such as citizens' science and data philanthropy, also enable networked governance. Moreover, networked governance might even be considered as a paradigm shift through its distinctive orientation away from government, which could be summarised as follows:

*   Its emphasis on process instead of a government entity. Networked governance does not focus on one entity, but on a networked arrangement of multiple stakeholders;

58 *Theory*

- Its emphasis on networked collaboration and co-design of digital governance amongst multiple stakeholders;
- Its horizontal focus on digital *governance* instead of a more traditional vertical focus on digital *government*; and
- Its decentralised and distributed nature.

As an example, Dutton (2009; 2012) points at the emergence of a "Fifth Estate" enabled by the Internet. As a result, the Fifth Estate is not simply a new media (i.e. an adjunct to the news media) but a distributed array of networked individuals who use the Internet as a platform to source and distribute data and information to be used to challenge the media and play a potentially important political role without the institutional foundations of the Fourth Estate, such as holding the government of the day more accountable on a particular public policy issue (Dubois & Dutton, 2014: 239). The Fifth Estate is not a social movement either; it is composed of the distributed activities of one or many individuals acting on their own or collaboratively in a decentralised network that crosses the boundaries of existing institutions and organizations and which can equally hold the leadership of social movements better to account (Dubois & Dutton, 2014: 239–240). Also, it doesn't replace existing democratic governance structures, such as representative political institutions, with forms of direct democratic control, but it does allow citizens to question the decisions of these institutions, provide input and demand accountability: in other words, power is being checked and re-balanced, and with it, the networked individual is becoming a player in public policy in new ways (Dubois & Dutton, 2014: 251; see also Chapter 7).

8. A surveillance state perspective

It is often expected that new and fast-moving technological developments will profoundly affect relationships between government and citizens. For example, in the early 1990s, some scholars believed that rapid technological developments around the Internet would lead to an Orwellian surveillance state where government has enhanced control over its citizens (van de Donk & Tops, 1995). Similarly, to date, we can observe that many scholars support a perspective that the introduction and use of digital technologies and data will lead to increased surveillance of citizens or even a new data-driven government panopticon and, with that, to substantial information imbalances in citizen-government relationships (London School of Economics, 2005; Lyon, 2001; Lyon, 2003; Murakami-Wood *et al*, 2006; Meijer, 2015; Kitchin, 2016). This "surveillance state" perspective on digital technology– and data-enabled government reform anticipates erosion of trust and has profound implications for social, ethical and democratic citizens' rights (see also Chapters 6 and 8).

According to this surveillance state perspective, new digital technologies and forms of data innovation are acknowledged as surveillance technologies or surveillance systems which can trace, track and monitor people's movements,

Different theories and perspectives   59

behaviours and sentiments as well as generate, collect, process and analyse people's personal data (see Chapters 6 and 8). In general, surveillance can be defined as "any collection and processing of personal data, for the purposes of influencing or managing those whose data have been garnered" (Lyon, 2001: 2). Interestingly, this same definition could also apply to a so-called service state perspective on governments helping individual clients by meeting their complex government service needs, for example (Lips, Taylor & Organ, 2009).

However, many scholars point to a smart technology of surveillance creeping into all aspects of society, including in government's relationships with citizens (e.g. Lyon, 2001; Lyon, 2003; Meijer, 2015; Kitchin, 2014; Kitchin, 2016). The use of surveillance technologies and systems can support the modern state in its efforts not only to gather more and better knowledge but also to enhance speed, control and co-ordination (Taylor, Lips & Organ, 2009; Lips, Taylor & Organ, 2009). Governments embracing NPM ideas and models appear to be particularly amenable to using these new surveillance technologies and systems as the needs and behaviours of citizens, being perceived as customers, can be systematically traced, tracked, monitored, processed and analyzed in order to be used for more personalised public services, political marketing and other behavioural economics activities targeting individuals (Lips, Taylor & Organ, 2009; Taylor, Lips & Organ, 2009; Bennett & Raab, 2003; see Chapters 6 and 8).

These scholarly viewpoints are further supported by public statements of various practitioners around the world. For example, in 2006, the UK Information Commissioner made a public statement about his fears that the UK was "sleep-walking into a surveillance society" (Lips, Taylor & Organ, 2009). In similar vein, in 2008, the UK House of Commons' Home Affairs Committee called on the UK central government to give proper consideration to the risks associated with increasing surveillance in British society as the resulting loss of privacy erodes trust and can change the nature of the relationship between citizens and the state (House of Commons, 2008, in: Lips, Taylor & Organ, 2009: 840). In 2009, the UK House of Lords' Select Committee on the Constitution similarly concluded that, although the processing of personal data has always been part of government, there has been a profound and continuous expansion in the surveillance apparatus of the State (House of Lords, 2009, in: Lips, Taylor & Organ, 2009: 840). In the view of this select committee, the development of surveillance has become pervasive, routine and almost taken for granted in British society, with data being collected on the entire population and not just on traditional suspects (Lips, Taylor & Organ, 2009: 840).

However, surveillance in citizen-government relationships does not happen as a result of the availability of new smart technologies in the public domain but is only determined by the actual use of these technologies by government (Lips, Taylor & Organ, 2009; Lyon, 2001). As mentioned before, this could just as easily mean that governments are actually using digital technologies and data to serve individual citizens, rather than to surveil them. Interestingly, empirical research into the actual use of digital citizen identity management systems and technologies by UK government organizations in varying digital government case studies

60　*Theory*

shows that characteristics of both surveillance state and service state perspectives were indeed visible in these UK case studies, simultaneously and in parallel (Lips, 2011: 255; Lips, Taylor & Organ, 2009). Moreover, all observed citizen identity information practices were within the legal restrictions of UK data protection legislation and did not violate the privacy rights of UK citizens (Lips, Taylor & Organ, 2009). This then suggests that digital government outcomes vary and can be either surveillance- or service-oriented, depending on the actual use of smart technologies and digitised citizen data in a particular socio-technical assemblage within the context of digital government relationships. These research findings not only reconfirm the critical importance of conducting empirical research but also suggest the existence of discrepancies between a government's intentions and the actual use of citizens' personal data (Lips, 2011).

9. A good governance perspective

More recently, we can observe the emergence of a "good governance" perspective around the use of digital technologies and data in the context of digital government and its democratic relationships with citizens. A popular perspective in countries in the Asia-Pacific region – Africa, and South-America for example – it considers government's application of digital technologies and data as an opportunity to standardise government processes and activities to reduce corruption, increase transparency and improve government accountability and effectiveness. A major implication of establishing technology- and data-enabled good governance is that it will enhance citizens' trust in government and promote public participation and collaboration in forms of democratic governance.

The following objectives and activities are commonly associated with good governance enabled by digital technologies and data (e.g. Bertot, Jaeger & Grimes, 2012; Anderson, 2009; Shim & Eom, 2008):

- Enhanced transparency, including greater access to government data and information;
- Less government and more involvement from citizens through collaboration and co-design;
- Participatory democratic processes;
- Improved government accountability and responsiveness;
- Better public policy-making;
- Increased government effectiveness and efficiency;
- Establishment of rule of law;
- Enhanced regulatory quality;
- Professionalisation and enhanced quality of government personnel; and
- Control of corruption

Similar to a networked governance perspective, good governance is distinct from government as it doesn't focus on a single entity but on key technology-enabled

Different theories and perspectives 61

relationships within and between government organizations and their multiple stakeholders. Moreover, good governance usually takes place at different levels of the public sector and in different relationships, including (see also Chapter 10):

- Good "corporate governance" at the level of a government organization. This usually includes (good) digital technology or IT governance;
- Good "accountable governance" at the level of government as a whole, aimed at social and economic prosperity and anti-corruption; and
- Good "democratic governance" in government's relationships with citizens.

However, in acknowledging the absence of definitional consensus amongst scholars, we need to be aware that good governance in fact has different meanings in different countries at different times in history (Gregory, 2013). This not only has implications for measuring the effectiveness of good governance in the sense that there is no one-best-way model, but also makes it a situational and context-relative concept. Consequently, the socio-historical development of politics and government in a particular country, including government's use of digital technologies and data, is of critical importance to assess good governance in that country. Moreover, the best way to explore and assess technology-enabled good governance in a particular country is empirically through the lived experience of citizens. This then implies that, in order to understand and explain technology- and data-enabled good governance, we need to take into account the local circumstances, conditions, culture, technology adoption and use, conditions, norms and values within a particular digital governance context in a country at a certain moment in time.

Box 3.2 Digital-Era Governance: which perspectives?

Digital-Era Governance is a model developed by Dunleavy *et al* (2006a); Dunleavy *et al* (2006b). This model is briefly summarised next. Explore which perspectives on public sector reform can be recognised in this model.

Dunleavy *et al* (2006a; 2006b) argue that the new public management model of governing is dead in the digital age and is replaced by a digital-era governance (DEG) model. Based on new digital technology and pervasive information-handling capabilities, this DEG model is seen as a response to emerging public sector problems resulting from NPM reforms (Dunleavy *et al*, 2006b). DEG can be characterised under the following three themes (Lips, 2012: 252; Dunleavy *et al*, 2006b):

- *Reintegration*: digital technologies will put back together many of the functions and expertise clusters that NPM separated into single-function organizational units across government. Examples are the use of digital identity management systems to facilitate joined-up government or re-strengthen central processes in order to reduce duplication across government;

- *Needs-based holism*: digital technologies will simplify and change the entire relationship between government organizations and their clients, moving away from the NPM focus on business process management and towards a citizen- or needs-based foundation for government organization. Examples are digital-enabled public service reorganizations around a single client group or ask-once processes supported by reusing already-collected citizen information;
- *Digitisation changes*: digital channels become the central feature of administrative and business processes in government. Examples are new forms of automated processes where no human intervention is needed in a government administrative or business operation, such as electronic monitoring of customers (e.g. patients) or increasing transparency and allowing citizens to track and self-monitor the processing of their public service applications.

An alternative perspective of complex public management[1]

As discussed earlier, none of these nine common perspectives is in fact sufficient to fully observe, understand and explain technology- and data-enabled changes and outcomes in socio-technical assemblages in the context of digital government. Consequently, we broaden our perspective on digital government and introduce an alternative, complex public management way of seeing digital government. This complex public management perspective helps us to both empirically and more comprehensively explore, understand and explain the complexity of this socio-technical phenomenon.

The features of this complex public management lens can be briefly described as follows (Eppel, Turner & Wolf, 2011: 187–190; Eppel & Lips, 2016; see Eppel, 2010 for a more comprehensive description):

- *A digital government system whole*: a complex digital government system cannot be understood as the sum of its parts or reduced to its parts to assist understanding. A digital government system whole is made up of individual human actors, interacting in social groups, which may be formal (e.g. government organizations or units) or informal, and non-human actors or digital technologies and data. These human and non-human actors mutually shape each other as part of a socio-technical construct or assemblage in the context or system of digital government. Human and non-human actors

Different theories and perspectives 63

can be part of vertical networks or hierarchies of actors, non-hierarchical networks of actors or both;

- *Nested, interacting and interdependent systems*: complex socio-technical assemblages embedded in digital government systems are part of larger and more complex systems. With components in common, these nested systems show "self-similarity" because the characteristics identified at one level of the system (e.g. the individual) are also present at successive levels of organization within the larger system (e.g. the government organizational unit, whole of government or even supranational levels). Understanding any part of these interdependent systems needs a simultaneous holistic view of other parts of the larger system and who is interacting;

- *Nested socio-technical assemblages as part of the larger digital government system*: human and non-human actors comprise socio-technical assemblages or interconnected, interdependent, nested networks within the larger digital government system. In interactions with each other and with digital technologies and data, human actors socially construct, design, apply, process, manage, use and re-use digital technologies and data. These complex assemblages change and are changed by other systems they interact with;

- *Multiple interactive systems create feedback mechanisms*: reflexive influence patterns, which arise from the ongoing interaction between human and non-human actors in the digital government system, can result in feedback loops. Positive feedback loops amplify changes by reinforcing the direction of change and can cause sudden, unpredictable and destabilising outcomes; negative feedback loops reverse or compensate for changes elsewhere. Internal features of government organizations, such as structures, hierarchies, rules, controls, cultures and power relations, are held in place by feedback loops locking an organization into a particular stable pattern;

- *Adaptation and co-evolution within and between systems*: over time, reflexive interactions between human actors lead to adaptation between groups or networks of actors constituting a system. From a complexity perspective, the external environment is an interacting system and, therefore, not only will changes in the environment stimulate digital government system change, but the environment will also undergo changes in response. As a result, there is co-evolution and adaptation of one group of actors (or level of the system) and their environment;

- *Change through self-organization and emergence*: human actors socially construct their uses of digital technologies and data, reflect on their experiences and recognise and respond to patterns that help them make sense of their environment. Humans respond to the complexity of their environment by either sidestepping complexity through the simplification and codification of responses or by holding multiple representations of environmental variety and, with that, retaining a repertoire of responses. Every change produces the stimulus for further change in each actor by self-reference to the individual actor's internal sense-making. This self-organization by multiple actors can lead to the emergence of new relations and patterns of actors

64 *Theory*

when seen from a more macro level, for example. Without any external direction, a repeated change at the individual actor level is reinforced by changes in other actors and their actions and results in a new trajectory of change and ultimately a new pattern. This overall change in the digital government system occurs as a result of feedback loops, adaptation and emergence of hitherto unknown new levels of order. The latter occurs through self-organization of system parts in reinforced patterns around "attractors";

- *Open systems and socially constructed boundaries:* groups or networks of human actors socially construct digital technologies and data in socio-technical assemblages or nested systems, and, together, make up a digital government system. These systems are open to their environment, with the boundaries of these systems being social constructs themselves. For example, a digital government system is open to a flow of energy (political, social), actors, technologies, data, information and ideas;
- *Construction of new socio-technical assemblages:* new socio-technical assemblages emerge from the complex interaction and adaptation between (networks or groups of) actors, other or larger systems (e.g. digital government system), and the environment (McLoughlin & Wilson, 2013). In this process the technology (or data) is shaping (networks or groups of) actors and systems, and actors and systems are in turn shaping their use of the technology for improved outcomes (Flichy, 2007). Because the interactions between (networks or groups of) actors and the technology are iterative and ongoing, no one actor is allowed to optimise the technology for itself at the expense of the other actors. Over time these repeated processes of adaptation lead to a co-evolution between digital government system structures and processes, nested socio-technical assemblages or systems, actors and digital technologies and data, to modify the performance landscape and achieve more advantageous adaptive peaks for all the actors as part of the system (Rhodes, 2013);
- *Stability, but not equilibrium:* complex digital government systems are far from equilibrium and can appear stable due to the cancelling interactions of feedback loops creating an impression of no change. However, such systems can suddenly and unpredictably undergo change unrelated in magnitude to any stimulus. Far-from-equilibrium digital government systems often exhibit tensions and paradoxical phenomena when changes to the stable pattern of feedback loops destabilise the system; and
- *The history of the system influences its starting point for change:* the history of earlier changes, starting points and feedback loops create "path dependencies" in the digital government system. Stabilizing path dependencies arise when negative feedback loops undo externally imposed change or limit what happens next. Stable systems are more likely when there is a single, strong attractor influencing feedback loops; less-stable systems are characterised by multiple, weak attractors. Furthermore, the size, timing and nature of change in a complex digital government system cannot be predicted in advance because of the sensitivity of the system to its initial

Different theories and perspectives 65

starting position and contingency of the interactions between the system parts.

This complex public management lens helps us to empirically explore, understand and explain the complexity of digital government phenomena. In order to apply this lens, we will need to use a qualitative research methodology, which could involve a social constructionist or constructivist approach for example. Useful qualitative research methods for this lens include case-study research, (historical) document analysis, narratives, semi-structured or open interviews and ethnographic observations.

Now that we are able to see digital government through a complex public management lens, we are able to empirically observe and analyse complex digital government systems in action, including nested socio-technical assemblages or systems; (networks or groups of) human actors; non-human actors or digital technologies and data; sense-making, reflecting, constructing, responding, learning, organizing and interacting activities (Weick, 1995); changes as well as stability; feedback loops; attractors and the system's boundaries and environment. We discuss the leadership, governance and managerial implications of using a complex public management lens to understand the socio-technical phenomenon of digital government in Chapters 10 and 11.

Box 3.3   Exercise 3.1

Read the following summary of the SmartGate case study (Eppel & Lips, 2016). Apply the complex public management perspective to this empirical case study and describe which complex features of digital government you see through this lens.

Learning, adaptation and co-evolution

SmartGate is an automated passenger clearance system that is available to eligible passport holders arriving at and leaving major international airports in New Zealand and arriving at Australia's eight international airports.

SmartGate was initially developed as a response to the government's wish to provide a better, smoother experience for travellers. In its essence, special kiosks read a microchip embedded in e-passports and use stored biometric data and photo-matching technology to validate passports and travellers to provide accurate and fast automated clearance. New Zealand Customs Service (Customs), as the government's agent at the border, promoted the introduction of SmartGate to government as a way of dealing with increasing visitor numbers, particularly during the Rugby World

66 *Theory*

Cup in 2011, but also as a response to an economic development strategy involving increased tourism in New Zealand.

On one level, SmartGate could be viewed as a relatively straightforward and conventional substitution of a relatively slow and inefficient human-mediated process with a technology-mediated process. SmartGate processed more passengers more quickly and surpassed all targets in its first two years of operation.

SmartGate was installed quickly and within specified parameters and budget because Customs drew on knowledge and experience from Australia's use of the same device through their networking with that government's sister organization and also on the experience and knowledge of the airport companies and the New Zealand–based airline operators who had installed their own smart check-in and boarding systems in airports. This resulted in adaptation and co-evolution of the SmartGate concept via these actors during the implementation process.

Firstly, the political and organizational priority accorded to SmartGate by the Prime Minister and Customs meant that the government made resources available for the project, and the project team was able to rely on Customs obtaining and allocating the resources it needed to complete the job on time. The project also benefited from alignment of the result to be achieved through SmartGate with organizational strategy, organizational commitment, organization-wide planning, sound project management methodology and choosing the best people within the organization to do the job – the project manager saw this as the most important factor in the project's success. There was in effect a mutually reinforcing feedback loop between the SmartGate project design team and the commitment to the particular organizational goals of the Chief Executive and the government.

During the design of SmartGate's deployment, Customs was able to benefit from Australia's investment in SmartGate's development and design. Customs used a borrowed Australian device to create a test environment to more fully explore SmartGate's potential. This experience led Customs to advise the government to buy SmartGate and meant that Customs had a head start on introducing SmartGate and integrating it into their in-house information system, CusMod. It also meant that Customs was able to design and use SmartGate faster and more cheaply.

A third factor which allowed Customs to design and roll out SmartGate effectively and on time was Customs' close collaboration with business partners. These included organizations within government (for whom Customs carries out some aspect of business), non-government partners such as the airlines and airports where SmartGate was expected to work and the vendor Morpho. By working collaboratively, Customs had better relationships with the organizations and had commitments from them to prepare business improvement strategies to make the most of SmartGate.

The government endorsed Customs' plan to build SmartGate in March 2009; in December 2009, the first SmartGate went into service in Auckland; SmartGate was progressively installed in the arrival and departure halls of Auckland, Wellington and Christchurch airports and was fully operational in the three airports by August 2011. By May 2012, Customs was using 22 gates and 54 kiosks continuously and processing passenger numbers far exceeding initial assumptions. In the first year of operation, more than 500,000 passengers used SmartGate. By April 2011, more than a million had used SmartGate. By December 2011, two million had, and the three-millionth passenger used SmartGate successfully in May 2012. By 2012, SmartGate was fully integrated with CusMod, and more than half of eligible trans-Tasman airline travellers were choosing to use SmartGate at Auckland, Wellington and Christchurch airports and airports in Australia. It is now used by most international airport arrivals on a range of trusted passports, rather than just the original Australian and New Zealand users.

Co-evolution and emergence of new patterns

At the New Zealand border, Customs also carries out activities on behalf of many other government agencies. SmartGate's introduction had immediate and downstream implications for some or all of these agencies.

Although SmartGate initially was not a favoured solution in partner agencies because they didn't see it as having sufficient potential to transform, Customs' adoption of SmartGate organized the business processes in ways the partner agencies wanted, which enhanced the working relationships between Customs and these partner agencies in unforeseen ways. The speed of SmartGate's introduction and the resulting more effective and efficient processing of travellers enhanced Customs' reputation as a trusted and efficient agency with the public, airlines, airports and other important stakeholders; SmartGate created confidence that Customs would do what it said it would do. SmartGate delivered on the government's vision for an improved experience for trans-Tasman travellers in line with Australia's automated border processes, a vital step towards the vision of a domestic-like travel experience between Australia and New Zealand. The primary processing of passengers at airports became more accurate, and the cost of the primary processing of arriving passengers went down, freeing up resources for assessing more complex risks. More arriving passengers were processed with no need for extra staffing or space. In 2010, more than 84 percent of users reported that they would probably use SmartGate again; in March 2012, 55 percent of eligible passengers who used SmartGate were repeat users; and more efficiency was achieved as processing became faster (an average of 16 minutes from

68 *Theory*

aircraft arrival at air-bridge to clearing Customs for SmartGate, compared with 20 minutes for non-SmartGate passengers in March 2012), so queues and waiting times were shorter.

Unexpected and/or unplanned benefits included new opportunities, such as providing arrival and departure information and extending Smart-Gate's use to a wider group of passengers when leaving the country. Realisation of these unplanned benefits is best seen as an adaptive and emergent process. SmartGate's initial success in meeting its implementation targets on time and within budget was a catalyst for Customs to think further about how to exploit SmartGate's capability, uptake and performance to do things differently. The SmartGate project programme manager said: "We picked a strategy and now we are aiming to derive the fullest value from it." From the start, Customs focused on monitoring SmartGate's performance and making changes to bring about more benefits, such as allowing 16-year-olds and 17-year-olds to use SmartGate. Customs saw the SmartGate technology as a platform from which to build its next phase of business changes and continued to invest to get the best performance possible from it.

Political and organizational support for the SmartGate project boosted energy, confidence and commitment in staff responsible for designing and delivering on the benefits, which in turn helped them to achieve results (mutual reinforcement).

Good relationships with vendors and others needed to help realise benefits were a powerful contributor to success. The indirect and intangible benefits of these collaborations extended beyond the life of the project. After the design and rollout of SmartGate, Customs had better relationships and commitments to keep working on business improvement strategies to make the most of SmartGate. Customs' regard for its reputation and keeping the trust of others created an organization-wide commitment to getting the job done.

Customs was pragmatic enough to avoid obstacles, learn as it went, and take advantage of what it learned. Introducing SmartGate in steps helped learning and kept project management costs down. Customs prepared well, picked a strategy, then planned and managed risks to make the strategy work. Customs continues to try to make SmartGate do as much as possible for its business transformation and uses it as a platform for further business change.

Discussion questions

1   Try and find a practical or empirical digital government case study that you can apply at least three of the ten perspectives to. What do you see through each of these lenses? What changes and outcomes are expected through each of these lenses?

Different theories and perspectives 69

2 What are the possible implications for citizen-government relationships if you support the reinforcement thesis in a particular digital government context? Motivate your answer.

Note

1 This section is largely based on the PhD Thesis of Dr Elizabeth A. Eppel (2010), a joint contribution of Eppel, Turner and Wolf (2011) and a joint contribution of Eppel and Lips (2016). The author would like to acknowledge Dr Eppel's invaluable contribution in constructing a new lens for seeing complex public management.

References

Allison, G.T. (1971) *Essence of Decision: Explaining the Cuban Missile Crisis*. Boston, MA: Little Brown.

Ananny, M. & Crawford, K. (2018) Seeing without knowing: Limitations of the transparency ideal and its application to algorithmic accountability. *New Media & Society*, 20 (3), 973–989.

Andersen, K.V. & Henriksen, H.Z. (2005) The first leg of e-government research: Domains and application areas 1998–2003. *International Journal of Electronic Government Research*, 1 (4), 26–44.

Andersen, K.V. & Henriksen, H.Z. (2006) E-government maturity models: Extension of the Layne and Lee model. *Government Information Quarterly*, 23, 236–248.

Anderson, T.B. (2009) E-government as an anti-corruption strategy. *Information Economics and Policy*, 21, 201–210.

Baum, C. & Di Maio, A. (2000) *Gartner's Four Phases of e-Government Model*. Stamford, CA: Gartner Group.

Bellamy, C. & Taylor, J.A. (1998) *Governing in the Information Age*. Buckingham: Open University Press.

Benkler, Y. (2006) *The Wealth of Networks: How Social Production Transforms Markets and Freedom*. New Haven, CT: Yale University Press.

Bennett, C.J. & Raab, C.D. (2003) *The Governance of Privacy: Policy Instruments in Global Perspective*. Aldershot: Ashgate.

Bertot, J.C., Jaeger, P.T. & Grimes, J.M. (2012) Promoting transparency and accountability through ICTs, social media, and collaborative e-government. *Transforming Government: People, Process and Policy*, 6 (1), 78–91.

Borins, S. (2007) Is IT transforming government? Evidence and lessons from Canada. In: Borins, S., Kernaghan, K., Brown, D., Bontis, N., 6, P. & Thompson, F. (eds.) *Digital State at the Leading Edge*. Toronto: University of Toronto Press, pp. 355–383.

Bovens, M.A.P. & Zouridis, S. (2002) From street-level bureaucracy to system-level bureaucracy: How information and communication technology is transforming administrative discretion and constitutional control. *Public Administration Review*, 62 (2), 174–184.

Brown, J.S. & Duguid, P. (2000) *The Social Life of Information*. Boston, MA: Harvard Business School Press.

Castells, M. (1996) *The Rise of the Network Society: The Information Age: Economy, Society and Culture*. Vol. 1. Oxford: Blackwell Publishers.

Danziger, J. & Andersen, K.V. (2002) The impacts of information technology on public administration: An analysis of empirical research from the "golden age" of transformation. *International Journal of Public Administration*, 25 (5), 591–627.

70 Theory

Dubois, E. & Dutton, W.H. (2014) Empowering citizens of the internet age: The role of a fifth estate. In: Graham, M. & Dutton, W.H. (eds.) *Society & the Internet: How Networks of Information and Communication Are Changing Our Lives*. Oxford: Oxford University Press, pp. 238–253.

Dunleavy, P., Margetts, H., Bastow, S. & Tinkler, J. (2006a) New public management is dead: Long live digital-era governance. *Journal of Public Administration Research and Theory*, 16 (3), 467–494.

Dunleavy, P., Margetts, H., Bastow, S. & Tinkler, J. (2006b) *Digital Era Governance: IT Corporations, the State, and E-Government*. Oxford: Oxford University Press.

Dutton, W.H. (2009) The fifth estate emerging through the network of networks. *Prometheus*, 27 (1), 1–15.

Dutton, W.H. (2010) The fifth estate: Democratic social accountability through the emerging network of networks. In: Nixon, P.G., Koutrakou, V.N. & Rawal, R. (eds.) *Understanding E-Government in Europe: Issues and Challenges*. London: Routledge, pp. 3–18.

Dutton, W.H. (2012) The fifth estate: A new governance challenge. In: Levi-Faur, D. (ed.) *The Oxford Handbook of Governance*. Oxford: Oxford University Press, pp. 584–598.

Eppel, E.A. (2010) *The Contribution of Complexity Theory to Understanding and Explaining Policy Processes: A Study of Tertiary Education Policy Processes in New Zealand*. Unpublished PhD Thesis. Wellington: Victoria University of Wellington. Available from: http://researcharchive.vuw.ac.nz/handle/10063/1202 [accessed 4 December 2018].

Eppel, E.A. & Lips, A.M.B. (2016) Unpacking the black box of successful ICT-enabled service transformation: How to join up the vertical, the horizontal and the technical. *Public Money & Management*, 36 (1), 39–46. Available from: https://doi.org/10.1080/09540962.2016.1103417

Eppel, E.A., Turner, D. & Wolf, A. (2011) Complex policy implementation: The role of experimentation and learning. In: Ryan, B. & Gill, D. (eds.) *Future State: Directions for Public Management in New Zealand*. Wellington: Victoria University of Wellington, pp. 182–212.

Flichy, P. (2007) *Understanding Technological Innovation*. London: Edward Elgar.

Foley, P. & Alfonso, X. (2009) eGovernment and the transformation agenda. *Public Administration*, 87 (2), 371–396.

Fountain, J.E. (2001) *Building the Virtual State: Information Technology and Institutional Change*. Washington, DC: Brookings Institution Press.

Fountain, J.E. (2008) Bureaucratic reform and e-government in the United States: An institutional perspective. In: Chadwick, A. & Howard, P.N. (eds.) *The Routledge Handbook of Internet Politics*. Abingdon: Routledge, pp. 99–113.

Frissen, P.H.A. (1998) Public administration in cyberspace: A postmodern perspective. In: Snellen, I.Th.M. & van de Donk, W.B.H.J. (eds.) *Public Administration in an Information Age: A Handbook*. Amsterdam: IOS Press, pp. 33–46.

Garson, D.G. (2006) *Public Information Technology and E-Governance: Governing the Virtual State*. Raleigh, NC: Jones and Bartlett Publishers.

Gregory, R. (2013) *Assessing 'Good Governance' and Corruption in New Zealand: 'Scientific' Measurement, Political Discourse, and Historical Narrative*. Working Paper No. 13/03, Institute for Governance and Policy Studies. Wellington: Victoria University of Wellington. Available from: https://www.victoria.ac.nz/__data/assets/pdf_file/0009/1286280/WP1303-Assessing-good-governance.pdf [accessed 4 December 2018].

Grönlund, A. (2005) State of the art in e-gov research: Surveying conference publications. *International Journal of Electronic Government Research*, 1 (4), 1–25.

Heeks, R. & Bailur, S. (2007) Analyzing e-government research: Perspectives, philosophies, theories, methods, and practice. *Government Information Quarterly*, 24, 243–265.

Different theories and perspectives   71

Henman, P. (2010) *Governing Electronically: E-Government and the Reconfiguration of Public Administration, Policy and Power*. Basingstoke: Palgrave MacMillan.

Homburg, V. (2008) *Understanding E-Government: Information Systems in Public Administration*. London: Routledge.

Kallinikos, J. (2011) *Governing Through Technology: Information Artefacts and Social Practice: Technology, Work and Globalization*. Basingstoke: Palgrave MacMillan.

Kitchin, R. (2014) *The Data Revolution: Big Data, Open Data, Data Infrastructures & Their Consequences*. London: Sage.

Kitchin, R. (2016) The ethics of smart cities and urban science. *Philosophical Transactions of the Royal Society A*, epub, 374: 20160115. Available from http://dx.doi.org/10.1098/rsta.2016.0115

Klievink, B. & Janssen, M. (2009) Realizing joined-up government: Dynamic capabilities and stage models for transformation. *Government Information Quarterly*, 26, 275–284.

Kraemer, K.L. & King, J.L. (2006) Information technology and administrative reform: Will e-government be different? *International Journal of Electronic Government Research*, 2 (1), 1–20.

Layne, K. & Lee, J. (2001) Developing fully functional e-government: A four stage model. *Government Information Quarterly*, 18 (2), 122–136.

Lee, G. & Kwak, Y.H. (2012) An open government maturity model for social media-based public engagement. *Government Information Quarterly*, 29, 492–503.

Lips, A.M.B. (2011) 'E-government is dead: Long live networked governance': Fixing system errors in the New Zealand public management system. In: Ryan, B. & Gill, D. (eds.) *Future State: Directions for Public Management in New Zealand*. Wellington: Victoria University of Wellington, pp. 248–261.

Lips, A.M.B. (2012) E-government is dead: Long live public administration 2.0. *Information Polity*, 17, 239–250.

Lips, A.M.B. (2014) Transforming government: By default? In: Graham, M. & Dutton, W.H. (eds.) *Society & the Internet: How Networks of Information and Communication Are Changing Our Lives*. Oxford: Oxford University Press, pp. 179–194.

Lips, A.M.B. (2017) Transforming government services over time: Meanings, impacts, and implications for citizen-government relationships. In: Chen, Y. & Ahn, M.J. (eds.) *Routledge Handbook on Information Technology in Government*. London: Routledge, pp. 11–26.

Lips, A.M.B. & Schuppan, T. (2009) Transforming e-government knowledge through public management research. *Public Management Review*, 11 (6), 739–749.

Lips, A.M.B., Taylor, J.A. & Organ, J. (2009) Managing citizen identity information in e-government service relationships in the UK: The emergence of a surveillance state or a service state? *Public Management Review*, 11 (6), 833–856.

London School of Economics. (2005) *The Identity Project: An Assessment of the UK Identity Cards Bill and Its Implications*. London: LSE Identity Project Final Report, June.

Lyon, D. (2001) *Surveillance Society: Monitoring Everyday Life*. Buckingham: Open University Press.

Lyon, D. (ed.) (2003) *Surveillance & Social Sorting: Privacy, Risk and Digital Discrimination*. London: Routledge.

MacKenzie, D.A. & Wajcman, J. (eds.) (1999) *The Social Shaping of Technology*. 2nd ed. Buckingham: Open University Press.

McLoughlin, I. & Wilson, R., with Martin, M. (2013) *Digital Government @ Work: A Social Informatics Perspective*. Oxford: Oxford University Press.

Meijer, A.J. (2015) *Bestuur in de datapolis: Slimme stad, blije burger?* Den Haag: Boom Bestuurskunde.

72 Theory

Mergel, I. (2013) *Social Media in the Public Sector: A Guide to Participation, Collaboration, and Transparency in the Networked World*. San Francisco, CA: Jossey-Bass.

Murakami-Wood, D., Ball, K., Lyon, D., Norris, C. & Raab, C.D. (September 2006) *A Report on the Surveillance Society*. For the Information Commissioner by the Surveillance Studies Network.

O'Neill, R.R. (2009) *E-Government: Transformation of Public Governance in New Zealand?* PhD Thesis. Wellington: Victoria University of Wellington. Available from: http:// researcharchive.vuw.ac.nz/handle/10063/929 [accessed 4 December 2018].

O'Reilly, T. (2010) Government as a platform. In: Lathrop, D. & Ruma, L. (eds.) *Open Government: Collaboration, Transparency, and Participation in Practice*. Sebastopol, CA: O'Reilly, pp. 11–39.

Rainie, L. & Wellman, B. (2012) *Networked: The New Social Operating System*. Cambridge, MA: Massachusetts Institute of Technology Press.

Rhodes, M.L. (2013) Innovation in complex public service systems. In: Osborne, S.P. & Brown, L. (eds.) *Handbook of Innovation in Public Services*. London: Edward Elgar.

Schokker, J.T. (1996) *Wet- en Informatiesysteem in de maak: Een onderzoek naar processen van wetgeving en systeemontwikkeling vanuit een taalspel-perspectief*. Delft: Eburon.

Shim, D.C. & Eom, T.H. (2008) E-government and anti-corruption: Empirical analysis of international data. *International Journal of Public Administration*, 31, 298–316.

Snellen, I.Th.M. (2005) E-government: A challenge for public management. In: Ferlie, E., Lynn, L.E. & Pollitt, C. (eds.) *The Oxford Handbook of Public Management*. Oxford: Oxford University Press, pp. 398–421.

Snellen, I.Th.M. & van de Donk, W.B.H.J. (eds.) (1998) *Public Administration in an Information Age: A Handbook*. Amsterdam: IOS Press.

Taylor, J.A. (1998) Informatization as X-ray: What is public administration for the information age? In: Snellen, I.Th.M. & van de Donk, W.B.H.J. (eds.) *Public Administration in an Information Age: A Handbook*. Amsterdam: IOS Press, pp. 21–32.

Taylor, J.A. (2012) The information polity: Towards a two speed future? *Information Polity*, 17, 227–237.

Taylor, J.A. & Lips, A.M.B. (2008) The citizen in the information polity: Exposing the limits of the e-government paradigm. *Information Polity*, 13 (3–4), 139–152.

Taylor, J.A., Lips, A.M.B. & Organ, J. (2009) Identification practices in government: Citizen surveillance and the quest for public service improvement. *Identity in the Information Society*, 1 (1), 135–154.

UK Office of Public Service. (1996) *Government. Direct: A Prospectus for the Electronic Delivery of Government Services*. Cm 3438. London: HMSO.

van de Donk, W.B.H.J. & Tops, P.W. (1995) Orwell or Athens? Informatization and the future of democracy. In: van de Donk, W.B.H.J., Snellen, I.Th.M. & Tops, P.W. (eds.) *Orwell in Athens: A Perspective on Informatization and Democracy*. Amsterdam: IOS Press, pp. 13–32.

Webster, F. (2004) Transformations: Introduction. In: Webster, F. (ed.) *The Information Society Reader*. London: Routledge, pp. 185–189.

Weick, K.E. (1995) *Sensemaking in Organizations*. Thousand Oaks/London/New Delhi: Sage.

West, D. (2005) *Digital Government: Technology and Public Sector Performance*. Princeton, NJ: Princeton University Press.

Williams, R. & Edge, D. (1996) The social shaping of technology. In: Dutton, W.H. (ed.) *Information and Communication Technologies: Visions and Realities*. Oxford: Oxford University Press, pp. 53–67.

Woolgar, S. (2002b) Five rules of virtuality. In: Woolgar, S. (ed.) *Virtual Society? Technology, Cyberbole, Reality*. Oxford: Oxford University Press, pp. 1–22.

Zouridis, S. (1999) *Digitale disciplinering: Over ICT, organisatie, wetgeving en het automatiseren van beschikkingen*. Delft: Eburon.

Zuboff, S. (1988) *In the Age of the Smart Machine: The Future of Work and Power*. New York, NY: Basic Books.

Zuurmond, A. (1998) From bureaucracy to infocracy: Are Democratic institutions lagging behind? In: Snellen, I.Th.M. & van de Donk, W.B.H.J. (eds.) *Public Administration in an Information Age: A Handbook*. Amsterdam: IOS Press, pp. 259–272.

Further reading

Brown, J.S. & Duguid, P. (2000) *The Social Life of Information*. Boston, MA: Harvard Business School Press.

Dunleavy, P., Margetts, H., Bastow, S. & Tinkler, J. (2006b) *Digital Era Governance: IT Corporations, the State, and E-Government*. Oxford: Oxford University Press.

Dutton, W.H. (2012) The fifth estate: A new governance challenge. In: Levi-Faur, D. (ed.) *The Oxford Handbook of Governance*. Oxford: Oxford University Press, pp. 584–598.

Eppel, E.A. & Lips, A.M.B. (2016) Unpacking the black box of successful ICT-enabled service transformation: How to join up the vertical, the horizontal and the technical. *Public Money & Management*, 36 (1), 39–46. Available from: https://doi.org/10.1080/09540962.2016.1103417

Flichy, P. (2007) *Understanding Technological Innovation*. London: Edward Elgar.

Fountain, J.E. (2001) *Building the Virtual State: Information Technology and Institutional Change*. Washington, DC: Brookings Institution Press.

Gregory, R. (2013) *Assessing 'Good Governance' and Corruption in New Zealand: 'Scientific' Measurement, Political Discourse, and Historical Narrative*. Working Paper No. 13/03, Institute for Governance and Policy Studies. Wellington: Victoria University of Wellington. Available from: https://www.victoria.ac.nz/__data/assets/pdf_file/0009/1286280/WP13-03-Assessing-good-governance.pdf [accessed 4 December 2018].

Kitchin, R. (2014) *The Data Revolution: Big Data, Open Data, Data Infrastructures & Their Consequences*. London: Sage.

Kraemer, K.L. & King, J.L. (2006) Information technology and administrative reform: Will e-government be different? *International Journal of Electronic Government Research*, 2 (1), 1–20.

Lyon, D. (2001) *Surveillance Society: Monitoring Everyday Life*. Buckingham: Open University Press.

Lyon, D. (ed.) (2003) *Surveillance & Social Sorting: Privacy, Risk and Digital Discrimination*. London: Routledge.

McLoughlin, I. & Wilson, R., with Martin, M. (2013) *Digital Government @ Work: A Social Informatics Perspective*. Oxford: Oxford University Press.

Rhodes, M.L. (2013) Innovation in complex public service systems. In: Osborne, S.P. & Brown, L. (eds.) *Handbook of Innovation in Public Services*. London: Edward Elgar.

Taylor, J.A. (1998) Informatization as X-ray: What is public administration for the Information Age? In: Snellen, I.Th.M. & van de Donk, W.B.H.J. (eds.) *Public Administration in an Information Age: A Handbook*. Amsterdam: IOS Press, pp. 21–32.

Taylor, J.A. & Williams, H. (1991) Public administration and the information polity. *Public Administration*, 69 (2), 171–190.

Part III

Areas of public sector reform

4 The service state

Learning objectives

By the end of this chapter you should be able to:

- Understand the different digital government service reform models available thus far;
- Indicate the main characteristics of each digital government service reform model;
- Identify differences between traditional forms of public service provision and digital government service provision; and
- Understand and classify emerging issues and barriers to digital government service reform.

Key points of this chapter

- Governments have launched a number of different digital government service reform strategies over the years, with each reform strategy having different characteristics and implications;
- Multiple digital divides are emerging, including around digital government services. This issue will be further discussed in Chapter 9;
- Digital government service reform ambitions are highly complex to achieve. Not only do they raise a number of issues and barriers, but outcomes are also often less successful and quite different than originally expected;
- Traditional public service organizations and provision are based on different public management principles than emerging digital forms of public service provision, requiring a trade-off between traditional values in government and emerging values in digital government. This then requires the establishment of a new ethical framework of contextual integrity in digital government service provision (see Chapter 6); and
- Service relationships between street-level bureaucrats and individual citizens are changing in the digital age, especially as a result of the introduction of data-enabled government. However, human expert–based decision-making continues to be of critical importance for effective digital government service outcomes.

78 *Areas of public sector reform*

Key terms

- *M-government:* digital government services provided via mobile technologies and devices.
- *Integrating government:* a public sector reform vision that aims to break down the vertical silos within government and deliver government services to the general public in a much more integrated, customer-centric and responsive way.
- *Citizen-centric government:* a public sector reform vision that puts the citizen first by taking a holistic "outside-in" perspective to their individual needs.
- *Digital-by-default government:* governments are replacing traditional paper-based and face-to-face service channels with a variety of digital channels and data as their standard way or "default setting" in government service provision.
- *Data-enabled government:* greater sharing and use of aggregated, de-identified and open data across the public sector offers new opportunities for government organizations to segment clients into groups, get more insights about each group and design more targeted, effective government services for clients with similar backgrounds. Also, governments use behavioural data and social media data in order to better predict certain events or situations and offer more effective and efficient government service interventions as a result.

Introduction

With the widespread uptake of digital technologies in societies around the world, such as the Internet, social media and mobile devices, scholars and practitioners have become convinced that digital government services will be critical to government and governance in the digital era (e.g. Chen & Ahn, 2017; Dunleavy *et al*, 2006; Lips, 2011; Lips, 2014; OECD, 2009a; Weerakkody & Reddick, 2012; European Union, 2013). Ever since the adoption of the Internet in the early 1990s, governments have presented bold visions about re-engineering government, joining up different government agencies into a service state where citizens can be supported in their individual service needs 24/7 without the hassle of physically visiting many public service counters and duplicating their citizen data in order to get access to a particular service. Furthermore, the increasing application of smart technologies and data innovation solutions only adds to the wide range of digital-era options available for governments to fundamentally change their public service provision.

It may not be surprising therefore that, in the last few decades, governments around the world have launched quite a few different digital government service reform strategies and related concepts, such as electronic government, mobile or m-government, integrating government, citizen-centric government, digital-by-default government and, more recently, data-enabled government. Also, we can witness the efforts of countries that are considered digital

The service state 79

government front-runners, such as New Zealand, Estonia, Korea, the UK, Canada, Israel, Uruguay and, more recently, Mexico and Portugal, to regularly get together and share their successes as the so-called Digital 9 countries group or D9. This group of digital government leaders has the objective of not only learning from each other's best practice but also collaborating on shared issues and future digital government service applications. At the same time, we can observe countries in the Asia-Pacific region, the Americas and Africa, who have only recently started to design and develop digital government services. With limited Internet uptake in individual households and often using Internet-enabled community hubs and smartphones therefore, many of these countries have started to replace large human-based bureaucratic public service channels with leaner and more standardised digital government channels in order to increase government transparency, accountability and effectiveness and, with that, achieve good governance.

However, although many digital government service concepts have been championed by governments since the 1990s and are still being pursued to date (e.g. Treasury Board of Canada Secretariat, 2018; UK Government Digital Service, 2017; Danish Agency for Digitisation, 2016), the outcomes of these technology- and data-enabled public sector reform efforts have been less successful and are often quite different than originally expected (Lips & Schuppan, 2009). For example, expected efficiency gains and cost savings have not been achieved, citizens' uptake of new digital government services turned out to be disappointing and traditional public service channels, such as telephone-based and face-to-face public service provision, continue to be popular (Lips, 2014; Lips, 2017; Kraemer, Dutton & Northrop, 1981; Heeks, 2006; Institute for Government, 2010). This suggests that turning this bold and ambitious vision of a technology- and data-enabled service state into a reality is often much more difficult and complex than expected.

Furthermore, an important question is what these digital government service reform efforts' actual impacts on and implications for governments' relationships with citizens are. Unfortunately, we only have limited scholarly insights available to date as most research activities have focused on either the technical and organizational aspects of digital government service provision to citizens (Lips & Schuppan, 2009) or the inherent capabilities of digital technologies to transform public service provision (Dunleavy et al, 2006). However, we do have some good empirical insights into these changing and increasingly digital government service relationships (e.g. Lips, 2014; Lips, 2017; McLoughlin & Wilson, 2013; Eppel & Lips, 2016; Heeks, 1999; Lips, Taylor & Organ, 2009a; Lips, Taylor & Organ, 2009b; Weerakkody & Reddick, 2012; Chen & Ahn, 2017; Lips et al, 2010; Lips, Barlow & Woods, 2016).

In this chapter, we explore the transitions that governments are making away from a traditional bureaucratic, vertically siloed and paper-based past and towards a digital government service future. We consider various visions and diverging realities around digital government service provision to citizens to date: governments' ambitions of becoming service states on the basis of newly

80 *Areas of public sector reform*

available technology and data affordances have been more difficult to achieve than originally expected. Consequently, we discuss emerging issues and barriers to achieving digital government service reform ambitions. And finally, we consider the institutional and democratic implications of digital government service reform.

From traditional public service provision to digital-era public services

As we discussed earlier, not much changed in the way governments provided public services to citizens in the past 150 years until governments started to adopt the Internet (UK Office of Public Service, 1996; Fountain, 2001). Until then at least, most governments were bureaucratic governments founded on the rational-legal ideal type of Weberian bureaucracy. The main principles and characteristics of this Weberian bureaucracy can be summarised as follows (Fountain, 2001: 45–46):

1 The principle of *official jurisdictional areas*, which are generally ordered by laws, rules and administrative regulations. This means:

    a   Regular activities required for the purposes of the bureaucratically governed jurisdiction or agency are assigned as official duties;

    b   The authority to give commands required for the discharge of these duties is distributed in a stable way and is strictly delimited by rules;

    c   Only people who qualify under general rules are employed;

2 The principles of *office hierarchy* and *channels of appeal* stipulate a clearly established system of super- and subordination in which lower offices are supervised by higher offices;

3 The principle of *written files or records*: office management is based on written documents, which are preserved in their original or draft form, and on an office staff of officials and scribes. Office staff and files are compartmentalised into "bureaus" or agency units;

4 The principle of *professionalisation and training*: office management usually presupposes thorough training in a field of specialisation;

5 The principle of *full-time job commitment*: official activities demand the full working capacity of the official; and

6 The principle of *general office rules*: the management of the office follows general rules, which are more or less stable and exhaustive and which can be learned. Knowledge of these rules represents a special technical expertise, which the officials possess. It involves jurisprudence and administrative or business management.

Institutional settings are not easy to change, which explains how deeply embedded in modern governments the traditional rules, hierarchical bureaucratic structures, functions, roles, processes and activities associated with the Weberian model are. This applies not only to strong vertical accountability and control structures

The service state 81

in modern government, but also to the vertical compartmentalisation of public records, files, data and information into segmented and separated functional areas (Bellamy & Taylor, 1998). Consequently, in many countries around the world, application of these Weberian bureaucratic principles has led to a modern state presence of many rule-based, vertical government jurisdiction areas or agencies both next to each other within a horizontal layer of government, such as an economic development government department, a treasury department and a government taxation office being part of a national government, and as segmented vertical administrative layers, such as federal government, state government and local government within a country. How widespread these vertical silo structures within and across different layers of government can be is illustrated by a real-life case study conducted in the UK mid-2000, when it became clear that a UK citizen dealing with a case of bereavement was required to visit at least 44 separate public counters to meet her specific service need (Varney, 2006).

Service provision to citizens by these traditional government bureaucracies was typically rule driven, siloed with separate citizen-facing public counters for each government functional domain and supported by paper-based files and public records stored in the filing cabinets of individual government agencies (Lips, Taylor & Organ, 2009a). Implementation and application of these government rules in individual relationships with clients was usually undertaken by a street-level bureaucrat (Lipsky, 1983) or frontline public official representing the government and with relevant functional expertise. In cases where government rules left room for discretion, the public servant would seek to apply existing administrative values based on the notion of administrative equivalence as far as possible, e.g. through considering case law on the matter (Lips, Taylor & Organ, 2009a: 722; Lipsky, 1983; Snellen, 1998). In general, application of this administrative equivalence principle covered the following three different forms of administrative equity in citizen-government relationships (Lips, Taylor & Organ, 2009a: 721):

- *Access rights to services*: equal service access for all citizens within any particular governmental jurisdiction;
- *Procedure*: equal and fair treatment during the service process; and
- *Legal entitlement to a specific standard of service*: equal service outcomes for similarly assessed cases, in accordance with legally embedded norms.

As a result, the street-level bureaucrat's discretionary capacity for decision-making was based on his control of the two-way information flow between government and individual clients: on the one hand, the frontline public official was the client's major source of information about the government's rules, processes and procedures; on the other hand, this public official was the government's major source of information about the particular circumstances of individual clients (Snellen, 1998: 500). The powerful discretionary role of street-level bureaucrats in public decision-making is further illustrated by the following four ways in which these government officials in theory could alter the two-way information flow between government and individual clients (Snellen, 1998: 500):

82 *Areas of public sector reform*

Table 4.1 Emerging managerial principles vs. traditional managerial principles

Emerging principles of "new" public management in the digital age	*Traditional principles of "old" public management*
• Targeted service provision in search of efficiency and effectiveness;	• Uniformity of service provision;
• Loose-tight network structures in enabling public service;	• Hierarchical top-down structures in bureaucratic organizations;
• Convergence and integration of services; and	• Functional division of work; and
• Responsive relationships to the "whole person" of "customer" citizens.	• Paternalistic relationships to clients.

- Not providing explicit and clear information about citizens' rights and entitlements to the client;
- Not requesting specific information needed from the client;
- Not asking the client for more details that are needed; and
- Providing the client with the terms and conditions under which the client needs to provide specific information to other government organizations.

In general, many technology-enabled public sector reform efforts are aimed at breaking these rule-driven government silo structures and powerful street-level bureaucratic relationships with individual clients and replacing them with a joined-up, customer-focused and responsive "whole of government." Indeed, a new set of managerial principles or "business logic" has become available to governments in the digital age, which are described and compared with traditional managerial principles in government in Table 4.1 (Bellamy & Taylor, 1998: 151).

However, Bellamy and Taylor (1998) warn us that application of these emerging digital-era public management principles requires the establishment of a new ethical order in digital government. In other words, it will require a trade-off between traditional values in government, such as universalism, equity and privacy, and emerging values in digital government, such as particularism and selectivity, efficiency and transparency (Bellamy & Taylor, 1998). We discuss this matter further in Chapter 6 in particular, when we consider a new ethical framework of contextual integrity for digital government.

Digital forms of public service provision

Although it is often thought that digital government service provision started with government's adoption of the Internet, digital technologies and data had already been used in government for quite some time by then. As we discussed in Chapter 1, the impact of digital technologies on government in the pre-Internet era should not be underestimated. For instance, without these decades-long developments of automating government through the application of computers and IT systems, many of the digital government service reform visions later proposed by governments could not have been realised (Lips, 2017). This "quiet revolution" took place particularly within individual government agencies and

The service state   83

led to an organizational shift towards more centralisation: for example, control of senior managers increased as a result of more decision-making power (Lips, 2017). The public sector workforce is another area where automating government had a major impact; not only did jobs disappear as a result of government computing, but new jobs in government also emerged, such as computer and programming experts. In particular, the introduction of PCs in government had an important influence on the professionalisation and training of public servants.

Citizen–government relationships were hardly affected by these technology-enabled changes in government organizations, except perhaps in areas where large volumes of data were processed, such as in the areas of taxation and social welfare, leading to a higher turnaround of citizens' service files and application forms. However, although these centralised computing solutions had an impact on government organizations for at least another decade or so, some changes started to happen in government with the adoption of the Internet. While IT and communication technologies (CT) had been used separately in government since the 1960s (Kraemer, Dutton & Northrop, 1981), the converging, networked, decentralised and ubiquitous nature of the Internet led people to believe that a new era had arrived when these new digital technologies would shape and deliver the government of the future (Lips, 2014).

Electronic government (e-government)

In September 1993, shortly after the World Wide Web became publicly available, the US federal government launched one of the first visions on digital government:

> Today, IT can create the government of the future, the electronic government. Electronic government overcomes the barriers of time and distance to perform the business of government and give people public information and services when and where they want them. It can swiftly transfer funds, answer questions, collect and validate data, and keep information flowing smoothly within and outside government.
>
> (Lips & Frissen, 1997: 117).

New digital technologies were expected to create a government that would work better and cost less: in other words, the adoption of digital technologies in government would lead not only to a radically streamlined bureaucracy, cost savings and more cost efficiency, but also to a government which would be much more responsive to the needs of individual citizens (Bellamy & Taylor, 1998: 41).

According to Fountain (2001), this public sector reform effort was different from earlier reform activities by the US federal government in the sense that there was no need for a restructuring of government agencies: it left government organizational and institutional structures, processes and procedures undisturbed. Instead, it emphasised redesigning process flows and enhancing the capacity of government in a way that government organizations could patch new digital technology solutions onto existing government structures and maintain the status quo (Fountain, 2001: 19).

84 *Areas of public sector reform*

As a result, with the White House as one of the leading government organizations, government agencies all over the world started to use the Internet as an additional government service channel to create their own public websites without changing their existing organizational structures. In so doing, they used a so-called yellow pages approach by putting the same public information on their websites as they offered in paper-based brochures and forms, including their official staff contact information (e.g. telephone numbers, email addresses) (Lips, 2017). Moreover, Internet domain name policy became of importance to governments, as they wanted their public websites to be found by people who started to navigate this new digital channel. A good illustration of the critical importance of both a robust domain name policy and a trusted and easy-to-find Internet domain name for citizens was provided in the early days of e-government, when the White House experienced the online public availability of a commercial site with illegal content using an almost identical Internet domain name.[1]

Government's relationship with the citizen didn't change much as a result of these early e-government service efforts, with the exception perhaps of both citizens and government officials starting to find their way on the Internet and having online access to government information, which was still designed in a traditional format: that is, exactly the same as government information published on paper and structured from a government organizational point of view.

An additional emerging issue for governments was their traditional democratic obligation based on the administrative equivalence principle that all citizens, without any exception, would be able to access and use government websites. This had implications not only for citizens who did not have Internet access but also for those who could not use government websites for reasons beyond their control (e.g. visual impairment). As a result, governments started to develop public policies aimed at closing these emerging digital divides amongst their citizens, such as promoting Internet access for all by installing Internet kiosks in public places and the development of web standards and guidelines to improve government website usability and user friendliness amongst all citizens (Lips & Frissen, 1997; see also Chapter 9).

Gaining citizens' trust in the new digital channel became of critical importance to government organizations, especially to provide these new Internet users with the confidence that the government agency's website was authentic and safe to use and had some added value (e.g. convenience) compared to the traditional paper-based and face-to-face channels available to the general public.

A further emerging Internet policy issue for governments in those early e-government days was around Internet navigation and making sure that citizens were able to find the government agency websites they were looking for. As a result, several governments around the world started investing in developing their own government Internet search engines, which, later on, with the widespread societal adoption of commercial Internet search engines like Google, became an issue for public debate: whether having a government search engine for navigating government websites was of added value to Internet-navigating citizens, when they also could use an existing commercial search engine with the downside of receiving commercially driven search outcomes (Lips, 2017).

The service state 85

Mobile government (m-government)

Many governments introduced mobile government or m-government as a digital government service channel when people started to use mobile devices, such as smartphones or iPads, combined with wireless access to the Internet. Especially in developing countries where access to mobile technology is much higher compared to more costly fixed broadband access, governments are using mobile government applications in order to deliver digital government services and engage with citizens online (OECD, 2011; Lips, 2017). Also, mobile technologies can provide access to government services where the infrastructure required for Internet-enabled service or wired phone service is not a viable option, which creates the opportunity for governments to reach out to a much greater number of people: for example, citizens in remote areas can receive m-health assistance and emergency or disaster response and enjoy e-learning content when they have limited access to public education (OECD, 2011; Lips, 2017).

As an example, in Cameroon, the widespread adoption of mobile phones has enabled the government to sidestep paying for expensive digital infrastructure (OECD, 2011). Mobile phones are used in digital government health service provision to track patients and remind them about appointments and vaccination schedules. Also, farmers receive text messages with information to help improve the productivity of their land and to provide information about available subsidies (OECD, 2011).

Furthermore, digital technologies in these countries are often seen by governments as means to introduce standardised digital government services, which guarantee more equitable treatment of all citizens than non-standardised human-based government services and, with that, enable good governance through a reduction of corruption (Lips, 2017). According to the OECD (2011: 12), m-government can help improve government performance and strengthen good governance, provided that the emphasis is not placed on the "m"; instead, the focus of m-government should be on the needs of both governments and citizens in establishing improved digital government service provision.

A practical example of m-government can be found in Malaysia, where citizens can verify their political voting information by using Short Message Service (SMS) (Lallana, 2008). Another practical example is from Indonesia, where the federal government has set up the online reporting system Lapor! (which means "report" in Bahasa Indonesian); citizens can provide feedback and report complaints about government performance and activities via SMS or mobile app to a public website.[2] The Lapor! website is managed by a government team that follows up on citizens' reports, which can range from bribery by traffic officers to corruption by politicians (Lukman, 2013). This website receives about 1,000 reports every day.

Integrating government

Since those early e-government days, we can observe a gradual shift away from government-centric ways of providing digital government services, such as

86 Areas of public sector reform

government information structured from a government organizational logic point of view, towards more customer-centric ways of digital government service provision. This development was influenced by governments' embracement of NPM thinking at the time: the application and use of new digital technologies like the Internet created an interesting strategic alignment with NPM objectives for governments to deliver more efficient and responsive public services and, with that, improve customer orientation (Homburg, 2004; Homburg, 2008). This strategic alignment then led to the development of a public sector reform vision around integrating government: the idea that digital technologies offered a major opportunity to break down the vertical silos within government and deliver government services to the general public in a much more integrated, customer-centric and responsive way (Lips, 2017).

Governments saw this opportunity of integrating government in three different technology-enabled public sector reform areas (Lips, 2017): firstly, making use of virtual integration and integrated web portals; secondly, facilitating the vertical integration of public services provided in different policy domains or government sectors (e.g. all public services provided in the wider social sector) through integrated government counters or "one-stop shops" and thirdly, facilitating horizontal integration of the physical front and/or back offices of government organizations. The option of facilitating horizontal integration of the physical back offices of government organizations, such as through the adoption and use of shared services horizontally across government agencies in areas like finance, procurement and human resources management (HRM), does not have much of an impact on digital government relationships with citizens other than some potential efficiency gains, perhaps, and is not further discussed here for that reason.

Governments around the world particularly embraced the first public sector reform strategy of virtual integration and the creation of web portals as it was a relatively easy customer-centric strategy to implement with no need to restructure any of the government organizations involved; digital network technology facilitated the virtual integration of government information and services provided by various government organizations in one public web portal. Moreover, this virtual integration of government information and services also allowed the same government information and services to be provided through an individual government agency's own website, which only required a few more clicks for citizens to access them. Consequently, the real-world organizational structure and functioning of government agencies stayed completely intact and only needed to solve technology-related issues, such as standardisation and interoperability (Lips, 2017; Luna-Reyes & Gil-Garcia, 2014; West, 2005).

Several years later, however, after a proliferation of government websites and web portals with increasingly high costs involved in the design and maintenance of these sites, several governments introduced website rationalisation strategies, which usually involved expanding the use of a single government web portal, strongly reducing the number of websites and the duplication of information and service provision across government (Lips, 2017).

The service state   87

Box 4.1   The GOV.UK portal

In 2011, the UK central government introduced a new and expanded single GOV.UK portal, which replaced the two web portals Directgov (for citizens) and Business Link (for businesses), whilst at the same time closing down 74 redundant government websites (Lips, 2017). Centrally led by the Government Digital Service (GDS), a unit in the UK government's Cabinet Office, and with active involvement of digital leaders from different government agencies in order to gain the experience, expertise and buy-in of those government agencies, the strategy and implementation of the portal was part of the UK government's reform ambition to offer digital-by-default public services. The main objectives of the GOV.UK portal were to provide citizens, businesses and government users with streamlined, accurate and comprehensive government services and information.

The GOV.UK portal serves as a one-stop information and services hub for all government departments in the UK. It uses several data sets to help make the website better. Many of these data sets are used under the Open Government Licence (see also Chapter 5). GDS work closely with every UK government organization to make sure all the information on GOV.UK is accurate and up to date. Also, the portal is updated based on results from user research and feedback from members of the general public. Although GDS tracks how people use GOV.UK, they do so without collecting or storing any personal information on users. Google Analytics software is used to track what webpages users visit, how long they use the site, how users got to the site and what links they clicked on.

Within a year of its launch, the portal had saved approximately £42 million GBP in UK government spending; in October 2013, it had two million visits in one day for the first time (Dilmegani, Korkmaz & Lundqvist, 2014). The success of the GOV.UK portal has led the GDS to open its code, which has been reused by governments around the world.

Another customer-centric development around integrating government was that governments started to offer their virtually integrated digital government services in a more interactive, dynamic and responsive way (Luna-Reyes & Gil-Garcia, 2014). Also, governments set up technology-enabled transactional services to individuals, involving the online exchange of personal data between government and the individual, which strongly adds to the complexities of achieving efficient and effective integrated digital government services (see also Chapter 8). This particularly applies to governments with large populations, such as India and Indonesia, where the introduction of new digital citizen identity management systems at the national level and the further integration of

88 *Areas of public sector reform*

these identity management systems into digital government transactional service provision, also shifting away from traditional face-to-face and paper-based government transactions, turned out to be a massive and highly complex undertaking. In general, the following types of services have been identified in digital government relationships with citizens around the world (Homburg, 2008: 93):

- *Information and data services*: digital access to government information provided via websites and portals, downloading government forms and brochures, policy documents, (draft) regulation and legislative documents, public records and other official documents. Also, access to government search functionalities (e.g. searching in government databases) and open government data services (see Chapter 5) are provided to citizens;
- *Contact services*: digital options to contact government organizations in order to ask a question, talk to a government agency staff member or make a complaint. These digital contact options include the use of email, online forms, text, online chat and other social media, and chatbots;
- *Transaction services*: the digital intake and further handling of digital government service applications and requests, such as the application for a building permit, vehicle license, passport, driver's licence, taxation assessment or student loan. Usually, a citizen's personal data need to be exchanged in order to get access to the required digital government service (see Chapter 8). Another area of digital government transaction services is around citizen identity management services, such as online citizen identity verification and authentication (see Chapter 8); and
- *Participation services*: technology- and data-enabled public participation options available to citizens, such as online discussion forums, engagement around open government data (see Chapter 5), submissions to draft public policy or legislation and engagement with government via social media (see Chapter 7).

Furthermore, several governments around the world, especially in Scandinavia and Western Europe, had already initiated public sector reform efforts to facilitate the vertical integration of public services through integrated government counters or one-stop shops when digital technologies provided new technology-enabled options for integrating government (Hagen & Kubicek, 2000; Lammers & Lips, 2000). Especially in local government, where most public services are provided to citizens in these countries, the vertical clustering and integration of government services in a particular service domain and provided via one single physical counter was considered to not only more holistically meet the multiple complex service needs of citizens, but also reduce the number of agencies a citizen must contact in order to meet a particular service need (Kubicek & Hagen, 2000; Lammers & Lips, 2000; Homburg, 2008). Digital technologies were seen as a critical infrastructure for this public sector reform movement as they facilitated the connection between the integrated front office with multiple, separated back offices in different government organizations

The service state   89

(Hagen & Kubicek, 2000). Moreover, they enabled digital access at the integrated counter to expert systems and government databases in various back offices so that relevant customer data from various government agencies were immediately available to the front-desk staff member if needed (Lips, 2017).

Again, the adoption and use of digital technologies supported governments in their public sector reform efforts to keep parts of the government organizational structure, especially the back offices of the various government agencies involved, more or less intact. However, the substantial changes needed to establish integrated counters did have a profound impact on front-desk staff members who needed to be retrained and reskilled in order to serve customers in a more holistic and integrated way (Lips, 2017). Moreover, the use of vertically integrated front offices in order to improve public service provision to customers required an increased sharing of a client's personal data between the integrated counter and the various back offices of government organizations, a development which was commonly not supported by existing privacy legislation (Lips, 2017; Dunleavy *et al*, 2006).

The public sector reform idea of facilitating horizontal integration of the physical front and back offices of government organizations has a much more profound impact on the organizational structures and process flows within and between government organizations as it requires the restructuring of both front and back offices of government agencies as well as front and back offices of other government service delivery partners (e.g. community service providers). Digital technologies, such as cloud computing, are considered critical enablers of joining up and integrating government front and back offices. Although some governments experimented with the implementation of this horizontal integration reform idea, such as the Dutch national government through its Government Counter 2000 Programme introduced in 1996, existing institutional arrangements across government, including accountability structures, organizational autonomy and legislation (e.g. privacy legislation), turn out to be important barriers for horizontal integration.

Citizen-centric government

Citizen-centric government became popular amongst governments in response to narrower customer-centric thinking around digital government service provision. It acknowledges the unique nature of government's service relationships with citizens in two important ways (Lips, 2017; OECD, 2009b): firstly, the fact that citizens' rights and obligations are quite different from more narrowly defined customer rights; and secondly, that governments need to balance the distinct interests and needs of different groups of citizens within the broader framework of the public interest. The latter implies that governments cannot use a one-size-fits-all approach in their digital government service design and, consequently, need to shift from a traditional government-centric service provision paradigm towards a more differentiated citizen-centric service design paradigm (OECD, 2009b; Lips, 2017).

90 *Areas of public sector reform*

The main differences between these two different government service paradigms can be described as follows (OECD, 2009b): where a traditional government-centric paradigm takes an "inside-out" perspective by emphasizing the organizational logic and coherence of government, including its focus on government processes and procedures, improving efficiency and effectiveness and increasing government performance and productivity, a citizen-centric paradigm on the other hand takes an "outside-in" perspective by emphasizing the context of the citizen and their specific service needs. This then creates an external, citizen-centric logic for organizing government service provision, including a focus on social factors (e.g. a citizen's socio-economic or ethnic background), organizational factors and institutional factors. This then leads to the following characteristics of citizen-centric government (OECD, 2009a; OECD, 2009b):

- Taking an "outside-in" instead of an "inside-out" perspective;
- Individuals are not just *customers* of government agencies, but *citizens* with rights and duties;
- Many "customers" of government are "involuntary customers";
- An externally focused, citizen-centric logic for organizing government service provision;
- Providing integrated government services tailored to the individual needs of citizens;
- Allowing for cross-government data sharing to support personalised government service provision and remove duplicated efforts of citizens to provide personal data to government;
- Co-design of government services between government organizations and citizens;
- Collaboration between multiple service providers depending on the citizen's service needs; and
- A networked perspective of the wider public sector.

However, as individualised forms of government service provision heavily rely on the sharing of personal data between the citizen and government as well as across government, the reality is that these forms of government service provision are usually limited due to existing privacy legislation. Moreover, human rights advocates have argued that a personalised amazon.com–type experience in government service provision can lead to undemocratic situations where citizens no longer receive any government information outside their immediate customer interests (Lips, 2017; Sunstein, 2007).

An early practical example of how digital technologies can enable citizen-centric forms of digital government is the application of the so-called life event model in Internet-enabled provision of government information and services. First introduced and used by the Singaporean government, this life event model clusters, integrates and presents government information and services in accordance with the major life events of citizens, such as looking for work, setting up a business, buying a house, having a child and retiring (Lips, 2017). Another practical example is the introduction of administrative simplification initiatives in governments around the world, where citizens do not need to submit the same personal data (e.g. change of address) over and over again to multiple government organizations any longer but only need to tell government once.

Box 4.2   Citizen–centric service provision around the birth of a child in New Zealand

Aimed at providing people with a single place to go for a wide range of government services and information they need when they are about to have a baby, SmartStart (https://smartstart.services.govt.nz/) was collaboratively designed by four New Zealand government organizations, namely the Department of Internal Affairs, the Ministry of Social Development, Inland Revenue and the Ministry of Health. This so-called cross-agency life event project gives people online access to integrated government information, services and support related to each phase of pregnancy and the first years of early childhood development. Available government services and information are structured around key events in people's lives, rather than how government agencies are organized. The goals of SmartStart are to save soon-to-be parents and caregivers time and effort by eliminating the need to call or visit various government agencies and other relevant organizations, fill out paperwork and provide the same identity information repeatedly to different government agencies.

SmartStart users can create a profile and add their due date to personalise the timeline with key dates that align with the important tasks they need to complete, such as choosing a lead maternity carer and ordering a birth certificate. Specific tasks, such as registering the birth of a new baby, can be completed online. As part of the same process, users can consent to sharing their baby's registration information with Inland Revenue to apply for an Inland Revenue number for their baby and with the Ministry of Social Development to update their benefit entitlement details. Also, users can get tips and advice on keeping themselves and the baby healthy and safe, as well as contact details for organizations that offer help and support. Moreover, SmartStart users can view the location of nearby services, such as antenatal classes and breastfeeding support.

The SmartStart cross-agency project team identified pain points through customer experience workshops in order to find out user needs and requirements for the life event service. They also delivered a working prototype to undertake customer user testing and gain feedback and used this to further develop the product. SmartStart went live in December 2016. In the first month, 15,000 people had used the integrated services and information tool. More than 170,000 users made use of SmartStart in its first year.

92 *Areas of public sector reform*

Further practical examples of technology- and data-enabled citizen-centric government can be found around so-called technology-enabled citizen prosumer (a combination of "producer" and "consumer") options, where citizens are actively involved in public service functions and activities that traditionally have been performed by government organizations. A good example is FixMyStreet, a project originally developed in the UK and later adopted by many governments around the world.

Box 4.3   FixMyStreet website and FIXiT app

The online initiative FixMyStreet (www.fixmystreet.com) was originally developed by the non-profit organization mySociety in the UK. As it uses an open-source code, the site has been adopted by many local governments around the world and incorporated into their workflow. More recently, a smartphone app FIXiT with similar functionalities also has been introduced in local governments across the globe.

The website FixMyStreet allows citizens in the UK to report any problems that need fixing, cleaning or clearing in their neighbourhood to their local council, such as potholes, graffiti, broken streetlights or dog fouling. They can do so by typing in their postcode on the website and using text and photos taken with their mobile phone to report their issue. People need to put the pin in the map to show exactly where the problem is. The report is forwarded to the relevant local council staff and published publicly on the FixMyStreet website so that others in the community can read, discuss and offer advice where needed. People can sign up on FixMyStreet to receive an email every time someone reports a problem in their chosen area. Posts on the FixMyStreet website are published anonymously. The status of a post can be changed to "fixed" when the reported problem has been resolved.

The city of Seattle uses the Find It, Fix It smartphone app to allow mobile users to report selected issues to the appropriate government department for response. Users can snap a photo with their smartphone, add detailed information, pinpoint the location and submit the report to their local council. The app offers the following service request categories:

- Abandoned Vehicle: report vehicles parked in a public right of way more than three days;
- Clogged Storm Drain: report a clogged storm drain;
- Graffiti Report: report graffiti, including what it is on – parking meter, utility pole or building – so it gets automatically routed to the appropriate department for response;

The service state   93

- Illegal Dumping: report illegal dumping – junk, garbage or debris – on public property, including roadsides, open streets and paved alleys;
- Parking Enforcement: make an inquiry regarding a parking concern;
- Pothole: report a pothole;
- Sign and Signal Maintenance: report damaged street signs and malfunctioning traffic signals;
- Streetlight Report: report a streetlight outage or damaged streetlight; and
- Other Inquiry: this miscellaneous category is for making an inquiry or request not listed under the other categories. Also, users can provide feedback via this category.

In summary, if governments would like to shift towards a citizen-centric approach to digital government service provision, the following managerial, institutional, democratic, organizational and government service design questions will be of major importance to them (Lips, 2011: 258–259; OECD, 2009a):

- How can governments enable and support a participatory and inclusive approach to digital government service design and delivery in order to ensure that citizen needs and expectations are met?
- How can governments use digital technologies to empower citizens to create their own services that meet their individual needs?
- How can the public sector itself change into a coherent whole, meeting users on their terms and not under the terms set by governments' traditions, organizations and cultures? and
- How can the current division of responsibilities and the organizational structures within the public sector be rethought to accommodate a whole-of-public-sector approach to digital government service design and delivery?

Digital-by-default government

Many governments around the world have launched digital government strategies to become digital by default. In general, this means that these governments are replacing traditional paper-based and face-to-face service channels with a variety of digital channels (e.g. web services, smartphone apps, SMS, social media) and data as their standard way or default setting in government service provision (Lips, 2014). For example, in Denmark, citizens are required to use a personal digital mailbox for all correspondence with government, instead of using paper-based mail options. It may not be surprising therefore that governments are expecting substantial efficiency gains and cost savings as a result of these digital-by-default government service reform efforts. In general, there

94 *Areas of public sector reform*

are six main reasons why governments want to become digital by default (Lips, 2014: 183):

1 To follow fundamental changes in society and seize the digital opportunity to transform themselves;
2 To promote substantial efficiency and cost savings;
3 To become customer-centric and provide better quality services;
4 To improve the availability and accessibility of open government data;
5 To move away from siloed approaches and duplications across the public sector by introducing common digital technology platforms; and
6 To promote the adoption of digital government services through enhanced security and privacy protection.

In order to further facilitate the use of digital government services, governments are removing legislative barriers preventing the development towards digital-by-default government, such as existing legislation made before the digital era (Lips, 2014).

Thus far, two main approaches can be observed in governments becoming digital by default (Lips, 2014): a service-centric approach, which basically converts traditional ways of government service provision into digital equivalents and a data–centric approach, which makes open government data publicly available for use to create new information products, services and applications that are most useful to consumers of that information (see Chapter 5). As an example, the city of San Francisco uses digital technologies, such as the Internet and application programming interfaces (APIs), to make its raw public transportation data on train routes, schedules and updates freely available to members of the general public. This has enabled citizen developers to write over ten different mobile applications to help individuals navigate San Francisco's public transport systems and provide more information services than the city can provide (The White House, 2012: 5–6).

Another substantial difference in national digital-by-default government service reform strategies can be observed in the implementation focus. For instance, some countries, such as the UK and Australia, focus on developing digital-by-default government services at the level of individual government organizations, whereas other countries, such as the United States and Denmark, focus on developing government-wide digital-by-default solutions, such as open government datasets and public registers, which can be used in government–agnostic, programme–agnostic and device–agnostic ways (Lips, 2014: 186).

However, governments' digital-by-default reform ambitions raise major issues around the existence of multiple digital divides amongst citizens. For instance, some population groups do not have any choice regarding the uptake of digital government services, such as vulnerable people highly dependent on social services, which could lead to even more inequalities around the access and use of government services. We discuss these important issues in Chapter 9.

In an attempt to actively support people who do not use the Internet or are less capable of accessing digital government services, the UK central government introduced a so-called assisted digital programme as part of their digital-by-default strategy (Lips, 2014). This assisted digital programme aims to gain customer insights from those who use digital government services and apply these insights in order to identify the support requirements and assistance needed for citizens who are not using the Internet (Lips, 2014). Also, the UK central government expects that they can persuade Internet users to use digital government services by improving their quality and making people aware of their availability. Another way of making it more attractive for citizens to use digital government services is the use of a positive incentive scheme, including passing on lower costs to digital government service users, allowing later deadlines for digital government service process completion and offering entries into prize draws for digital government service users (Cabinet Office, 2012: 30). However, as mentioned, assisting vulnerable population groups with using digital government services may in fact add to the costs involved with establishing digital-by-default government, which might be against the UK central government's objectives for digital-by-default government in the first place (Lips, 2014).

Data-enabled government

New innovative forms of data use are finding their way into the public sector for more effective and efficient digital government service delivery (see also Chapter 6). Greater sharing and use of aggregated, de-identified and open data across the public sector offers new opportunities for government organizations to segment clients into groups; get more insights about each group, such as what government interventions worked or didn't work and, on the basis of this knowledge, design more targeted, effective government services for clients with similar backgrounds (Lips, 2017). Another innovative opportunity for governments is to use behavioural data (e.g. mobile phone data) or social media data (e.g. Twitter feeds) in order to better predict certain events or situations and offer more effective and efficient government service interventions as a result: for example, in Indonesia, people's tweets about floods are being analysed in order to detect patterns in rising water levels in particular areas and prevent flooding more effectively[3] (Lips, 2017) (see also Box 7.3). Another example is the creation of real-time health maps[4] in certain geographical areas, where real-time behavioural and social media data are being harvested, integrated, visualised and publicly shared so that citizens and governments can monitor, detect and prevent emerging diseases and other public health threats at an early stage.

The New Zealand Ministry of Social Development (MSD) has worked with economic and data analysts to create a "forward liability" data model in order to estimate the financial risks of welfare dependency among their most vulnerable client groups (Taylor Fry, 2011). The data analysis showed that those who received an unemployment benefit accounted for only 5 percent

96 *Areas of public sector reform*

of actual welfare recipients, whereas people with the highest liability turned out to be those who went on a benefit before the age of 18 and sole parents (Ministry of Social Development, 2012; Taylor Fry, 2013). By matching and analysing data available across government, MSD was able to predict the probability of youth under the age of 18 going on to an adult benefit and, with that, the cost to the New Zealand government of future welfare services (SAS, 2013: 1).

These findings and predictive modelling techniques formed the basis for a new innovative "investment approach" to welfare services in New Zealand: the use of data and data analytics to better understand which social services have the most effective impact on different client groups of the most vulnerable people over longer periods of time (Lips, 2017). This improved evidence base is used in public decision-making around the development and design of government service provision to particular client groups and to shift government funding to those government service intervention programmes where the evidence suggests it is most needed. The reallocation of government funding may also include investing in programmes and services delivered by other service providers (e.g. community service providers), where the evidence base shows that those service interventions have the most positive impact on the lives of specific client groups.

However, as we discussed in Chapter 2, this development raises important issues about what evidence in data-enabled government service provision actually is, who interprets the data and converts it into information and knowledge, what the respective contributions of data analysts and expert frontline staff members to the creation of this evidence base are and the quality of the underlying data sets that are used in public decisions that are affecting people's lives. We will explore these issues further in Chapter 6.

Traditionally, as discussed earlier, frontline public servants with relevant expertise have a critical role in public service relationships with individual clients to not only interpret data and match the resulting information with government rules and regulations around public service provision, but also, in cases where government rules leave room for discretion, make decisions based on public service values and similar cases about appropriate government service provision to a particular client. Considering this innovative development where data analysts and algorithms seem to be replacing at least part of this room for discretion in public decision-making at the front line, we need to be aware that, in 1968, Vickers explained that human systems are different from mechanical systems in the sense that they are informed by appreciation and the "art of judgement": according to Vickers, the world is not a set of data but a socio-technical construct, a collective work of art (Vickers, 1968: 85). Facts are only reality judgements of "what is" and in themselves mean nothing without value judgements of "what ought"; it is the interaction between these two types of judgements which will lead to action judgements in public service provision about what to do, how to do it, what action to take and what solutions are good enough (Vickers, 1968).

The service state 97

In other words, we can observe potential ethical risks emerging as a result of public sector reform changes that are causing a shift away from traditional public decision-making in the course of public service provision based on equitable treatment and fairness and towards a more customised, preferential treatment of individual clients driven by their data-enabled, segmented client profiles in digital government service provision. Considering Vickers's arguments, this development suggests that human experts should continue to have a critical role in the decision-making process around appropriate public service provision to individual clients in the context of data-enabled government. In Chapter 6, we explore and discuss a new ethical framework of contextual integrity that would mitigate these emerging ethical risks in data-enabled government.

Emerging issues and barriers

If we consider these developments in digital government service provision to date, we can observe a wide range of emerging issues and barriers to technology- and data-enabled public sector reform. Public managers of digital government initiatives will need to deal with these issues and barriers in order to achieve digital government service reform. Interestingly, digital technology seems to be one of the least problematic issues in achieving the digital government service reform ambitions of governments. We briefly discuss each of these issues and barriers next and point to potential strategies on how to manage these issues and barriers wherever possible.

- *A relatively low uptake of digital government services compared to Internet use in other societal domains and activities*: the success of digital government service provision is dependent on citizens being aware of the existence of digital government services as well as willing and able to use these services (e.g. Eurostat, 2016; OECD, 2009a). Moreover, many citizens are mandatory customers of digital government services; they do not have any choice but to use them, especially when governments are becoming digital by default. Also, besides the fact that people may not be aware of the existence of digital government services, we should not underestimate the fact that most people do not need to use government services on a frequent basis, such as the renewal of a driver's licence, getting a building permit or renewing a passport. However, many governments demonstrate a so-called build-and-they-will-come attitude in their design and delivery of digital government services thus far. Consequently, it is critical for governments to take a citizen-centric perspective and understand the demands, needs, conditions and requirements of different groups of citizens in the context of digital government service relationships;
- *Citizens not having access to or using digital government services*: although not having access to digital technologies may cause a digital divide for large parts of the world, the more important digital divide issue here is that large groups of citizens, often the most vulnerable groups in society, do not have access to or use digital government services. We discuss this issue further in Chapter 9;

98 *Areas of public sector reform*

- *Governments' firm belief in citizens' desire to shift from traditional to digital government service channels*: as many people are regular users of digital technologies in their daily lives, governments often believe that the existence or supply of better quality and customer-centric digital government services will make people shift from traditional to online channels. However, empirical support for this common belief is often lacking and, where empirical research is available, also points towards people's multi-channel behaviours in digital government service relationships, including their preferred use of traditional telephone-based and face-to-face government service channels over digital channels (e.g. Lips, Barlow & Woods, 2016). For example, research findings from a 2013 EU survey show that, even though people can be daily Internet users, they can be unwilling to use digital government services for a variety of reasons, including preferring personal contact (62 percent), anticipating that the service requires face-to-face contact (34 percent) or seeing other channels as more convenient (19 percent) (European Union, 2013: 4);
- *Trust in digital government service provision*: trust in digital government is a complex and dynamic issue, which can be different for various people from different countries and at different moments in time (Bennett & Raab, 2003; Raab, 1998). It is also a context-relative issue, in the sense that people trust or distrust a digital government service relationship with a particular government organization through a particular digital channel or device: for instance to share their personal data by submitting a web-based service application form (Lips *et al*, 2010; Nissenbaum, 2010). Furthermore, it is easier to destroy trust than to gain it (Bennett & Raab, 2003). With that, digital security and privacy protection become closely associated with people's perception of trust in digital government: for instance, increasing numbers of data breaches in digital environments around the world, including in digital government, may affect people's trust in using digital channels in their service relationships with government (see Chapter 8). But the authenticity and quality of government service provision in digital environments also may influence people's trust perceptions. However, in several countries around the world, the use of digital channels in government service relationships with citizens can also enhance people's trust in government and establish good governance;
- *Security of digital government service provision*: digital security is closely associated with people's trust perceptions of digital government (see the discussion in Chapter 8);
- *Privacy protection vs. the need for increased cross-government data sharing*: with the gradual shift in government's public sector reform ambitions to become more citizen-centric, there is an increasing tension around the necessity to increase cross-government data sharing in order to achieve those ambitions, whilst simultaneously protecting the privacy of citizens in accordance with existing privacy legislation. More in general, we can observe that privacy legislation is often standing in the way of governments' efforts to

improve the effectiveness of public service provision to individual clients. In Chapters 6 and 8, we discuss further how this important dilemma for governments of providing more effective government services whilst protecting fundamental citizen rights, such as the individual's privacy (Bellamy *et al*, 2008), can be managed in the context of digital government service relationships;

- *Achieving citizen-centric government requires co-design of government services, collaboration between service providers and a networked perspective of the wider public sector*: this requires not only a horizontal orientation on digital government service provision but also a different way of managing (see Chapter 7);
- *Legislative barriers*: many existing laws applicable to the context of digital government were made prior to the (increased) use of digital technologies and data in digital government service relationships with citizens and, as a result, often stand in the way of governments' public sector reform ambitions;
- *A government-centric logic in providing digital government services*: many governments apply a government-centric, organizational logic to designing, structuring and providing government information and services through digital channels. A good example is the fact that more or less every individual government organization has its own public website, usually in addition to an official government-wide web portal through which the same government information and services can be accessed by citizens through a few additional clicks. Moreover, many digital government services have issues regarding their usability and user friendliness (see Chapter 9). As this puts the burden of navigating digital government on the citizen, applying a citizen-centric logic to the design, structuring and delivery of digital government services would support a further uptake of these services;
- *Complexity of providing government services through digital channels*: as government services are often intangible, provided within regulatory frameworks aimed at compliance with traditional administrative values (e.g. equity, universalism, fairness) and required to meet the varying service needs and demands of different groups of citizens entitled to them, the standardisation and simplification processes needed for digitisation of government services are very complex and difficult to achieve. Also, empirical research in New Zealand demonstrates that digitally provided standardised forms usually do not offer individuals the option of explaining their unique circumstances in digital government relationships (Lips *et al*, 2010). Consequently, digital government service users hold the view that government agencies are not always asking them for the right information in these standardised digital government service relationships (Lips *et al*, 2010). They therefore prefer direct service interaction with a public official via traditional channels, such as telephone or face to face, not only to make sure that government agencies understand their unique personal circumstances, but also to get instant confirmation of the requested government service (Lips *et al*, 2010; Lips, 2014);

100 *Areas of public sector reform*

- *Ethical issues around the use of data in data-enabled government service provision*: this development raises important issues about what evidence in data-enabled government service provision actually is, who interprets the data and converts it into information and knowledge, what the respective contributions of data analysts and expert frontline staff members to the creation of this evidence base are, and the quality of the underlying data sets used in public decisions that affect people's lives. We discuss these issues further in Chapters 6 and 8 in particular;
- *A tension between a government-wide, horizontal view on digital government reform and the perspective and needs of individual, vertical government agencies*: different perspectives and needs at different organizational levels and layers of government raise issues around leadership, horizontal versus vertical accountability, cross-government coordination, collaboration, funding, governance and the autonomy of government organizations (e.g. Brown, 2007);
- *The transition process from traditional government services to digital government service provision*: this process requires management of a wide variety of institutional, organizational, cultural, social, ethical, legal and technological changes, both within and across government organizations, and in service relationships with citizens, especially when new digital government services will be provided in more citizen-centric and integrated ways;
- *Required re-skilling and re-training of public servants involved in digital government service provision*: the re-skilling and re-training of public servants becomes more relevant in digital government service reform initiatives when they are geared towards more integrated, citizen-centric and data-enabled forms of digital government service provision;
- *Leadership of digital government service reform is critically important*: both political and public management leadership in digital government service relationships are critically important. We discuss this issue further in Chapter 10;
- *A favourable climate for public service innovation and risk taking*: the political environment of digital government service innovation usually is risk averse as a result of the failure of many high-profile digital government projects and the high costs involved with most digital government service reform initiatives;
- *Existence of legacy systems in digital government service provision*: legacy systems can stand in the way of investment in and use of new digital technologies and systems in digital government service provision. The reasons for this can be the political risks associated with the introduction of a new large government technology project and the high costs involved in not only replacing these legacy systems, but also managing the various changes related to introducing and using new digital technologies and applications in digital government. This also needs to be seen in the context of limited available public funds and annual budget cycles;
- *Technology issues*: technology issues important for digital government service reform include standardisation, interoperability, Internet domain name policy, investment in critical back-up digital infrastructure and investment in and adoption of new digital infrastructure, technologies, systems, datasets and applications.

Institutional and democratic implications of digital government service reform

Digital technologies and data are increasingly embedded in the fabric of government's service relationships with citizens. In general, we can observe a development from using centralised mainframe computers to process government service applications of citizens more quickly to an increasing use of digital technologies and data for more integrated, citizen-centric and personalised forms of digital government service provision. However, as we discussed earlier, digital technologies and data do not determine the outcomes of digital government service reform; digital government service outcomes depend on the actual use of digital technologies and data in a particular socio-technical assemblage within the context of digital government service relationships with citizens. As these contexts are different in countries around the world, we most likely will see different digital government service outcomes emerging from the use of similar digital technologies but in different contexts and socio-technical assemblages. Consequently, gaining more empirical insight into these socio-technical assemblages and why and how digital technologies and data are being used in the context of digital government service relationships in each country is critically important.

In general, what becomes clear from our discussion thus far is that the traditional institutional and democratic foundations of government and its relationships with citizens are increasingly challenged as a result of using digital technologies and especially data. For instance, we can observe an increasing tension between newly required horizontal institutional arrangements for digital government service provision and traditional vertical institutional settings, such as accountability structures and the vertical organization and handling of citizen data. Moreover, as Bellamy and Taylor (1998) predicted earlier, we are increasingly witnessing a required trade-off between traditional values in government, such as universalism, equity, fairness and privacy, and emerging values in digital government, such as particularism and customer differentiation, citizen-centricity, effectiveness and efficiency. This then requires the establishment of a new ethical order or framework for the context of digital government service relationships. We discuss this important ethical foundation for the future of digital government more specifically in Chapters 6 and 8.

Box 4.4 Exercise 4.1

Explore to what extent each of the digital government services models differs from the main principles and characteristics of the traditional Weberian bureaucracy. What has changed, why and how?

102 *Areas of public sector reform*

Discussion questions

1   Which digital government service reform model would be most suitable for providing digital government services to citizens in your country, and why? Motivate your answer.
2   Which traditional public service values do you consider to be of continued importance in the digital age, if any, and why? Motivate your answer.
3   What are the issues and barriers for a government that wants to introduce an integrating government service reform model? Motivate your answer.
4   Find a government website and explore which website features use a government-centric logic and which features use a citizen–centric logic. In general, what would governments in your country need to do in order to become more citizen–centric in digital government service provision from your personal point of view?
5   What are the pros and cons of governments becoming digital by default in their service provision relationships with citizens?
6   In your view, what are the three most critical issues and barriers that emerge around digital government service reform and why? Motivate your answer.

Notes

1 Whitehouse.com instead of whitehouse.gov
2 Lapor!, available from: https://www.lapor.go.id/ [accessed 23 June 2018].
3 Floodtags, available from: https://www.floodtags.com/ [accessed 23 June 2018].
4 HealthMap, available from: https://www.healthmap.org/en/ [accessed 23 June 2018].

References

Bellamy, C., 6, P., Raab, C.D., Warren, A. & Heeney, C. (2008) Information-sharing and confidentiality in social policy: Regulating multi-agency working. *Public Administration*, 86 (3), 737–759.
Bellamy, C. & Taylor, J.A. (1998) *Governing in the Information Age*. Buckingham: Open University Press.
Bennett, C.J. & Raab, C.D. (2003) *The Governance of Privacy: Policy Instruments in Global Perspective*. Aldershot: Ashgate.
Brown, D. (2007) The government of Canada: Government on-line and citizen-centred service. In: Borins, S., Kernaghan, K., Brown, D., Bontis, N., 6, P. & Thompson, F. (eds.) *Digital State at the Leading Edge*. Toronto: University of Toronto Press, pp. 37–68.
Cabinet Office. (November 2012) *Government Digital Strategy*. London: Cabinet Office.
Chen, Y. & Ahn, M.J. (eds.) (2017) *Routledge Handbook on Information Technology in Government*. London: Routledge.
Danish Agency for Digitisation. (May 2016) *Digital Government Strategy 2016–2020: Digitaliseringsstyrelsen*. Available from: https://en.digst.dk/policy-and-strategy/digital-strategy/ [accessed 20 December 2018].
Dilmegani, C., Korkmaz, B. & Lundqvist, M. (December 2014) *Public-Sector Digitization: The Trillion-Dollar Challenge*. McKinsey & Company. Available from: https://www.mckinsey.com/business-functions/digital-mckinsey/our-insights/public-sector-digitization-the-trillion-dollar-challenge [accessed 7 January 2019].

The service state   103

Dunleavy, P., Margetts, H., Bastow, S. & Tinkler, J. (2006) *Digital Era Governance: IT Corporations, the State, and E-Government.* Oxford: Oxford University Press.

Eppel, E.A. & Lips, A.M.B. (2016) Unpacking the black box of successful ICT-enabled service transformation: How to join up the vertical, the horizontal and the technical. *Public Money & Management*, 36 (1), 39–46. Available from: https://doi.org/10.1080/09540962.2016.1103417

European Union. (2013) *Public Services Online Digital by Default or by Design? Assessing User Centric eGovernment Performance in Europe – eGovernment Benchmark 2012.* Final Insight Report, European Commission, Directorate-General of Communications Networks, Content and Technology. European Union: European Commission.

Eurostat. (2016) *Internet Access and Use Statistics – Households and Individuals.* Available from: http://ec.europa.eu/eurostat/statistics-explained/index.php?title=Archive:Internet_access_and_use_statistics_-_households_and_individuals [accessed 19 June 2018].

Fountain, J.E. (2001) *Building the Virtual State: Information Technology and Institutional Change.* Washington, DC: Brookings Institution Press.

Hagen, M. & Kubicek, H. (eds.) (2000) *One-Stop-Government in Europe: Results from 11 National Surveys.* Bremen: University of Bremen.

Heeks, R. (ed.) (1999) *Reinventing Government in the Information Age: International Practice in IT-Enabled Public Sector Reform.* London: Routledge.

Heeks, R. (2006) *Implementing and Managing eGovernment: An International Text.* London: Sage.

Homburg, V. (2004) *E-Government and NPM: A Perfect Marriage?* Proceedings of the 6th International Conference on Electronic Commerce, ACM, pp. 547–555.

Homburg, V. (2008) *Understanding E-government: Information Systems in Public Administration.* London: Routledge.

Institute for Government. (2010) *System Error: Fixing the Flaws in Government IT.* London: Institute for Government.

Kraemer, K.L., Dutton, W.H. & Northrop, A. (1981) *The Management of Information Systems.* New York, NY: Columbia University Press.

Kubicek, H. & Hagen, M. (2000) One-stop-government in Europe: An overview. In: Hagen, M. & Kubicek, H. (eds.) *One-Stop-Government in Europe: Results from 11 National Surveys.* Bremen: University of Bremen, pp. 1–36.

Lallana, E.C. (2008) *mGovernment: Mobile/Wireless Applications in Government.* Available from: https://www.egov4dev.org/mgovernment/ [accessed 20 December 2018].

Lammers, K. & Lips, A.M.B. (2000) One-stop-government in The Netherlands. In: Hagen, M. & Kubicek, H. (eds.) *One-Stop-Government in Europe: Results from 11 National Surveys.* Bremen: University of Bremen, pp. 403–466.

Lips, A.M.B. (2011) 'E-government is dead: Long live networked governance': Fixing system errors in the New Zealand public management system. In: Ryan, B. & Gill, D. (eds.) *Future State: Directions for Public Management in New Zealand.* Wellington: Victoria University of Wellington, pp. 248–261.

Lips, A.M.B. (2014) Transforming government: By default? In: Graham, M. & Dutton, W.H. (eds.) *Society & the Internet: How Networks of Information and Communication Are Changing Our Lives.* Oxford: Oxford University Press, pp. 179–194.

Lips, A.M.B. (2017) Transforming government services over time: Meanings, impacts, and implications for citizen: Government relationships. In: Chen, Y. & Ahn, M.J. (eds.) *Routledge Handbook on Information Technology in Government.* London: Routledge, pp. 11–26.

Lips, A.M.B., Eppel, E.A., Cunningham, A. & Hopkins-Burns, V. (August 2010) *Public Attitudes to the Sharing of Personal Information in the Course of Online Public Service Provision.* Final Research Report. Wellington: Victoria University of Wellington.

104 *Areas of public sector reform*

Lips, A.M.B. & Frissen, P.H.A. (1997) *Wiring Government: Integrated Public Service Delivery Through ICT in the UK and the USA*. NWO/ITeR-series, Vol. 8. Alphen aan den Rijn: Samsom BedrijfsInformatie bv, pp. 67–164.

Lips, A.M.B. & Schuppan, T. (2009) Transforming e-government knowledge through public management research. *Public Management Review*, 11 (6), 739–749.

Lips, A.M.B., Taylor, J.A. & Organ, J. (2009a) Identity management, administrative sorting and citizenship in new modes of government. *Information, Communication & Society*, 12 (5), 715–734.

Lips, A.M.B., Taylor, J.A. & Organ, J. (2009b) Managing citizen identity information in e-government service relationships in the UK: The emergence of a surveillance state or a service state? *Public Management Review*, 11 (6), 833–856.

Lips, A.M.B., Barlow, L. & Woods, L. (March 2016) *Conditions for Channel Shift Behaviours and Simplification in Business Individuals' and Small Businesses' Online Interactions with Government*. Survey Research Report. Wellington: Victoria University of Wellington.

Lipsky, M. (1983) *Street-Level Bureaucracy: Dilemmas of the Individual in Public Services*. New York, NY: Russel Sage Foundation.

Lukman, E. (21 October 2013) Indonesia's anti-corruption website is now getting 1,000 crowdsourced reports every day. *Tech in Asia*. Available from: https://www.techinasia.com/lapor-indonesia-200000-users [accessed 23 June 2018].

Luna-Reyes, L.F. & Gil-Garcia, J.R. (2014) Digital government transformation and internet portals: Co-evolution of technology, organizations and institutions. *Government Information Quarterly*, 31, 545–555.

McLoughlin, I. & Wilson, R., with Martin, M. (2013) *Digital Government @ Work: A Social Informatics Perspective*. Abingdon: Oxford University Press.

Ministry of Social Development. (12 September 2012) *Investment Approach Refocuses Entire Welfare System*. MSD Media release.

Nissenbaum, H. (2010) *Privacy in Context: Technology, Policy, and the Integrity of Social Life*. Stanford, CA: Stanford University Press.

OECD. (2009a) *Rethinking e-Government Services: User-Centred Approaches*. Paris: OECD.

OECD. (2009b) *Citizen-Centric Government*. Paris: OECD.

OECD. (2011) *m-Government: Mobile Technologies for Responsive Governments and Connected Societies*. Paris: International Telecommunication Union, OECD.

Raab, C.D. (1998) Electronic confidence: Trust, information and public administration. In: Snellen, I.Th.M. & van de Donk, W.B.H.J. (eds.) *Public Administration in an Information Age: A Handbook*. Amsterdam: IOS Press, pp. 113–133.

SAS. (2013) *Transforming Social Welfare with Analytics: SAS Customer Story*. Wellington: SAS.

Snellen, I.Th.M. (1998) Street level bureaucracy in an information age. In: Snellen, I.Th.M. & van de Donk, W.B.H.J. (eds.) *Public Administration in an Information Age: A Handbook*. Amsterdam: IOS Press, pp. 497–505.

Sunstein, C. (2007) *Republic.com 2.0*. Princeton, NJ: Princeton University Press.

Taylor Fry. (2011) *Ministry of Social Development and The Treasury – Actuarial Advice of Feasibility: A Long-Term Investment Approach to Improving Employment, Social and Financial Outcomes from Welfare Benefits and Services*. Wellington: Ministry of Social Development and The Treasury.

Taylor Fry. (2013) *Ministry of Social Development and The Treasury – Actuarial Valuation of the Benefit System for Working-age Adults as at 30 June 2013*. Wellington: Ministry of Social Development and The Treasury.

The White House. (2012) *Digital Government: Building a 21st Century Platform to Better Service the American People*. Executive Office of the President of the United States. Washington, DC: The White House.

The service state   105

Treasury Board of Canada Secretariat. (2018) *Digital Operations Strategic Plan: 2018–2022*. Available from: https://www.canada.ca/en/government/system/digital-government/digital-operations-strategic-plan-2018-2022.html [accessed 20 December 2018].

UK Government Digital Service. (2017) *Government Transformation Strategy*. London: The National Archives. Available from: https://www.gov.uk/government/publications/government-transformation-strategy-2017-to-2020/government-transformation-strategy [accessed 20 December 2018].

UK Office of Public Service. (1996) *Government.Direct: A Prospectus for the Electronic Delivery of Government Services*. Cm 3438. London: HMSO.

Varney, D. (2006) *Service Transformation: A Better Service for Citizens and Businesses, A Better Deal for the Taxpayer*. London: HSMO. Available from: https://assets.publishing.service.gov.uk/government/uploads/system/uploads/attachment_data/file/229012/011840489X.pdf [accessed 20 December 2018].

Vickers, G. (1968) *Value Systems and Social Process*. London: Tavistock Publications.

Weerakkody, V. & Reddick, C.G. (eds.) (2012) *Public Sector Transformation Through e-Government: Experiences from Europe and North America*. New York, NY: Routledge.

West, D. (2005) *Digital Government: Technology and Public Sector Performance*. Princeton, NJ: Princeton University Press.

Further reading

Bellamy, C. & Taylor, J.A. (1998) *Governing in the Information Age*. Buckingham: Open University Press.

Chen, Y. & Ahn, M.J. (eds.) (2017) *Routledge Handbook on Information Technology in Government*. London: Routledge.

Heeks, R. (2006) *Implementing and Managing eGovernment: An International Text*. London: Sage.

McLoughlin, I. & Wilson, R., with Martin, M. (2013) *Digital Government @ Work: A Social Informatics Perspective*. Abingdon: Oxford University Press.

OECD. (2009b) *Citizen-Centric Government*. Paris: OECD.

OECD. (2011) *m-Government: Mobile Technologies for Responsive Governments and Connected Societies*. Paris: International Telecommunication Union, OECD.

Weerakkody, V. & Reddick, C.G. (eds.) (2012) *Public Sector Transformation Through e-Government: Experiences from Europe and North America*. New York, NY: Routledge.

5 Open and transparent government

Learning objectives

By the end of this chapter you should be able to:

- Understand the practical meaning of meaningful transparency in open and transparent government;
- Point out the complexities, issues and barriers to achieving open and transparent government; and
- Identify strategies to promote open and transparent government.

Key points of this chapter

- Transparency is a guiding democratic principle in citizen–government relationships with many meanings, types and forms attached to it, including meanings which do not seem to refer to an ideal image of transparency at all;
- A transparency paradox could emerge in digital government relationships; with more and more government information being publicly released via digital channels, citizens may have increasing difficulty finding the government information they need or search for;
- Another transparency paradox refers to the fact that, although government data and information can be made visible to the general public, it is unlikely that they are understood, relevant and meaningful to the actionable choices citizens must make;
- A problematic popular conception of the transparency ideal is the idea that, for citizens to be able to see an object, such as a government document, is the same as being able to understand it and act upon it;
- "Open data" and "openness" mean different things to different government organizations, citizens and other external stakeholders;
- Opening up government data has its limitations, with several types of government data requiring protection;
- Open government data initiatives usually assume that all citizens are capable users of open data; and

Open and transparent government   107

- Opening up government data will not automatically lead to open and transparent government, nor will data *per se* lead to enhanced forms of public participation, collaboration and good governance; a shift of focus towards the actual use and citizen-users of open government data is critically important in order to make some further progress with public sector reform ambitions around establishing open and transparent government.

Key terms

- *Transparency in digital government relationships*: is not simply a precise outcome in which the technology-enabled release of government information or data is accessible, visible, understandable and actionable for citizen-users, but a process of social construction and making sense of the socio-technical assemblage of which government information, government data and digital technologies are integral parts.
- *Open government data*: need to be seen on a spectrum from completely open to completely closed or protected.

Introduction

Governments around the world have embraced new innovative opportunities enabled by the use of digital technologies and data to become more open and transparent in the digital age. For decades if not centuries in some countries around the world, such as Sweden, principles of openness and transparency in government and its societal relationships have been acknowledged as critical foundations of democracy and, as such, have been institutionalised and usually codified via legislation. For example, improving public access to government information and other public records became an important strategy for governments to support these democratic principles in the 20th century, leading to the adoption of freedom of information legislation in many countries around the world. The arrival of digital technologies, especially the Internet, has further accelerated this development towards better and easier public access to government information, as we discussed in Chapter 4.

Moreover, governments, too, have acknowledged the potential of innovative data use in order to promote open and transparent government and have started to make their digitised datasets more accessible and publicly available. For many governments around the world, challenges posed by the global financial crisis have created an incentive to think outside the box and use public assets, such as government-held non-personal data, to develop new opportunities for innovation, job creation and public sector reform. For instance, data innovation holds the promise of generating new forms of data sharing and collaborative knowledge production, leading to novel insights and a better understanding of a wide variety of complex public policy problems, such as air pollution, natural disasters, water quality and poverty (Benkler, 2006; United Nations, 2013). Also,

108   *Areas of public sector reform*

data innovation and the use of open government data are expected to gain substantial economic benefits through the development of new products and services: for example, according to Manyika *et al* (2013), the use of open data across the economic domains of education, transportation, consumer products, electricity, oil and gas, health care and consumer finance could unlock an estimated US$3 trillion in annual economic potential.

Further opportunities around opening up government data are perceived by governments, especially those in the developing world, to build societal trust and establish more democratic good governance through enhanced transparency and accountability. A 2011 OECD report points out that, for many countries, promoting an open and transparent government serves the following double objective (OECD, 2011):

- to provide a vehicle to restore trust in government and align the public sector with modern information management practices where citizens are looking for easily accessible digitised government information and services; and
- to create policy levers to facilitate capacity for change and for more efficient, sustainable reform in the public sector in partnership with external stakeholders from the private sector and civil society.

More in general, digital technologies and data are increasingly seen as critical enablers of establishing open and transparent government in many respects, including improving public access, quality and accuracy of government data and information; enabling data sharing and open innovation; enabling better informed public decision-making; preventing corruption and enhancing participatory democracy (Bertot, Jaeger & Grimes, 2012). This development towards open and transparent government has been further driven by international organizations and programmes, such as the United Nations (2013), the World Bank's open data initiative,[1] and the endorsement of the 2011 Open Government Declaration by many countries through their membership in the Open Government Partnership.[2]

However, thus far there is little consensus, either in academia or amongst practitioners, what "openness" and "transparency" actually mean. Answers to these questions are particularly important now that governments are using digital technologies and data to become open and transparent; important questions, then, are how, when, and under what conditions these public sector reform ambitions will be actually achieved. We explore these issues in this chapter, including how digital technologies and open government data are affecting governments' public sector reform efforts to date. Firstly, we explore the meaning of the concept of transparency and how governments are using digital technologies to become more transparent. Secondly, we consider several problems around this transparency ideal for governments. Thirdly, we look more closely at governments' ambitions to open up government data. Fourthly, we explore some of the complexities around opening up government data; there are several emerging issues and barriers that can be identified to governments becoming

Open and transparent government 109

more open and transparent. And finally, we will consider some strategies for governments to become more open and transparent.

Towards more transparent government

Traditionally, achieving the public sector reform ambition of more transparent government has been associated with better public access to government information (e.g. Mergel, 2013; de Vries, 2005). In some countries, such as Sweden, this democratic principle of enhanced public access to government information has been supported by government for centuries: for instance, in 1766, Sweden started legislating press freedom through its Freedom of the Press Act (*Tryckfrihetsforordningen* law), which gave publishers rights of statutory access to government records (Ananny & Crawford, 2018: 975). In other countries, public access to government information often has been regulated in the last century, as in the USA, where citizens have the right to request access to government information and public records held by US federal government organizations through their 1967 Freedom of Information Act (FOIA), except to the extent that records are protected from disclosure by an exemption contained in the law.

Commonly, freedom of information acts around the world are promoting government transparency, accountability, and openness as they facilitate making key public policy documents and government decision-making documents and information transparent and accessible to the general public (Kitchin, 2014; de Vries, 2005). According to Janssen and van den Hoven (2015), transparency is a critical democratic mechanism from a checks-and-balances point of view as it allows citizens to hold government to account. This democratic checks-and-balances mechanism is growing in importance, now that governments are able to use digital technologies and data in ways in which the citizen becomes more transparent to government (Dutch Scientific Council, 2016; Brin, 1998): for instance, Brin (1998) argues that, in this digital era in which governments can easily monitor citizens, it has become crucial for citizens to "watch the watchers." At the same time, however, the use of digital technologies and data to support this democratic checks-and-balances mechanism can also promote trust in government, reduce corruption and enhance good governance (Bertot, Jaeger & Grimes, 2012).

As becomes clear, there is little scholarly consensus about the definition of transparency (Meijer, 2013; Grimmelikhuijsen, 2012; Albu & Flyverbom, 2016). Instead, scholars observe transparency as a guiding democratic principle in citizen-government relationships with many meanings, types and forms attached to it, including meanings which do not seem to refer to an ideal image of transparency at all. For instance, scholars have identified the following typologies of government transparency (Ananny & Crawford, 2018: 976; Heald, 2006: 27–33; Grimmelikhuijsen, 2012):

- *Fuzzy transparency* versus *clear transparency*: in other words, provided government information that does not reveal the actual government performance

110 *Areas of public sector reform*

and/or is unreliable versus provided government information that does reveal reliable insights about government performance;

- Transparency that creates *soft accountability* (i.e. government organizations must answer for their actions without legal consequences) versus *hard accountability* (i.e. government organizations face sanctions and/or legal action);
- *Transparency upwards* (i.e. the hierarchical principal can monitor the performance of the hierarchical agent) versus *transparency downwards* (i.e. the hierarchical agent can monitor the performance of the hierarchical principal or the ruled the performance of their rulers) versus *transparency outwards* (i.e. the hierarchical agent can monitor what is happening outside the organization) versus *transparency inwards* (i.e. when those outside can monitor what is going on inside the organization);
- *Transparency as event* (i.e. the inputs, outputs or outcomes that define the objects of transparency) versus *transparency as process* (i.e. the organizational rules, regulations and procedures that define the conditions of transparency); and
- *Transparency in retrospect* (i.e. an organization's *ex post* account of stewardship and management) versus *transparency in real time* (i.e. the accountability window is always open as monitoring is continuous).

Transparency can also be considered through its contrasting democratic principle of secrecy (e.g. Meijer, 2013). There are very good reasons for democratic societies to keep government data and information secret, such as the need to fight crime and terrorism threats. Indeed, for government to make assessments about what government information should be opened up and what needs to stay secret, or at least confidential from a public good point of view, is a delicate balancing act which is commonly supported by legislation (e.g. legal exemptions under the FOIA).

How easy it is nowadays to reverse the balance between transparency and secrecy as a result of the use of digital technologies is demonstrated by practical examples like Wikileaks. In this particular case, individuals put secret government documents and information on the Internet, so the information has become publicly available for Internet users all over the world: a technology-enabled outcome, which might be considered as a case of enhanced or even radical transparency (Roberts, 2006). Another well-known example involves a former contractor for the US National Security Agency, Edward Snowden, who made the top-secret files of one of the world's most powerful intelligence organizations publicly available via independent third parties from the free press, such as the UK newspaper *The Guardian* (Harding, 2014). He revealed that digital technologies were used by these intelligence organizations for mass surveillance (Harding, 2014). Edward Snowden described his motivation for this massive intelligence breach as follows:

> I don't want to live in a world where everything that I say, everything I do, everyone I talk to, every expression of creativity or love or friendship is recorded.
>
> (In: Harding, 2014: 5).

Open and transparent government 111

As these practical examples make clear in dramatic ways, digital technologies nowadays have the potential to enhance transparency and, with that, empower citizens to hold governments to account (Janssen & van den Hoven, 2015). According to de Vries, digital technologies have the following impact on citizens' access to government information in digital government relationships (de Vries, 2005: 659–660):

- *Digital technologies enable new forms of interaction and communication between citizens and government*: government websites, email, apps, SMS and social media in digital government relationships enable citizens to have faster, easier and more interactive access to digitised government information and public records, regardless of time or location;
- *Government has the technology-enabled capability to make much more government information publicly accessible compared to the paper-based era*: enhanced public access to digitised government information implies that citizens should be able to find, use and understand government information. Standardisation, web guidelines and search functionalities can further support this new government capability in the digital age;
- *Digital technologies are influencing the power balance between government and citizens:* as citizens are able to access and monitor more information about government performance and activities, they can better hold government to account. This then can also lead to a more active involvement of citizens in public policy- and decision-making; and
- *The use of digital technologies has reduced the costs of publicly releasing and accessing government information*: digital technologies have greatly reduced the costs for governments to produce, publish, manage, store and disseminate government information and even create new government information products using public websites, social media, SMS and smartphone apps, for example. At the same time, the costs for citizens to publicly access government information have been reduced as well.

As a result of these technological developments, governments increasingly release public sector information pro-actively via digital channels. However, de Vries (2005) warns us of the possibility of a transparency paradox: with more and more government information being publicly released via digital channels, such as the Internet, citizens may have increasing difficulty finding the government information they need or search for. As we saw in Chapter 4, taking a more citizen-centric approach to the structuring and provision of government information may be of support in this respect. Another emerging issue in this respect is the existence of multiple digital divides, with some population groups being excluded from technology-enabled public access to government information. We explore this issue further in Chapter 9.

A problematic transparency ideal

However, Ananny and Crawford (2018) point us at a problematic popular conception of the transparency ideal: namely, the idea that being able to

112 *Areas of public sector reform*

see an object, such as a government document, is the same as being able to understand it and act upon it. And yet, many technology-enabled government transparency strategies are based on this very transparency ideal: that citizens being able to see and monitor government information implies that they are able to understand how governments work and hold them to account. The roots of this transparency conception can be traced to dominant positivist thinking in science around evidence and, more specifically, the objective to uncover a singular truth: the more that is known about a government's performance and activities, the better it can be held accountable (Ananny & Crawford, 2018). It presumes the presence of the following critical conditions (Christensen & Cheney, 2015; Ananny & Crawford, 2018; Grimmelikhuijsen, 2012):

- Government information is easily visible and clear;
- Citizen-users are competent, involved and able to comprehend the information made visible; and
- Citizen-users act to hold government to account.

However, transparency in digital government relationships is not simply a precise outcome or end state in which the technology-enabled release of government information is accessible, visible, understandable and actionable for citizen-users, but a process of social construction and making sense of the socio-technical assemblage of which government information and digital technologies are integral parts (Meijer, 2013). Consequently, this popular transparency ideal of accountability through visibility is problematic in many respects (Ananny & Crawford, 2018). In general, the following ten shortcomings of this transparency ideal can be observed in digital government relationships, or perhaps even a transparency illusion, as it promises accountability that transparency alone cannot deliver (Ananny & Crawford, 2018: 978–982; Meijer, 2013; Grimmelikhuijsen, 2012; Heald, 2006):

1   *Transparency can be disconnected from power:* if transparency has no meaningful effects, (e.g. if corruption continues after government information has been made transparent), then the idea of transparency can lose its purpose. In fact, it can even lead to reverse outcomes, such as more cynicism and other behaviours that are immune to transparency;

2   *Transparency can be harmful:* if transparency is implemented without a notion of why government information should be revealed, it has the potential to threaten public and private interests, such as people's privacy, safety and proprietary rights. Some level of confidentiality or secrecy is sometimes a necessity (e.g. to protect an individual's privacy or safety) but can also be functional: for example, consider the necessity for governments to protect ongoing trade negotiations or for public servants to have some protection in order to explore potential public policy options before firming up any particular alternative;

Open and transparent government   113

3   *Transparency can obscure*: transparency can be applied in ways that it becomes counter-productive or even useless. A distinction can be made between unintentional opacity, a situation where transparency leads to large volumes of available government information so that critical information becomes hidden, and strategic opacity, such as when an actor purposefully makes so much government information visible that it will take a lot of time and effort to sift through. As a result, people get distracted from the key information that this actor wishes to conceal (Stohl, Stohl & Leonardi, 2016). Another example of concealing information is using a particular form of presenting or visualizing data which focuses the public's attention on selective facts or outcomes (Brooke, 2011; Levitin, 2016). Consequently, increased transparency from a provider's point of view can in fact lead to an information overload and, with that, to reduced transparency from a receiver's point of view;

4   *Transparency can create false binaries*: transparency as an instrument of accountability should not be treated as a binary matter of visibility, i.e. a choice between complete secrecy and total openness, but needs to be considered in a much more subtle and nuanced way by asking the following question: What kinds of transparency lead to what kinds of accountability and under what conditions? (Fox, 2007: 663);

5   *Transparency can invoke neoliberal models of agency*: the transparency ideal presumes that individuals are able to find government information, to interpret that information and to determine its significance. It embraces modernist beliefs that information symmetry exists between citizens and government as a result of the provided transparency, with transparency maximizing citizens' empowerment and minimizing government interference, and that, consequently, putting government information in the hands of the public will enable people to make informed choices that will lead to improved social outcomes (Schudson, 2015);

6   *Transparency does not necessarily build trust*: although transparency is often thought to enhance citizens' trust in government organizations, there is little empirical evidence to support this (Albu & Flyverbom, 2016). Moreover, there is empirical evidence available that people from various backgrounds (e.g. socio-economic, age, ethnic, gender) and in different countries trust government organizations differently (Bennett & Raab, 2003; Raab, 1998). This then requires differentiated approaches of digital government transparency towards different groups of the general public;

7   *Transparency entails professional boundary work*: transparency can be restricted as a result of public sector professionals protecting the exclusivity of their expertise. This requires management of professional boundaries around who can have access to professional information and how public sector professionals will be held accountable for providing reliable and understandable professional information;

114 *Areas of public sector reform*

8 *Transparency can privilege seeing over understanding*: as mentioned, visibility of government information does not necessarily mean understanding what it means or how government works;

9 *Transparency can have technical limitations*: digital technologies may have flaws, which can create problems or obstacles in seeing. For example, Google's photo app unexpectedly tagged black people as gorillas, whereas similar problems have emerged with Google's system when people of all races were misidentified as dogs (Dougherty, 2015); and

10 *Transparency has temporal limitations*: different moments in time may require or produce different kinds of accountability as decisions about when to make information or systems visible reveal a great deal about what people think "the system" or "the information" is and what kind of knowledge is required (Ananny & Crawford, 2018: 982). The temporal dimension of transparency is further complicated by the fact that knowledge and systems may change over time.

These ten shortcomings demonstrate that the transparency ideal is based on a misconceived truth or certainty: namely, that understanding goes hand in hand with looking and seeing.

Consequently, the authoritative knowledge required for robust accountability in digital government relationships is not present in many situations where technology-enabled transparency has been introduced as a tool for accountability and good governance. Some authors refer to this situation as the "transparency paradox": although government data and information can be made visible to the general public, it is unlikely that they are understood, relevant and meaningful to the actionable choices citizens must make (Crawford, 2016; Nissenbaum, 2010; Nissenbaum, 2011).

Towards open and transparent government

Since 2009, when the Obama administration took office in the USA, the traditional notion of transparency has been reconceptualised in a way that it involves the pro-active, public release of government data so that citizens and other stakeholders can re-use them (Noveck, 2015; Noveck, 2017; Mergel, 2013). This so-called open data approach is a government strategy to enhance transparency radically different from traditional right-to-know strategies as embodied in freedom of information laws in the sense that it not only involves *ex ante* rather than *ex post* disclosure of government data, but also aims to enhance citizens' active participation in the public sector instead of promoting litigation (Noveck, 2017).

In his first day in office, President Obama issued a Memorandum on Transparency and Open Government, in which he expressed his commitment to creating an unprecedented level of openness in government through enhancing transparency, accountability, public participation and collaboration (The White House, 2009). By pro-actively opening up non-personal, non-sensitive

Open and transparent government 115

and historical government datasets held by US state and federal organizations and making them publicly available via a government website (see Box 5.1), Obama's objectives were to strengthen democracy, enhance people's trust and increase efficiency and effectiveness in government (The White House, 2009). Open government data can be tagged, shared, secured, mashed up and presented in the way that is most useful for the consumer of that information (The White House, 2012: 3). By using open standards and web APIs, the US federal government is able to make government datasets freely available for use by various stakeholders and in a programme- and device-agnostic way (Lips, 2014). This has the advantage that, rather than having the government itself build out all of the applications that use government data, providing APIs to citizens and the private sector allows members of the public and software developers to come up with innovative uses for government data (O'Reilly, 2010).

Box 5.1   Data.gov

Data.gov (www.data.gov) is the US federal government's open data programme and is managed and hosted by the US General Services Administration's technology transformation service unit. Here you can find open datasets from US government agencies and tools and resources to conduct research, develop applications and design data visualisations. In June 2017, Data.gov hosted approximately 200,000 open datasets, representing about 10 million data resources. Data.gov does not host data directly, but rather aggregates metadata about open data resources in one centralised location. Once an open data source meets the necessary format and metadata requirements, the Data.gov team can pull directly from it as a harvest source. While most datasets are from US federal government agencies, agencies from other administrative levels of government (e.g. state, county, city) also make their datasets available through Data.gov.

In accordance with the 2013 US Federal Government Open Data Policy, each US federal government agency is responsible for its own data. Newly generated federal government data are required to be made available in open, machine-readable formats, while continuing to ensure privacy and security. Also, US federal government agencies are required to catalogue their data assets and create a single agency data inventory, publish a list of their data assets that are public or could be made public, set up feedback mechanisms to engage members of the general public and identify public points of contact for agency datasets.

116   *Areas of public sector reform*

Impacts of using open US government data include cost savings, efficiency, fuel for business, improved public services, informed public policy, performance planning, research and scientific discoveries, transparency and accountability and increased public participation in the democratic process. Data.gov presents some examples of case studies where open government data have been used, including the following:

- *HD Scores*: this app helps to search for and discover restaurants, churches, schools, hospitals, hotels, convenience stores and supermarkets and checks their health inspection scores. The app has 2600 daily users;
- *Farmlogs*: farmers can use visualisations of land and crops to get insight on how well fields perform;
- *Realtor.com*: this app has real estate listings for millions of homes for sale in regions across the US and Canada. It has 23 million users each month;
- *AccuWeather*: users are provided with minute-by-minute precipitation forecasts, including precipitation type, intensity and start and end times. The app predicts weather for the next 15 days and provides severe weather alerts. The app is available for use in the US, Canada, the UK, Ireland, Japan, France, Germany, Belgium, Switzerland and the Netherlands;
- *Simple Energy*: users can compare their energy consumption with their neighbours'.

Another important development for open data has been the promotion of the semantic web as the development from a web of documents to a web of data or Big, Open and Linked Data (BOLD) (Berners-Lee, 2009). This vision of a machine-readable web recognises that all the information shared on the web contains a rich diversity of data which are not necessarily formally identified as such or structured in a way that they can be easily harvested and used (Kitchin, 2014). By encoding and structuring documents using unique identifiers and a mark-up language, it is possible to make visible the data they contain, enabling others to automatically incorporate, process and understand them and to link them with other related data (Miller, 2010, in: Kitchin, 2014: 52–53).

Around the world, many governments at different administrative levels and international organizations, such as the European Union and the United Nations Development Programme (UNDP), have followed this US federal government initiative by opening up thousands of previously restricted government datasets for public re-use.

Box 5.2 Open data case studies from New Zealand

- *A Mobility Marketplace*: the New Zealand Transport Agency (NZTA) uses open data to provide individuals with a better way to view and choose any mode of transport option, including bus, taxi, water taxi, train, shuttle and rideshare, across the whole transport network in the city of Auckland. Accessible via smartphone, this one-stop shop provides up-to-date, dynamic information on all available transport options. Individuals can make the best decision for themselves by comparing all options in real time. Developed and built in house by the NZTA, the Mobility Marketplace operates on a real-time data processing platform that is open to all compliant transport providers in the region and does not store any data from individual transactions. By providing the digital transport infrastructure needed to connect transport services and customers, government not only wanted to help connect people to their best transport options in a cost-effective way but also to make sure that it is a fair marketplace, where every customer and provider can participate;
- *ANZ Truckometer*: the ANZ bank uses open government data from the New Zealand Transport Agency to construct an indicator of the momentum of the New Zealand economy. The so-called ANZ Truckometer uses traffic volume data from state highways in New Zealand. Traffic flows are a real-time and real-world proxy for economic activity this particularly applies to New Zealand, where a large proportion of freight is moved by road. The ANZ found that heavy traffic volumes showed a strong contemporaneous relationship with GDP: for instance, when heavy traffic volume grew in a three-month period, GDP also grew in those three months. They also found that light traffic volumes serve as an indicator of what GDP will be doing in six months' time. Using statistical techniques, they optimised the two constructed ANZ Truckometer indexes, the ANZ Heavy Traffic Index and the ANZ Light Traffic Index, and mapped them to quarterly GDP growth. Understanding where the New Zealand economy is headed over the coming six months is an important insight for stakeholders (e.g. businesses, individuals) to make better planning decisions, such as investment or spending decisions.

Datasets in government have traditionally been predominantly closed in nature, locked inside an archive or filing cabinet within a government agency and with access restricted to approved users. However, as a result of this open data movement, governments around the world are now making public sector data, such as census data, weather data and geospatial data, widely publicly

118 *Areas of public sector reform*

available and accessible by using digital technologies like the Internet. Gurin (2014) describes open government data as:

> accessible public data that people, companies, and organisations can use to launch new ventures, analyse patterns and trends, make data-driven decisions, and solve complex problems.
>
> (p. 9)

In general, the following five government objectives for making open government data publicly available and accessible can be identified (Kitchin, 2014; Huijboom & van der Broek, 2011; Noveck, 2015; Noveck, 2017; Janssen, 2012):

1) *Enabling public accountability*: open government data provide citizens with an opportunity to assess and evaluate the efficiency and effectiveness of government programmes and initiatives. Moreover, external monitoring and (re-)use of open government data can also contribute to the quality and reliability of these datasets;
2) *Promoting active citizenship and participatory democracy*: people can become more informed about public policy- and decision-making. Moreover, open government data can support citizens in making better decisions, facilitate choice regarding public service consumption and encourage active citizenship and democratic involvement, such as in government "hackathons" or other open data events where people actively collaborate on open data solutions (see also Chapter 7);
3) *Improving organizational performance*: government agencies can use open government data to improve their organizational efficiency and productivity through new evidence-based insights, internal and external government monitoring, better public decision-making and external feedback;
4) *Building public trust and agency reputation*: making open government data publicly available raises the public profile of a government agency as being innovative and entrepreneurial whilst serving the public mission. It also increases connections and enables collaboration with end users; and
5) *Creating economic value and supporting innovation*: many public sector datasets have integrated with existing business datasets to add value, create new applications and services and improve knowledge and decision-making.

Box 5.3 Find and compare schools in England

This UK government website uses non-personal open data in order to compare the performance of schools in geographical locations across England.
www.compare-school-performance.service.gov.uk/

In general, government's aim in making government data available is to facilitate re-use in new ways for social, economic and democratic benefit. Some governments, including the New Zealand government, view government data funded by taxpayer money as a national asset that must be open by default. Similarly, the US federal government wants to better leverage the wealth of public data for new innovative applications and services by ensuring that data is open and machine readable by default (The White House, 2012: 2).

In some countries, such as in the United States, access to (certain types of) government data (e.g. census data) is provided free of charge; in other countries, such as in the United Kingdom, many government documents are under Crown copyright and some high-utility datasets are controlled by trading funds which act as monopolies (e.g. map data within Ordnance Survey, weather data within the Met Office) (Kitchin, 2014; Pollock, 2006). Many countries, including the UK and the United States, increasingly offer a mixture of (open) access arrangements for public sector data, with different funding and intellectual property rights models attached to them.

However, even when government datasets have been relatively open and accessible, they have required specialist equipment and digital tools (e.g. software), skills (e.g. statistical expertise) and knowledge about a particular field or topic to make sense of them, much of which is beyond the capabilities of the general population (Kitchin, 2014: 48). This reminds us of the fact that open government data are not just data, but they are part of a socio-technical assemblage in the context of digital government relationships (Ananny & Crawford, 2018; Ananny, 2016). We consider some further complexities, issues and barriers around open government in the next few sections.

What is "open" government?

Several scholars have expressed some scepticism about governments' reform ambitions of achieving open government (e.g. Huijboom & van der Broek, 2011; Kitchin, 2014; Borgman, 2015). First of all, there seems to be little consensus on what "open" data actually means (Borgman, 2015: 44). Where some define open data in a more narrow sense as machine-readable information that is made available to others (Manyika *et al*, 2013), others, such as the Open Knowledge Foundation, have much higher expectations around openness and define data as open if anyone can freely access, use, modify and share the data for any purpose.[3] The latter definition has the following implications for opening up government-held data, according to the United Nations (United Nations, 2013: 23–24):

- *Availability and Access*: the data must be available as a whole at no more than a reasonable reproduction cost, preferably through downloading over the Internet. The data must also be available in a convenient and modifiable form;
- *Re-use and Redistribution*: the data must be provided under terms that permit re-use and redistribution, including integration with other datasets; and

120 *Areas of public sector reform*

- *Universal Participation*: everyone must be able to use, re-use and redistribute – there should be no discrimination against fields of endeavour or against persons or groups. For example, non-commercial restrictions that would prevent commercial use and restrictions of use for certain purposes (e.g. only in education) are not allowed.

In practice however, "open data" and "openness" mean different things to different government organizations and external stakeholders, as is the case with intellectual property rights. For example, a user might be able to freely access an opened-up government dataset but may only be allowed to re-use the data under specific conditions (e.g. not to rework the data for profit or to resell it) (Kitchin, 2014). Other examples are for a government organization to only make the associated metadata freely available but not provide access to the underlying primary data or to allow only specific groups of users access to the data.

In order to achieve a better shared understanding of what openness means, many organizations have set out and adopted a set of ideal characteristics or principles of open data. We need to be aware that the ideal of full openness cannot be achieved in most cases, but there are gradations of openness (Gurin, 2014). For example, OpenGovData[4] uses the following nine principles of open data (in: Kitchin, 2014: 50–51):

1) *Data must be complete*: All data are made available, subject to statutes of privacy, security or privilege limitations;
2) *Data must be primary:* Data are published as collected at the source, with the finest possible level of granularity, not in aggregate or modified forms;
3) *Data must be timely:* Data are made available as quickly as necessary to preserve the value of the data;
4) *Data must be accessible:* Data are available to the widest range of users for the widest range of purposes;
5) *Data must be machine-processable:* Data are reasonably structured to allow automated processing of them;
6) *Access must be non-discriminatory*: Data are available to anyone, with no requirement of registration;
7) *Data formats must be non-proprietary:* Data are available in a format over which no entity has exclusive control;
8) *Data must be licence-free:* Data are not subject to any copyright, patent, trademark or trade secret regulation. Reasonable privacy, security and privilege restrictions may be allowed as governed by other statutes; and
9) *Compliance must be reviewable:* A contact person must be designated to respond to people trying to use the data or complaints about violations of the principles, and another body must have the jurisdiction to determine if the principles have been applied appropriately.

Other organizations, such as the OECD (2008), have proposed that open data needs to be accompanied by asset lists and mechanisms of data discovery, to

Open and transparent government 121

issue indications of data quality and reliability, to use open data formats and standards that enhance interoperability and to provide easy-to-use data infrastructures that facilitate regular publication and promotion of new datasets and access to these datasets, as well as suites of basic and specialist tools that enhance open data use and analysis (Kitchin, 2014: 50–52).

Furthermore, many have argued that opening up government data has its limitations, with several types of government data requiring protection. This particularly applies to personal data, confidential data, commercially sensitive data and classified data, such as data in the interest of public safety and national security. Consequently, opening up government data is not a universal end goal, and open and closed are not binary categories, but government data need to be seen on a spectrum from completely open to completely closed or protected. For instance, Manyika *et al* (2013: 3) point out that government datasets range from completely open to completely closed across the following four dimensions of openness:

- *Degree of access/accessibility*: a wide range of users is permitted to access the data;
- *Machine readability*: the data can be processed automatically;
- *Cost*: data can be accessed free or at negligible cost; and
- *Rights*: limitations on the (re-)use, integration and distribution of data are minimal.

Also, given the resources required to produce and maintain open government datasets, access to government data has generally been restricted through public policy, licensing or fees (Kitchin, 2014).

Another issue is that multiple stakeholders involved in open government initiatives are likely to have different perspectives on the nature and drivers of opening up government data. Research points at the general existence of four different stakeholder perspectives (Gonzales-Zapata & Heeks, 2015):

1   A *bureaucratic perspective:* sees open government data as a government policy to support improvements in public service provision and the quality of internal processes through greater efficiency and effectiveness of data management, regulations, strategies and processes within government. The main stakeholders promoting this perspective are public servants;
2   A *technological perspective:* perceives open government data as a technological innovation focused on changes in government data systems and the design of data formats, processes and standards that are used to handle government data, with the intention of creating an improved data infrastructure across government. The main stakeholders supporting this perspective are digital technology staff and data experts;
3   A *political perspective:* conceives open government data as a fundamental right for all citizens. According to this perspective, the intention of open government data is to achieve better governance through increased transparency, improved accountability of government officials and greater participation

122 *Areas of public sector reform*

and empowerment of citizens and other civil society stakeholders in public sector decision-making. The main stakeholders representing this perspective are citizens; and

4 An *economic perspective*: treats open government data as a means to generate economic value through the development of new products and services and the creation of jobs. The main stakeholders promoting this perspective are private-sector firms and entrepreneurs.

These four different perspectives point not only to different incentives for stakeholders to participate in open government initiatives, but also to varying stakeholder roles, capacities and involvement in public sector reform initiatives towards more open and transparent government: for instance, some stakeholders may not be that interested in or may not have the capacity to achieve these open data-enabled government reform ambitions.

Similarly, some scholars have observed that, as many open government data initiatives have high expectations around citizens as stakeholders in realising open government, they usually assume that all citizens are capable users of open government data (e.g. Meijer, Curtin & Hillebrandt, 2012; Janssen, Charalabidis & Zuiderwijk, 2012; Zuiderwijk *et al*, 2012). However, Zuiderwijk *et al* (2012) point to the following ten categories of barriers around open government data use that are usually encountered by citizens:

1 Problems around the availability and access of open government data;
2 Limited search ability by the user;
3 Usability;
4 Limited user understanding of open government data;
5 Issues around open government data quality;
6 Issues around linking and merging of open government data;
7 Lack of interoperability;
8 Lack of metadata;
9 Issues around the interaction with the open government data provider; and
10 Issues around opening and uploading government data.

These research findings are further supported by an empirical study of the functionalities and contents of open government data portals in US cities (Thorsby *et al*, 2017). In general, the empirical study findings show that open government data portals in these US cities are in a very early stage of development and need a great deal of work to improve user support and data analysis functionalities (Thorsby *et al*, 2017). Whilst search functionalities and tools to visualise or analyse data were common features of these open government portals, open government data policies, demonstrations of tools and interpretations of the data were not available in many cases (Thorsby *et al*, 2017). Also, it would have been of great assistance to citizen-users if there were portal functionalities that could help them understand the data, such as data visualisations, charts and data analysis (Thorsby *et al*, 2017).

Open and transparent government   123

Emerging issues and barriers

In general, in emphasizing the promises of open data whilst ignoring the barriers, Janssen, Charalabidis and Zuiderwijk (2012) demonstrate that many advocates of open government data use the rather simplistic and idealised view that open government data will automatically lead to open, transparent and accountable government. Moreover, policy-makers often prefer to simply make the raw government data publicly available. Not surprising perhaps, the success of opening government data is often considered on the basis of the number of datasets that have been published (Bertot, McDermott & Smith, 2012).

However, as Janssen, Charalabidis and Zuiderwijk (2012) point out, the source data often cannot be used immediately but needs modification and quality assessment first. Also, data cannot be easily found if essential metadata is not available or inadequate. As the value of open data is created through its use, publication of the data in a user-friendly way is a critical requirement. Moreover, another critical requirement is that users are aware of the public availability of government data from a citizen-centric, not a government-centric, logic. In other words, it is not enough for individual government agencies to simply make their raw data available for re-use; they should be taking into account the needs and expectations of users (e.g. Helbig *et al*, 2012; Janssen, Charalabidis & Zuiderwijk, 2012; Kitchin, 2014).

However, government efforts have been dominantly focused on the supply side of providing open government data access and creating open data initiatives, rather than on how open data are being used and the sustainability of open data initiatives (Kitchin, 2014; Helbig *et al*, 2012). A study of various open data projects by Helbig *et al* (2012) points out that too many projects are not well organized and are too technically focused, operating more as data holdings and lacking clean, high-quality, validated and interoperable data that comply with data standards and have appropriate metadata. Many projects fall short on preservation, backup, auditing, data re-use, privacy and ethics policies. Moreover, many do not have appropriate administrative, management and governance arrangements and lack financial stability and a long-term development plan (Helbig *et al*, 2012). Also, the released datasets are often low-hanging fruit, in the sense that they are easy for a government agency to release but do not have high utility for citizen end users. Another issue is the lack of government follow-up on and longer-term sustainability of open data-based solutions created during government hackathons or other open data events.

Consequently, it is likely that opening up government data will not automatically lead to open and transparent government, nor will data *per se* lead to enhanced forms of public participation, collaboration and good governance; a shift in focus towards the actual use and citizen-users of open government data is critically important to make further progress with public sector reform ambitions around establishing open and transparent government.

Further emerging issues and barriers to achieving governments' reform ambitions of open and transparent government can be briefly described as

124 *Areas of public sector reform*

follows (e.g. Mergel, 2013; Huijboom & van der Broek, 2011; Grimmelikhuijsen, 2012; Kitchin, 2014):

- *The lack of robust evidence of societal impact*: thus far, there is only a limited uptake of open government data initiatives and related applications and outcomes amongst substantial parts of the population. Moreover, research shows that most open government data users are young and educated and have high degrees of technical knowledge (McClean, 2011). In general, a problem with measuring the impact and outcomes of open government data initiatives is that a robust empirical evidence base is lacking;
- *The existence of multiple digital divides around data and digital technologies*: see Chapter 9.
- *Institutional issues and barriers*: traditionally, government data have been collected, managed and disseminated in vertical ways. This traditional vertical orientation on data also explains why there can be substantial differences in opening up government data between government agencies at the same administrative level. However, open government data are increasingly shared and used horizontally across government and with external stakeholders, such as citizens, the private sector and civil society. Existing rules and regulations around data in government usually date from the pre-digital age, are vertically focused and don't support the increasing horizontal needs and requirements;
- *Cultural issues and barriers*: many government organizations are reluctant or resistant to opening up their data. This particularly applies to datasets of high utility to end users;
- *Government data services have been contracted out to third parties*: in many countries, public sector data services have been contracted out to third parties to manage and run on behalf of government. Usually, these third parties add proprietary value and/or make the data available at a cost. Many third-party data resellers are actively lobbying against the opening up of government data as it destroys their business model;
- *Financial cost issues and barriers*: considering the budgetary constraints in many government agencies, one of the most substantial barriers is the cost associated with opening up government data, managing open data initiatives and (new) data systems and infrastructures. Moreover, opening up public sector data is not simply a matter of publishing them online in the form held by government agencies: most datasets need to be repurposed and curated through anonymisation and aggregation to enable them to be made open in a non-sensitive and non-personal way (see also Chapter 8);
- *Privacy and security issues:* many government datasets contain highly sensitive and personal data, such as those in the domains of social services, health, criminal justice, education and taxation. These government datasets were not created with a view toward making them publicly available. Consequently, public expectations are that the privacy of individuals in these datasets will be protected, which can be done by anonymising and aggregating

the data. However, even when data have been adequately anonymised and aggregated, the possibility of citizen identification or re-identification exists, especially when different datasets are merged (see also Chapter 8);

- *Regulatory issues and barriers*: there are tensions between governments' reform ambitions of more openness and proprietary rights (e.g. copyright, IPR); and
- *Data and technology issues in government*: the lack of (open) standards, lack of interoperability and the existence of legacy data systems as well as legacy data formats.

Strategies for open and transparent government

The following strategies and lessons for designing open and transparent government can be identified for governments around the world:

- *For governments to become open by default:* a commitment for governments to release all their non-personal and non-sensitive government datasets pro-actively by default. In support of this strategy to maximise the release of open government data, many national and local governments, including national governments from the UK, New Zealand, South Korea, Canada, Uruguay, Australia and Mexico, have adopted the International Open Data Charter,[5] which contains the following six principles to further maximise the public value of opening up government data:

1 Open by Default;
2 Timely and Comprehensive;
3 Accessible and Useable;
4 Comparable and Interoperable;
5 For Improved Governance and Citizen Engagement; and
6 For Inclusive Development and Innovation.

These six principles were developed on the basis of extensive experience with releasing government data in countries around the world. The following lessons were built into this charter[6]:

- It promotes the comparability and interoperability of open government data for increased data use and societal impact;
- It acknowledges global challenges, such as the digital divide, and the significant opportunities of open government data for inclusive development;
- It recommends standardisation (e.g. data and metadata);
- It encourages cultural change;
- It recognises the importance of safeguarding the privacy of citizens and their right to influence the collection and use of their own personal data;
- It fosters increased engagement with citizens and civil society; and
- It promotes increased focus on data literacy, training programs and entrepreneurship.

126 *Areas of public sector reform*

- *Make the opening up of government data mandatory and embed open government data sharing in legislation*: this strategy goes one step further than adopting an open by default strategy or an International Open Data Charter. It meets the vertical rule–based culture of Weberian bureaucracies, as discussed in Chapter 4. This institutional enabling of open government data release will further maximise the value of using open government data;
- *Use transparency-enhancing technologies (TETs) and transparency by design*: transparency by design refers to a principle where data about the functioning of government are automatically opened, can be easily accessed and interpreted and are not being manipulated, predefined or pre-processed (Janssen & van den Hoven, 2015). Transparency by design should ensure that information for effective public oversight is made available and that this information is clear and not ambiguous (Janssen & van den Hoven, 2015: 365);
- *Adopt a service-oriented approach, instead of a product approach, to open government data management*: this includes the involvement of citizen end users in the planning, development and management of open government data initiatives; education and training of citizen end users to be able to manage, process and analyse government data appropriately and effectively and robust empirical evaluation of the societal impact of open government data initiatives (Gurstein, 2013).

More in general, O'Reilly (2010) points out that a radical redesign of government is needed in order to achieve an ideal state of open and transparent government. He sets out a vision for government to become an open "platform" that allows people inside and outside government to share, use and produce open data for a wide range of innovative solutions (sometimes called Government 2.0: see Chapter 7). This radical departure from the existing hierarchical model of government also requires rethinking the role of government as one that is collaborative and on more equal grounds with citizens: this includes being the facilitator or manager of the open platform, accepting that public sector outcomes are not specified beforehand but instead evolve through interactions between government and citizens and treating open data produced and shared via this platform as a public asset (O'Reilly, 2010). Learning from the success of technological platforms like the Internet, O'Reilly (2010) uses the open platform metaphor as a source of inspiration to fundamentally reconsider the design of government. He points at the following seven lessons for designing open government (O'Reilly, 2010: 15–38):

1) *Open standards spark innovation and growth*: history shows that platforms that are the most generative of new economic activity are those that are the most open. Standardisation has played an important role in these developments;
2) *Build a simple system and let it evolve*: with the development of the Internet in mind, O'Reilly's lesson is about applying a philosophy of simplicity to government's involvement. He sees designing foundations that others can build on as an important part of applying platform thinking to government:

Open and transparent government 127

"It's about creating the starting point, something that others can re-use and extend" (O'Reilly, 2010: 19);

3) *Design for participation*: successful open digital systems, such as the Internet, have demonstrated the critical importance of having clear rules for cooperation and interoperability. These open-by-default settings of the Internet have created new platform opportunities to bring people together to share data and information and collaborate on innovative solutions (e.g. shared editing of entries on Wikipedia);

4) *Learn from your hackers*: the most innovative ideas about how an open platform can be used do not necessarily come from the platform creators, but from its users and in particular from those who do unexpected things, such as leading users who break existing rules or develop new rules, or hackers. Open systems get better the more people are using them. (O'Reilly, 2010: 31);

5) *Data mining allows you to harness implicit participation:* based on user behaviour patterns, government organizations are capable of better understanding users, which helps to enhance user participation and the co-creation of value;

6) *Lower the barriers to experimentation*: in many cases, government programmes are designed as though there is only one right answer and with the assumption that the project specification developed by a dedicated project team must be correct by definition (O'Reilly, 2010: 35). However, in reality, failure is often an option for governments too. Being agile and open to experimentation are equally important features for digital government programmes and initiatives. However, this will require a cultural change in government in order to empower government employees to experiment, "fail forward fast" and be able to learn from it. The sharing of best practices across government would help to establish this cultural change; and

7) *Lead by example*: showing what can be done via the open platform – more specifically, how open government data can be effectively used and the societal impact of open government data use – is critical for successfully achieving open government.

Box 5.4   Exercise 5.1

Look up a government website with information for citizens about an open data programme. Design a strategy of meaningful transparency for all groups of citizens for the information and data provided through this website.

Discussion questions

1   Try and find practical examples for the ten shortcomings of the transparency ideal in digital government relationships. What recommendations

128 *Areas of public sector reform*

would you make to resolve the shortcomings you found? Motivate your answer.

2   Look up an open data programme of a government organization. Consider how this government organization could further enhance transparency and openness from a citizen's perspective in digital government relationships.

3   Some people refer to Wikileaks as a case of radical transparency (e.g. Roberts, 2006). Do you agree? Motivate your answer.

4   What recommendations would you make to enhance understanding, relevance and meaningfulness of government information and data for citizens? Motivate your answer.

5   What are the three most important principles of open government data in your view? Motivate your answer.

6   Which two issues or barriers do you personally find most problematic in governments' reform efforts to become more open and transparent in digital government relationships?

Notes

1 Worldbank, available from: https://data.worldbank.org/ [accessed 23 June 2018].
2 The Open Government Partnership, available from: https://www.opengovpartnershiporg/ [accessed 23 June 2018].
3 Open Knowledge Foundation, the Open Definition, available from: http://opendefinition. org/ [accessed 23 June 2018].
4 OpenGovData, available from: https://www.opengovdata.org/ [accessed 23 June 2018].
5 Open Data Charter, available from: https://opendatacharter.net/ [accessed 23 June 2018].
6 Open Data Charter, available from: https://opendatacharter.net/history/ [accessed 23 June 2018].

References

Albu, O.B. & Flyverbom, M. (2016) Organizational transparency: Conceptualizations, conditions, and consequences. *Business & Society*, Epub, DOI: 10.1177/0007650316659851
Ananny, M. (2016) Toward an ethics of algorithms: Convening, observation, probability, and timeliness. *Science, Technology & Human Values*, 41 (1), 93–117.
Ananny, M. & Crawford, K. (2018) Seeing without knowing: Limitations of the transparency ideal and its application to algorithmic accountability. *New Media & Society*, 20 (3), 973–989.
Benkler, Y. (2006) *The Wealth of Networks: How Social Production Transforms Markets and Freedom*. New Haven/London: Yale University Press.
Bennett, C.J. & Raab, C.D. (2003) *The Governance of Privacy: Policy Instruments in Global Perspective*. Aldershot: Ashgate.
Berners-Lee, T. (2009) *Linked Data*, 18 June 2016. Available from: https://www.w3.org/ DesignIssues/LinkedData.html [accessed 23 June 2018].
Bertot, J.C., Jaeger, P.T. & Grimes, J.M. (2012) Promoting transparency and accountability through ICTs, social media, and collaborative e-government. *Transforming Government: People, Process and Policy*, 6 (1), 78–91.
Bertot, J.C., McDermott, P. & Smith, T. (4–7 January 2012) *Measurement of Open Government: Metrics and Process*. Proceedings of the 45th Annual Hawaii International Conference on Systems Sciences, (HICSS-45), Maui, HI.

Open and transparent government 129

Borgman, C.L. (2015) *Big Data, Little Data, No Data: Scholarship in the Networked World.* Cambridge, MA: Massachusetts Institute of Technology Press.

Brin, D. (1998) *The Transparent Society: Will Technology Force Us to Choose Between Privacy and Freedom?* New York, NY: Basic Books.

Brooke, H. (2011) *The Silent State.* London: Windmill Books.

Christensen, L.T. & Cheney, G. (2015) Peering into transparency: Challenging ideals, proxies, and organizational practices. *Communication Theory*, 25 (1), 70–90.

Crawford, K. (2016) Can an algorithm be agonistic? Ten scenes from life in calculated publics. *Science, Technology & Human Values*, 41 (1), 77–92.

de Vries, M. (2005) ICT en overheidsinformatie. In: Lips, A.M.B., Bekkers, V.J.J.M. & Zuurmond, A. (eds.) *ICT en Openbaar Bestuur: Implicaties en uitdagingen van technologische toepassingen voor de overheid.* Utrecht: Lemma BV, pp. 651–670.

Dougherty, C. (1 July 2015) Google photos mistakenly labels black people 'gorillas'. *The New York Times.* Available from: http://bits.blogs.nytimes.com/2015/07/01/google-photos mistakenly-labels-black-people-gorillas/ [accessed 23 June 2018].

Dutch Scientific Council. (2016) *Big Data in een vrije en veilige samenleving.* Wetenschappelijke Raad voor het Regeringsbeleid, 95, Den Haag: WRR.

Fox, J. (2007) The uncertain relationship between transparency and accountability. *Development in Practice*, 17 (4–5), 663–671.

Gonzales-Zapata, F. & Heeks, R. (2015) The multiple meanings of open government data: Understanding different stakeholders and their perspectives. *Government Information Quarterly*, 32, 441–452.

Grimmelikhuijsen, S. (2012) A good man but a bad wizard: About the limits and future of transparency of democratic governments. *Information Polity*, 17, 293–302.

Gurin, J. (2014) *Open Data Now: The Secret to Hot Startups, Smart Investing, Savvy Marketing, and Fast Innovation.* New York, NY: McGraw-Hill Education.

Gurstein, M. (3 February 2013) Should 'Open Government Data' be a product or a service (and why does it matter?). *Gurstein's Community Informatics.* Available from: http://gurstein.wordpress.com/2013/02/03/is-open-government-data-a-product-or-a-service-and-why-does-it-matter/ [accessed 23 June 2018].

Harding, L. (2014) *The Snowden Files: The Inside Story of the World's Most Wanted Man.* London: Guardian Books.

Heald, D. (2006) Varieties of transparency. *Proceedings of the British Academy*, 135, 25–43.

Helbig, N., Cresswell, A.M., Burke, G.B. & Luna-Reyes, L. (2012) *The Dynamics of Opening Government Data: A White Paper.* Center for Technology in Government, State University of New York, Albany. Available from: https://www.ctg.albany.edu/publications/reports/opendata/opendata.pdf [accessed 23 June 2018].

Huijboom, N. & van der Broek, T. (2011) Open data: An international comparison of strategies. *European Journal of ePractice*, 12 (March–April), ISSN: 1988–625X. Available from: https://www.epracticejournal.eu/ [accessed 23 June 2018].

Janssen, K. (2012) *Open Government Data: Right to Information 2.0 or Its Rollback Version?* ICRI Working Paper, 8/2012. Available from: http://papers.ssrn.com/sol3/papers.cfm?abstract_id=2152566 [accessed 23 June 2018].

Janssen, M., Charalabidis, Y. & Zuiderwijk, A. (2012) Benefits, adoption barriers and myths of open data and open government. *Information Systems Management*, 29, 258–268.

Janssen, M. & van den Hoven, J. (2015) Big and Open Linked Data (BOLD) in government: A challenge to transparency and privacy? *Government Information Quarterly*, 32, 363–368.

Kitchin, R. (2014) *The Data Revolution: Big Data, Open Data, Data Infrastructures & Their Consequences.* London: Sage.

130 Areas of public sector reform

Levitin, D.J. (2016) *A Field Guide to Lies and Statistics: A Neuroscientist on How to Make Sense of a Complex World*. London: Viking Penguin Random House.

Lips, A.M.B. (2014) Transforming government: By default? In: Graham, M. & Dutton, W.H. (eds.) *Society & the Internet: How Networks of Information and Communication Are Changing Our Lives*. Oxford: Oxford University Press, pp. 179–194.

Manyika, J., Chui, M., Farrell, D., Van Kuiken, S. & Groves, P. (2013) *Open Data: Unlocking Innovation and Performance with Liquid Information*. McKinsey. Available from: https://www.mckinsey.com/business-functions/business-technology/our-insights/open-data-unlocking-innovation-and-performance-with-liquid-information [accessed 23 June 2018].

McClean, T. (1–4 September 2011) *Not with a Bang but a Whimper: The Politics of Accountability and Open Data in the UK*. Paper presented at the American Political Science Association Annual Meeting, Seattle, WA. Available from: http://papers.ssrn.com/sol3/papers.cfm?abstract_id=1899790 [accessed 23 June 2018].

Meijer, A.J. (2013) Understanding the complex dynamics of transparency. *Public Administration Review*, 73 (3), 429–439.

Meijer, A.J., Curtin, D. & Hillebrandt, M. (2012) Open government: Connecting vision with voice. *International Review of Administrative Sciences*, 78 (1), 10–29.

Mergel, I. (2013) *Social Media in the Public Sector: A Guide to Participation, Collaboration, and Transparency in the Networked World*. San Francisco, CA: Jossey-Bass.

Nissenbaum, H. (2010) *Privacy in Context: Technology, Policy, and the Integrity of Social Life*. Stanford, CA: Stanford University Press.

Nissenbaum, H. (2011) A contextual approach to privacy online. *Daedalus*, 140 (4), 32–48.

Noveck, B.S. (2015) *Smart Citizens, Smarter State: The Technologies of Expertise and the Future of Governing*. Cambridge, MA: Harvard University Press.

Noveck, B.S. (2017) Rights-based and tech-driven: Open data, freedom of information, and the future of government transparency. *Yale Human Rights and Development Law Journal*, 19 (1), 1–10.

OECD. (2008) *OECD Recommendation of the Council for Enhanced Access and More Effective Use of Public Sector Information*. Paris: OECD.

OECD. (28 March 2011) *The Call for Innovative and Open Government: An Overview of Country Initiatives*. Paris: OECD.

O'Reilly, T. (2010) Government as a platform. In: Lathrop, D. & Ruma, L. (eds.) *Open Government: Collaboration, Transparency, and Participation in Practice*. Sebastopol, CA: O'Reilly, pp. 11–39.

Pollock, R. (2006) The value of the public domain. *IPPR*. Available from: https://www.ippr.org/publication/55/1526/the-value-of-the-public-domain [accessed 23 June 2018].

Raab, C.D. (1998) Electronic confidence: Trust, information and public administration. In: Snellen, I.Th.M. & van de Donk, W.B.H.J. (eds.) *Public Administration in an Information Age: A Handbook*. Amsterdam: IOS Press, pp. 113–133.

Roberts, A. (2006) *Blacked Out: Government Secrecy in the Information Age*. New York, NY: Cambridge University Press.

Schudson, M. (2015) *The Rise of the Right to Know*. Cambridge, MA: Belknap Publishing.

Stohl, C., Stohl, M. & Leonardi, P.M. (2016) Managing opacity: Information visibility and the paradox of transparency in the digital age. *International Journal of Communication Systems*, 10, 123–137.

Thorsby, J., Stowers, G.N.L., Wolslegel, K. & Tumbuan, E. (2017) Understanding the content and features of open data portals in American cities. *Government Information Quarterly*, 34 (1), 53–61.

Open and transparent government 131

United Nations. (2013) *Guidelines on Open Government Data for Citizen Engagement.* Department of Economic and Social Affairs, Division for Public Administration and Development Management, ST/ESA/PAD/SER.E/177. New York, NY: United Nations.

The White House. (2009) *Open Government Directive.* Executive Office of the President of the United States. Washington, DC: The White House.

The White House. (2012) *Digital Government: Building a 21st Century Platform to Better Service the American People.* Executive Office of the President of the United States. Washington, DC: The White House.

Zuiderwijk, A., Janssen, M., Choenni, S., Meijer, R. & Alibaks, R.S. (2012) Socio-technical impediments of open data. *Electronic Journal of e-Government*, 10 (2), 156–172.

Further reading

Brin, D. (1998) *The Transparent Society: Will Technology Force Us to Choose Between Privacy and Freedom?* New York, NY: Basic Books.

Gurin, J. (2014) *Open Data Now: The Secret to Hot Startups, Smart Investing, Savvy Marketing, and Fast Innovation.* New York, NY: McGraw-Hill Education.

Harding, L. (2014) *The Snowden Files: The Inside Story of the World's Most Wanted Man.* London: The Guardian Books.

Helbig, N., Cresswell, A.M., Burke, G.B. & Luna-Reyes, L. (2012) *The Dynamics of Opening Government Data: A White Paper.* Center for Technology in Government, State University of New York, Albany. Available from: https://www.ctg.albany.edu/publications/reports/opendata/opendata.pdf [accessed 23 June 2018].

Kitchin, R. (2014) *The Data Revolution: Big Data, Open Data, Data Infrastructures & Their Consequences.* London: Sage.

Lathrop, D. & Ruma, L. (eds.) (2010) *Open Government: Collaboration, Transparency, and Participation in Practice.* Sebastopol, CA: O'Reilly.

Noveck, B.S. (2015) *Smart Citizens, Smarter State: The Technologies of Expertise and the Future of Governing.* Cambridge, MA: Harvard University Press.

Roberts, A. (2006) *Blacked Out: Government Secrecy in the Information Age.* New York, NY: Cambridge University Press.

6 Smart government

Learning objectives

By the end of this chapter you should be able to:

- Ask critical questions around the use of smart technologies, data and algorithms in smart government relationships with citizens;
- Develop a comprehensive smart government strategy; and
- Apply the revised ethical framework of contextual integrity to the context of smart government and relationships with citizens.

Key points of this chapter

- Governments are shifting from data-informed to data-enabled smart governments in their relationships with citizens. This development has major ethical, democratic, governmental and managerial implications;
- A rigorous definition of big data does not exist thus far. Often, the dominant focus is on either the technical characteristics or the data-driven aspects of big data;
- Besides opportunities for governments to use innovative big data solutions in order to improve public policy- and decision-making, they can also use small data solutions in order to do so;
- Data legacy systems, digital technology legacy systems and the legacy of a centralised government statistics department will have an impact on the design and application of smart government initiatives;
- A comprehensive view is needed, involving 14 interrelated dimensions, in order to develop an effective smart government strategy; and
- The reconceptualised contextual integrity framework offers an appropriate, broader sphere of justice around personal and non-personal data flows and data (re-)use in smart, socio-technical assemblages within the context of digital government and its relationships with citizens.

Key terms

- *Datafication:* The societal phenomenon of deriving billions of digitised data dynamically in real time from locations, movements and social activities.

- *Big data*: are generally related to large volumes of data; a large variety of datasets derived from different sectors and domains; the speed at which data are generated, processed and analysed and the capacity to analyse structured and/or unstructured data.
- *Data science*: involves new forms of data analytics that utilise machine learning techniques designed to process and analyse enormous datasets, such as data mining and pattern recognition, data visualisation and visual analytics, statistical analysis, prediction, simulation and optimisation modelling (Kitchin, 2016: 3).
- *Smart cities*: smart technologies and innovative data solutions embedded into the fabric of urban environments, e.g. to monitor various objects, locations, activities, movements, sentiments and behaviours and continually send data to a wide range of control and management systems, which can process and respond to the data flow in real time.
- *Smart government*: a government that uses a comprehensive contextual approach to introducing and using smart technologies and innovative data solutions as part of its operations and in its relationships with citizens.
- *Data determinism*: the misconception that data *per se* are driving outcomes, including outcomes that are based on predictions of the future (Kitchin, 2016).

Introduction

Nowadays, data are proliferating in many forms (Borgman, 2015). Fast-moving digital technology and data developments, including big data, the Internet of Things (IoT), driverless cars, wearable technologies, robotics and AI, are expected to transform how we live, work, travel, shop, play, learn, communicate and think (Mayer-Schönberger & Cukier, 2013; Manyika *et al*, 2011; Pentland, 2014). In general, these technological developments not only hold the promise of generating better information and knowledge, but are also becoming increasingly critical to the functioning of society. For instance, we can increasingly observe innovative digital technology applications and data uses regulate traffic, energy consumption and water consumption; monitor public sentiment; operate street lights; monitor public safety through networked surveillance cameras and track vehicle movements and driverless cars (Gil-Garcia, Pardo & Nam, 2016b; van Zoonen, 2016; Kitchin, 2014). Indeed, several reports have pointed to the replacement of human beings by these smart technologies and a huge loss of jobs within the next few decades as a result (e.g. BBC, 2017).

It is clear that this pervasive data-driven development is leading to profound changes in our society, including in digital government relationships with citizens. On the one hand, substantial societal and economic value creation are expected from the application of these smart technologies, including significantly enhancing quality of life (Harrison *et al*, 2010); on the other hand, the fact that people are increasingly observable, traceable and knowable as a result of the digital footprints and bread crumbs they leave behind raises fundamental ethical issues around these emerging forms of "dataveillance," increasing information asymmetries in society and a potential development towards new

134 *Areas of public sector reform*

panopticons (Pentland, 2014; Kitchin, 2016; van Dijck, 2014; Meijer, 2015). Consequently, a major challenge for data-driven public sector reform of digital government into smart government would be how to maximise the benefits whilst minimising the risks (NZDFF, 2014).

It is the combination of networked digital technologies and new data collection, processing, analysing, use and re-use opportunities in particular that is driving public sector reform ambitions of governments to become smart or even smarter. This includes the development of smart cities: smart technologies embedded into the fabric of urban environments include digital cameras, sensors, transponders, meters, actuators, GPS and transduction loops that monitor various objects, locations, activities, movements, sentiments and behaviours and continually send data to a wide range of control and management systems, such as city operating systems, centralized control rooms, dashboards, intelligent transport systems, logistics management systems, smart energy grids and building management systems that can process and respond in real time to the data flow (Kitchin, 2016; van Zoonen, 2016).

For governments, smart technology applications and innovative data uses offer the potential for new forms of knowledge which, compared to traditional forms of knowledge, are dynamic and generated in real time and seem to have greater breadth, depth and longitude, both retrospectively and predictively. Indeed, these new forms of knowledge are expected to enable much more effective and efficient public service provision to citizens as well as solutions to a wide range of complex public policy problems, such as climate change, natural disasters, obesity, an aging society, water quality, poverty and child abuse (Pentland, 2014; Mayer-Schönberger & Cukier, 2013). For instance, the United Nations (2014) has embraced these new data opportunities in its UN Global Pulse initiative with the objective of establishing improved forms of sustainable development through innovative data use (see Box 6.1). However, with large volumes of data being generated in real time, the risk of "data smog" (Shenk, 1997) could be a realistic scenario for digital government as well; therefore, a major challenge for smart governments is how to manage these new datasets and derive useful information and knowledge from them.

Box 6.1 UN Global Pulse

The United Nations Global Pulse initiative (www.unglobalpulse.org/, accessed 6 May 2019) was established based on a recognition that big data offers the opportunity to gain a better understanding of changes in human well-being and to get real-time feedback on how well public policy responses are working. Its vision is a future in which big data is harnessed safely and responsibly as a public good. And its mission is to accelerate discovery, development and scaled adoption of big data innovation for sustainable development and humanitarian action. To this end, UN Global Pulse is working to promote awareness of big data opportunities for sustainable development and humanitarian action, forge public-private data sharing partnerships, generate high-impact analytical tools and approaches through its network of big data innovation labs (Pulse Labs) and drive broad adoption of useful innovations across the UN system.

As data need to be understood in context in order to gain insights that are actionable for global development policy-makers, it is important to understand how different cultures and communities use digital media and services, such as mobile phones and social media. For this reason, UN Global Pulse is organized into a network of Pulse Labs in different regions of the world with a headquarters lab in New York; a lab in Jakarta, Indonesia and a lab in Kampala, Uganda. Pulse Labs co-create big data research projects together with expert organizations including UN organizations, public sector institutions, private sector partners and academic partners. UN Global Pulse uses innovation challenges and hackathons to unite research problems with problem solvers and share sample datasets with creative technical experts. Each Pulse Lab is guided by an annual research agenda determined in consultation with stakeholders and with wide-ranging topics, such as food security, humanitarian logistics, economic well-being, gender discrimination and health. By sharing their findings, Pulse Labs help establish global best practices of how big data research may be used to help policy-makers understand, in real time, what is happening to vulnerable populations.

Examples of UN Global Pulse big data research projects include the following:

- *Data visualisation and interactive mapping to support response to disease outbreak in Uganda* (www.unglobalpulse.org/projects/mapping-infectious-diseases, accessed 6 May 2019): from January 2015 to May 2015, a typhoid outbreak occurred in Uganda. In coordination with the World Health Organization, and in collaboration with the Uganda Ministry of Health, Pulse Lab Kampala produced a series of data visualisations to support the early response to the disease. Visualisations of weekly reports from health centres were produced with interactive maps at district, sub-county and individual health facility levels. The visualisations allowed decision-making for the allocation of medicine, medical personnel and health centres, as well as targeting training areas.
- *Using big data analytics for improved public transport* (www.unglobalpulse. org/projects/improving-transport-planning-with-data-analytics, accessed 6 May 2019): Pulse Lab Jakarta collaborated with Jakarta Smart City on a project to enhance transport planning and operational decision-making through real-time data analytics. Using data

136 *Areas of public sector reform*

from the city's rapid bus transit system (TransJakarta) and passenger stations, the project mapped origin-destination trends and identified bottleneck locations, information which can be used to identify whether new routes are needed. The project also explored the possibility of using real-time data to determine passenger-waiting times in order to enhance the efficiency of the bus dispatching system. The collaboration contributed to improvements in TransJakarta's operations and enhanced capacity within Jakarta Smart City.

- *Using Twitter data to analyse public sentiment on fuel subsidy policy reform in El Salvador* (www.unglobalpulse.org/projects/fuel-subsidy-el-salvador, accessed 6 May 2019): in 2011, El Salvador made policy reforms to a national subsidy on propane gas, causing widespread public disaffection and a series of strikes by distributor companies. The World Bank and UN Global Pulse collaborated on a research project analyzing the content and sentiment of tweets in order to better understand public opinion around the reforms. The study demonstrated that public opinion as expressed in social media could complement and potentially replace household survey data if none were available. While a decline in negative sentiment was observed around several issues, including the gas distributor strikes, household survey data from the same period showed an increase in positive sentiment on the reform. This discrepancy showed that analysing social media could help reveal unexpected impacts of issues and events related to public policy. In the case of the fuel reform, the research findings showed that the distributor strikes might have contributed to changes in public perception more than previously acknowledged.

- *Using financial transaction data to measure economic resilience to natural disasters* (www.unglobalpulse.org/projects/using-financial-transaction-data-measure-economic-resilience-natural-disasters, accessed 6 May 2019): this project explored how financial transaction data can be analysed to better understand the economic resilience of people affected by natural disasters. The project used the Mexican state of Baja California Sur as a case study to assess the impact of Hurricane Odile on livelihoods and economic activities over a period of six months in 2014. The project measured daily point of sale transactions and ATM withdrawals at high geospatial resolution to gain insight into the way people prepare for and recover from disaster. The study revealed that people spent 50 percent more than usual on items such as food and gasoline in preparation for the hurricane and that recovery time ranged from two to forty days, depending on characteristics such as gender and income. Findings suggest that insights from transaction data could be used to target emergency response and to estimate economic loss at the local level in the wake of a disaster.

Smart government   137

Furthermore, we should not forget that the promise of better information and knowledge for government is not new. For many years we have seen the collection, management and use of government statistics; census data; the development of databases in a wide range of government activities; national and local registers; various forms of citizen identity information (see Chapter 8) and, most recently, the opening up of government data (see Chapter 5), for example. For decades if not centuries, many traditional, what could be called small datasets have been catering to the need of government to be data informed and continue to do so. Another important question for governments is then what the role and contribution of these traditional data legacy systems are in an environment where new smart technologies and innovative data uses are being adopted.

In general, these developments raise some important questions about the nature of digital government's relationship with its citizens, the extent to which it is changing as a result of the adoption of smart technologies and innovative data uses and what the ethical, democratic, governmental and managerial implications are. Thus far, however, there is hardly any empirical understanding available of what is happening around governments becoming smart. Based on scholarly insights available to date, we explore these issues in this chapter.

First of all, we look at what is happening in societies around big data and datafication. We conceptualize big data and explore some critical issues around this phenomenon raised by scholars. However, as data-based relationships with citizens are not new for government, we discuss a brief history of data-informed government, including three different data legacy systems for smart government. Also, we further conceptualize "smartness" in government, including the use of algorithms, data science applied to smart government, the benefits of smart government and the need for a more comprehensive view on smart government. Governments that want to become smart are being challenged by a number of issues as identified in scholarly literature; we discuss these issues later in this chapter. And finally, we reconceptualise Nissenbaum's theory on contextual integrity in order to construct a broader new ethical framework of contextual integrity for governments in the digital age, especially smart governments.

Datafication and big data

Worldwide, we can observe a radical expansion in the volume, variety and granularity of data being generated about people, things and places (Pentland, 2014; Mayer-Schönberger & Cukier, 2013; Kitchin, 2016). As these new data are created through the application of emerging smart technologies, their digital nature makes it easy to combine, integrate, process, analyse, model, share, use or re-use them. Indeed, a new multidisciplinary area of study has developed in parallel with the arrival of these smart technologies and innovative data applications: data science involves new forms of data analytics that utilise machine learning techniques designed to process and analyse enormous datasets, such as data mining and pattern recognition, data visualisation and visual analytics, statistical analysis, prediction, simulation and optimisation modelling (Kitchin, 2016: 3).

138 *Areas of public sector reform*

This societal phenomenon of deriving billions of digitised data dynamically in real time from locations, movements and social activities is also referred to as datafication (Mayer-Schönberger & Cukier, 2013; van Dijck, 2014; Kitchin, 2016). To datafy a phenomenon is to put it in a quantified format so it can be tabulated and analysed (Mayer-Schönberger & Cukier, 2013: 78). Moreover, as processes of datafication are increasingly common in our society as a result of the application of sensing technologies and networks, such as wearing a smart watch or a Fitbit whilst exercising, patients being monitored remotely by doctors and nurses and the use of driverless cars, they allow us to analyse patterns of human life through data (Pentland, 2009).

Newly generated datasets can be used by governments or private sector organizations in real-time decision-making and problem solving and also in simulations and models to predict future patterns in social activities and behaviours (Matheus, Janssen & Maheshwari, 2018; Kitchin, 2016). The following examples of datasets generated by a wide range of organizations give a further impression of current datafication processes in society (Kitchin, 2016: 2):

- data on the use of electricity, gas and water, generated by utility companies;
- data on travel flow, locations and movements, generated by transport providers;
- data on smartphone app use and behaviours, locations and movements, generated by mobile phone operators;
- data on locations, movements, reviews and consumption, generated by travel and accommodation providers;
- data on preferences, attitudes, sentiments, consumption behaviours, opinions, locations and movements, generated by social media providers;
- data on public service consumption and satisfaction and government performance, generated by government agencies;
- data on security, crime, policing, emergency responses and fire alarms, generated by policing organizations and emergency services;
- data on weather events and patterns, generated by weather service organizations;
- data on consumption, shopping behaviour and expenditure, credit card use, generated by retailers and financial institutions;
- data on people's locations and behaviours, generated by security firms; and
- data on people's use and behaviours, consumption and preferences, generated by home appliances and entertainment systems.

With the exception of some publicly available government data sets, many of these newly generated datasets are considered commercially or privately owned and, with that, are not publicly accessible. More in general, Pasquale (2015) warns us of increasing information asymmetries in our society; although more and more data is being generated through processes of datafication, the valuable information that can be derived from these datasets is often out of reach for ordinary citizens in his view. More specifically, he points at the following

Smart government 139

societal changes as a result of new technological and data affordances in the hands of large corporations and governments and at the costs of public values and the interests of individuals (Pasquale, 2015: 191–194):

- *a rule of scores and bets*: the importance of credit reputation grows as public assistance shrinks;
- *a development of separate and unequal economies*: reputational systems for ordinary citizens and for high financiers have diverged to the point that they hardly operate in the same economy;
- *a development towards invisible powers*: the rise of algorithmic authorities replacing human wisdom; and
- *wasteful arms races and unfair competitions*: in more and more aspects of our lives, computers are authorised to make decisions without human intervention;

Pasquale (2015) makes the following recommendations to reduce these increasing information asymmetries in society:

- increasing transparency and openness, e.g. by promoting open uses of technology and data;
- educated citizenship to better understand public and private decision-making;
- a public check on the quality of data and the information derived from them;
- a public safety net for cases in which decisions made on the basis of algorithms are unjust or unfair; and
- a restorement of human authority in decision-making based on algorithms.

More or less, what Pasquale (2015) is alluding to here is a new ethical framework that is needed to assess these asymmetries in societal relationships, including in digital government relationships with citizens. We discuss this matter further later in this chapter and propose an alternative ethical framework of contextual integrity.

Conceptualising "big data"

Recent hype around so-called big data require us to further explore the empirical meaning and validity of this new concept. In a submission to the UK House of Commons Science and Technology Committee's inquiry into big data, Research Councils UK provided the following description (UK House of Commons Science and Technology Committee, 2016):

> What constitutes big data varies between disciplines and sectors. It goes beyond the extremely large and complex datasets generated by, for example, the Large Hadron Collider, DNA sequencing, Earth observation,

140 *Areas of public sector reform*

government records and transactions, commercial or online interactions, to include data from new technologies. Smaller scale data of high complexity and variability, for example from environmental monitoring and the IoT, where sensors capture and process large amounts of fast-moving (and often personal) data, is such technology. Regardless of the source, big data is about gaining value and insights from extremely large, complex, fast moving or combined data, across a range of sectors.

(p. 7)

As becomes clear from this description, big data are generally related to large volumes of data; a large variety of datasets derived from different sectors and domains (e.g. scientific research data, commercial data, government records, personal data); the speed at which data are generated, processed and analysed and the capacity to analyse structured and/or unstructured data from sources as diverse as web logs, social media, mobile communications, sensors and financial transactions (OECD, 2013; Dutch Scientific Council, 2016). As data analysis is becoming more and more complex, the use of algorithms and machine-learning techniques is increasing as well. Data can be generated through overt (mandatory) data collection processes, in automated or digital processing or through voluntary data donations or "data philanthropy," for example. Moreover, the rise of Big and Open Linked Data makes it easier to link, share and integrate data from different domains (Janssen & van den Hoven, 2015). Further characteristics of big data are (e.g. Dutch Scientific Council, 2016):

1   A *data-driven method of analysis*: the aim here is to inductively find correlations and patterns in the data – that is, without using any hypotheses deducted from theory – and use these correlations and data patterns for a particular purpose;
2   The *capacity to conduct retrospective analysis, real-time analysis or "nowcasting" and predictive analysis or "forecasting"*;
3   *Cross-sector and cross-domain use of data*: for example, personal data can be integrated with scientific research data and government data from the public health sector in order for public health professionals to make better decisions about effective solutions for tackling obesity; and
4   The *use of data to derive actionable knowledge*: patterns derived from aggregated data can be used in public decision-making at an individual or group level.

However, as these big data characteristics represent a wide-ranging overview of what is possible and not an actual phenomenon in which all these characteristics can be identified, several scholars point out that a rigorous definition of big data does not exist thus far (Manovich, 2011; Mayer-Schönberger & Cukier, 2013; Dutch Scientific Council, 2016). Also, many authors tend to focus in their definitions on either the technical characteristics of big data, such as volume, computer processing, data analytics software and storage technologies,

Smart government 141

or the data-driven aspects of big data analysis (e.g. Gil-Garcia, Pardo & Nam, 2015; Pentland, 2014; Mayer-Schönberger & Cukier, 2013). Moreover, with fast-moving technological developments in this area, such definitions are in continuous flux (OECD, 2013). For instance, according to the UK House of Commons Science and Technology Committee (2016), the exponential growth of big data and datafication processes in our society can be illustrated by the following observations:

- 90 percent of all data on the Internet were created within the last two years;
- In 2014, every minute, more than 200 million emails were sent, 4 million Google search queries were conducted and more than 2.4 million Facebook posts were shared; and
- the total amount of global data is predicted to grow 40 percent year on year for the next decade.

Besides the lack of scholarly consensus about a rigorous definition of big data, scholars also have different views on the nature of big data applications and innovative forms of data use and the extent to which they will actually lead to new forms of knowledge. Boyd and Crawford (2012), for instance, observe that the current trend of big data is less about data that is "big," such as earlier large data sets that are not considered big data (e.g. census data) than it is about this new capacity to search, aggregate and cross-reference large data sets. They emphasize the need to see big data not as a technology-driven or data-driven phenomenon, but as a socio-technical construct that requires further empirical investigation. Empirical insights into how information and knowledge are derived from big data applications in specific contexts would also help to debunk some popular myths around big data, including the widespread belief that large data sets offer a higher form of intelligence and knowledge that can generate insights which were previously impossible and with the aura of truth, objectivity and accuracy (Boyd & Crawford, 2012: 663; van Dijck, 2014). Mayer-Schönberger and Cukier (2013), too, more sceptically point out that big data is mainly about predictions as it seeks to apply mathematics to huge quantities of data in order to infer probabilities. They warn that data are not similar to information or knowledge as interpretation of data is needed in order to achieve those. Consequently, they see big data as only pointing at the "what" and not the "why" of a phenomenon (Mayer-Schönberger & Cukier, 2013).

Critical issues around big data

In general, several scholars have raised some critical questions about the underlying assumptions of big data and data-driven ways of thinking, which can be summarised as follows.

First of all, as discussed earlier, the application of big data does not automatically lead to information, knowledge or even evidence, for that matter, with data or numbers not speaking for themselves (Gonzalez-Bailon, 2013). Intellectual

142 *Areas of public sector reform*

analysis and interpretation continue to be of critical importance in converting data into information and, subsequently, into knowledge within a particular context (Kitchin, 2014; see also Chapter 2). Indeed, some scholars claim that social scientific theory and interpretation are more necessary than ever before if we are to find the appropriate interpretation of data (Gonzalez-Bailon, 2013). This then also implies that claims about the objectivity of big data are misleading as working with big data, including making research design decisions, identifying meaningful correlations in a particular context and understanding potential biases in the data set, is a critical subjective activity conducted by people (Gonzalez-Bailon, 2013; Boyd & Crawford, 2012).

Secondly, although big data involves the application of large volumes of data, it does not mean that the sample size of big data research is not important, as some people are suggesting, or that using big datasets means that the entire population is included (n = all) (Gonzalez-Bailon, 2013). For example, in analysing big data research on Google search engine behaviours in Australia, Schroeder (2014) points at some problematic research methodological issues, including the representativeness of the Australian population among Google users; restricted access to commercial data, which prevents further insights into the origins of the data and the fact that the research is not replicable. Potential biases in the sampling always have to be taken into account when data are interpreted, as they can lead to incorrect conclusions (Gonzalez-Bailon, 2013).

Thirdly, although the dominant focus both in scholarly work and amongst practitioners currently is on big data and datafication, this doesn't mean that traditional small datasets, such as government statistics, qualitative research data or occasional survey data, are not relevant or of importance any longer (Lindstrom, 2016; Kitchin, 2014; Kitchin, 2016). For example, in his book on small data, Lindstrom (2016) makes a compelling case for the benefits of qualitative research, such as ethnographic research and qualitative interviews, in order to get a rich and in-depth understanding of the daily lives of individuals from their own socio-cultural perspective, empirical insights which are impossible to get when only big datasets are being harvested and analysed, stripped of their social contexts and realities. For this reason, Lindstrom (2016) points to the value of mixed-method research and triangulation in order to get more robust research outcomes.

Fourthly, although rapid processes of datafication seem to suggest that more or less every societal phenomenon is being put into a quantified format (Mayer-Schönberger & Cukier, 2013; Pentland, 2014), there are still phenomena that do not have any data on them or where data is not available for big data research (Borgman, 2015). An example of phenomena that do not have any data on them at all are groups of unidentified people living in very remote places, such as on some of the Indonesian islands or in the Amazon rainforests. Other examples are unidentified natural species from the biological world of animals, insects, sea creatures and plants. Closer to home, in the area of digital government, many governments have difficulty collecting data on homeless people living in their respective jurisdictions. Examples of datasets that are not available

Smart government   143

for use in big data research often are closed in nature and have proprietary issues (e.g. IPR) or formats, which bring up complex problems and restrictions around data ownership in big data research (Borgman, 2015; Schroeder, 2014).

Fifthly, when big datasets including personal data, such as Twitter feeds, are publicly available, it does not mean that they can be used or re-used without people's consent (Boyd & Crawford, 2012; Schroeder, 2014). As re-identification of anonymised data is a realistic option, even in situations where large aggregated data sets have been used, privacy protection is an important issue to consider in conducting big data research, particularly as informed consent prior to data collection becomes increasingly difficult when data is being re-used more and more. Moreover, Internet users are not necessarily aware of all the multiple uses, profits and other gains that come from personal information they have posted online, which might have prevented them from giving permission for their data to be used for other purposes (Boyd & Crawford, 2012). Other emerging ethical risks are potential misuse of data and preferential treatment of or even discrimination against individuals on the basis of data (re-)use.

And finally, whilst a critical consideration of these big data issues is of importance, it is also clear that the trade-offs people are willing to make in big data initiatives when they disclose their personal data in return for a particular value are not well understood either (Gonzalez-Bailon, 2013; Polonetsky, Tene & Jerome, 2014). In the end, the benefits and risks of big data applications will depend on how the data are actually used in a particular context (NZDFF, 2014; Gonzalez-Bailon, 2013). Consequently, maximising the potential of innovative data uses requires a new ethical framework that is context oriented and focuses on the integrity of data use in terms of both value creation and protection against any harm within that particular context (e.g. NZDFF, 2014; Nissenbaum, 2010; Nissenbaum, 2011; Schintler & Kulkarni, 2014; Polonetsky, Tene & Jerome, 2014). We explore what such a new ethical framework could look like later in this chapter.

A short history of data-informed government

Rapid datafication processes in society do not necessarily imply a similar uptake of smart technologies and big data applications in digital government relationships with citizens. Nor does it imply that data-based relationships with citizens are completely new for government. Governments around the world have been data informed for centuries: for example, population counts were used by rulers in order to be able to collect taxes from people living within the ruler's jurisdiction (Agar, 2003). Drafting male inhabitants for the military in wartime was another way in which population counts were used by kings and other rulers.

These early population counts were relatively simple; however, over time, we can observe the changing and expanding capacities of government around data collection and compilation, which relied on the application of new technologies (Agar, 2003: 3). For example, in 1831, standardised paper-based forms were used in the fourth British census of population (Agar, 2003). In

144 *Areas of public sector reform*

the 19th century, cities started collecting, processing and analysing population data through civil registrations, government and commercial records, surveys and mapping, supporting city planning and decision-making (van Zoonen, 2016). Government records, surveys, mapping and population registers became important means for many governments to collect and compile data related to citizens. Later on, punch-card machines, mainframe computers and networked PCs were successively introduced to help governments collect, process, analyse and store data on citizens in files and databases. The Second World War turned out to be influential, with funding available to governments to invest in R&D on computers and computing. Also the UK's experience during the Second World War influenced the UK central government not to set up a universal population register, as was common practice in many continental European countries at the time.

Since those early days of data collection and information gathering by governments in their relationships with citizens, governments have been using centralised data or knowledge departments directly accessible to those who govern (Agar, 2003). Underlying the preference for a centralised data department was a modernist, technocratic idea that centralised data would create more information and knowledge in one place, which would lead to more control and better governing (Agar, 2003). From that perspective, until the Second World War, each UK government department had its own statistics office to produce the statistics it needed for governing (Agar, 2003). Modernisation also led to the arrival of statistical experts in government to further support governing and the governors.

However, unlike the more recent data science methods applied to large volumes of data, traditional statistical methods have been designed to perform "data-scarce" science: i.e. to identify significant relationships from small, clean sample sizes with known properties (Kitchin, 2016). Data-informed government traditionally uses small data that, unlike big datasets, have been sampled, are generated on an occasional basis, and are limited in scope (Kitchin, 2014; Kitchin, 2016; Lindstrom, 2016).

From this short overview, we can derive three types of legacy systems of data-informed government that are likely to have an impact on the design and application of smart government initiatives. For example, these legacy systems may clash with the use of big datasets and algorithms in smart government initiatives (Janssen & Kuk, 2016). Other options are that they may be standing in the way of the implementation of smart government initiatives (e.g. due to a lack of available government funding for new initiatives) and that they are merged into smart government (e.g. the use of open government data and statistical datasets in big data research):

1   *Data legacy systems:* involving concrete, structured datasets (e.g. official statistics, census data, population data), metadata and databases or registers. These data and metadata can be integrated with other datasets and used in big data applications;

2   *Digital technology legacy systems:* including information systems, network technologies, hardware and software. These legacy systems may need to be replaced by smart technologies in order for governments to become smart(-er); and

3   *Legacy of government statisticians and statistical expertise:* although statistics is an important discipline within the new field of data science, it is not the only discipline of relevance to data science applied to the public sector. This means that government statisticians will need to be retrained if they want to perform data science activities. Moreover, the real-time generation, processing and analysis of big data does not sit very well with a centralised statistical function in government that is separated from real-time expert decision-making at the frontline; as a result, developments towards smart government will likely see a disintermediation of the centralised statistical function and, simultaneously, horizontal integration of data and data expertise across government in order to put data directly in the hands of expert decision-makers in real time.

Interestingly, now that governments around the world are investing in fundamentally changing from being data informed to data driven or smart, objectives similar to those of the early days of governments' data collection and information gathering in their relationships with citizens can be observed: to have more and better knowledge about their operations and functioning, which would then lead to more control and better governing (Meijer, 2015; Kitchin, 2016). Next, we explore how digital governments are trying to achieve these smart ambitions.

Smartness in digital government

Conceptualising "smartness" in government

Increasingly, governments around the world are adopting emerging digital technologies and innovative data applications in their ambition to become smart, including wireless and network technologies, sensors, ubiquitous systems, digital and physical infrastructures, cloud computing, mobile services, broadband, interconnected computing networks, service-oriented architectures, big data, open government data, social networking, web design and smartphone applications (Gil-Garcia, Pardo & Nam, 2016a; Naphade *et al*, 2011; Criado, Sandoval-Almazan & Gil-Garcia, 2013). These smart technologies enable new innovative applications in the public sector, such as Internet-connected street lamps, networked surveillance cameras, sensors that monitor air and water quality, sensing visitor movements, monitoring of public sentiment, crowd control, predictive policing and the monitoring of vehicle movements and traffic, for example (Scoblete, 2018; van Zoonen, 2016). Increasingly, these digital technologies and applications are connected through the IoT, which enables the integration of sensors, radio-frequency identification and Bluetooth in the real-world

146 *Areas of public sector reform*

environment using highly networked services (Hashem *et al*, 2016). IoT devices can be further empowered by new innovative forms of AI: for example, AI-empowered networked surveillance cameras are able to digest thousands of gigabytes of video data in real time, perform machine vision and object detection on those feeds and identify potential trouble spots (Scoblete, 2018).

But what does smart government actually mean in practice? Is it something new or different perhaps from smart operations and practices in the commercial sector, for example? Are we actually witnessing a smart paradigm shift in how governments are operating in comparison with the past?

Similar to other smart technology–enabled societal developments, emerging smart technologies and innovative data uses are critical elements of smart government initiatives (Gil-Garcia, Pardo & Nam, 2016a; Gil-Garcia, Pardo & Nam, 2016b). However, it is in using these smart technologies and data as part of socio-technical assemblages in the context of digital government and its relationships with citizens that we can observe some outcomes different from those in the private sector, for example. For instance, one of the major strengths of big data is the high accuracy of data at an aggregated level, which can be used to enhance the effectiveness of public policy solutions and public service provision to different groups of the population; much better than in the past, smart government are now able to use data in order to analyse what works and what doesn't in terms of potential solutions to public policy problems and approaches in public service provision to particular client groups (Dutch Scientific Council, 2016). Moreover, big data analyses increasingly influence government interventions, making them more effective and efficient and improve public decision-making. However, with that, statistical probabilities, instead of actual facts, are increasingly used in smart government operations as well (Dutch Scientific Council, 2016). To date, many smart city initiatives demonstrate the following innovative forms of data use enabled by digital technologies and networks, such as the IoT (Harrison *et al*, 2010):

1) The use of real-time data that is captured from a variety of connected physical and digital sensors;
2) Integration of these captured datasets into a government enterprise computing platform which can be accessed and used across various public services; and
3) The application of complex data analytics, models, data optimisation and data visualisation in operational business processes in order to make better operational decisions.

These innovative data uses are often supported by data visualisation via smart government dashboards, which can be designed for use by government officials or by members of the public. Smart government dashboards can be used for a variety of purposes, including increased transparency and accountability, faster and more accurate public decision-making, increased effectiveness and efficiency of government business operations and processes, facilitating public participation and generating public feedback (Matheus, Janssen & Maheshwari, 2018). A practical example can be found in The Netherlands, where the Dutch national government has created an online dashboard where Dutch citizens can monitor progress on and investments in all large government ICT projects[1] and, as a result, hold the Dutch government better to account.

Box 6.2 Smart city: Songdo, South Korea

Songdo is a smart city built from scratch in South Korea through public-private partnership arrangements. Around 100,000 people are living in Songdo at the moment. Developing a new smart city has the advantage that sensors and computers can be built into a wide range of new city infrastructure, such as buildings and streets, and used in a variety of service areas. Data is collected in real time 24 hours a day via sensor devices, traffic detectors and CCTV cameras. The collected data is stored in a database connected to an integrated operations control platform operated by the city administration and monitored and analysed by application services in order to provide citizens with useful services in real time in areas of traffic, parking, public transport, crime prevention, emergency and disaster response services, environmental services (e.g. pollution levels, weather), energy services, urban infrastructure and facilities management (e.g. water, street lights) and waste disposal.

A smart traffic signal control system regulates traffic flows on the basis of real-time data gathered through sensors throughout the city. This intelligent traffic management system collects and provides traffic information, parking information, public transportation information and data used as input for crime prevention. Citizens are informed in real time about available spaces for public parking, with cases of illegal parking being monitored and intervened in by the authorities. CCTV cameras have been installed at bus stops to inform citizens when a bus will arrive and monitor possible bus service issues that may arise, but also to check for unusual activity.

Moreover, CCTV cameras have been installed throughout the city in order to monitor any unusual activity in real time. If an unusual activity is detected, the operator is informed immediately, and information on the location and situation is forwarded to the police for immediate action. Crime prevention also takes place through the use of automatic number plate recognition (ANPR) cameras. These cameras collect the license plate number data of passing vehicles in real time. Data are analysed to filter out stolen vehicles, vehicles of people who have unpaid tax and vehicles used by criminals. This information is then forwarded to the police, the tax office and other relevant organizations for their immediate response.

148 *Areas of public sector reform*

In terms of disaster response services, Songdo collects data in real time via sensors and emergency operation services on emergencies, such as fires, and natural disasters, including earthquakes, tsunamis, floods and typhoons. The data is forwarded on to the integrated operation centre, the National Disaster Management System and emergency management for their immediate response. At times of an emergency, citizens are informed about the situation through web and mobile services and speakers in public places.

Environment detecting sensors are installed at Songdo's parks, shopping areas, schools and housing areas to measure weather and atmosphere conditions, including pollution levels. Road surface detecting sensors and weather sensors installed at main roads and bridges collect real-time data on weather-related road conditions and road visibility, such as frost and fog. A predictive analysis informs citizens via web-based and mobile channels of current road conditions and those expected in the near future.

IoT sensors are installed at houses and buildings to provide real-time information to consumers on how much energy has been used and what measures can be taken to minimise utility bills. Songdo residents can control lighting, heating, air conditioning and opening the front doors in their homes with a push of a button on a control panel or remotely via their mobile phones. Also, smart water pipes prevent drinkable water from being wasted in showers and toilets.

Furthermore, the city has a smart pneumatic waste disposal system, where people need to throw their garbage into smart pipes. Sensors determine whether garbage has been properly separated and correct garbage bags have been used. If so, the pipes will suck the garbage underground, disposing of waste and recycling what can be recycled.

Songdo provides citizens with information on urban infrastructure and facilities (e.g. water, street lights) via dedicated public terminals. Here, citizens can also search for any city-related information that they need. Another option people have is to contact the city administration from their televisions at home.

Algorithms in digital government relationships

Other critical elements of smart government initiatives are algorithms or sets of operational rules. The increasing complexity of big data analyses requires the application of more sophisticated and higher quality algorithms, particularly as a result of the necessity of using qualitative small datasets in smart government data analysis. In this respect, the Dutch Scientific Council (2016: 127) points to the emerging issue of "the unreasonable effectiveness of data": average-performing algorithms using large volumes of data deliver better outcomes than good-quality algorithms using a small dataset. The scientific robustness of algorithms applied in big data analysis is a major issue for smart government; according to Janssen and Kuk (2016), algorithms can systematically introduce unintentional bias, reinforce stereotyping and discrimination, favour a political orientation or reinforce undesired practices, for example.

In general, design choices made during the analysis of big data have a major impact on the research results. However, "algorithmic accountability" hardly exists in smart government initiatives (Diakopoulos, 2013, in: Dutch Scientific Council, 2016). Although algorithms do not operate independently of the data and data use applications in smart government initiatives, they become increasingly autonomous and invisible to the public eye for scrutiny (Janssen & Kuk, 2016; Dutch Scientific Council, 2016). Moreover, public access and scrutiny become even more problematic when smart government initiatives use commercial, proprietary algorithms as part of their data analysis (Dutch Scientific Council, 2016).

Based on these developments and insights, the Dutch Scientific Council (2016) warns of a "transparency paradox" emerging in smart government relationships with citizens, leading to major power imbalances: citizens becoming more transparent for smart governments as a result of the application of smart technologies and big data analyses, whilst algorithms, profiles and big data research methods deployed by smart governments are not at all transparent to citizens or available for public scrutiny (Dutch Scientific Council, 2016: 135).

More recently, several scholars have pointed at the benefits of considering algorithmic transparency as a way to offer opportunities for public scrutiny and governance, which could prevent forms of bias, overrepresentation or discrimination in big data analysis (e.g. Ananny & Crawford, 2018; Dutch Scientific Council, 2016). However, we need to be very careful here about using a technology-driven perspective that considers algorithms as independent and objective agents driving outcomes (Crawford, 2016; Ananny & Crawford, 2018); seeing the algorithm doesn't mean that people will have authoritative knowledge on how the algorithmic system actually works and delivers outcomes, i.e. on the whole social-technical assemblage of human and non-human actors around algorithms within the context of digital government, where political choices are made about appropriate criteria and datasets (Ananny & Crawford, 2018; Ananny, 2016; Crawford, 2016). Consequently, holding such a socio-technical assemblage around algorithms accountable in an effective way requires broadening the perspective in order to see and understand how the whole public decision-making process around big data analysis in smart government works (Ananny & Crawford, 2018; Crawford, 2016).

Data science applied to smart government

A new multidisciplinary area of study that covers an important part of these innovative forms of data analysis and data use in government is data science applied to the public sector: the extraction, interpretation and presentation of

150 *Areas of public sector reform*

insights from unstructured and structured government data and other datasets that can be either closed or open (Matheus, Janssen & Maheshwari, 2018). Nowadays, governments collect enormous amounts of data in a large variety of areas, such as traffic, infrastructure, housing, energy and water consumption, economy, employment, social services, education, health, taxation, environment, conservation, primary industries and policing. These data can be combined or enriched with data from smart devices and other sources including social media, data held by NGOs and private sector data (Matheus, Janssen & Maheshwari, 2018; Janssen, Matheus & Zuiderwijk, 2015).

In order to understand data analysis and data use in the context of digital government, and particularly its implications, government data scientists need not only knowledge and skills around data analytics, statistics, (predictive) modelling, simulations and data visualisation techniques, but also an in-depth understanding of the government context, including public sector values, unique citizen-government relationships, institutions, organizations, public policy, public service provision, legislation and politics (Matheus, Janssen & Maheshwari, 2018; Kitchin, 2014). Taking into account the unique context of smart digital government and its relationships with citizens, it is in this applied form of government data science that data analysis and use can enable, as part of socio-technical assemblages, the production of effective digital government outcomes, such as more effective public services. However, in order to do so, expert public servants will need to be part of those socio-technical assemblages in order to interpret the data and derive valuable, context-relative information, which enhances the outcomes' effectiveness.

Benefits of smart government

Scholars have identified a number of benefits of smart government, including the following.

New forms of data use enable the adaptation of city services to the behaviours of city inhabitants and, with that, a more optimal use of available physical infrastructure and resources, such as monitoring energy and water consumption and managing transportation systems, whilst enhancing quality of life (Harrison *et al*, 2010). Moreover, empirical research in fourteen smart cities has demonstrated that the innovative use of digital technologies and data in cities is a driver of innovation and productivity and strongly promotes economic growth and development (Vinod Kumar, 2017). Some claim that cities that embrace the smart city paradigm can expect to see between 2 and 5 percent additional GDP growth (Scoblete, 2018). Further benefits of smart government are considered to be (Matheus, Janssen & Maheshwari, 2018; UK House of Commons Science and Technology Committee, 2016; Dutch Scientific Council, 2016; Gil-Garcia, Pardo & Nam, 2016b):

- Increased operational efficiency;
- Predictive analysis of future activities or developments;

Smart government 151

- Reconstruction of events in the past (e.g. natural disasters, terrorist attacks);
- Better, faster and real-time public decision-making;
- Better public services more tailored to citizens;
- Improved public engagement;
- Better public policy-making;
- Improved effectiveness and efficiency;
- More sustainable cities and other government jurisdictions;
- Enhanced transparency, accountability and governance; and
- Improved stakeholder engagement, creating collaborative innovation communities around smart government initiatives (e.g. citizens, business firms, knowledge institutions and national and local government agencies).

Box 6.3   Smart government initiatives in the USA

- *Reducing traffic fatalities in the city of San José*
  The city of San José aims to reduce traffic fatalities to zero. In 2015, San José had 60 traffic fatalities, the highest annual total in 20 years (Miller, 2016). The city's department of transportation (DOT) has used data analytics and GIS analysis in order to identify 14 Priority Safety Corridors: i.e. places where a significant share of fatal and major injury collisions occur. A data analysis of five years of collision data showed that, while pedestrian-related collisions made up a very small share of priority corridor collisions, they comprised over two-thirds (67 percent) of the fatal collisions on those roadways (Miller, 2016). Furthermore, a majority (51 percent) of the pedestrian fatality reports indicated that pedestrians may have been illegally in the roadways or crossing roadways outside of crosswalks (Miller, 2016). These findings have clear implications for the city's traffic fatality elimination strategy and have had an impact on the activities of frontline police officers, such as deployment times aligned more closely with the peak times of traffic collisions and providing police officers with smartphone access to GIS maps of high-incident intersections with detailed intelligence.
- *Early intervention of vulnerable individuals at risk in the justice system*
  Vulnerable individuals struggling with complex multidimensional problems, including homelessness, mental illness, substance abuse and chronic health conditions, are often in contact with different parts of the justice system (e.g. jails, emergency rooms, mental-health facilities, social services) without being tracked across the system, making it difficult for government to provide coordinated care to these individuals. Typically, outcomes for the individuals are poor, and costs for government interventions are high. By combining data from

different organizations and multiple separate datasets, officials can understand and address the individual's challenges and underlying conditions: individuals are matched across these multiple datasets to explore where they have interacted with different parts of the system. Also, predictive modelling can help officials to identify individuals at risk of interacting with parts of the system at an early stage with the opportunity to intervene before long-term harm is done.

The Data Science and Public Policy team (DSaPP) at the University of Chicago developed such a predictive early intervention model. In 2015, DSaPP partnered with Johnson County, Kansas, and generated a list of 200 people most at risk of coming into contact with the criminal justice system (Data–Smart City Solutions, 2017).[2] This list provided officials with a prioritised group most in need of early intervention, saving government money by doing so and reinvesting these funds in preventative measures.

Box 6.4   Smart government strategy in Singapore

Singapore has developed a strategy to become a smart government. This Digital Government Blueprint can be accessed here: www.smartnation.sg/docs/default-source/default-document-library/dgb_booklet_june2018.pdf (accessed 6 May 2019).

The need for a comprehensive view of smart government

However, Gil-Garcia, Pardo and Nam (2015) point out that the large majority of academic studies in the field of smart government put a strong and narrow emphasis on the digital technology and data aspects of smart government initiatives. For instance, Harrison *et al* (2010) define smart cities as urban areas that exploit operational data from across various public service areas in order to optimize the operation of city services. Similarly, Kitchin (2016) observes a tendency of cities to adopt a narrow, instrumental perspective of what he sees as "data-driven urbanism" as their guiding vision: a computational understanding of city systems that reduces urban life to rationalized logic and calculative rules and procedures. He warns that the result of using this linear data-driven approach may be a new form of "panopticon" urban governance in which digital technologies and big data systems are determining, knowing and controlling the urban environment, solving urban issues through technical solutions (Kitchin, 2016).

Cities should move away from these technocratic forms of governance, as they produce a limiting and reductionist understanding of the actual functioning of

Smart government 153

cities, and acknowledge a more organic, complex, multifaceted and wicked nature of urban issues and their environments (Kitchin, 2016; Macke *et al*, 2018). In line with this thinking, a more productive approach would be to adopt an empirical non-linear perspective in order to understand and explain the mutual shaping of emerging smart technologies, data, social relationships, people, organizations and institutions in an urban context and their outcomes. Consequently, several scholars have emphasised the need to consider smart government initiatives not just through a technology- or data-driven lens, but taking a much more comprehensive view on the socio-technical construct or assemblage of smart technologies, data, people, institutions, organizations, stakeholders, regulations and resources, in the context of smart, digital government (Kitchin, 2014; Gil-Garcia, Pardo & Nam, 2016a). Moreover, smartness is not a black-and-white category but needs to be considered as a wide range of multiple dimensions (Gil-Garcia, Pardo & Nam, 2016a). It is only through such a comprehensive approach that governments can achieve an effective and efficient smart paradigm shift in how they operate.

However, thus far, there is no scholarly consensus about the broader meaning of smartness in government (Gil-Garcia, Pardo & Nam, 2016a; Gil-Garcia, Pardo & Nam, 2016b). Moreover, if we consider the scholarly literature to date, there are only a few studies looking at smart government at the national level (e.g. Gil-Garcia, Pardo & Nam, 2016a); the large majority of studies focus on smartness in the slightly different context of local government, in particular smart cities (Gil-Garcia, Pardo & Nam, 2016b; Meijer, 2016; Meijer & Bolivar, 2016). In an attempt to characterize smartness in different branches and levels of government, Gil-Garcia, Pardo and Nam (2016a) have identified the following fourteen interconnected smart government dimensions based on a scholarly literature review of available studies into smart government developments:

1) *Cross-government data sharing and integration* allow for better public service provision through improved cross-government communication, response and coordination;
2) *Innovation* enables a government to become smarter by continuously incorporating new and improved ways to deliver public services and manage operational business processes;
3) *Evidence-based decision-making and the intensive use of data* enable governments to make more informed decisions and improve the effectiveness of public policy and public service provision at the frontline;
4) *Citizen-centricity* implies that governments know what citizens want and use smart technologies and data to fulfil citizens' needs and provide more tailored public services to individuals;
5) *Sustainability* refers to the ecological implications of developing smart cities, governments and countries that are viable in the long term and improve the quality of life for generations;
6) *Creativity* refers to the role of governments in promoting a public sector environment in which creativity and innovation in partnerships with

154 *Areas of public sector reform*

citizens, businesses, NGOs and other stakeholders is encouraged, as well as being creative in their own public policy and public service interventions;

7) *Effectiveness* goes beyond supplier-led public service provision with the objective of truly enhancing the quality of life of individual citizens from various backgrounds and solving complex public policy problems;

8) *Efficiency* refers to governments being able to provide more value to citizens with fewer resources;

9) *Equality* refers to the role of governments in improving the quality of life for all citizens and therefore fighting any existing social inequalities by using smart technologies, data and appropriate strategies to reduce social exclusion and promote social justice;

10) *Entrepreneurialism* implies that governments develop a broad and comprehensive strategy on knowledge-based and innovation-oriented economic development in order to promote a healthy business environment and, with that, increase the attractiveness of cities or countries. As empirical research has demonstrated that the dynamics of smart city GDP creation take different pathways (Vinod Kumar, 2017), it is important for smart governments to take their own socio-cultural, economic, governmental, technological and regulatory context as a starting point for developing an effective economic development strategy;

11) *Citizen engagement* enables collaboration, public participation, and other forms of two-way communication in relationships between citizens and government in ways that foster collective forms of intelligence and smartness;

12) *Openness* refers to governments opening up their data and using these datasets in smarter ways to become more transparent, accountable, collaborative and effective in their relationships with citizens, businesses, NGOs and other stakeholders;

13) *Resiliency* implies that governments use data and smart technologies to be able to quickly respond in cases of emergency and disaster, recover quickly and re-establish their service operations in relationships with citizens, businesses and other stakeholders; and

14) *Technology savviness* provides the necessary knowledge, competencies and skills to select, implement and use smart technology applications and strategies to make government smarter.

These 14 interconnected dimensions are critical elements of a comprehensive and effective smart government strategy.

Box 6.5   Exercise 6.1

Use the 14 interrelated dimensions and develop a comprehensive and effective smart city strategy for a particular urban environment in your country.

Smart government 155

Emerging issues and barriers

A number of issues and barriers have been identified in the scholarly literature around the application of smart technologies and big datasets that are causing challenges for governments trying to become smart. Most of these issues have been discussed or raised throughout this chapter and in some instances also in other chapters of this book. Without the claim of being comprehensive, the following is a list of emerging issues and barriers that require the attention of public managers in smart government initiatives:

- *Ethical implications of the application and use of smart technologies and data in relationships with citizens*: many scholars point to major risks around increasing power imbalances, information asymmetries and potential individual harm in increasingly smart relationships between government and citizens (e.g. Drew, 2016; Dutch Scientific Council, 2016; Gil-Garcia, Pardo & Nam, 2015; Gil-Garcia, Pardo & Nam, 2016b). In the next section, we explore a strategy for smart government in order to deal with ethical issues in its relationships with citizens, including privacy matters, data breaches and data misuse, by adopting a new ethical framework of contextual integrity;
- *Human expert–based decision-making in the context of smart government relationships with citizens is critical*: human experts are critical to interpret the data and convert them into valuable, context-relative information and knowledge.
- *Data integration*: different government agencies generate their own datasets. These datasets are usually not shared.
- *Data visualisation*: many smart governments use a data dashboard which displays (integrated) data on a screen, usually using maps and charts. Users of these dashboards typically are unaware of underlying subjective decisions in selecting and processing data.
- *Data quality*: is a critical issue for smart government as public decision-making depends on the use of high-quality data (Chengalur-Smith, Ballou & Pazer, 1999; Matheus, Janssen & Maheshwari, 2018; Dutch Scientific Council, 2016). Robust data standards play an important role in this respect;
- *Data accuracy*: is particularly relevant for public decision-making based on data or data analysis. Moreover, it is a critical issue when governments want to integrate, share, improve or disseminate data (Gil-Garcia, Pardo & Nam, 2016a);
- *Data transparency*: having raw data doesn't necessarily mean that people have the information or knowledge needed for robust evidence-based decision-making. Moreover, too much data can lead to data smog;
- *Data (re-)use*: a major problem in current regulatory approaches (e.g. privacy legislation) is that collected data cannot be used or re-used for another purpose. This issue is standing in the way of value creation through data (re-)use in smart government initiatives. A potential solution would be a regulatory shift from a dominant focus on data collection to data (re-)use for a particular purpose;

156   *Areas of public sector reform*

- *Data and information security*: see the discussion in Chapter 8;
- *Data governance*: involves both the technical and organizational aspects of how data are collected, processed, analysed, used, re-used, stored, made accessible, shared and integrated, all within the context of digital government (OECD, 2013). However, oversight of the various (meta-)data sets, data bases, data flows, data sharing and data-integration activities tends to be lacking in smart government initiatives (Meijer & Rodriguez Bolivar, 2016);
- *Data access:* data should be accessible to those who need it (OECD, 2013). However, not every citizen has access to data, for a variety of reasons. In Chapter 9, we discuss the existence of multiple digital divides around data;
- *Data availability*: datasets can be closed or open by nature. Many commercial and proprietary datasets are closed and, with that, are not available for public access. However, non-sensitive government data are increasingly publicly available, including for use in smart government initiatives (see also Chapter 5). Another issue is that some societal phenomena do not have any data on them, as discussed earlier;
- *Data aggregation, anonymization and re-identification of individuals*: see the discussion in Chapter 8;
- *Data bias:* bias in datasets used in big data research can be reproduced and reinforced in the data analysis. Data bias can also be caused by the use of algorithms;
- *Data determinism*: or the misconception that data *per se* are driving outcomes, including outcomes that are based on predictions of the future (Kitchin, 2016);
- *Data-driven analysis:* a major risk in data-driven analysis and public decision-making is to consider statistical probabilities and correlations as proven causalities (Dutch Scientific Council, 2016);
- *False positives and false negatives in data analysis*: every data analysis based on probabilities will produce false positives (e.g. accusation of "good" people) and false negatives (e.g. problems continue to exist unnoticed) in smart government initiatives (Bellamy *et al*, 2008). Additional research and public decision-making are needed to assess these cases, preferably using the revised contextual integrity framework introduced in the next section;
- *Algorithm quality*: algorithms need to meet scientific research criteria and robust standards (Dutch Scientific Council, 2016);
- *Algorithm transparency:* transparency of the whole public decision-making process instead of the algorithm *per se* is critically important (Crawford, 2016);
- *Blurring of boundaries between different data domains*: the blurring of the domain of personal data with other, non-personal data domains is a major issue in smart government initiatives. This issue will be further discussed in Chapter 8;
- *Legacy systems*: as discussed, legacy systems related to data, statistics and (older) digital technologies, such as centralised government statistics

Smart government   157

departments removed from frontline decision-making, could stand in the way of governments' use of new innovative data solutions. Consequently, governments need to rethink what to do with these legacy systems when they want to operate under the new smart government paradigm.

Governments becoming smart: adopting a new ethical framework of contextual integrity

An alternative perspective on online privacy protection

In 2010, influenced by major concerns around the impact of digital technologies on people's privacy, especially the Internet, and how online privacy might be protected, Helen Nissenbaum introduced a new concept of "contextual integrity" (Nissenbaum, 2010). Building on the idea of spheres of justice developed by political philosopher Michael Walzer, Nissenbaum wanted to overcome a fundamental flaw in dominant legalistic thinking about privacy protection at the time: namely, the assumption that individuals can understand all facts relevant to true choice at the moment of pair-wise contracting between individuals and [personal ML] data gatherers online (Nissenbaum, 2011: 32).

In general, Nissenbaum (2010; 2011) observes new and different personal information flows in Internet-based environments compared to the real world, creating major privacy threats. Personal data in these digital environments have become a hidden currency, with the profits going to large corporations rather than to the individuals to whom these personal data belong. Good examples are a large variety of personal data generated as by-products of people's online activities, such as cookies, clicks, IP addresses and browsing histories, all commercially benefiting private sector entities, including third parties. Nissenbaum simultaneously observes new and different principles governing these flows of personal data online, with default constraints on personal information flow only responding to the logic of technical possibility (i.e. whatever the Internet allows) and not to social, ethical and political logic (Nissenbaum, 2011).

Nissenbaum (2010) points out that, whilst promoting and complying with an individual's right to privacy is already difficult to undertake in the real world, it has become even more complex to do so in Internet-based environments. The increased complexity of promoting an individual's right to privacy in online environments is caused by shifting recipients of online personal data flow, the types of personal data that are being exchanged online, and the limited constraints under which personal data flows online (Nissenbaum, 2011). A good example of the latter is that third parties in many cases have access to people's online personal data, especially those data generated as by-products of people's online activities, even when people only interact with family or known friends online through social media networks like Facebook, Twitter and Instagram.

Unfortunately, the dominant approach thus far to addressing these online privacy concerns has failed in the eyes of Nissenbaum: this so-called notice-and-consent' or informed-consent approach aims to inform individuals of

158 *Areas of public sector reform*

online personal data practices and provide them with the choice to either engage or disengage online (Nissenbaum, 2011: 34). The underlying assumptions of this dominant approach are twofold (Nissenbaum, 2011): first of all, there is an assumption of a person's right to privacy consideration or, put differently, a right to control information about themselves; a second assumption is that the notice-and-consent approach is compatible with the paradigm of a competitive free market. In an ideal competitive marketplace, buyers are informed of a seller's online practices around collecting and using their personal data and, on that basis, can make free and rational purchase decisions regarding the asking price, including personal data collection and use, for a particular online service or good.

However, Nissenbaum (2011) points out that the current opt-out model for online consumers is not only not fit for purpose, but also deeply problematic:

> A deeper ethical question is whether individuals indeed freely choose to transact (e.g. accept an offer, visit a website, make a purchase online, participate in a social network) given how these choices are framed as well as what the costs are for choosing not to do so.
>
> (p. 35)

As a result, individuals are paying the price for meeting their individual needs of engaging online in a wide range of activities. Moreover, as people do not read and understand online privacy policies through which informed consent is being sought from them, the unrealistic burden put on individuals for their online engagement needs only further increases.

Considering the severeness of online privacy breaches at the time and the fact that the Internet was predominantly a commercial enterprise in 2010, Nissenbaum was keen to rebalance individual and commercial interests around online personal data protection and use through an alternative way of thinking. Conceiving the Internet as a public good, she proposed an alternative approach of so-called contextual integrity; this contextual approach considers an individual's privacy protection by applying context-relative informational norms that constrain what personal data websites can collect, with whom they can share these data and under what conditions they can be shared (Nissenbaum, 2011: 32). Key parameters of these context-relative informational norms are actors (subject, sender, recipient), attributes (types of information) and transmission principles (constraints under which personal data flows):

> Generally, when the flow of information adheres to entrenched norms, all is well; violations of these norms, however, often result in protest and complaint. In a health care context, for example, patients expect their physicians to keep personal medical information confidential, yet they accept that it might be shared with specialists as needed. Patients' expectations would be breached and they would likely be shocked and dismayed if they learned that their physicians had sold the information to a marketing company.

In this event, we would say that informational norms for the health care context had been violated.

(Nissenbaum, 2011: 33)

Contextual integrity ties adequate protection for privacy to the informational norms of specific contexts, demanding that personal data collection and use be appropriate to that context and obey the context-relative informational norms. Rules governing personal data flow will not be driven by a particular digital technology like the Internet but are embedded in and derived from real world social contexts, such as government or the private home environment, and social roles; according to Nissenbaum (2011), as the Internet is deeply embedded in social life, context-specific informational norms need to be extended to corresponding online activities. She explains the application of contextual integrity as follows:

> The decision heuristic derived from the theory of contextual integrity suggests that we locate contexts, explicate entrenched informational norms, identify disruptive flows, and evaluate these flows against norms based on general ethical and political principles as well as context-specific purposes and values.
>
> (Nissenbaum, 2011: 38)

Furthermore, contextual informational norms, like other social norms, are not fixed and static but dynamic, with technology being a significant agent of change (Baracos & Nissenbaum, 2014).

Reconceptualising contextual integrity for digital government relationships to date

Nissenbaum's contextual-integrity theory is an invaluable attempt to reconsider complex issues around personal data flow in online environments and to protect online privacy in these socio-technical assemblages within a certain context. However, a lot has changed since Nissenbaum presented her contextual integrity theory in 2010. First of all, Nissenbaum developed her theory on the basis of observations derived from Internet-based socio-technical assemblages within particular contexts. Rapid developments of datafication and big data had not arrived in our society yet. Secondly, her concerns are exclusively focused on the contextual integrity of personal data flow or, put differently, on personal data integrity. A third observation is that her transmission principles focus exclusively on constraints under which personal data are collected and used: on personal data integrity protection, in other words, and not so much on enabling personal data use supported by contextual informational norms.

As we discussed earlier in this chapter, we can observe a radical expansion in the volume, range and granularity of data being generated about people, things and places (Pentland, 2014; Mayer-Schonberger & Cukier, 2013;

160 *Areas of public sector reform*

Kitchin, 2016). As these new data are being created through the application of emerging smart technologies, their digital nature makes it easy to combine, integrate, process, analyse, model, share, use or re-use them. In their report "Big Data in a Free and Safe Society," the Dutch Scientific Council (2016) concludes that traditional regulatory approaches around data are dominantly focused on the collection of data, such as in the case of data protection legislation and public safety legislation. Such regulatory approaches are no longer tenable in an increasingly datafied world. Instead, they recommend a shift towards regulation, monitoring and governance of data analysis and data use in a big data era, as decisions made in the process of data analysis, including around the application of algorithms, profiling, categorisation and research criteria, as well as actual data use or re-use, influence the outcome of big data-enabled processes and activities. A similar observation about a necessary shift in regulatory focus towards data use was made earlier by the New Zealand Data Futures Forum (2014).

Based on these observations and in current times, I would like to argue that a reconceptualised contextual integrity theory would offer an appropriate, broader sphere of justice around personal and non-personal data use in the context of digital government relationships with citizens in an age of new smart technologies, datafication and big data. Even more so than in Nissenbaum's socio-historical context of Internet-enabled environments, the traditional notice-and-consent model is not working at all in an increasingly smart, data-enabled world: for example, how are people going to receive notice and give informed consent around the harvesting of data via sensing lights at airports (NZDFF, 2014)? Consequently, we will need an alternative contextual approach in order to deal with ethical issues, including privacy, that are emerging around new data flows as part of smart socio-technical assemblages within the digital government context.

A reconceptualised version of Nissenbaum's contextual integrity theory suitable for application in the context of digital government relationships with citizens would involve the following changes in my view:

- Extend the theory of contextual integrity to include all data flows and not just personal data flows;
- Extend the contextual integrity transmission principles to constrain not just (personal) data flows, with a focus on the protection of privacy and the prevention of other harms, but also to include the support of data (re-)use and data flows where data (re-)use is not causing any risks but is enhancing people's lives;
- Apply the revised theory of contextual integrity to the context of digital government relationships with citizens to date: i.e. determining which democratic government-related informational norms need to be considered in identifying and evaluating data (re-)use and data flows in socio-technical assemblages within the digital government context, with privacy protection being one of them.

- Be transparent about the rules that govern data (re-)use and data flows in the (digital) government context, including the government-related informational norms and transmission principles (e.g. via legislation);
- Apply minimum quality assurance standards for data and data analysis research methods in the context of digital government relationships;
- As smart technologies are not determining the rules that govern data (re-)use and data flows but the social context of government is, expert public servants who are able to make a robust assessment of the data and translate these into information and knowledge need to be the authoritative agents of decision-making on data (re-)use in digital government relationships with citizens: i.e. emerging technologies, algorithms or the data *per se* should not be driving or determining public decision-making on data use. Also, public servants should be accountable for appropriate and robust application and use of algorithms in the digital government context, not the algorithms *per se*;
- Increase transparency around data (re-)use and data analysis, including methods and techniques, in the digital government context for citizens and other external stakeholders to be able to understand, monitor and review;
- Create an independent governance board as a safety net for all stakeholders involved in digital government in order to address potential mistakes and (unintended) harms as a result of innovative data (re-)use in digital government relationships. Moreover, this governance board should also have the authority to independently evaluate and audit smart government initiatives on their compliance with the contextual integrity framework;
- Invest in education and training public servants, politicians and the independent governance board members on applied data science in the context of digital government, including context-related informational norms and transmission principles and statistical knowledge; and
- Invest in education of citizens on statistical knowledge, data science and digital government context-related informational norms and values.

General ethical principles and context-specific values in digital government relationships

As we discussed earlier, Nissenbaum (2011) recommends evaluating data flows against norms based on general ethical and political principles[3] as well as context-specific purposes and values. The question is then what these general ethical principles and context-specific norms and values would look like in the context of smart government relationships with citizens. In terms of general ethical principles to evaluate data flows in digital government relationships, the following principles have been identified in the literature (Baracos & Nissenbaum, 2014; Janssen & van den Hoven, 2015; Dutch Scientific Council, 2016; van Zoonen, 2016):

- Fairness;
- Equality;
- Social justice;

162 *Areas of public sector reform*

- Digital inclusion;
- Privacy;
- Security;
- Openness and transparency
- Freedom;
- Freedom of expression;
- Democratic participation;
- Autonomy;
- Dignity; and
- Welfare

Application of these ethical principles, together with digital government context-specific norms within a particular jurisdiction, would support and protect the sphere of justice in the context of digital government relationships with citizens. As an example of what context-specific norms might look like for digital government at the national level, the New Zealand State Services Commission (SSC) has published a Code of Conduct for the State Services,[4] which can be considered the social contract between the New Zealand State Services and New Zealand citizens and residents. This New Zealand Code of Conduct has identified the following norms and values as the ethical foundations on which New Zealand public servants should operate in their relationships with members of the general public: fair, impartial, responsible and trustworthy.

Fair:

- Treat everyone fairly and with respect;
- Be professional and responsive;
- Work to make government services accessible and effective; and
- Strive to make a difference to the well-being of New Zealand and all its people.

Impartial:

- Maintain the political neutrality required to enable us to work with current and future governments;
- Carry out the functions of our organisation, unaffected by our personal beliefs;
- Support our organisation to provide robust and unbiased advice; and
- Respect the authority of the government of the day.

Responsible:

- Act lawfully and objectively;
- Use our organisation's resources carefully and only for intended purposes;
- Treat information with care and use it only for proper purposes; and
- Work to improve the performance and efficiency of our organisation.

Trustworthy:

- Be honest;
- Work to the best of our abilities;
- Ensure our actions are not affected by our personal interests or relationships;
- Never misuse our position for personal gain;
- Decline gifts or benefits that place us under any obligation or perceived influence; and
- Avoid any activities, work or non-work, that may harm the reputation of our organisation or of the State Services.

Examples of the type of ethical issues that could emerge around data use in the context of smart government include the following (Baracos & Nissenbaum, 2014):

- Unfair treatment;
- Preferential treatment;
- Discrimination;
- Being limited in one's life choices;
- Being trapped inside stereotypes;
- Being wrongly assessed or judged;
- Breach of privacy; and
- Breach of confidentiality.

Box 6.6 Exercise 6.2

Use a theoretical case of a real-life practical example of potential child abuse of a six-year-old girl by one of her family members. The family is from a low socio-economic background; has multiple complex problems, such as unemployment and the use of drugs and is well known to local community service providers and police. This case has been detected by a social worker, who would like to get other service providers involved and work out an effective approach, using smart technologies and innovative data solutions.

Use the revised contextual integrity framework to describe, analyse and evaluate the various data flows. Which context-relative and general ethical principles are at stake here? Which data flows should be either enabled or protected by government officials and other service providers as a result of your analysis? How could data flows be enabled or protected in this particular case? Do your findings differ from the real-life situation in your country around enabling and protecting data flows in this particular case?

164 *Areas of public sector reform*

Discussion questions

1 What are the pros and cons of using 1) big data; 2) algorithms; and 3) small data in the context of digital government relationships with citizens? Motivate your answer.
2 Find a real-life case of smart government in a particular relationship with citizens in your country and apply the revised ethical framework of contextual integrity to that particular case. What are your findings? Are they different from what government is currently doing in the data space? Motivate your answer.
3 Why is it important to treat the 14 dimensions of a smart government strategy as closely interrelated dimensions? Motivate your answer.
4 From your perspective, what are the five most critical issues and barriers for governments to become smart governments? Motivate your answer.
5 What would governments in your country need to do in order to institutionalise the proposed ethical framework of contextual integrity as part of their smart government operations and activities? Motivate your answer.
6 How could governments in your country take an effective citizen-centric approach in becoming smart governments? Motivate your answer.

Notes

1 Rijks ICT Dashboard, available from: https://www.rijksictdashboard.nl/ [accessed 24 June 2018].
2 Data–Smart City Solutions (2017) A Catalog of Civic Data Use Cases, 19 July 2017, Harvard Kennedy School Ash Center for Democratic Governance and Innovation. Available from: https://datasmart.ash.harvard.edu/news/article/how-can-data-and-analytics-be-used-to-enhance-city-operations-723 [accessed 14 January 2019].
3 I use the general ethical and political principles of democratic societies in this chapter, with the recommendation that each government should apply context-relative norms and values first to find out if, and if so to what extent, these general principles are appropriate within their own context.
4 State Services Commission, Code of conduct for the State Services, available from: https://www.ssc.govt.nz/node/2069 [accessed 23 June 2018].

References

Agar, J. (2003) *The Government Machine: A Revolutionary History of the Computer.* Cambridge, MA: Massachusetts Institute of Technology Press.
Ananny, M. (2016) Toward an ethics of algorithms: Convening, observation, probability, and timeliness. *Science, Technology & Human Values,* 41 (1), 93–117.
Ananny, M. & Crawford, K. (2018) Seeing without knowing: Limitations of the transparency ideal and its application to algorithmic accountability. *New Media & Society,* 20 (3), 973–989.
Baracos, S. & Nissenbaum, H. (2014) Big data's end run around anonymity and consent. In: Lane, J., Stodden, V., Bender, S. & Nissenbaum, H. (eds.) *Privacy, Big Data, and the Public Good: Frameworks for Engagement.* New York, NY: Cambridge University Press, pp. 322–358.
BBC. (29 November 2017) *Robot Automation Will 'Take 800 Million Jobs by 2030' - Report.* Available from: https://www.bbc.com/news/world-us-canada-42170100 [accessed 23 June 2018].

Bellamy, C., 6, P., Raab, C.D., Warren, A. & Heeney, C. (2008) Information-sharing and confidentiality in social policy: Regulating multi-agency working. *Public Administration*, 86 (3), 737–759.

Borgman, C.L. (2015) *Big Data, Little Data, No Data: Scholarship in the Networked World*. Cambridge, MA: Massachusetts Institute of Technology Press.

Boyd, D. & Crawford, K. (2012) Critical questions for big data: Provocations for a cultural, technological, and scholarly phenomenon. *Information, Communication & Society*, 15 (5), 662–679.

Chengalur-Smith, I.N., Ballou, D.P. & Pazer, H.L. (1999) The impact of data quality information on decision making: An exploratory analysis. *IEEE Transactions on Knowledge and Data Engineering*, 11 (6), 853–864.

Crawford, K. (2016) Can an algorithm be agonistic? Ten scenes from life in calculated publics. *Science, Technology & Human Values*, 41 (1), 77–92.

Criado, J.L., Sandoval-Almazan, R. & Gil-Garcia, J.R. (2013) Government innovation through social media. *Government Information Quarterly*, 30, 319–326.

Drew, C. (2016) Data science ethics in government. *Philosophical Transactions: Series A, Mathematical, Physical, and Engineering Sciences*, 374 (2083).

Dutch Scientific Council. (2016) *Big Data in een vrije en veilige samenleving*. Wetenschappelijke Raad voor het Regeringsbeleid, 95, Den Haag: WRR.

Gil-Garcia, J.R., Pardo, T.A. & Nam, T. (2015) What makes a city smart? Identifying core components and proposing an integrative and comprehensive conceptualization. *Information Polity*, 20 (1), 61–87.

Gil-Garcia, J.R., Pardo, T.A. & Nam, T. (2016a) A comprehensive view of the 21st century city: Smartness as technologies and innovation in urban contexts. In: Gil-Garcia, J.R., Pardo, T.A. & Nam, T. (eds.) *Smarter as the New Urban Agenda: A Comprehensive View of the 21st Century City*. Springer International Publishing, ebook, pp. 1–19.

Gil-Garcia, J.R., Pardo, T.A. & Nam, T. (eds.) (2016b) *Smarter as the New Urban Agenda: A Comprehensive View of the 21st Century City*. Springer International Publishing, ebook.

Gonzalez-Bailon, S. (2013) Social science in the era of big data. *Policy and Internet*, 5 (2), 147–160.

Harrison, C., Eckman, B., Hamilton, R., Hartswick, P., Kalagnanam, J., Paraszczak, J. & Williams, P. (2010) Foundations for smarter cities. *IBM Journal of Research and Development*, 54 (4), 1–16, DOI: 10.1147/JRD.2010.2048257

Hashem, I.A.T., Anuar, N.B., Chang, V. & Chiroma, H. (2016) The role of big data in smart city. *International Journal of Information Management*, 36 (5), 748–758.

Janssen, M. & Kuk, G. (2016) The challenges and limits of big data algorithms in technocratic governance. *Government Information Quarterly*, 33, 371–377.

Janssen, M., Matheus, R. & Zuiderwijk, A. (2015) Big and open linked data (BOLD) to create smart cities and citizens: Insights from smart energy and mobility cases. *Electronic Government*, 79–90.

Janssen, M. & van den Hoven, J. (2015) Big and Open Linked Data (BOLD) in government: A challenge to transparency and privacy? *Government Information Quarterly*, 32, 363–368.

Kitchin, R. (2014) *The Data Revolution: Big Data, Open Data, Data Infrastructures & Their Consequences*. London: Sage.

Kitchin, R. (2016) The ethics of smart cities and urban science 374. *Philosophical Transactions of the Royal Society A: Mathematical, Physical and Engineering Sciences*. Available from: http://dx.doi.org/10.1098/rsta.2016.0115

Lindstrom, M. (2016) *Small Data: The Tiny Clues That Uncover Huge Trends*. London: John Murray Learning.

166 Areas of public sector reform

Macke, J., Casagrande, R.M., Sarate, J.A.R. & Silva, K.A. (2018) Smart city and quality of life: Citizens' perception in a Brazilian case study. *Journal of Cleaner Production*, 182, 717–726.

Manovich, L. (2011) Trending: the promises and the challenges of big social data. In: Gold, M.K. (ed.) *Debates in the Digital Humanities*. Minneapolis, MN: University of Minnesota Press.

Manyika, J., Chui, M., Brown, B., Bughin, J., Dobbs, R., Roxburgh, C. & Hung Byers, A. (May 2011) *Big Data: The Next Frontier for Innovation, Competition and Productivity*. McKinsey Global Institute.

Matheus, R., Janssen, M.F.W.H.A. & Maheshwari, D. (2018) Data science empowering the public: Data-driven dashboards for transparent and accountable decision-making in smart cities. *Government Information Quarterly*. Available from: https://doi.org/10.1016/j.giq.2018.01.006

Mayer-Schönberger, V. & Cukier, K. (2013) *Big Data: A Revolution That Will Transform How We Live, Work and Think*. London: John Murray.

Meijer, A.J. (2015) *Bestuur in de datapolis: Slimme stad, blije burger?* Den Haag: Boom Bestuurskunde.

Meijer, A.J. (2016) Smart city governance: A local emergent perspective. In: Gil-Garcia, J.R., Pardo, T.A. & Nam, T. (eds.) *Smarter as the New Urban Agenda: A Comprehensive View of the 21st Century City*. Springer International Publishing, ebook, pp. 73–85.

Meijer, A.J. & Rodriguez Bolivar, M.P.R. (2016) Governing the smart city: A review of the literature on smart urban governance. *International Review of Administrative Sciences*, 82 (2), 392–408.

Miller, K. (16 March 2016) *San José Improves Traffic Safety with Data*. Data-Smart City Solutions. Ash Center for Democratic Governance and Innovation, Harvard Kennedy School. Available from: https://datasmart.ash.harvard.edu/news/article/san-jose-tackles-traffic with-data-802 [accessed 14 January 2019].

Naphade, M., Banavar, G., Harrison, C., Paraszczak, J. & Morris, R. (2011) Smarter cities and their innovation challenges. *Computer*, 44 (6), 32–39.

New Zealand Data Futures Forum (NZDFF). (2014) The following three discussion papers were published by the NZDFF and can be downloaded from their website (www.nzdatafutures.org.nz/): 1) New Zealand's Data Future; 2) Navigating the Data Future: Four Guiding Principles; and 3) Harnessing the Economic and Social Power of Data.

Nissenbaum, H. (2010) *Privacy in Context: Technology, Policy, and the Integrity of Social Life*. Stanford, CA: Stanford University Press.

Nissenbaum, H. (2011) A contextual approach to privacy online. *Daedalus*, 140 (4), 32–48.

OECD. (18 June 2013) *Exploring Data-Driven Innovation as a New Source of Growth: Mapping the Policy Issues Raised by 'Big Data'*. Paris: OECD, DSTI/ICCP(2012)9/Final.

Pasquale, F. (2015) *The Black Box Society: The Secret Algorithms That Control Money and Information*. Cambridge, MA: Harvard University Press.

Pentland, A. (2009) Reality mining of mobile communications: Toward a new deal on data. In: *World Economic Forum (2009) The Global Information Technology Report 2008–2009*, pp. 75–80.

Pentland, A. (2014) *Social Physics: How Good Ideas Spread: The Lessons from a New Science*. New York, NY: Penguin Press.

Polonetsky, J., Tene, O. & Jerome, J. (September 2014) *Benefit-Risk Analysis for Big Data Projects*. Washington, DC: Future of Privacy Forum. Available from: https://www.futureofprivacy.org [accessed 23 June 2018].

Schintler, L.A. & Kulkarni, R. (2014) Big data for policy analysis: The good, the bad, and the ugly. *Review of Policy Research*, 31 (4), 343–348.

Schroeder, R. (2014) Big data: Towards a more scientific social science and humanities? In: Graham, M. & Dutton, W.H. (eds.) *Society and the Internet: How Networks of Information and Communication Are Changing Our Lives*. Oxford: Oxford University Press, pp. 164–176.

Scoblete, G. (2018) Welcome to the age of smart cities. *TWICE*, 33 (1), 40–41.

Shenk, D. (1997) *Data Smog: Surviving the Information Glut*. New York, NY: HarperCollins Publishers.

UK House of Commons Science and Technology Committee. (2016) *The Big Data Dilemma Report*. London: UK House of Commons Science and Technology Committee.

United Nations. (November 2014) *A World That Counts: Mobilising the Data Revolution for Sustainable Development*. Independent Expert Advisory Group on a Data Revolution for Sustainable Development.

van Dijck, J. (2014) Datafication, dataism and dataveillance: Big data between scientific paradigm and ideology. *Surveillance & Society*, 12 (2), 197–208.

van Zoonen, L. (2016) Privacy concerns in smart cities. *Government Information Quarterly*, 33, 472–480.

Vinod Kumar, T.M. (ed.) (2017) *Smart Economy in Smart Cities International Collaborative Research: Ottawa, St. Louis, Stuttgart, Bologna, Cape Town, Nairobi, Dakar, Lagos, New Delhi, Varanasi, Vijayawada, Kozhikode, Hong Kong*. Singapore: Imprint Springer.

Further reading

Borgman, C.L. (2015) *Big Data, Little Data, No Data: Scholarship in the Networked World*. Cambridge, MA: Massachusetts Institute of Technology Press.

Gil-Garcia, J.R., Pardo, T.A. & Nam, T. (eds.) (2016b) *Smarter as the New Urban Agenda: A Comprehensive View of the 21st Century City*. Springer International Publishing, ebook.

Lane, J., Stodden, V., Bender, S. & Nissenbaum, H. (eds.) (2014) *Privacy, Big Data, and the Public Good: Frameworks for Engagement*. New York, NY: Cambridge University Press.

Mayer-Schönberger, V. & Cukier, K. (2013) *Big Data: A Revolution That Will Transform How We Live, Work and Think*. London: John Murray.

Meijer, A.J. & Bolivar, M.P.R. (2016) Governing the smart city: A review of the literature on smart urban governance. *International Review of Administrative Sciences*, 82 (2), 392–408.

Nissenbaum, H. (2010) *Privacy in Context: Technology, Policy, and the Integrity of Social Life*. Stanford, CA: Stanford University Press.

Nissenbaum, H. (2011) A contextual approach to privacy online. *Daedalus*, 140 (4), 32–48.

Pentland, A. (2014) *Social Physics: How Good Ideas Spread: The Lessons from a New Science*. New York, NY: Penguin Press.

7 Participatory democracy and public engagement

Learning objectives

By the end of this chapter you should be able to:

- Understand the difference between traditional vertical forms of public engagement enabled by digital technologies and data and emerging horizontal forms of participatory governance facilitated by digital technologies and data;
- Identify a number of issues and barriers to these new technology- and data-enabled participatory forms of governance; and
- Identify strategies to promote new participatory ways of working in digital government and governance relationships.

Key points of this chapter

- Many research findings around innovative forms of e-democracy in the 1990s were highly speculative and technology driven;
- Governments have been using digital technologies to conduct many democratic experiments with ambitions of achieving electronic democracy or "teledemocracy"; however, most of these Internet-enabled democratic experiments have been following an add-on strategy to existing government institutions and procedures;
- Several scholars have identified opportunities for hybrid technology-enabled democratic reform of citizen-government relationships, containing elements of both participatory and representative forms of democracy and including more actively engaged citizens;
- Empirical research suggests a digital technology- and data-enabled renovation of government institutions, instead of innovation of those institutions (Bekkers, 2005);
- Empirical research suggests that citizens may not always want to engage with government via social media channels but may prefer other channels for (digital) engagement with government;
- Networked citizens socially construct whatever "public good" means to them and use digital technologies and data in those situations where they

Participatory democracy   169

feel they can make a difference: in other words, they don't need to go to government agencies (first) to do so;

- Innovative uses of digital technologies and the sharing of data allow governments to gather information, knowledge, expertise and assistance from a diverse range of citizen experts and use these informational sources for co-creating and co-designing better public policy- and decision-making and more effective public services; and
- More robust empirical research is needed in order to understand and explain the use of digital technologies and data in emerging horizontal participatory forms of governance.

Key terms

- *Direct democracy*: the citizen is directly and actively involved in democratic practices.
- *Virtual public sphere*: a new public domain on the Internet.
- *Social media/social networking/social technologies*: web services that allow users to create online profiles and that also enable user-generated content, crowd-sourcing and online collaboration (Boyd & Ellison, 2008).
- *Government 2.0*: the use of Web 2.0 applications, such as social media, in digital government. This concept focuses on government as a platform: Internet technology is used as a collaborative governance platform between government and citizens for active user participation, harnessing collective intelligence and using the principle of open access (O'Reilly, 2005).
- *Networked citizen*: enabled by digital technologies, the citizen-user as the driver of democratic innovation through self-actualised networking with other citizens, government organizations and other stakeholders (Loader & Mercea, 2012a).
- *Participatory governance*: horizontal, decentralised, collaborative and open practices where government agencies, together with citizens, solve public policy problems and create public good.

Introduction

Ever since the arrival of the Internet in the early 1990s, scholars and practitioners have been intrigued by the innovation potential of digital technologies and data, including Web 2.0, social media, smart technologies, open government data and new innovative data uses, to address existing democratic deficits in the public sector (e.g. van de Donk & Tops, 1992; Schalken, 1998; Chadwick, 2006; Chadwick & Howard, 2008; Coleman & Blumler, 2001; Dutton, 2012; Hague & Loader, 1999b; Loader & Mercea, 2012b; Noveck, 2009; Noveck, 2015). Ranging from visions about direct democracy, electronic democracy, a virtual public sphere, a civic commons, deliberative democracy, Government 2.0, participatory democracy and collaborative governance, fast-moving digital technology and data developments are widely expected to enable a paradigm

170   *Areas of public sector reform*

shift from traditional representative, spectator, and passive forms of citizenship towards more participatory, empowered and active forms of citizenship (e.g. Noveck, 2015; Coleman, 1999; Coleman & Blumler, 2009; Dutton, 2012; Loader & Mercea, 2012b; Mergel, 2013). For example, Noveck (2015) points to the opportunity for governments to use digital technologies and data in order to shift from a top-down and closed public policy-making approach *for* citizens towards more horizontal, decentralised, collaborative and open practices where government agencies, together *with* citizens, solve public policy problems and create public good.

In general, digital technologies and data are seen by governments as strong contributors to enhanced democratic participation and engagement in many respects, including better informed public decision-making; more effective public policy, government service provision and public engagement; enhanced collaboration and the development of stronger communities; improved social and democratic inclusion; stronger civic culture; more open innovation and collective forms of data sharing for achieving public good and enhanced digital collectivism and citizen activism (Chadwick & Howard, 2008; Loader & Mercea, 2012b; Mergel, 2013; Noveck, 2009; Noveck, 2015; White, 2012). However, in practice, these innovative public sector reform ideas turn out to be rather complex to achieve (Bekkers, 2005; Loader & Mercea, 2012a; Snellen, 2005).

Consequently, in this chapter, we explore and discuss scholarly insights into the use of digital technologies and data in digital government relationships to establish innovative participatory forms of governance, the impact of these innovations and their outcomes. In so doing, we predominantly focus on potential new forms of active citizenship in digital government relationships with executive government; this implies that we do not consider in great detail the political aspects, including the representative democracy dimension, of these technology-enabled forms of participatory governance in this chapter.[1]

Firstly, we discuss some of the early scholarly ideas about the Internet displacing traditional representative democratic systems, leading to new forms of direct democracy and active citizenship. Secondly, we consider second-generation scholarly thinking about the democratic reform potential of digital technologies in the public sector, which are often referred to as Web 2.0 and Government 2.0; here, we discuss the introduction and use of social media in digital government relationships in particular in order to establish more interactive and participatory forms of governance and, with that, more effective forms of public engagement. Thirdly, we explore scholarly insights into emerging innovative, networked forms of participatory and collaborative governance in digital government relationships, including modes of governance, such as the "Fifth Estate" (Dutton, 2009), which can be even beyond any direct involvement of government. Fourthly, we discuss emerging issues and barriers around governments' use of digital technologies and data to establish participatory and collaborative forms of governance as well as more effective public

Participatory democracy 171

engagement. And finally, we consider some strategies and design principles in order to achieve the public sector reform ambitions of enhanced participatory democracy.

Towards direct democracy?

Many scholars have claimed that the Internet will lead to enhanced forms of democracy and democratic citizenship, such as a new virtual public sphere strongly aligned with the thinking of philosopher Jürgen Habermas (e.g. van de Donk & Tops, 1992; Schalken, 1998; Hague & Loader, 1999b; Chadwick, 2006; Ward & Vedel, 2006). Revolutionary ideas about an Internet-enabled paradigm shift to overhaul traditional representative forms of democracy and adopt new virtual forms of direct democracy where the newly empowered citizen would be actively engaged with politics and the wider public sector, cutting out the political and parliamentary middle men (cf Coleman, 1999), were very popular at the time (e.g. Frissen, 1998; Frissen, 1999; van de Donk & Tops, 1992; Hague & Loader, 1999a; Hague & Loader, 1999b; Moore, 1999; Grönlund, 2001; Norris & Reddick, 2013). For instance, many scholars introduced concepts in order to express this new technology-enabled democratic vision, such as electronic democracy or e-democracy (see Chapter 1), teledemocracy, cyber democracy, virtual democracy, e-participation, e-engagement and digital democracy; however, only few authors actually specify what they mean by these terms (Norris & Reddick, 2013).

As an example, as one of the few scholars who does define electronic democracy, Moore (1999: 55) understands it as:

> the use of electronic networking to bring about a more direct form of democracy, to short-circuit the representative process and look more to net-supported plebiscites and "official" online debates in deciding issues of government policy.

In his view, electronic democracy holds out the promise of cutting through bureaucratic red tape, reducing the role of corrupt politicians and special interests and allowing the will of the people to be expressed (Moore, 1999: 55). Indeed, "everyone a pamphleteer" has been an iconic claim about the Internet and its impact on democratic citizenship since the early 1990s (Benkler, 2006: 177).

However, based on a review of available scholarly literature in the early days of Internet technology, van de Donk and Tops (1992) conclude that the research findings are highly speculative and seem to be technology driven. Moreover, Schalken (1998: 159) empirically observes that, although governments around the world have been using digital technologies to conduct many democratic experiments with ambitions of achieving electronic democracy or teledemocracy, most of these Internet-enabled democratic experiments have been following an add-on strategy to existing government institutions and procedures.

172 *Areas of public sector reform*

Since then, digital technologies and data are widely considered to offer new opportunities to respond to some fundamental problems with the democratic deficit of the contemporary state, demonstrated for example by low voter turnout in elections, low levels of (pluralist) public participation in democratic processes and activities (e.g. public hearings, public submissions to draft policy and legislation) and a lack of trust in government amongst large groups of the population in many countries around the world (Castells, 1996; Hague & Loader, 1999b; Fischer, 2012; Froomkin, 2004; Bekkers, 2005; Norris & Reddick, 2013; Mergel, 2013). Consequently, a public sector reform ambition of achieving technology- and data-enabled participatory democracy is seen by many governments as an appropriate response to these democratic deficit problems as it gives all citizens an equal opportunity to participate in public decision-making and, with that, enhances the legitimacy of the contemporary state (Snellen, 2005; Hague & Loader, 1999a; Bekkers, 2005).

Moreover, governments consider the application of digital technologies and data as an opportunity to support the increasingly important horizontal, networked governance dimension of post-NPM systems, including in digital government relationships with citizens (Christensen & Laegreid, 2012; Snellen, 2005). This then could not only lead to new forms of co-production of public policy and public services in technology-enabled relationships between government organizations and active citizens, but also enhance the quality and effectiveness of public policy and service provision (Bekkers, 2005).

Box 7.1   Better Reykjavik website in Iceland

Better Reykjavik is a participatory website operated by the non-profit organization Citizens Foundation, where citizens can propose, debate and prioritise their ideas on how to improve the city of Reykjavik's operations and services. Each month, the Reykjavik City Council debates the 10 to 15 ideas that citizens have listed as top priorities. More than 70,000 people have used the website, out of a total population of 120,000, and over 6,800 ideas have been submitted. More than 3,000 ideas have been formally reviewed, and almost 1,000 have been accepted since 2011. In so doing, around 18 million euros have been allocated to projects since 2011.

Furthermore, from this latter perspective of governments' responding to the democratic deficit, instead of replacing political institutions, several scholars have identified opportunities for hybrid technology-enabled democratic reform of citizen- government relationships, containing elements of both participatory and representative forms of democracy and including more actively

Participatory democracy 173

engaged citizens (e.g. Hague & Loader, 1999a; Raab *et al*, 1996; Coleman, 1999; Coleman & Blumler, 2001; Noveck, 2009; Bekkers, 2005; Snellen, 2005).

Box 7.2   Participatory lawmaking in Taiwan

Taiwan is a digital consultation platform hosting a range of applications where people can participate in online discussions. Built in 2015, the platform enables citizens, civil society organizations, experts and elected officials to discuss proposed laws via its website as well as in face-to-face meetings and hackathons. Its goal is to help policy-makers make decisions that gain legitimacy through consultation (Horton, 2018). Taiwan uses open-source tools for soliciting proposals, sharing information and holding polls. One of its key digital discussion platforms is Pol.is, where topics are put up for debate. People can propose an idea, post comments on the topic and up-vote or down-vote other participants' comments. However, people cannot reply to each other's comments, which reduces the motivation for negative contributions. Also, a map of all participants in the debate is created on the basis of the up-votes and down-votes, which clusters together those people who have voted similarly. This then incentivises people to draft comments that will win votes from both sides of a divide. Moreover, people stop wasting time on divisive statements. In August 2018, although online consultations and petitions are not legally binding, the platform had been used in 26 cases, with 80 percent resulting in government action.

For instance, in 1999, Coleman (1999) proposed implementing the following Internet-enabled political mechanisms in UK representative government in order to realise forms of direct public deliberation and enhance democratic governance as a result (Coleman, 1999: 201–203):

- *The creation of a virtual public space*: to enable citizens to inform themselves about issues of the day, scrutinise the workings of Parliament and government and enter into dialogue with decision-makers in ways currently available to elites but rarely to average citizens;
- *Online policy proposals*: a constitutional requirement for all local councils, national parliaments and assemblies and government departments to publish policy proposals online. All proposed legislation should be accessible in the same way, not just so that citizens can inform themselves, but so that decision-makers can be informed by citizens;
- *Online consultation*: regular pre-legislative online consultations, from the white paper to the draft bill stage, and again during the standing committee

174 *Areas of public sector reform*

stage, in which the public will have its own virtual chamber to deliberate on both the principles and the details of major legislation;

- *Public involvement in select committees*: direct submission by citizens to select committees. Proceedings could be webcast, with regular opportunities for members of the public to feed into inquiries, both as invited guests via closed discussion lists and within an open forum, accounts of which could be summarised and published as appendices to Select Committee reports;
- *Online conferences*: the running of regular online conferences, hosted by Parliament, enabling wider groups of citizens to participate in public policy deliberation over a longer period of time;
- *Interactive information*: the provision of regularly updated, interactive information about Parliament, including deliberative fora for citizens to exchange ideas and perspectives with one another on various public policy issues; and
- *Online evaluation*: online deliberative evaluations of public policy areas could be established, involving random samples of the population. Online participants would control their own agendas, acting rather like select committees in choosing aspects of their particular policy areas to investigate and discuss.

In an attempt to separate popular rhetoric about new technology-enabled forms of participatory democracy from empirical reality, Wilhelm (1999) conducted a content analysis of a random sample of postings to political Usenet newsgroups on the Internet in order to explore whether these digital exchanges demonstrated characteristics of democratic deliberation. However, as his empirical findings were a range of overlapping, short-lived conversations, usually amongst like-minded individuals, his conclusions were that public debate in online forums would not provide governments with the required democratic input or influence to substantially improve public policy- and decision-making, let alone realizing the ideal of participatory democracy (Wilhelm, 1999).

More in general, Hague and Loader (1999a) point to the size and complexity of modern nation-states, which makes public sector reform ambitions around participatory democracy and more active involvement of citizens and their actual influence on public decision-making not very realistic. Similarly, Bekkers (2005) points to the lack of empirical research and, with that, robust evidence for scholarly claims around emerging new forms of either direct democracy or innovative forms of participatory governance. If anything, digital technologies and data are enabling the *renovation* of government institutions, but not *innovation* of those institutions or a revolution, according to Bekkers (2005).

However, this doesn't mean that experimenting with digital technologies and data to improve digital government relationships in a democratic sense, such as Coleman's (1999) proposals mentioned earlier, would not be very useful (Noveck, 2015; Hague & Loader, 1999a; Hague & Loader, 1999b). Moreover, we need to be aware that the introduction and use of digital technologies and data in order to achieve participatory democracy in digital government

Participatory democracy 175

relationships need to be observed as socio-technical constructs which can have multiple, context-relative outcomes (Malina, 1999). For instance, based on his personal involvement in several technology-enabled democratic experiments, Aikens (1999) sees the potential of digital technologies to promote various context-relative democratic outcomes in their facilitation of "multiple gateways to socialised public intelligence." We further explore Aikens' statement in the remaining sections of this chapter.

The use of social media in digital government

With the advent of social media platforms around the world, such as Facebook, YouTube, Snapchat, Twitter, WhatsApp, QQ, WeChat, Google, Tumblr, Instagram, Pinterest, wikis and the blogosphere, we can observe a second generation of scholarly interest in promoting participatory democracy and enhancing active citizenship in digital government relationships (Loader & Mercea, 2012a; Loader & Mercea, 2012b; Mergel, 2013; Coleman & Blumler, 2009). This renewed scholarly interest had a lot to do with the introduction of social media for public engagement in digital government relationships with citizens, a development which is sometimes referred to as Government 2.0; founded on the basis of new, so-called Web 2.0 principles, social media are Web 2.0 applications that use existing Internet technology as a collaborative platform for active user participation, harnessing collective intelligence and using the principle of open access (O'Reilly, 2005). A well-known example is the online encyclopedia Wikipedia.[2]

According to Mergel (2013), the terms "social media," "social technologies," and "social networking" are often used interchangeably to describe "web services that allow users to create an online profile and that also enable user-generated content, crowd-sourcing, and online collaboration" (Boyd & Ellison, 2008, in: Mergel, 2013: 12). For instance, in contrast to traditional media, social media allow for bidirectional interaction in real time, reach larger audiences and have users who co-create and share content (Mergel & Greeves, 2013). The four main activities that social media promote are mingling (rather than lecturing), networked collaboration, bidirectional communication and community building (Mergel & Greeves, 2013). In general, governments have the following three main drivers for using social media in their digital government relationships with citizens (Mergel & Greeves, 2013: 34):

1   Connectedness with citizens;
2   Expectations of "digital natives," or young people preferring to use social media in order to engage with government; and
3   Expectations around government agency cost reductions and customer service increases made possible by social media tools.

However, although governments may have invested in particular social media platforms for their digital engagement with citizens, such as Facebook, Twitter

176 *Areas of public sector reform*

and Instagram, we need to observe that the popularity of these social media is rapidly changing, especially amongst young people. Also, the rapid uptake of social media platforms in countries with large populations, such as Indonesia, China and India, can lead to rapid shifts in the worldwide popularity rankings of social media. In other words, citizens may have developed a different social media preference for their digital engagement with government than the social media platforms governments have invested in for public engagement in digital government relationships.

Also, Loader and Mercea (2012a) warn us of the fact that citizens' access to a social networking site does not in itself determine their engagement with government. Another consideration may be that citizens do not want to engage with government via a (particular) social media platform but may prefer other digital channels. Empirical research in New Zealand indeed confirms that citizens' use of social media in their digital engagement with government about government service provision is almost non-existent (Lips, Barlow & Woods, 2016). According to Coleman and Blumler (2009), this raises an important additional design question for public engagement in digital government relationships in the sense that this is not only about how government should engage with citizens, but also about how citizens should engage with government.

In general, Rainie and Wellman (2012) observe that the so-called triple revolution of converging and increasingly blurring uses of social media, the Internet and mobile technologies and devices has created a new information and media ecology in which increasingly networked individuals operate. This information and media ecology is distinct from the past in the following ways (Rainie & Wellman, 2012: 226–235):

- *The dramatic growth of information*: more and more information is generated and circulated at a rapid pace;
- *The differentiation of information use*: as all this information material is displayed and distributed online and as mobile devices and cloud computing allow Internet users access to media and data from anyplace at any time, users exercise more choice in their media consumption;
- *The greater variety of information*: on the one hand, there is a development that fewer organizations than before control traditional media, making it less diverse; on the other hand, a counterbalancing development leads to a situation where the Internet and mobile news apps enhance people's capacity to obtain diverse information, as does their involvement in multiple social networks;
- *The acceleration of information flows*: with high-speed broadband and always-accessible mobile devices, information flows through people's lives more quickly than at any time since most people lived in small villages. Also, the pace of communication, such as via emails, updates from social networking profiles, tweets, text messages and mobile phone calls, has accelerated and intensified;

- *Finding relevant information with greater ease:* the convenience of search engines like Google, information hubs like Wikipedia and other easily accessible sources gives people the instant ability to pull together masses of information directly related to every query of the moment. It also helps that people can set up alerts and receive personalised information of relevance to their individual preferences and tastes;
- *Emergence of new signposts of credible and trustworthy sources:* new markers of trustworthiness and credibility include the increasing popularity of user ranking, rating, commenting, tagging systems, Facebook's "like" and "recommend" buttons and personalised recommender systems built on aggregated user data and algorithms;
- *The intermixing of information and communication:* the social experience that underlies people's consumption of networked information also deeply connects it to communication. This then also changes and deepens the interplay of information flows, especially the feedback process between institutional information and interpersonal information becoming a continuous cycle to pin down and assess information (e.g. people obtaining information from their friends, then going to the Internet to check it and going back to their friends to discuss it, etc.); and
- *People use a number of strategies to help manage the abundance of information that is available to them both online and offline:* strategies include people's reliance on search engines, bookmarks, and tags; people developing ways to alert them to new information about issues that matter to them; people setting up websites with customised information and people choosing those they want to follow on social networking sites. Also, people exploit both institutional and interpersonal information to help them with their everyday decisions.

It is within this new information and media ecology, and increasingly also data ecology as a result of converging smart technologies (see also Chapter 6), that scholars observe the emergence of a networked, citizen-centred perspective providing opportunities to connect the private sphere of autonomous citizens to a multitude of chosen public spaces (Loader & Mercea, 2012a). This new networked citizen–perspective is a significant departure from the traditional, vertical government perspective of government providing a pre-defined public space for rational deliberation by dutiful citizens; instead, there is a focus on:

> the role of the citizen-user as the driver of democratic innovation through the self-actualised networking of citizens engaged in lifestyle and identity politics.
>
> (Loader & Mercea, 2012a: 2)

According to Coleman and Blumler (2009), this new form of citizenship has the potential to compete with established traditional forms of democratic citizenship, such as those related to representative democracy.

178 *Areas of public sector reform*

Several scholars have identified the following inherent democratic capabilities of networked social media, also compared to traditional mass media (Loader & Mercea, 2012a: 3):

- *Networked social media have the potential to reconfigure communicative power relations*: by making use of ever-easier social networking and user-centred innovation, citizens are able to challenge the monopoly control of media production and dissemination by state and commercial institutions;
- *Networked social media are accessible to most citizens*: in general, social media are perceived to be technologically, financially and legally accessible to most citizens living in advanced societies;
- *Networked social media enable citizens to share and publish their own perspective*: the citizen no longer has to be a passive consumer of government information or mass media news but is instead enabled to challenge discourses, share alternative perspectives and publish their own opinions; and
- *Networked social media can facilitate mass collaboration of citizens and government agencies*: the openness of social media platforms facilitates the potential of mass collaboration of citizens and government organizations who become the source of new innovations and ideas in democratic practices.

Although governments mostly use social media for the traditional activities of disseminating government information and, to a lesser extent, interaction with citizens (e.g. Kavanaugh *et al*, 2012; Lips, Barlow & Woods, 2016), there are a myriad of practical examples where governments use social media for networked collaboration or even empowerment of citizens (e.g. Noveck, 2009; Noveck, 2015; Mergel, 2013).

Box 7.3   Crowdsourcing flood reports from Twitter in Jakarta

Each year, the city of Jakarta experiences severe flooding during the rainy season. In 2014, researchers at the University of Wollongong in Australia teamed up with the Jakarta Emergency Management Agency and Twitter Inc. in the PetaJakarta project to develop a real-time map of flooding in the city based on crowdsourced flood reports from Twitter. This crowdsourced information was used by the Jakarta Emergency Management Agency to cross-validate formal reports of flooding from traditional sources, supporting the creation of information for flood assessment, response and management in real time.

However, based on a number of early empirical studies, Loader and Mercea (2012a: 4–5) express the following reasons for being cautious in proclaiming the democratic potential of using social media:

Participatory democracy 179

- Individual preferences for social networking sites reveal an unequal spread of social ties with a few giant commercial nodes, such as Facebook, YouTube and Google, attracting the majority of social media users. This could be seen to grant them a disproportionate authoritative influence over information sources for users, such as via search engine ranking algorithms, which privilege access to information;
- Although there is only limited empirical research available about social media use in the public sector, available empirical findings suggest that the most active political users are social movement activists, politicians, political party representatives, cognisant citizens and those who are already fully committed to political causes (Bengtsson & Christensen, 2012). Even the potential of citizen journalism in the public sphere appears to be restricted by the domination of a limited number of political bloggers;
- Instead of facilitating an increasing host of active citizen-users around public policy issues, social media use more typically focuses on other societal activities, such as online shopping, online entertainment and communication with family and friends (e.g. Mascheroni, 2012); and
- More detailed empirical research of citizens' actual use of social media in the public domain is needed before we can assess their democratic affordances.

The latter observation reconfirms our discussion thus far about the need for robust empirical research in order to better understand and explain the actual use of social media in socio-technical assemblages within the context of digital government relationships. However, it also reconfirms that it is that same context that determines the outcomes of mutual shaping processes around the use of social media in digital government relationships with citizens. Consequently, these outcomes are likely to be contingent, multiple and different for different contexts of digital government and its relationships with citizens. Based on the empirical insights we do have available, it does not seem the case thus far that governments have been successful in realising their public sector reform ambition of supporting and enhancing participatory democracy for all citizens.

Towards new forms of participatory governance

Increasingly, the emerging data, information and media ecology in which networked citizens operate is both fundamentally challenging existing government institutions and offering innovative opportunities for change towards networked participatory forms of governance. It is in this light that several scholars have identified an urgent need to move away from what they see as "eroding" traditional government institutions and procedures, towards a better-equipped participatory governance model for governing in the digital age (Noveck, 2015; Coleman & Blumler, 2009). The necessity of this shift is the more urgent in their view now that citizens are taking public matters into their own hands by using digital technologies and data in collaborative

180 *Areas of public sector reform*

peer-to-peer communities, which not only expose the limitations of contemporary government but also significantly reduce its legitimacy. Coleman and Blumler (2009) describe this current deficit in digital government relationships in more detail as follows:

> Frustrated and disappointed by government consultations in which they are not being genuinely consulted, media discussions in which the public voice is marginalised or manipulated and e-democracy projects which pay more attention to technological than political efficacy, the public – or, at least, significant numbers within it – have taken matters into their own hands and improvised a series of open-source solutions to the problems of social interaction, some of which have significant political ramifications. And yet fundamental features [of government institutions, ML] persist, foremost amongst which is the need to connect collective will formation to the exercise of state power.
>
> (Coleman & Blumler, 2009: 178)

In other words, networked citizens using the digital technology and data affordances of the current smart revolution have options nowadays. They use combinations of data and information from the Internet and compare those with reliable sources, such as friends and family, to make a difference in their own lives (Dutton, 2012; Rainie & Wellman, 2012). For example, networked citizens know which personalised education strategy, teacher and school are most suitable to meet the learning needs of their children; they know their personal health situation via their Fitbit, for example, and the best ways for them to deal with that health situation, and do not need to be told by their GP first; they know where they will get stuck in traffic that morning, upload their own traffic data and observations to the collective data pool via a smartphone app, and can learn via the same app which alternative route would be best for them to get to work; they have data and information about the condition of their immediate natural environment and know about a range of strategies to care best for it and they don't need to know, or care, about government for these insights and knowledge. That is, however, if they are in the luxurious position of being a networked citizen and not a victim of multiple digital divides for whatever reason (see Chapter 9).

Networked citizens socially construct whatever "public good" means to them and go where they can make a difference: in other words, they don't need to go to government agencies (first) to do so (e.g. Dutton, 2012). Moreover, they increasingly rely on the Internet as a collaborative platform for data sharing, information, connecting with people, expertise and exchange of other resources. We can observe plenty of practical examples where citizens of all ages support particular public good causes, often single issues, and collaborate with others primarily via open-source digital networks and an open data pool or "data commons" to achieve that goal (see for instance Box 7.4).

Box 7.4 Wheelmap.org

Wheelmap.org (https://wheelmap.org/search) is a crowdsourced real-time map, accessible via a website and an app, where anyone can contribute and mark public places around the world according to their wheelchair accessibility. People can mark public places on the basis of a traffic light system of green for fully wheelchair accessible places, yellow for partly wheelchair accessible places, and red for places that are not wheelchair accessible. They can also add photos of entrances to public places and public toilets. If a public place has not been marked yet, it has a grey marker on the map. Wheelmap.org is run by the non-profit organization Sozialhelden e.V. and is based on the world map OpenStreetMap. All datasets are published under the Open Database License, which makes them available for use by anyone.

Dutton (2009) calls this digital technology- and data-enabled development towards new horizontal modes of governance across sectors of increasingly networked societies, the Fifth Estate, as discussed in Chapter 3; as a result of reconfiguring their access to alternative sources of data, information, people and other resources, networked citizens can move across, undermine and go beyond the boundaries of existing government institutions, thereby opening new ways of increasing the accountability of government, politicians, press, experts and other loci of power and influence (Dutton, 2012: 584). According to Dutton (2012), a frequent response to this technology-enabled challenge from traditional institutions, such as government or the press media, is to suggest that they will retain their central position in present times. However, he also points out that uses of digital technologies and data result in different outcomes in different contexts and that no single actor is in control of how these Internet-enabled technologies are being used (Dutton, 2012) Instead, a pluralistic interplay among an ecology of actors who are socially constructing technologies as part of socio-technical assemblages within the context of digital government has given rise to the Fifth Estate and its role in governance (Dutton, 2012).

An important question then becomes how government could tap into this emerging-networked, open and collaborative data, information and media ecology and strategically align itself with these networked citizens to achieve shared public good objectives and ambitions? Noveck (2015) has some possible answers to this question and is convinced that traditional government will need to change. She points out that, as a result of professionalisation in traditional government institutions, the following three barriers are standing in the way of opening up government institutions in order to establish participatory forms of governance with citizens (Noveck, 2015: 29–30):

182 Areas of public sector reform

1   The "myth of spectator citizenship": the belief that only professional public servants possess the requisite skills and abilities to govern. Expertise is possessed only by elites with professional credentials;
2   A top-down decision-making culture: public professionals have cultivated a decision-making culture that is top-down in orientation, unnecessarily complex, and lacks the mind-set or skill set for experimentation. In accordance with traditional Weberian conceptions of the bureaucratic state, the dominant belief is that professionals trained in the science of governing can discover, in linear ways, the right solutions to virtually any problem; and
3   The lack of tangible "mental models" for knowing what the alternative to this professionalised way of governance or a smarter way of governing would be.

Traditionally, with barriers existing between citizens and professionals who govern, make public decisions, legislate, make public policies and deliver government services, governing has been predominantly the domain of an elite group of professionals working behind closed doors (Noveck, 2015). And yet, traditional vertical approaches to public decision-making are not designed to provide agile responses to increasingly complex and dynamic public policy problems. Consequently, Noveck (2015) considers traditional forms of centralised, hierarchical and closed-door governing out of date and suggests an alternative form of networked, decentralised, horizontal and open governance in collaboration with citizens.

"Smarter governing," as Noveck (2015) calls it, would require that governments adopt new "technologies of expertise"; innovative uses of digital technologies and data sharing allow governments to gather information, knowledge, expertise and assistance from a wide and diverse range of citizen-experts and use these informational sources for co-creating and co-designing better public policy- and decision-making and more effective delivery of public services. According to Noveck (2015), using these technologies of expertise in an open-source way would facilitate unlocking three types of human expertise that is hard to get: besides unlocking the expertise and skills of those working inside government and credentialed expertise from acknowledged experts outside government, a third and critically important type of human expertise that can be unlocked is the lived experiences, expertise, ideas, information, knowledge, practical proficiencies and skills of citizens.

Noveck (2015: 168–172) identifies the following five broad technology-enabled crowd-sourcing activities through which governments could establish open, participatory and collaborative forms of governance with citizens:

1)   *Crowd-sourcing ideas*;
2)   *Crowd-sourcing opinions*;
3)   *Crowd-sourcing funds* (or crowd funding);
4)   *Crowd-sourcing tasks* (or micro-tasking): involves distributing small bits of work or repetitive tasks to people in a participating group using a technology platform;

Participatory democracy   183

5) *Crowd-sourced data gathering, "data philanthropy" and citizens' science*: data are gathered with people's consent through mechanisms, such as SMS text messaging, social media or websites, and then leveraged toward a variety of ends. For example, Noveck (2015) refers to the Street Bump initiative in Boston, Massachusetts, as a crowd-sourcing project that draws on real-time data provided by local drivers to improve neighbourhood streets (see Box 7.5). Citizens can also voluntarily donate their personal data (data philanthropy) or submit their personal experience to various public good causes, such as creating a shared pool of data and knowledge around a certain disease (e.g. MS) (see Box 7.6), a public health issue (e.g. heatmap indicating geographical spread of a virus), pest control, a natural disaster or traffic congestion. Another area of crowd-sourced data use is citizens' science, where citizens are collecting and sharing data which influences public policy- and decision-making: for example, NASA uses citizens' observations to find out how galaxies form, and local authorities in the New Zealand Canterbury region use data collected by citizens who are measuring the water quality of regional rivers via a smartphone app in public policy- and decision-making.

Box 7.5   Street Bump in the city of Boston

Street Bump (www.streetbump.org/) is a crowd-sourcing project, developed in partnership between researchers and the Boston Mayor's Office of New Urban Mechanics, that helps residents improve their neighbourhood streets. Volunteers use the Street Bump mobile app to collect road condition data while they drive; the accelerometer (a motion detector) and GPS in mobile phones are utilised to sense when the driver of a vehicle hits a bump in the road. GPS records the location, and the phone transmits the data to a remote server. The results are reported on a public website. If three or more bumps occur at the same location, the city will inspect the obstacle. The data is aggregated and provides the city with real-time information to fix short-term problems and plan long-term investments.

Box 7.6   Health patients sharing their data

Over 600,000 patients from around the world share data on more than 2,800 chronic diseases to improve research and treatment of their conditions (McKenna, 2018). For instance, people who participate in the PatientsLikeMe online community share personal information and experience on a wide range of health-related topics, such as medication and treatment plans, symptoms, health outcomes and their emotional struggles. This information can then be turned into millions of data points about different chronic diseases and aggregated and organized to reveal new insights (McKenna, 2018). The philosophy of this online community is "give data, get data": every patient using the website to provide personal information has access to a wide range of crowd-sourced information. This information can also be shared with the healthcare and pharmaceutical industries to help develop better products and services.

In general, in order to shift from traditional closed-door government to innovative, participatory open-door governance, we will need to create technology- and data- enabled collaborative "laboratories of democracy" (Noveck, 2015). This then has the following implications for governments (Noveck, 2015: 263–264):

1   The adoption of new "technologies of expertise";
2   The development of an agenda for empirical research and experimentation to test the use of targeted crowd-sourcing at different stages of public decision-making, including identifying problems, prioritizing an agenda, identifying solutions, choosing which solutions to implement and assessing what works. Also, empirical research is needed to study the impact of crowd-sourcing on public policy-making and make recommendations for improvements;
3   The creation of supportive legal frameworks; and
4   The practical design of real-world implementations.

Other scholars, too, point to the benefits from an enhanced public value perspective of establishing new experimental forms of participatory governance which focus on a horizontal, collaborative production of a data commons, which facilitates the conversion of shared and integrated data into knowledge in order to solve complex public policy issues with the active participation of multiple and varying stakeholders, including citizens (e.g. Borgman, 2015; Hess & Ostrom, 2007; Benkler, 2006). However, thus far, there is a lack of empirical research into the use of digital technologies and data as part of new participatory forms of governance and the implications for government and citizens (Noveck, 2015; Loader & Mercea, 2012a).

How critically important it is to consider empirical research findings in light of assumptions that are held in government, amongst scholars and practitioners and, more widely, in the public domain is demonstrated by those empirical studies that are available to us. In many cases, they provide us with different insights and outcomes of digital government relationships than those we might

Participatory democracy 185

have considered originally. For example, in an empirical study into the use of digital technologies by traditional media organizations in Italy, Vaccari (2012) found that these media organizations weren't acting as independent watchdogs of democratic politics as might have been expected, but instead used these technologies to promote their own political agenda by enlisting the support of citizen-users to predefined political content rather than empowering these citizens to add their own voices to the political debate. Another empirical study in Finland found that citizens who were otherwise unengaged in (traditional) politics, including youth, used the Internet for political engagement (Bengtsson & Christensen, 2012).

That digital technologies can be used differently as part of a socio-technical assemblage within a different context of digital government relationships, leading to different outcomes, is perhaps best demonstrated by empirical research in The Netherlands. In his empirical study into the use of digital technologies and data in collective public policy- and decision-making around nursing homes in The Netherlands, van de Donk found that both government agencies and societal interest groups of citizens used digital technologies and data strategically to strengthen their own interests and positions in the public policy arena, as well as politically to confuse the "opposition" through strategic uncertainty reduction via "data wars" and "information politics" (van de Donk, 1998). Another interesting empirical observation from this public policy arena is that quantitative data and algorithms used in budget allocation models are considered of far more importance than the qualitative data that are used in discretionary policy- and decision-making (van de Donk, 1998: 395).

Van de Donk (1998: 391) summarises his empirical findings as follows:

> The real world of information processing in the domain of public policy-making does not at all comply with the [scholarly, ML] claim of a predominantly analytical and systematic use of scientific information. Instead, it is characterised by several types of information (manipulated statistics, high quality research, gossip, editorial comments, evaluation reports, corridor analysis); information pathologies (faulty receptors, failures in communication, information overload, systematic biases) and information politics (manipulation, non-registration, withholding, biased presentation, adding other information, timing, leaking and so on). This information behaviour is fueled by all kinds of ambiguities: ambiguity of preferences, ambiguities of relevance, ambiguities of intelligence in complex ecologies and ambiguities of meaning.

Based on these empirical findings, van de Donk (1998) concludes that the use of digital technologies in collective public policy-making leads to stronger top-down and hierarchical structures in digital government relationships and, at the same time, a decrease in both democratic participation and plural representation as well as the utilisation of democratic intelligence (van de Donk, 1998). In his view, the use of digital technologies in public policy-making reinforces

186   *Areas of public sector reform*

traditional forms of rule-driven public policy-making and promotes tunnel vision (van de Donk, 1998).

Emerging issues and barriers

A number of emerging issues and barriers to these new participatory forms of governance and democracy have been identified in the scholarly literature. We will provide a brief overview of these issues and barriers next.

Mergel (2013) provides a useful overview of issues and barriers to the use of social media in digital government relationships. She identifies the following five main categories of challenges, with a particular focus on social media use in the context of US digital government relationships (Mergel, 2013: 55–70):

1   *Systemic challenges*: the US federal government system leads to overlapping and intersecting lines of responsibility, authority and participation, but also to a large degree of autonomy for government units creating a considerable amount of freedom to make decisions around social media use for public engagement. This then creates the following issues:

    a   Each individual government agency has maximum freedom to adopt its own social technologies. Often, IT functional units are decentralised and intersect little with marketing, communications or public relations authority within the same agency. This then has implications for where the responsibility for social media use should be located in a government agency and where formal guidance should be coming from;

    b   Increasing use of social technologies by networked citizens is creating dramatic changes in the way people communicate and collaborate, which is challenging existing traditional, hierarchical ways of working in government agencies. For example, citizens are expecting instant feedback when they are willing to interact with government on social media sites, which is against traditional government operating procedures;

    c   Introducing new digital technologies is requiring government organizations to think about new rules, acceptable use standards, organizational institutions, resource allocation and adjustments of existing resources to the new requirements.

2   *Organizational and cultural challenges*: social technologies can have disruptive effects on the existing organizational norms and procedural elements of government organizations. This then creates the following challenges:

    a   Traditional forms of informing the public about government operations and decision-making processes, such as press releases, written government reports, interviews and written speeches, often have created a

Participatory democracy   187

culture of guardedness in public employees' communication. The learned, on-the-record, scripted communication style favoured by government officials is a barrier to their use of informal conversational technologies;

b   Government agencies' confidentiality agreements with individual clients and sworn secrecy statements of government officials prevent open exchanges on third-party platforms;

c   Blurring boundaries between government organizations as the sole authorities for information and other organizations and individuals, which leads to increasing organizational complexity. The informal nature of social media conversations does not match the highly formal nature of government records and processes;

d   In networked digital government relationships, social technologies can be used by government agencies to scan the environment and match issues that citizens are discussing online and offline with agency priorities;

e   Understanding the diverse group of citizens a government organization has to cater to is especially challenging in a (legal) environment in which measuring online activities and tracking user behaviour of citizens is highly restricted;

f   Social technologies (with the capability of creating a personalised profile for each user) provide the challenging opportunity for government officials to individualise their direct exchanges with individual citizens. As social media are often used as part of public service provision, this has the potential for government agencies to receive information from large numbers of citizen-users. Agencies might not have the capacity or resources to extract this information or customise their exchanges with individual citizens;

g   The issue of how to overcome organizational resistance to change and motivate government employees to participate in or start using social technologies in the context of government;

h   Citizens' interactive use of social technologies in relationships with elected officials has potentially disruptive effects on power balances in the sense that it might undermine government's mandate and sovereignty.

3   *Informational challenges*: faster and more interactive information publishing mechanisms (e.g. blogs, wikis, retweets, responses to Facebook comments) as a result of using social media are supporting governments to move from a "need-to-know" to a "need-to-share" culture (Dawes, Cresswell & Pardo, 2009). This has implications for traditional information-vetting procedures in government:

a   Government representatives might feel the threat of losing control over the information creation and dissemination process;

b   This issue causes challenges for information archiving and the democratic requirement for government agencies to create authentic public records;

188 *Areas of public sector reform*

    c   The issue of who owns content created by citizens on social media sites;

    d   The issue of protecting the privacy of contributing individuals;

    e   The issue of who determines how the created content or data are used.

4   *Technological challenges*:

    a   Legacy technology systems and databases can stand in the way of the system and knowledge integration required for effective engagement with citizens;

    b   Security concerns;

    c   The issue of existing digital divides (see also Chapter 9); and

5   *Legal challenges*: an ambiguous legal environment has hindered many government organizations from adopting social media applications.

The following further issues and barriers have been identified in the scholarly literature:

- *The recruitment of citizen participants in technology- and data-enabled participatory governance arrangements*: where to find citizens who want to participate, how to find them, and how to keep them?
- *The degree to which citizens are able to participate meaningfully in technology- and data-enabled participatory governance arrangements* (Fischer, 2012);
- *Governments need to learn and develop techniques to "mass-listen" to complement their facility of "mass-talking"* (Richard, 1999)
- *Governments need to consider how, when and by whom moderation of discourse between citizens and governments should be applied* (Richard, 1999);
- *Changing roles and requirements for government officials*: for instance, the changing role of the public manager as that of creating "digital communities of participation and collaboration" with citizens and the changing role of the public servant as facilitator of public participation via multiple digital channels and platforms in digital government relationships (Fischer, 2012). These changing roles will require different expertise, skill sets and training for government officials than traditional forms of professional expertise in government.
- *A lack of funds to invest in and sustain new horizontal forms of participatory governance*;
- *Government organizations seeking to leverage large volumes of data gathered from the crowd need the personnel, resources and strategies in place to make the most of that input* (Noveck, 2015: 172–173). A related issue is how to filter the information received from citizen experts through crowd-sourcing.
- *The evaluation of participatory democracy initiatives*: how do we measure or assess success? Also, the quality of evaluation and feedback to citizens is critically important from the perspective of managing citizens' expectations around their involvement in and contributions to networked participatory democracy arrangements.

Strategies for designing open and participatory governance

According to the OECD (2011), governments around the world see the increasing reliance on digital technologies and data as an opportunity to embrace a new open and participatory governance paradigm for the future public sector, where citizens will be empowered to take on greater responsibility and start more horizontal, collaborative partnerships with public sector organizations. In this chapter, we discussed the importance of reconceptualising government, governing and democratic citizenship in order to do so, including reconceptualising the citizen as a partner in and co-producer of public policy- and decision-making (Richard, 1999). Besides the scholarly thinking that has already been presented in this area, the following strategic advice is relevant to governments in their public sector reform ambitions to establish more open and participatory technology- and data-enabled governance arrangements with citizens.

For instance, Noveck (2015: 264) summarises new participatory ways of working for government organizations as follows:

- To embrace collaboration, co-production and co-creation;
- To make public consultation part of government operations on a day-to-day basis;
- To strive for constant conversation with an engaged and knowledgeable public; and
- To reinvent the conception of public service as co-creating and co-designing effective public services with citizen experts and of the public servant as the steward of such a conversation.

Ansell (2012) points out that the institutional design of participatory governance is critically important. The following general institutional design principles can be identified (Ansell, 2012: 506):

1. Citizens should co-produce public goods;
2. Community assets should be mobilised;
3. Expert knowledge should be shared;
4. Citizens should deliberate together;
5. Partnerships should be encouraged to be sustainable;
6. Assets and governance networks should be strategically mobilised and deployed;
7. Institutional cultures should be transformed to support community empowerment and civic problem solving; and
8. Mutual accountability among collaborative partners should be ensured.

And finally, the following conditions have been identified for more democratic forms of horizontal participatory governance arrangements (Papadopoulos, 2012: 518):

190 *Areas of public sector reform*

- The inclusiveness of collaborative forms, which allows equity and a fair amount of pluralism in participation and deliberation;
- The publicity of debate, which allows effective accountability, consent and contestation from outside; and
- The direct presence of, or indirect supervision by, elected officials, which prevents formally authorised representative bodies from being hollowed out by participatory governance.

Box 7.7   Exercise 7.1

Describe the ten main characteristics of traditional closed-door government on the one hand and of innovative participatory open-door governance on the other. Compare the two models and design a strategy for your government to shift from closed-door government to participatory open-door governance.

Discussion questions

1   How and under what conditions could technology- and data-enabled forms of participatory governance be meaningful for citizens to collaborate with government organizations? Motivate your answer.
2   From your perspective, what is the answer to Coleman and Blumler's (2009) question about how citizens should engage with government? Motivate your answer.
3   What would be effective strategies for governments to tap into the potential of expertise, knowledge and resources of networked citizens?
4   What do you consider to be the three most important barriers for governments to achieve more horizontal and participatory forms of governance using digital technologies and data? What would be strategies to overcome those barriers in your view?
5   How and under what conditions could effective technology- and data-enabled horizontal forms of participatory governance be sustained over a longer period of time?

Notes

1 This implies that we will not discuss new direct forms of so-called push-button democracy, such as e-voting, online referenda and online opinion polls.
2 Wikipedia, available from: https://en.wikipedia.org/wiki/Main_Page [accessed 16 January 2019].

References

Aikens, G.S. (1999) Deweyan systems in the Information Age. In: Hague, B.N. & Loader, B.D. (eds.) *Digital Democracy: Discourse and Decision Making in the Information Age*. London: Routledge, pp. 179–194.

Ansell, C. (2012) Collaborative governance. In: Levi-Faur, D. (ed.) *The Oxford Handbook of Governance*. Oxford: Oxford University Press, pp. 498–511.

Bekkers, V.J.J.M. (2005) Democratie en ICT: Institutionele renovatie of innovatie? In: Lips, A.M.B., Bekkers, V.J.J.M. & Zuurmond, A. (eds.) *ICT en Openbaar Bestuur*. Utrecht: Lemma, pp. 443–477.

Bengtsson, A. & Christensen, H.S. (2012) The political competence of Internet participants: Evidence from Finland. In: Loader, B.D. & Mercea, D. (eds.) *Social Media and Democracy: Innovations in Participatory Politics*. London: Routledge, pp. 131–149.

Benkler, Y. (2006) *The Wealth of Networks: How Social Production Transforms Markets and Freedom*. New Haven/London: Yale University Press.

Borgman, C.L. (2015) *Big Data, Little Data, No Data: Scholarship in the Networked World*. Cambridge, MA: Massachusetts Institute of Technology Press.

Boyd, D.M. & Ellison, N.B. (2008) Social network sites: Definition, history, and scholarship. *Journal of Computer-Mediated Communication*, 13 (1), 210–230.

Castells, M. (1996) *The Rise of the Network Society: The Information Age: Economy, Society and Culture*. Vol. 1. Oxford: Blackwell Publishers.

Chadwick, A. (2006) *Internet Politics: States, Citizens, and New Communication Technologies*. Oxford: Oxford University Press.

Chadwick, A. & Howard, P.N. (eds.) (2008) *Routledge Handbook of Internet Politics*. London: Routledge.

Christensen, T. & Laegreid, P. (2012) Governance and administrative reforms. In: Levi-Faur, D. (ed.) *The Oxford Handbook of Governance*. Oxford: Oxford University Press, pp. 255–267.

Coleman, S. (1999) Cutting out the middle man: From virtual representation to direct deliberation. In: Hague, B.N. & Loader, B.D. (eds.) *Digital Democracy: Discourse and Decision Making in the Information Age*. London: Routledge, pp. 195–210.

Coleman, S. & Blumler, J.G. (2001) *Realizing Democracy Online: Towards a Civic Commons in Cyberspace*. London: Institute for Public Policy Research.

Coleman, S. & Blumler, J.G. (2009) *The Internet and Democratic Citizenship: Theory, Practice and Policy*. New York, NY: Cambridge University Press.

Dawes, S.S., Cresswell, A.M. & Pardo, T.A. (2009) From 'need to know' to 'need to share': Tangled problems, information boundaries, and the building of public sector knowledge networks. *Public Administration Review*, 69 (3), 392–402.

Dutton, W.H. (2009) The fifth estate emerging through the network of networks. *Prometheus*, 27 (1), 1–15.

Dutton, W.H. (2012) The fifth estate: A new governance challenge. In: Levi-Faur, D. (ed.) *The Oxford Handbook of Governance*. Oxford: Oxford University Press, pp. 584–598.

Fischer, F. (2012) Participatory governance: From theory to practice. In: Levi-Faur, D. (ed.) *The Oxford Handbook of Governance*. Oxford: Oxford University Press, pp. 457–471.

Frissen, P.H.A. (1998) Public administration in cyberspace. In: Snellen, I.Th.M. & van de Donk, W.B.H.J. (eds.) *Public Administration in an Information Age: A Handbook*. Amsterdam: IOS Press, pp. 33–46.

Frissen, P.H.A. (1999) *Politics, Governance, and Technology: A Postmodern Narrative on the Virtual State*. Cheltenham: Edward Elgar.

192 Areas of public sector reform

Froomkin, M. (2004) Technologies for democracy. In: Shane, P. (ed.) *Democracy Online: The Prospects for Political Renewal Through the Internet*. New York, NY: Routledge, pp. 3–20.

Grönlund, A. (2001) Democracy in an IT-framed society. *Communications of the ACM*, 44 (1), 23–26.

Hague, B.N. & Loader, B.D. (1999a) Digital democracy: An introduction. In: Hague, B.N. & Loader, B.D. (eds.) *Digital Democracy: Discourse and Decision Making in the Information Age*. London: Routledge, pp. 3–22.

Hague, B.N. & Loader, B.D. (eds.) (1999b) *Digital Democracy: Discourse and Decision Making in the Information Age*. London: Routledge.

Hess, C. & Ostrom, E. (eds.) (2007) *Understanding Knowledge as a Commons: From Theory to Practice*. Cambridge, MA: Massachusetts Institute of Technology Press.

Horton, C. (21 August 2018) The simple but ingenious system Taiwan uses to crowdsource its laws. *MIT Technology Review*. Available from: https://www.technologyreview.com/s/611816/the-simple-but-ingenious-system-taiwan-uses-to-crowdsource-its-laws/ [accessed 16 January 2019].

Kavanaugh, A., Fox, E., Sheetz, S., Yan, S., Li, L.T., Shoemaker, D., Natsev, A. & Xie, L. (2012) Social media use by government: From the routine to the critical. *Government Information Quarterly*, 29, 480–491.

Lips, M., Barlow, L. & Woods, L. (2016) *Conditions for Channel Shift Behaviours and Simplification in Business Individuals' and Small Businesses' Online Interactions with Government*. Survey Research Report. Wellington: Victoria University of Wellington.

Loader, B.D. & Mercea, D. (2012a) Networking democracy? Social media innovations in participatory politics. In: Loader, B.D. & Mercea, D. (eds.) *Social Media and Democracy: Innovations in Participatory Politics*. London: Routledge, pp. 1–10.

Loader, B.D. & Mercea, D. (eds.) (2012b) *Social Media and Democracy: Innovations in Participatory Politics*. London: Routledge.

Malina, A. (1999) Perspectives on citizen democratisation and alienation in the virtual public sphere. In: Hague, B.N. & Loader, B.D. (eds.) *Digital Democracy: Discourse and Decision Making in the Information Age*. London: Routledge, pp. 23–38.

Mascheroni, G. (2012) Online participation: New forms of civic and political engagement or just new opportunities for networked individualism. In: Loader, B.D. & Mercea, D. (eds.) *Social Media and Democracy: Innovations in Participatory Politics*. London: Routledge, pp. 207–223.

McKenna, J. (13 November 2018) These patients are sharing their data to improve healthcare standards. *World Economic Forum*. Available from: https://www.weforum.org/agenda/2018/11/these-patients-are-sharing-their-data-to-improve-their-treatment/ [accessed 16 January 2019].

Mergel, I. (2013) *Social Media in the Public Sector: A Guide to Participation, Collaboration, and Transparency in the Networked World*. San Francisco, CA: Jossey-Bass.

Mergel, I. & Greeves, B. (2013) *Social Media in the Public Sector Field Guide: Designing and Implementing Strategies and Policies*. San Francisco, CA: Jossey-Bass.

Moore, R.K. (1999) Democracy and cyberspace. In: Hague, B.N. & Loader, B.D. (eds.) *Digital Democracy: Discourse and Decision Making in the Information Age*. London: Routledge, pp. 39–59.

Norris, D.F. & Reddick, C.G. (2013) E-democracy at the American grassroots: Not now . . . not likely? *Information Polity*, 18, 201–216.

Noveck, B.S. (2009) *Wiki Government: How Technology Can Make Government Better, Democracy Stronger, and Citizens More Powerful*. Washington, DC: Brookings Institution Press.

Noveck, B.S. (2015) *Smart Citizens, Smarter State: The Technologies of Expertise and the Future of Governing*. Cambridge, MA: Harvard University Press.

OECD. (28 March 2011) *The Call for Innovative and Open Government: An Overview of Country Initiatives*. Paris: OECD.

O'Reilly, T. (30 September 2005) *What Is Web 2.0: Design Patterns and Business Models for the Next Generation of Software*. O'Reilly Media, Inc. Available from: https://www.oreilly.com/pub/a/web2/archive/what-is-web-20.html [accessed 23 June 2018].

Papadopoulos, Y. (2012) The democratic quality of collaborative governance. In: Levi-Faur, D. (ed.) *The Oxford Handbook of Governance*. Oxford: Oxford University Press, pp. 512–526.

Raab, C.D., Bellamy, C., Taylor, J.A., Dutton, W.H. & Peltu, M. (1996) The information polity: Electronic democracy, privacy, and surveillance. In: Dutton, W.H. (ed.) *Information and Communication Technologies: Visions and Realities*. Oxford: Oxford University Press, pp. 283–299.

Rainie, L. & Wellman, B. (2012) *Networked: The New Social Operating System*. Cambridge, MA: Massachusetts Institute of Technology Press.

Richard, E. (1999) Tools of governance. In: Hague, B.N. & Loader, B.D. (eds.) *Digital Democracy: Discourse and Decision Making in the Information Age*. London: Routledge, pp. 73–86.

Schalken, C.A.T. (1998) Internet as a new public sphere for democracy? In: Snellen, I.Th.M. & van de Donk, W.B.H.J. (eds.) *Public Administration in an Information Age: A Handbook*. Amsterdam: IOS Press, pp. 159–174.

Snellen, I.Th.M. (2005) E-government: A Challenge for Public Management. In: Ferlie, E., Lynn, L.E. & Pollitt, C. (eds.) *The Oxford Handbook of Public Management*. Oxford: Oxford University Press, pp. 398–421.

Vaccari, C. (2012) The news media as networked political actors: How Italian media are reclaiming political ground by harnessing online participation. In: Loader, B.D. & Mercea, D. (eds.) *Social Media and Democracy: Innovations in Participatory Politics*. London: Routledge, pp. 77–90.

van de Donk, W.B.H.J. (1998) Beyond incrementalism? Redistributive policy making, information systems and the revival of synopticism. In: Snellen, I.Th.M. & van de Donk, W.B.H.J. (eds.) *Public Administration in an Information Age: A Handbook*. Amsterdam: IOS Press, pp. 381–404.

van de Donk, W.B.H.J. & Tops, P.W. (1992) Informatization and democracy: Orwell or Athens? A review of the literature. *Informatization and the Public Sector*, 2, 69–196.

Ward, S. & Vedel, T. (2006) Introduction: The potential of the Internet revisited. *Parliamentary Affairs*, 59 (2), 210–225.

White, C.M. (2012) *Social Media, Crisis Communication, and Emergency Management: Leveraging Web 2.0 Technologies*. Boca Raton, FL: CRC Press.

Wilhelm, A.G. (1999) Virtual sounding boards: How deliberative is online political discussion? In: Hague, B.N. & Loader, B.D. (eds.) *Digital Democracy: Discourse and Decision Making in the Information Age*. London: Routledge, pp. 154–178.

Further reading

Benkler, Y. (2006) *The Wealth of Networks: How Social Production Transforms Markets and Freedom*. New Haven/London: Yale University Press.

Castells, M. (1996) *The Rise of the Network Society: The Information Age: Economy, Society and Culture*. Vol. 1. Oxford: Blackwell Publishers.

Chadwick, A. (2006) *Internet Politics: States, Citizens, and New Communication Technologies*. Oxford: Oxford University Press.

Chadwick, A. & Howard, P.N. (eds.) (2008) *Routledge Handbook of Internet Politics*. London: Routledge.

194 *Areas of public sector reform*

Coleman, S. & Blumler, J.G. (2009) *The Internet and Democratic Citizenship: Theory, Practice and Policy*. New York, NY: Cambridge University Press.

Dutton, W.H. (2012) The fifth estate: A new governance challenge. In: Levi-Faur, D. (ed.) *The Oxford Handbook of Governance*. Oxford: Oxford University Press, pp. 584–598.

Fischer, F. (2012) Participatory governance: From theory to practice. In: Levi-Faur, D. (ed.) *The Oxford Handbook of Governance*. Oxford: Oxford University Press, pp. 457–471.

Hague, B.N. & Loader, B.D. (eds.) (1999b) *Digital Democracy: Discourse and Decision Making in the Information Age*. London: Routledge.

Loader, B.D. & Mercea, D. (eds.) (2012b) *Social Media and Democracy: Innovations in Participatory Politics*. London: Routledge.

Mergel, I. (2013) *Social Media in the Public Sector: A Guide to Participation, Collaboration, and Transparency in the Networked World*. San Francisco, CA: Jossey-Bass.

Mergel, I. & Greeves, B. (2013) *Social Media in the Public Sector Field Guide: Designing and Implementing Strategies and Policies*. San Francisco, CA: Jossey-Bass.

Noveck, B.S. (2009) *Wiki Government: How Technology Can Make Government Better, Democracy Stronger, and Citizens More Powerful*. Washington, DC: Brookings Institution Press.

Noveck, B.S. (2015) *Smart Citizens, Smarter State: The Technologies of Expertise and the Future of Governing*. Cambridge, MA: Harvard University Press.

Rainie, L. & Wellman, B. (2012) *Networked: The New Social Operating System*. Cambridge, MA: Massachusetts Institute of Technology Press.

White, C.M. (2012) *Social Media, Crisis Communication, and Emergency Management: Leveraging Web 2.0 Technologies*. Boca Raton, FL: CRC Press.

Part IV
Emerging issues

8 Citizen identity, privacy, ethics and security

Learning objectives

By the end of this chapter you should be able to:

- Understand the existence of a privacy paradox between people's privacy concerns and their actual online behaviour;
- Identify different perspectives in citizens' perceptions of the digital government context in which they exchange their citizen identity data with government agencies; and
- Apply the contextual integrity framework to evaluate personal data flow in the context of digital government relationships with citizens.

Key points of this chapter

- Citizen identity data management in digital government relationships, including citizen identity verification and citizen identity authentication, has fundamentally changed compared to the paper-based past of citizen-government relationships;
- Citizens' personal data and processes of citizen identity construction, citizen identity attribution and citizen identity fixation have become critical enablers of digital government relationships;
- In digital government relationships, citizens usually do not have a choice whether to disclose or withhold their personal data if they want or need to have access to a particular government service;
- The collection and use of citizens' personal data, including potential privacy issues, must be understood in the context of digital government relationships; individuals only consider their privacy to be breached when they regard the collection, management and use of their personal data inappropriate or improper from the viewpoint of context-related informational principles and norms (Nissenbaum, 2010);
- As digital government outcomes depend on the actual use of technologies and data in a particular context, the use of digital technologies and citizen identity data by public servants in the context of digital government relationships can also lead to more effective and equitable public decision-making and decreased human prejudice;

198   *Emerging issues*

- Data determinism in the construction and use of an individual's predictive profile of what that person might do in the future could have a negative impact on how people are being treated today;
- Security is not a product but a process. Consequently, we should not be dominantly focused on a technology product solution but need to consider the use of the security technology as part of a socio-technical assemblage in the context of digital government relationships; and
- Contextual integrity in digital government relationships is a critical part of the social contract between government and citizens in the digital age.

Key terms

- *Citizen identity construction*: the process of using data to construct a profile of an individual citizen.
- *Citizen identity attribution*: the process of associating data with a certain individual citizen.
- *Citizen identity fixation*: the process of assigning data to causal explanations about a citizen.
- *Citizen data integrity*: Application of the contextual integrity framework to the flow of citizen data in digital government relationships in order to assess potential benefits and harms for the citizen concerned.

Introduction

Digitised citizen identity data have become significant underpinnings of digital government relationships with citizens and will be even more so with the further rollout of digital government, including the adoption of emerging smart technologies, AI and robotics in people's lives. For example, in Chapter 4, we discussed the development towards increasingly digitised transactional public service provision in digital government relationships, for which the submission of citizens' personal data is critical to proceed. And in Chapter 6, we looked at the adoption of smart technologies and innovative data uses in digital government relationships, including the use of citizens' personal data, and how they are having an impact on the construction, analysis and use of citizen identity data in public decision-making. This development towards increasingly smart government has the potential not only to provide much more effective and efficient public services to individuals but also to substantially enhance the quality of people's lives.

However, as citizens' personal data become increasingly critical as a foundation of digital government relationships, they also point towards fundamental changes happening in citizen-government relationships, including a potential impact on democratic citizen rights. For instance, several scholars observe a development towards increasing forms of surveillance of individuals, leading to substantial information imbalances in citizen-government relationships with a significant impact on the privacy of individuals (e.g. Lyon, 2003b; van Dijck, 2014; London School of Economics, 2005; Murakami-Wood *et al*, 2006). Likewise, in 2009, the UK House of Lords Select Committee on the Constitution concluded that, although the processing of citizen identity data has always been part of government, there has been a profound and continuous expansion in the surveillance apparatus of the state: in British society, with citizen identity data being collected on the entire population and not just on traditional suspects, the development of technology-enabled surveillance has become pervasive, routine and almost taken for granted (UK House of Lords, 2009). Others, too, observe an emerging transparency paradox in digital government relationships, where citizens are becoming more and more transparent for government as a result of various forms of digitised citizen data use, whilst at the same time government is becoming increasingly invisible and obscure for citizens through its data- and algorithmic-enabled operations (Dutch Scientific Council, 2016).

In this chapter we explore and discuss these potential changes happening around the collection, construction, processing, analysis, storage and use of citizens' identity data in digital government relationships and the privacy, ethical and security implications. Firstly, we explore the shift away from paper-based and face-to-face citizen identity reconstruction towards digital forms of citizen identity construction. Secondly, we look at privacy as a multifaceted, ambiguous notion. We particularly consider empirical research around the privacy paradox of people's privacy attitudes versus their actual online identity information behaviours in the context of digital government relationships. Thirdly, we discuss an overview of emerging issues, barriers and risks around citizens' personal data flow in digital government relationships. Fourthly, using the contextual integrity framework developed in Chapter 6, we explore and assess citizen data integrity issues in digital government relationships, in particular the privacy, ethical and security implications around personal data flow in digital government. And finally, we consider some citizen data integrity strategies for digital government.

Emerging digital forms of citizen identity construction

Enabled by fast-moving technological developments, governments are increasingly using digital technologies and data in their multiple relationships with citizens, including in public decision-making, public policy, service provision and democratic and public engagement. As a result, citizens' personal data have become a critical enabler of these digital government relationships. Moreover, this development towards increased sharing and use of citizens' personal data in digital government relationships is happening in parallel to a development where governments are moving away from and replacing traditional forms of citizen identification, or the process whereby a person's identity is revealed, and citizen authentication, or the process to establish that identity claims made by or about a person are true (Whitley & Hosein, 2010).

200 *Emerging issues*

For instance, where governments used to rely on paper-based citizen identification documents, such as a passport, driver's licence and birth certificate, in order to reconstruct a citizen's identity on the basis of face-to-face citizen identity authentication, they nowadays use digital citizen identity management systems to verify and authenticate a citizen's identity. These digital citizen identity management systems can be large and quite complex as the national identity management programme of India demonstrates: Aadhaar is a national register of citizens assigned a unique 12-digit number tied to their name, gender, address, date of birth and the biometric information of ten fingerprints and two irises. With 1.3 billion citizens enrolled, it has nearly universal coverage. In 2018, it was required or encouraged for almost every Indian government agency and programme, including welfare payments, government pensions, public health care, scholarships, birth and death certificates, and filing taxes.

Furthermore, where the sharing and use of a citizen's personal data in citizen-government relationships used to be minimal and proportional to the service needs of an individual, the adoption of smart technologies and big data research in digital government is changing the volume and types of personal data that governments are able to collect from their citizens, such as movements, gaits, behaviours, facial expressions and public sentiments. The pervasiveness of this development means that citizens leave more and more digital footprints behind, which makes them more observable, traceable and knowable (Kitchin, 2016).

Box 8.1   Digital driver's licence in Australia

In New South Wales, Australia, citizens can access and use their driver's licence in a digital format via an app on their smartphone or tablet device. The digital driver's licence can be used to verify a citizen's identity or prove their age. It includes a QR code that expires and reloads, a hologram and a watermark-matching licence photo. A person downloads the digital driver's licence on their smartphone and shows and/or scans it when they need to demonstrate that they hold a valid driver's licence or to prove their identity or age. A licence checker will get real-time customer information, including change of address updates.

In addition, it has become possible for smart governments to profile and construct a citizen's identity in real time on the basis of not only integrated personal data, but also integrated non-personal, aggregated or de-identified datasets and to construct and analyse data-driven predictions around a citizen's identity in the longer term, such as the likeliness of a repeat of a person's criminal behaviour or an effective solution for a benefit claimant to get a job. Such predictive analytics relates (meta-)data patterns to a citizen's actual or potential behaviour (van Dijck, 2014), which public decision-makers could translate into powerful information about who an individual citizen is, what they do and how government could offer more effective services to this individual.

Box 8.2 Social behaviour credit system in China

China has developed a plan to judge each of its citizens on their social behaviour (Bloomberg News, 2018[1]). For instance, the city of Beijing will adopt a lifelong points programme by 2021 that assigns personalised ratings to each resident. The city will pool data from several government departments, including tourism bodies, business regulators and transit authorities, to reward and punish citizens on the basis of their actions and reputations. Those with better social credit will get so-called green channel benefits through streamlined services while those who violate laws will find life more difficult as a result of restrictions and penalties. For example, in the city of Hangzhou, good social behaviours like volunteer work and blood donations are rewarded with personal credit points while those who violate traffic laws or charge under-the-table fees are punished with bad credit. In China, people with bad credit have been blocked from booking flights and high-speed train trips. The tracking of individual behaviour in China has become easier as economic life moves online, with apps being used for making payments, getting loans and organizing transport. Accounts are generally linked to mobile phone numbers, which in turn require government IDs.

In general, the following three processes can be distinguished in citizen identity management in digital government (Lips, 2013):

- Citizen identity construction: the process of using data to construct a profile of an individual citizen;
- Citizen identity attribution: the process of associating data with a certain individual citizen; and
- Citizen identity fixation: the process of assigning data to causal explanations about a citizen.

However, considering fast-moving and increasing data-driven developments in digital government relationships, several scholars warn of data determinism in the construction and use of individual predictive profiles of what people might do in the future, which could have a negative impact on how people are being treated today (e.g. Kitchin, 2016; van Dijck, 2014). For example, the Chicago police force uses predictive analytics to profile and identify

202 *Emerging issues*

individuals who are located within crime hotspots, on the basis of arrest records, phone records, social media and other data to construct the social networks of those arrested. They do so to identify who in their network is most likely to commit a crime in the future, designating them "pre-criminals" and visiting them to let them know that they have been flagged as potential threats (Kitchin, 2016: 10). Another data deterministic problem with predictive modelling is that it may cause predictive privacy harms: for example, tracking data revealing that a person regularly visits gay bars may lead to the inference that the person is gay (Kitchin, 2016). When such data-driven inferences lead to incorrect interpretations, they can cause stigma and harm, with an even bigger risk of producing inaccurate information in case of poor quality of the underlying data.

More in general, several scholars have pointed to the risk of so-called dataveillance: a mode of surveillance where forms of (meta-)data are increasingly used in digital government relationships in order to generate information on citizens (Lupton & Williamson, 2017; van Dijck, 2014; Kitchin, 2016). In Chapter 6, we discussed a common misconception of governments that having more data would mean more and better information and knowledge, which would create an opportunity for better governing in their view. Also, numerous scholars have identified a major risk with so-called social sorting capabilities of digital technologies, which, according to them, makes them in fact surveillance systems which collect, process and monitor individuals' personal data in unprecedented ways (Lyon, 2003a; Lyon, 2003b; Murakami-Wood *et al*, 2006). For example, citizens' personal data captured by these rationalised, automated surveillance systems can be used to classify them according to varying embedded codes, values and criteria to determine who should be targeted for special treatment, suspicion, eligibility, inclusion, access et cetera (Lyon, 2003a; Lyon, 2003b; Lyon, 2001; Murakami-Wood *et al*, 2006). Consequently, surveillance systems are discriminatory technologies as they sieve and socially sort through obtained personal data for the purpose of assessment. thus affecting people's life chances (Lyon, 2003: 20).

However, Lips, Taylor and Organ (2009a) warn of the popular use of a narrow technological deterministic perspective of "what can happen, will happen" around digital technologies, regardless of context: the misconception that, if the technological capability exists, then it will be used, thereby threatening a citizen's privacy and other democratic rights. Such a technological deterministic perspective is largely sustained by *a priori* reasoning rather than by a clear empirically derived evidence base that casts light on what is actually happening in the context of digital government relationships (Lips, Taylor & Organ, 2009a).

This then raises important empirical questions as to how, and to what extent, digital technologies and data have an effect on what may be called the administrative sorting activities of governments: those assessment processes enabled by government systems and depending on the contextual norms and values embedded in those systems which are necessary to the establishment of public service relationships with citizens, for example (Lips, Taylor & Organ, 2009a). To further illustrate this point, based on empirical research into the use of new forms of citizen identity and identification systems in digital government relationships in the UK, Lips, Taylor and Organ (2009a) observe that new digital citizen identification technologies and citizen identity data do not necessarily lead to the social sorting of citizens but can, in fact, support public servants in their administrative sorting activities in ways that *decrease* human prejudice, leading to more equitable public decision-making and, with that, more effective and higher-quality public service provision. However, in those cases where data-driven administrative sorting activities happen without the intervention of (expert) human beings, risks of discriminatory social sorting and other potential breaches of citizens' rights do come to the fore again (Lips, Taylor & Organ, 2009a).

In summary, citizen identity construction, citizen identity attribution and citizen identity fixation have completely changed in the age of smart government. Many scholars agree that these developments around citizens' personal data in increasingly digital relationships with government are causing fundamental changes in citizen-government relationships, with potentially major implications for citizens' rights (Lips, 2013; Lips, Taylor & Organ, 2009a; Lips, Taylor & Organ, 2009b; UK House of Lords, 2009; van Dijck, 2014; Kitchin, 2016). However, thus far, there is not much systematic empirical evidence about what changes are happening in these digital government relationships. Few available empirical research findings indicate that change outcomes depend on the actual use of a citizen's personal data in digital government relationships (Lips, Taylor & Organ, 2009a; Lips, Taylor & Organ, 2009b).

In other words, changes in citizen-government relationships are determined by how citizen identity is constructed, attributed and fixated as part of a particular socio-technical assemblage in the context of digital government (Lips, 2013). This particular context of digital government doesn't start from scratch, however, but has a certain history of citizen identity legacy systems; consequently, we can observe a shifting away from managing citizens' personal data on the basis of fixed citizen identity and uniform egalitarian citizenship conceptions in traditional real-life public service environments, such as via a passport or driver's license, towards a situation where citizens' personal data are being managed on the basis of data-enabled fluid citizen identity and differentiated, tailored citizenship conceptions in "onlife" digital government relationships (Lips, 2013; Floridi, 2014), such as the use of predictive analytics to assess pre-criminals and the attribution of risk scores of citizens in social welfare assessments.

Privacy attitudes vs. actual privacy behaviours

A lot has changed since Warren and Brandeis (1890) wrote their famous article about a citizen's right to privacy, highly concerned as they were at the time about people's photographs appearing in newspapers and the deep intrusion

204   *Emerging issues*

this was causing into people's private sphere. To date, public and scholarly concern focuses on the emergence of an Orwellian surveillance state: a technology- and data-driven smart government with seemingly panopticon-like capabilities (Lyon, 2003b; Lyon, 2007; van Dijck, 2014; Kitchin, 2014; Meijer, 2015). Indeed, when people are being asked in regular survey research if they are concerned about their privacy in digital environments, including in digital government relationships, the answer predominantly is confirmative (Bennett & Raab, 2003). At the same time, though, we need to take into consideration that survey research about people's privacy concerns in digital environments is diverse and contradictory in terms of theory, methods and outcomes (van Zoonen, 2014; van Zoonen, 2016).

Thus far, this surveillance state perspective is hardly supported by any empirical evidence demonstrating what is actually happening with the collection, processing, analysis, storage and use of citizen's personal data in increasingly digital relationships between the citizen and the state, both from a government and a citizen's perspective (Lips, Taylor & Organ, 2009a; Lips, Taylor & Organ, 2009b; Nissenbaum, 2010). Moreover, instead of clear and overall empirical support for an emerging surveillance state, the few empirical studies available show mixed findings of surveillance-like activities, including support for increased effectiveness of public service provision or even the empowerment of individuals (Lips, Taylor & Organ, 2009a; Lips, Taylor & Organ, 2009b; Nissenbaum, 2010). This seems to confirm Nissenbaum's thesis that the collection and use of citizens' personal data and related privacy issues must be understood in their social context; individuals only consider their privacy to be breached when they regard the collection, management and use of their personal data inappropriate or improper from the viewpoint of context-related informational principles and norms (Nissenbaum, 2010).

In general, we need to consider that privacy is not a straight-forward concept: it is a multifaceted, ambiguous notion which means many things to many people (Moore, 1984; 6, Lasky & Fletcher,1998; Nissenbaum, 2010; Buchanan *et al*, 2007). For instance, empirical research into individuals' privacy preferences in their behaviour around personal data sharing shows that people do not have a simple desire to control and withhold their personal data, but rather display finely tuned tendencies to disclose, share or withhold personal data depending on the context of data sharing, data recipients and the sensitivity of the data (Halperin & Backhouse, 2008; Institute for Insight in the Public Services, 2008; Nissenbaum, 2010; Viseu, Clement & Aspinall, 2004). For example, in being able to choose between service channels, including digital service environments where more personal data is collected on the customer, people prefer options that offer convenience, time savings, financial savings or public safety, rather than those that offer privacy (Regan, 1995; Nissenbaum, 2010).

Furthermore, research has identified an important privacy paradox between people's concerns and their actual behaviour (Young & Quan-Haase, 2013; van Zoonen, 2016): despite people's clearly expressed concerns about their privacy, there is a simultaneous lack of appropriate secure behaviour. For example, the

Identity, privacy, ethics and security 205

most popular pin code used is 1234, and many people use only one password for multiple accounts (van Zoonen, 2016: 474; van Zoonen, 2014). Another example is that people share their personal information on many social media sites despite the fact that they do not feel very secure on sites like Facebook (van Zoonen, 2016; Pew, 2015).

In the last decades, the broad societal adoption of digital technologies has further supported changes to people's conception of privacy and their resulting online behaviours (6, 1998; Raab, 2005). For example, empirical research findings demonstrate that youth have different privacy behaviours in digital environments compared to older generations, with youth usually being much more privacy savvy than older people (Lips *et al*, 2015; Boyd, 2014; Livingstone & Bober, 2004; Palfrey & Gasser, 2008; Madden & Smith, 2010). Furthermore, what individuals consider private information varies with context and relationships. Indeed, ethnographic research findings from two highly different cultures confirm that an individual's conception of privacy is culture- and context-specific (Moore, 1984). Consequently, the disclosing of personal data considered appropriate in the context of one relationship may not be considered appropriate in another (Moore, 1984; Schoeman, 1984; Wacks, 1989; 6, Lasky & Fletcher, 1998; Nissenbaum, 2010). For example, an individual usually considers their medical data more sensitive than their address or a mobile phone number (Wacks, 1989; Nissenbaum, 2010); however, disclosing medical information to your doctor usually is considered less sensitive than to your employer. In other words, whether disclosing personal data in a particular context is considered appropriate or not depends on the assessment of the contextual integrity of the personal data flow and whether a person's privacy may be breached.

In general, research points to three consistent factors influencing people's privacy considerations (van Zoonen, 2016):

1 The type of data involved, e.g. personal or non-personal data; highly sensitive personal data, such as medical, financial and civic data or less sensitive personal data, such as age, gender, and nationality;
2 The purpose of personal data collection and use; and
3 The organization or people collecting and using the data.

These three consistent factors all refer to the relevance of the context in which personal data are being shared. Moreover, research has shown that people assess the benefits of providing their personal data in a particular context: when these benefits are considered of personal relevance (e.g. public service access, commercial gain), most people are willing to share their personal data with the organization asking for them (Acquisti, John & Loewenstein, 2013; van Zoonen, 2016). However, people do consider the trade-off between the amount of personal data asked for and the benefits received in return (van Zoonen, 2016; Acquisti, John & Loewenstein, 2013).

In an empirical study of the online identity information behaviours of New Zealanders from various backgrounds in varying digital relationships, Lips *et al*

206 Emerging issues

(2015) found that, although online privacy was of importance to all research participants without exception, people belonged to one of the following four "privacy behavioural types," revealing people's context-relative preferences and differences in digital behaviour, including in digital relationships with government:

- *Privacy pragmatist*: depending on the transactional relationship, privacy is a commodity for the privacy pragmatist (*"personal information helps you to get the services you want/need"*). Identity information is traded for convenience, cost and time efficiency and particular services;
- *Privacy victim*: a loss of privacy is inevitable in order to use the service; a privacy victim sees no choice. They stop using the online service when the informational demands are too intrusive;
- *Privacy optimist*: privacy optimists are willing to keep doing things online they think might be risky until something bad happens to confirm it; and
- *Privacy fatalist*: a major breach of privacy and power imbalance are inevitable and unescapable in the view of the privacy fatalist.

Citizens' online identity information behaviours in digital government relationships

Several scholars have pointed to the unique context of digital government relationships in which citizens share their personal data with government agencies (e.g. Lips, Taylor & Organ, 2009a; Lips, Taylor & Organ, 2009b). For instance, in many digital government service relationships, citizens do not have a choice about whether to disclose or withhold their personal data if they want to have access to a particular service; also, they usually need to disclose personal data for identity verification and authentication purposes in their relationships with digital government (Lips, Taylor & Organ, 2009a; Lips, Taylor & Organ, 2009b; Birch, 2007).

Moreover, whether citizens are disclosing or withholding personal data in digital government relationships also depends on their trust in government. International research findings show that citizens' trust in government fluctuates within and across countries, as well as over time (Van de Walle, Van Roosbroek & Bouckaert, 2008). Generally, an individual's trust in government goes hand in hand with their trust in the public service to do what is right, deliver value for the taxpayer's money and treat citizens fairly (Heintzman & Marson, 2005). However, people's evaluation of the quality of specific public services may differ substantially from public attitudes towards government, leading to a situation in which low trust in government and a positive image of specific public services can co-exist (Van de Walle, Kampen & Bouckaert, 2005). Furthermore, empirical research on the relationship between customer satisfaction with public service delivery and trust in government shows that the impact of a negative experience with a public agency is much more profound than the effect of a positive experience (Kampen, van de Walle & Bouckaert, 2006).

Identity, privacy, ethics and security 207

Also, trust in the security of the digital government service environment, including access management, the secure exchange of citizens' personal data in digital government relationships and the security of government databases and information systems is a critical enabler of the uptake of digital government services (Lusoli, Maghiros & Bacigalupo, 2008; OECD, 2009). 6, Lasky and Fletcher (1998) point out that individuals generally place high levels of trust in an organization's handling of personal data if they have the following observations: believing data to be kept securely, believing staff to be reliable with data and information, believing the organization to be law abiding, believing the organization only uses the information for notified purposes and believing public service provision is tailored and personalised.

One of the few available empirical studies into citizens' online identity behaviours in digital government relationships in New Zealand (Lips *et al*, 2015) shows that there is no strong and overall support among the research participants for a surveillance state perspective where the use of citizens' personal data in digital government relationships leads to the violation of citizens' privacy, substantial information imbalances to the advantage of the state or any other threats of evaporating standards and procedures of equitable citizenship. On the contrary, an alternative, what could be called "fair state" perspective of trusting, fair, beneficial, reciprocal and proportional information relationships between citizens and government is supported by most research participants and associated for them with the context of digital government relationships (Lips *et al*, 2015).

For instance, research participants pointed to the convenience of digital government service provision and the control they personally have over government's collection and processing of their personal data (Lips *et al*, 2015). Preferences for other service channels were based on either the desire to receive instant confirmation around the requested service or having more complex service-related questions that are not supported by the standardised set-up of digital government services.

The frustration of many participants with repetitive and duplicated processes of online personal data provision to various government agencies also shows that interviewees did not support the viewpoint of substantial information imbalances in favour of the state (Lips *et al*, 2015). Quite the opposite – many participants pointed to the individual and collective advantages of increased cross-government data sharing within a particular service cluster (i.e. social services, financial services and taxation, justice and health services) and saw the sharing of citizen identity data across government as an important public management tool to meet citizens' rights and obligations in a fair and more effective way.

Aware of existing privacy rules and principles, research participants were not indifferent about their privacy. Most of them were privacy pragmatists in the sense that they saw the disclosure of their personal data to government as having personal benefits (Lips *et al*, 2015). Also, research participants did not perceive a tension between increasing cross-government data sharing and their individual privacy rights, as long as the rules around privacy are met.

208   *Emerging issues*

Furthermore, most research participants did not support a surveillance state perspective by having high trust in the New Zealand government around its handling of citizens' personal data, even though the processing, use, storage and access of citizens' identity information across government were not transparent to them, including government's communication around these personal data management practices.

However, there were some notable exceptions to this emerging fair state perspective on citizens' identity information exchange in digital government service relationships, which do point towards some support for a surveillance state perspective in the context of digital government (Lips *et al*, 2015). For instance, several research participants indicated that they don't feel comfortable about sharing their personal data with government agencies if they don't know them and understand what they do. Moreover, some interviewees expressed their concern about not being able to see the personal data government agencies hold on them and to check these for data accuracy. Furthermore, for some participants, negative experiences with citizen identity data management by particular government agencies led to uncomfortable feelings about these government organizations. Also, research participants of 65 years and older in particular did not like the amount of personal data they were obliged to provide in digital government relationships and preferred face-to-face exchanges with government.

Features of a surveillance state perspective became visible, too, among particular groups of research participants (Lips *et al*, 2015). For instance, research participants who strongly distrusted the collection, management and use of citizens' personal data in digital government relationships were most commonly vulnerable individuals highly dependent on social services, people from the Pacific Islands or Pasifika and indigenous New Zealanders or Māori (Lips *et al*, 2015). High social services users strongly perceived a power imbalance in their personal data exchanges with government in the sense that they do not have a choice about providing the requested information as they need the service. They indicated that they disclose their personal data to government reluctantly and only if they have to and regard citizen identity information that might contribute to a negative service response or lead to a misjudgement in service provision as private (Lips *et al*, 2015).

Pasifika, too, strongly distrusted government agencies and preferred face-to-face information exchange with government over digital government service environments. They also felt powerless about cross-government data sharing in particular and rather preferred no data sharing at all. Māori participants had a general distrust of government agencies and their staff members and were particularly sceptical about potential misuse of their identity information once they have provided it to government. Moreover, they considered the personal information requested by government sometimes out of proportion to the services being sought and had strong reservations about cross-government data sharing (Lips *et al*, 2015). Consequently, for these research participants, distrust of government, a privacy-violating perception of the handling and sharing

Identity, privacy, ethics and security 209

Table 8.1 Surveillance state vs. fair state perspective

	Surveillance State Perspective	*Fair State Perspective*
Changing information relationships between citizens and government	Negative impact on privacy	More convenience
Increasing cross-government data sharing	Substantial power and information imbalances to the advantage of the state	Enhanced effectiveness and efficiency of public service provision
Privacy	Privacy fundamentalists	Privacy pragmatists
Trust in government	Distrust	High trust in the New Zealand government
Information security	Low trust in the government's handling of citizen identity data; misuse of identity data	High trust in the government's handling of citizen identity data
Transparency	Lack of transparency around citizen identity information management leads to individuals' reluctance to provide their identity data to government	Lack of transparency around citizen identity information management leads to individuals' desire for more and better communication from government about the handling of their identity data

Source: Lips *et al.* (2015)

of citizens' personal data by the data recipient(s) and, with that, a strong tendency to withhold personal data are closely related to each other and are associated with the context of digital government relationships (Lips *et al*, 2015).

The surveillance state and fair state perspectives emerging from these empirical research findings are summarised in Table 8.1 (Lips *et al*, 2015). They reveal that people's perception of their relationship with government in the digital government context can be quite different, which also has implications for what these people would consider as contextual integrity in their digital government relationships.

Emerging issues, barriers and risks

A number of issues, barriers and risks around citizens' personal data in digital government relationships emerge from our discussion thus far. We will briefly discuss these issues and risks next.

- *The sharing of personal data and citizen identification have become default settings in digital government relationships*: citizens' personal data have become a critical enabler of digital government service provision and evidence-based public decision-making;

210 *Emerging issues*

- *Increasing cross-government data sharing*: many scholars observe tensions between an increased sharing of citizen identity information across government and the privacy rights of individuals (e.g. 6, Lasky & Fletcher, 1998; Murakami-Wood *et al*, 2006; Raab, 2005; Solove, 2004). However, several studies also point to the complex nature of actually achieving increased cross-government data sharing as a result of significant organizational, political, legal and technical barriers in digital government environments (6, Raab & Bellamy, 2005; Bellamy *et al*, 2007; Gil-Garcia, Chengalur-Smith & Duchessi, 2007);
- *The difficulty for individual citizens to opt out of sharing their personal data*: citizens, especially those highly dependent on government services, have no choice but to provide their personal data in digital government service relationships;
- *Citizens' personal data can be shared in non-personal ways, such as aggregated or de-identified data*: there is an increasing awareness that citizens' personal data are not always needed in evidence-based public decision-making, for example. Open government data are a good example of non-personal data that can be shared (see also Chapter 5);
- *Combinations of non-personal data can generate personal information*: combinations of non-personal data, such as open data, can generate personal information about individual citizens: for example, only a limited number of people living in a rural town in New Zealand will be 6 foot 8 and belong to a certain age group;
- *Meta-data can be identifiable personal data*: meta-data, such as telephone logs, can reveal a citizen's identity;
- *The ease of re-identification*: the application of big data techniques in particular can make the re-identification of de-identified data relatively straightforward, unless the data are fully de-identified by removing both unique identifiers and quasi-identifiers (Kitchin, 2016; Baracos & Nissenbaum, 2014);
- *Government legacy systems of citizen identification can influence dominant thinking about new digital forms of citizen identification*: similar to the dominant role of the passport or birth certificate in citizen-government relationships in the paper-based era, having a single digital citizen identifier is often seen as the holy grail. However, having a single citizen identifier for many service interactions in digital government relationships, such as the Social Security number in the USA, also can cause major security concerns around the attractiveness of such a citizen identifier for identity fraud or theft;
- *Centralised personal data storage in digital government is risky*: potential risks include criminals trying to get access to the centralised database, misuse of data and hacking. Instead, to ensure that no government or person has sole control of citizens' personal data, digital identity information systems used in digital government relationships should be distributed, transparent, trustworthy and user-controlled, and they should adhere to privacy-by-design and transparency-by-design principles (Janssen & van den Hoven, 2015: 365).

Identity, privacy, ethics and security 211

- *There is no 100 percent information security solution*: all technology solutions can be broken deliberately (e.g. hacking, malware, data abuse, identity fraud, identity theft) or unconsciously; the human factor is the weakest link in any information security solution as people often don't understand the technology and can access data or make mistakes, for example (Schneier, 2000);
- *Third-party access to citizens' personal data in digital government relationships*: the use of social media sites (e.g. Facebook) and apps in digital government relationships can lead to third-party access to citizens' personal data. Such third-party access is usually out of sight and not transparent for individual citizens;
- *Notice and informed consent can be either absent, difficult to achieve or an empty exercise in smart government applications*: increasingly, the application of smart technologies in digital government relationships, such as sensors, makes it difficult if not impossible to ask citizens for informed consent to collect their personal data (e.g. sensing lights in airports collecting data on people's movements, data collected on people's movements in traffic);
- *Opacity of personal data (re-)use in digital government*: scholars point out that digital government service access and consumption are generating largely unseen forms of citizens' personal data that often underpin digital government service relationships, such as people's click behaviour and use of government websites (Lips, Taylor & Organ, 2009a; Lips, Taylor & Organ, 2009b). More in general, empirical research findings show that people have little awareness of what citizen identity data are held by government (MORI, 2003). A further problem is that, although the application of digital technologies for the collection and management of citizen identity information is not necessarily hidden to individuals, these systems and practices are usually not transparent (Gandy, 1993; Solove, 2004; Lyon, 2007). These issues undermine fair information practice principles at the heart of privacy regulation, making it difficult for citizens:

  - to seek access to their personal data;
  - to know how personal data collected about them are being (re-)used;
  - to assess how fair any actions taken on their personal data are; and
  - to hold data users or controllers to account.

Consequently, several scholars and practitioners consider enhanced and meaningful transparency as a way to better protect citizen identity data, improve citizen control over their own personal data and enhance trust (OECD, 2008; Lusoli, Maghiros & Bacigalupo, 2008; Nissenbaum, 2010).

Citizen data integrity in digital government

In Chapter 6 we proposed a new ethical framework of contextual integrity for assessing and evaluating data flow in the context of digital government relationships. This includes the flow of citizens' personal data in such relationships. The

212 *Emerging issues*

value of applying this ethical framework to assess potential benefits and harms of personal data flow in digital government relationships has been confirmed in an empirical study of online identity information behaviours of New Zealanders in their digital relationships with government (Lips *et al*, 2015). Research participants in this study pointed to the critical importance of the context in which they share their personal data online: according to them, sharing personal data in digital relationships is about trust and who they are dealing with (Lips *et al*, 2015). The large majority of the research participants indicated that they trusted the New Zealand government in particular with their personal data, compared with other governments in the world (Lips *et al*, 2015).

Ethical norms around personal data flow in digital government

However, although research participants did indicate that they have high level of trust in digital government relationships with the New Zealand government, it is often not clear to them which New Zealand government agency or who they are actually dealing with (Lips *et al*, 2015). This problem of blurring boundaries in digital environments between various actors, sectors and domains is a generic societal development, as we discussed in Chapter 6; with increasing uptake of smart technologies and innovative data use, further blurring and integration of domains is widely expected (Gil-Garcia, Pardo & Nam, 2016). However, from a contextual integrity point of view, this blurring or even crossing of boundaries including a loss of "line of sight" for citizens around the use of their personal data in digital government relationships is highly problematic (see Box 8.3).

Box 8.3   Case study: Online provisional driver's licence application in the UK

UK citizens wanting to apply for a provisional driver's licence used to go to a local post office branch where they submitted a form including their demographic details, accompanied by paper-based proofs of identity (e.g. passport). Since 2006, the UK Driver and Vehicle Licensing Agency (DVLA) also has offered this service online through the UK central government's Direct.gov web portal, which uses the Government Gateway authentication infrastructure. Users needed to register separately for online access to the DVLA service and to the Government Gateway infrastructure.

When registering for the online DVLA service, applicants needs to complete an online form providing identity information including surname, date of birth, UK passport number, National Insurance number, driver number, credit card details and previous addresses over the

Identity, privacy, ethics and security 213

past three years. After submission, the identity information is digitally matched with DVLA's database to retrieve any existing data for the applicant, including previous applications and driving disqualification information. If this data-matching process doesn't provide any matches, then the applicant can continue with the online application process, creating a new record. Likewise, the applicant can proceed in case of one match with the DVLA database that potentially could prohibit progression (e.g. common surname). However, if multiple matches occur, the application will need to be checked by a staff member and cannot be completed online.

In those cases where the applicant is allowed to proceed, the applicant's identity information is automatically transferred to a commercial information solutions provider who searches for data matches and checks the reliability of the submitted information in a variety of private-sector and public-sector databases (e.g. mail-order catalogues, banking). Based on the hits during this digital footprint assessment, a "trust score" is generated and used by DVLA to determine whether the application can be completed online. An applicant who has failed the assessment receives an instruction to complete the application through the traditional paper-based process. If the applicant proceeds through the assessment, they need to submit medical details to assess their qualification as a provisional driver (e.g. eye problems) and their passport number, which allows the UK Identity and Passport Service (IPS) to electronically transfer the digital passport photograph and signature from the applicant's passport records to the DVLA for use on the applicant's provisional driver's licence. The applicant then proceeds to online payments using a credit or debit card and, finally, will be able to check through the full application details on a verification screen.

Source: Lips (2013)

What this case study shows us is in fact a breach of contextual integrity in digital government: ethical decision-making that should have taken place in accordance with digital government context-relative norms, such as fairness, social justice and equality, has been outsourced to a third party in the private sector where other context-relative principles and norms are supported. In accordance with digital government contextual integrity, citizens have the right to know if any contextual boundaries around digital government are being crossed or merged and have the right to correct and challenge any citizen data exchanges and decision-making taking place outside the digital government context that has an impact on their relationships with government. Moreover, as governments are accountable for protecting and maintaining contextual

214 *Emerging issues*

integrity in digital government relationships, they should enforce digital government context-relative norms and principles on any third-party involved in digital government operations.

Security of personal data flow in digital government

Protecting and maintaining digital government's contextual integrity involves not only managing blurring boundaries between different domains but also providing security for data flows in digital government. The good thing about information security is that it also protects data privacy at the same time. According to Schneier (2015), the most important privacy-enhancing technology (PET) is encryption, which, of course, is an information security solution. Many governments around the world have adopted encryption in their digital government relationships with citizens.

However, Schneier (2000) also alludes to the fact that security in the context of digital government is not a product but a process in which human beings work with technologies. As mentioned, humans are the weakest link in this digital security process, as they can access the data or make mistakes, for example. Consequently, we should not be exclusively focused on technology products as potential security solutions for digital government but need to consider the whole socio-technical assemblage around a particular security technology in the context of digital government relationships.

More recently, blockchain technology is becoming an option for governments to consider in their digital government relationships. Several governments around the world, including Estonia, have adopted this technology. Not only is blockchain both a PET and a SET (security-enhancing technology), but it also provides citizens with more control over their personal data.

Box 8.4 Blockchain use in Estonia

Blockchain is a mathematically ensured cyber security technology for rapid and immutable identification of modifications in digital data and intelligent devices; every change in data can be instantly detected based on traces left in the pattern across connected blocks of the chain. The connected blocks in the chain cannot be changed without leaving a trace behind. These connected blocks are distributed in millions of computers all over the world. When changes are made, the chain instantly reflects all these changes that mismatch the mathematical code in the chain. No data is stored on a blockchain, but changes in the pattern instantly reveal who has accessed the data, when and how. The blockchain is an Internet-hosted network which stores information as a shared database.

The Estonian blockchain technology protects a wide range of digital government and other e-services, including the e-Health Record, e-Prescription database, e-Law and e-Court systems, e-Police data, e-Banking, e-Business Register and e-Land Registry. For example, in order to keep health information secure and at the same time accessible to authorised individuals, the electronic ID-card system used by the Estonian e-Health Record uses blockchain technology to ensure data integrity and mitigate internal threats to the data. Patients own their own health data in Estonia, which is available in digital format. Typically, an e-Health record contains medical case notes, test results, digital prescriptions and X-rays, as well as a full log-file tracking access to the data. Each Estonian has exclusive access to their own record and can control which doctors or family members have access to these data online (Tapscott & Tapscott, 2018: 198).

With blockchain technology, every occurrence of data use and misuse is detectable, and major damages to a person's health can be prevented (such as the wrong medicine or the wrong dose). Similarly, blockchain technology helps to detect who changed data about real estate in the e-Land register or statements documented in the e-Court system, when and how. Or when information about a company was changed in the e-Business Register and why. Also, blockchain technology helps to ensure that no one has manipulated smart devices, such as intelligent transportation or smart war machines that could become life-threatening.

In the digital government context, there are of course legitimate needs of government for law enforcement and intelligence gathering. We sometimes learn about governments creating back-door options in security arrangements in order to be able to access personal data in the fight against terrorism, for example. However, legitimate law enforcement can be done in accordance with context-relative norms and without any violations of privacy, subverting of security or infringing on citizens' right to be free of unreasonable suspicion and observation (Schneier, 2015: 257).

Contextual integrity is a critical part of the social contract

In summary, contextual integrity of digital government is a critical part of the social contract between citizens and government in an increasingly data-enabled world; citizens trust that they have provided their personal data to government in digital government relationships, not to a commercial company or a financial institution like a credit reference agency. This then also raises some questions around government's use of third-party social media networks (e.g. Facebook, Google and YouTube) and their personal data collection and use behaviours, in governments' democratic and public engagement activities with

216 *Emerging issues*

the general public, without the enforcement of digital government context-relative norms on these third parties (see also Chapter 7).

In general, application of the revised contextual integrity framework suggests that all citizens have the right to the integrity of their personal data in accordance with context-relative norms and general ethical principles for digital government relationships, including fairness, social justice, privacy protection and security (see also Chapter 6).

Citizen data integrity strategies for digital government

Considering our discussion thus far, the following citizen data integrity strategies could benefit the design and further development of digital government:

- *The reconceptualization of personal data in digital government relationships*: we are witnessing a proliferation of digitised types of personal data in accordance with existing legal definitions, which are very broad and non-contextual. The implications of using such a broad definition of personal data is that not only will privacy legislation be easily breached, but legal compliance may even become unmanageable. This suggests the need to rethink and reconceptualise personal data in digital government relationships. In accordance with the theory of contextual integrity, it may be more appropriate for the digital government context to make a distinction between citizens' personal data from their private sphere, and citizens' identity data as assigned by government (e.g. Social Security number, National Health Service number, driver's licence number). Consequently, a narrower definition of "personal data" can be used in digital government relationships, which can not only support legal compliance with privacy legislation, but also better enable cross-government sharing and use of citizen data for the benefit of individual citizens and enhancing people's lives;
- *Provide citizens with more control over their personal data and their citizen data*: enhanced transparency of how people's personal data, including citizen data, are managed will lead to increased control of citizens and enhanced trust in digital government relationships;
- *Adoption of blockchain technology in digital government relationships can provide citizens with more control over their personal data*: a technology solution like blockchain can be used to enhance the privacy and security of the data flow in digital government relationships, prevent blurring of boundaries between different sectors and provide citizens with more control over their personal data;
- *Minimise the sharing and use of identifiable citizen data in digital government relationships*: as discussed, citizens' data do not always need to be used in identifiable ways but can be shared and used in aggregated, de-identified forms. Moreover, governments could use the strategy to only collect and use citizen and other personal data that are absolutely necessary in order to achieve government objectives;

- *Use anonymisation strategies:* the privacy of individuals can be protected through anonymisation strategies, including the use of pseudonyms instead of real information, aggregation of personal data and de-identification of personal data;
- *Make re-identification of de-identified citizen data illegal*;
- *Use privacy-by-design principles, including the application of privacy-enhancing technologies (PETs) and privacy impact assessments*;
- *Use transparency-by-design principles, including the application of transparency-enhancing technologies (TETs) and transparency impact assessments*; and
- *Use security-by-design principles, including the application of security-enhancing technologies (SETs) and security impact assessments.*

Box 8.5 Exercise 8.1

Conduct qualitative interviews with three citizens from different backgrounds in your country and explore the following:

1 Do they indicate having online privacy concerns that are different than their online behaviour in digital government relationships?
2 Do they consider sharing their personal data with government in digital government relationships to be different than sharing their data with commercial entities online? In what way(s)?
3 What considerations do they have in sharing their personal data with or protecting it from government agencies via different digital channels and for different purposes (e.g. health data, tax data, driver's licence data, benefit data, address data)?
4 Compare similarities and differences in answers between the three citizens.

Discussion questions

1 Apply the contextual integrity framework to a theoretical situation where citizens need to apply for a social benefit online, and algorithms are used in the background to construct a risk profile for each applicant. What would be the outcome of your evaluation assessment: which ethical norms are at play here, and how are they either supported or violated?
2 In your view, what are the three best strategies for governments to support citizen data integrity in digital government relationships? Motivate your answer.
3 Informed consent of citizens is not possible any longer in many smart government applications. What would be your solution to this problem?

218 *Emerging issues*

Note

1 Bloomberg News, Beijing to judge every resident based on behavior by end of 2020, November 21, 2018, available from: https://www.bloomberg.com/news/articles/2018-11-21/beijing-to-judge-every-resident-based-on-behavior-by-end-of-2020 [accessed 4 February 2019].

References

6, P. (1998) *The Future of Privacy: Vol. 1: Private Life and Public Policy.* London: Demos.

6, P., Lasky, K. & Fletcher, A. (1998) *The Future of Privacy: Vol. 2: Public Trust and the Use of Private Information.* London: Demos.

6, P., Raab, C.D. & Bellamy, C. (2005) Joined-up government and privacy in the United Kingdom: Managing tensions between data protection and social policy: Part 1. *Public Administration,* 83 (1), 111–133.

Acquisti, A., John, L.K. & Loewenstein, G. (2013) What is privacy worth? *The Journal of Legal Studies,* 42 (2), 249–274.

Baracos, S. & Nissenbaum, H. (2014) Big data's end run around anonymity and consent. In: Lane, J., Stodden, V., Bender, S. & Nissenbaum, H. (eds.) *Privacy, Big Data, and the Public Good: Frameworks for Engagement.* New York, NY: Cambridge University Press, pp. 322–358.

Bellamy, C., 6, P., Raab, C.D., Warren, A. & and Heeney, C. (2008) Information sharing and confidentiality in social policy: Regulating multi-agency working. *Public Administration,* 86 (3), 737–759.

Bellamy, C., Raab, C.D., Warren, A. & Heeney, C. (2007) Institutional shaping of interagency working: Managing tensions between collaborative working and client confidentiality. *Journal of Public Administration Research and Theory,* 17 (3), 405–435.

Bennett, C.J. & Raab, C.D. (2003) *The Governance of Privacy: Policy Instruments in Global Perspective.* Aldershot: Ashgate.

Birch, D.G.W. (2007) *Digital Identity Management: Perspectives on the Technological, Business and Social Implications.* Aldershot: Gower Publishing Limited.

Boyd, D. (2014) *It Is Complicated: The Social Lives of Networked Teens.* New York, NY: Yale University Press.

Buchanan, T., Paine, C., Joinson, A.N. & Reips, U. (2007) Development of measures of online privacy concern and protection for use on the internet. *Journal of the American Society for Information Science and Technology,* 58 (2), 157–165.

Dutch Scientific Council. (2016) *Big Data in een vrije en veilige samenleving.* Wetenschappelijke Raad voor het Regeringsbeleid, 95, Den Haag: WRR.

Floridi, L. (2014) *The Fourth Revolution: How the Infosphere Is Reshaping Human Reality.* Oxford: Oxford University Press.

Gandy, O. (1993) *The Panoptic Sort: A Political Economy of Personal Information.* Boulder, CO: Westview Press.

Gil-Garcia, J.R., Chengalur-Smith, I. & Duchessi, P. (2007) Collaborative e-government: Impediments and benefits of information sharing projects in the public sector. *European Journal of Information Systems,* 16, 121–133.

Gil-Garcia, J.R., Pardo, T.A. & Nam, T. (eds.) (2016) *Smarter as the New Urban Agenda: A Comprehensive View of the 21st Century City.* Springer International Publishing, ebook.

Halperin, R. & Backhouse, J. (2008) A roadmap for research on identity in the information society. *Identity in the Information Society,* 1 (1), pp. 71–87.

Heintzman, R. & Marson, B. (2005) People, service and trust: Is there a public sector service value chain? *International Review of Administrative Sciences,* 71 (4), 549–575.

Identity, privacy, ethics and security 219

Institute for Insight in the Public Services. (2008) *Data and Privacy: How Concerned Are Citizens About Data Sharing in the Public Service?* London: Institute for Insight in the Public Services.

Janssen, M. & van den Hoven, J. (2015) Big and Open Linked Data (BOLD) in government: A challenge to transparency and privacy? *Government Information Quarterly*, 32, 363–368.

Kampen, J.K., van de Walle, S. & Bouckaert, G. (2006) Assessing the relation between satisfaction with public service delivery and trust in government: The impact of the predisposition of citizens toward government on evaluations of its performance. *Public Performance & Management Review*, 29 (4), 387–404.

Kitchin, R. (2016) The ethics of smart cities and urban science. 374, In: *Philosophical Transactions of the Royal Society A: Mathematical, Physical and Engineering Sciences*, epub. Available from: http://dx.doi.org/10.1098/rsta.2016.0115

Lips, A.M.B. (2013) Reconstructing, attributing and fixating citizen identities in digital-era government. *Media, Culture and Society*, 35 (1), 61–70.

Lips, A.M.B., Taylor, J.A. & Organ, J. (2009a) Identity management, administrative sorting and citizenship in new modes of government. *Information, Communication & Society*, 12 (5), 715–734.

Lips, A.M.B., Taylor, J.A. & Organ, J. (2009b) Managing citizen identity information in e-government service relationships in the UK: The emergence of a surveillance state or a service state? *Public Management Review*, 11 (6), 833–856.

Lips, A.M.B., Eppel, E., Barlow, L., Löfgren, B., Löfgren, K. & Sim, D. (February 2015) *Kiwis Managing Their Online Identity Information*. Final Research Report. Wellington: Victoria University of Wellington.

Livingstone, S. & Bober, M. (2004) *UK Children Go Online: Surveying the Experiences of Young People and Their Parents*. Research Report. London: London School of Economics and Political Science.

London School of Economics. (June 2005) *The Identity Project: An Assessment of the UK Identity Cards Bill and Its Implications*. London: LSE Identity Project Final Report.

Lupton, D. & Williamson, B. (2017) The datafied child: The dataveillance of children and implications for their rights. *New Media & Society*, 19 (5), 780–794.

Lusoli, W., Maghiros, I. & Bacigalupo, M. (2008) E-ID policy in a turbulent environment: Is there a need for a new regulatory framework? *Identity in the Information Society*, 1 (1), 173–187.

Lyon, D. (2001) *Surveillance Society: Monitoring Everyday Life*. Buckingham: Open University Press.

Lyon, D. (2003a) Surveillance as social sorting: Computer codes and mobile bodies. In: Lyon, D. (ed.) *Surveillance & Social Sorting: Privacy, Risk and Digital Discrimination*. London: Routledge, pp. 13–30.

Lyon, D. (ed.) (2003b) *Surveillance & Social Sorting: Privacy, Risk and Digital Discrimination*. London: Routledge.

Lyon, D. (2007) *Surveillance Studies: An Overview*. Cambridge: Polity Press.

Madden, M. & Smith, A. (2010) *Reputation Management and Social Media: How People Monitor Their Identity and Search for Others Online*. Washington, DC: Pew Internet & American Life Project, Pew Research Center.

Meijer, A.J. (2015) *Bestuur in de datapolis: Slimme stad, blije burger?* Den Haag: Boom Bestuurskunde.

Moore, B. (1984) *Privacy: Studies in Social and Cultural History*. Armonk, NY: M.E Sharpe.

MORI. (2003) *Privacy and Data Sharing for Department for Constitutional Affairs: Survey of Public Awareness and Perceptions*. London: Department of Constitutional Affairs.

220 Emerging issues

Murakami-Wood, D., Ball, K., Lyon, D., Norris, C. & Raab, C.D. (September 2006) *A Report on the Surveillance Society*. The Information Commissioner by the Surveillance Studies Network.

Nissenbaum, H. (2010) *Privacy in Context: Technology, Policy and the Integrity of Social Life*. Stanford, CA: Stanford University Press.

OECD. (2008) *At the Crossroads: 'Personhood' and Digital Identity in the Information Society*. Working Paper 2007/7, Directorate for Science Technology and Industry, Information and Communication Technologies. Paris: OECD.

OECD. (2009) *The Role of Digital Identity Management in the Internet Economy: A Primer for Policy Makers*. Directorate for Science Technology and Industry. Paris: OECD.

Palfrey, J. & Gasser, U. (2008) *Born Digital: Understanding the First Generation of Digital Natives*. New York, NY: Basic Books.

Pew. (2015) *Americans' Privacy Strategies Post-Snowden*. Research Report, Pew Research Center. Available from: https://www.pewinternet.org/files/2015/03/PI_Americans PrivacyStrategies_0316151.pdf [accessed 24 June 2018].

Raab, C.D. (2005) Perspectives on 'personal identity'. *BT Technology Journal*, 23 (4), 15–24.

Regan, P. (1995) *Legislating Privacy*. Chapel Hill, NC: University of North Carolina Press.

Schneier, B. (2000) *Secrets and Lies: Digital Security in a Networked World*. Indianapolis, IN: Wiley Publishing, Inc.

Schneier, B. (2015) *Data and Goliath*. New York, NY: W.W. Norton & Company, Inc.

Schoeman, F. (1984) *Philosophical Dimensions of Privacy: An Anthology*. Cambridge: Cambridge University Press.

Solove, D. (2004) *The Ditigal Person: Technology and Privacy in the Information Age*. New York, NY: New York University Press.

Tapscott, D. & Tapscott, A. (2018) *Blockchain Revolution: How the Technology Behind Bitcoin and Other Cryptocurrencies Is Changing the World*. London: Penguin Random House UK.

UK House of Lords Select Committee on the Constitution. (2009) *Surveillance: Citizens and the State*. Vol. 1 Report. London: The Stationery Office Ltd.

Van de Walle, S., Kampen, J.K. & Bouckaert, G. (2005) Deep impact for high-impact agencies? Assessing the role of bureaucratic encounters in evaluations of government. *Public Performance & Management Review*, 28 (4), 532–549.

Van de Walle, S., Van Roosbroek, S. & Bouckaert, G. (2008) Trust in the public sector: Is there any evidence for a long-term decline? *International Review of Administrative Sciences*, 74 (1), 47–64.

van Dijck, J. (2014) Datafication, dataism and dataveillance: Big Data between scientific paradigm and ideology. *Surveillance & Society*, 12 (2), 197–208.

van Zoonen, L. (2014) *What Do Users Want from Their Future Means of Identity Management?* Final Report. Available from: http://imprintsfutures.org/assets//images/pdfs/End%20 report%20IMPRINTS.pdf [accessed 24 June 2018].

van Zoonen, L. (2016) Privacy concerns in smart cities. *Government Information Quarterly*, 33, 472–480.

Viseu, A., Clement, A. & Aspinall, J. (2004) Situating privacy online: Complex perceptions and everyday practices. *Information, Communication and Society*, 7 (1), 92–114.

Wacks, R. (1989) *Personal Information: Privacy and the Law*. Oxford: Clarendon Press.

Warren, S.D. & Brandeis, L.D. (1890) The right to privacy. *Harvard Law Review*, 4 (5), 193–220.

Whitley, E.A. & Hosein, I. (2010) *Global Challenges for Identity Policies*. London: Palgrave Macmillan.

Young, A.L. & Quan-Haase, A. (2013) Privacy protection strategies on Facebook: The internet privacy paradox revisited. *Information, Communication & Society*, 16 (4), 479–500.

Further reading

6, P., Raab, C.D. & Bellamy, C. (2005) Joined-up government and privacy in the United Kingdom: Managing tensions between data protection and social policy: Part 1. *Public Administration*, 83 (1), 111–133.

Bellamy, C., 6, P., Raab, C.D., Warren, A. & and Heeney, C. (2008) Information sharing and confidentiality in social policy: Regulating multi-agency working. *Public Administration*, 86 (3), 737–759.

Bennett, C.J. & Raab, C.D. (2003) *The Governance of Privacy: Policy Instruments in Global Perspective*. Aldershot: Ashgate.

Boyd, D. (2014) *It Is Complicated: The Social Lives of Networked Teens*. New York, NY: Yale University Press.

Lips, A.M.B. (2013) Reconstructing, attributing and fixating citizen identities in digital-era government. *Media, Culture and Society*, 35 (1), 61–70.

Lips, A.M.B., Taylor, J.A. & Organ, J. (2009a) Identity management, administrative sorting and citizenship in new modes of government. *Information, Communication & Society*, 12 (5), 715–734.

Lips, A.M.B., Taylor, J.A. & Organ, J. (2009b) Managing citizen identity information in e-government service relationships in the UK: The emergence of a surveillance state or a service state? *Public Management Review*, 11 (6), 833–856.

Lips, M., Eppel, E., Barlow, L., Löfgren, B., Löfgren, K. & Sim, D. (February 2015) *Kiwis Managing Their Online Identity Information*. Final Research Report. Wellington: Victoria University of Wellington.

Lyon, D. (ed.) (2003b) *Surveillance & Social Sorting: Privacy, Risk and Digital Discrimination*. London: Routledge.

Moore, B. (1984) *Privacy: Studies in Social and Cultural History*. Armonk, NY: M.E Sharpe.

Nissenbaum, H. (2010) *Privacy in Context: Technology, Policy and the Integrity of Social Life*. Stanford, CA: Stanford University Press.

Schneier, B. (2000) *Secrets and Lies: Digital Security in a Networked World*. Indianapolis, IN: Wiley Publishing, Inc.

Schneier, B. (2015) *Data and Goliath*. New York, NY: W.W. Norton & Company, Inc.

Solove, D. (2004) *The Ditigal Person: Technology and Privacy in the Information Age*. New York, NY: New York University Press.

Tapscott, D. & Tapscott, A. (2018) *Blockchain Revolution: How the Technology Behind Bitcoin and Other Cryptocurrencies Is Changing the World*. London: Penguin Random House UK.

9 Digital citizenship

Learning objectives

By the end of this chapter you should be able to:

* Understand that digital inclusion and digital exclusion are equally important areas that need to be considered on a continuum;
* Understand the critical impact of context on digital inclusion and exclusion issues;
* Identify relevant digital divides for digital government relationships in a particular country; and
* Identify relevant draft citizens' rights for digital government relationships in your country.

Key points of this chapter

* Digital inclusion and digital exclusion are equally important areas that need to be considered as a continuum rather than as binary categorisations, taking into account that forms and gradations in frequency of digital use and non-use can be different for different groups of the population in different social and cultural contexts as well as national contexts, may change over time and often depend on past personal experience or that of friends and family;
* An empirical non-linear approach needs to be adopted in digital inequalities research in order to better understand and explain the critical impact of the social, economic, geographical and temporal context on individual digital inclusion or exclusion behaviours. This also applies to the context of digital government relationships;
* As the context of digital government has a major impact on digital inclusion and exclusion issues in relationships between citizens and government, we need to consider dimensions of digital divides in those citizen-government relationships different than those of the digital divides existing in other contexts, such as commercial contexts and a social context with family and friends;

Digital citizenship 223

- Digital divides in the context of citizen-government relationships have six dimensions (i.e. access, ability, skills, knowledge, trust and use) and three digital government focus areas: digital technology divides, digital divides around data and digital government service divides; and
- Based on the needs of citizens in accordance with empirical research findings to date, a number of draft citizens' rights for digital government relationships can be proposed.

Key terms

- *Digital divide*: originally a division between population groups that have access to the Internet and those that do not. In this chapter, a case is made for the existence of multiple digital divides in different digital government focus areas: digital technologies, data and digital government services.
- *Digital inclusion*: a broader, multi-dimensional conceptualisation of digital divide issues focused on technology-enabled use as a social need.
- *Digital exclusion*: a much more complex and differentiated phenomenon then just the binary opposite of digital inclusion. It includes digital behaviours of non-use, low-use and ex-use around a specific Internet-enabled activity and in a certain context. These behaviours can also change over time.

Introduction

In 1995, the US federal government's National Telecommunications and Information Administration (NTIA) published a report "Falling Through The Net: A Survey of the 'Have Nots' in Rural and Urban America" (NTIA, 1995). It was one of the first reports signaling an emerging problem of social inequality for those American citizens from low socio-economic backgrounds who do not have access to the Internet and proposing projects and initiatives to overcome this divide between different groups of the American population (Lips & Frissen, 1997).

Since then, many studies have been published about the existence of a so-called digital divide affecting different parts of the population in countries around the world. However, scholarly assumptions and interpretations of the nature, meaning and extent of the digital divide have been varied, with Internet access not being considered the only digital divide, nor the sole requirement for people to enjoy the benefits of full digital inclusion, for example (e.g. van Dijk, 2005; Hargittai, 2002; Hacker & Mason, 2003).

In this chapter, we explore scholarly insights to date around the digital divide, which, over time, have identified multiple dimensions along which digital divides can be distinguished. We broaden this binary perspective on the digital divide to a continuum of digital inclusion and exclusion. We can observe that digital inclusion and exclusion issues are even more complex in the context of digital government; consequently, instead of applying a technology perspective that is exclusively focused on (access to) Internet technology

224 *Emerging issues*

(e.g. Anderson, 2012), an alternative, multi-dimensional understanding of digital divides is proposed which takes into account the wider socio-technical context of digital government and its unique relationships with citizens. Moreover, we further unpack and explore digital inclusion and exclusion issues for three different digital government focus areas where those unique digitised citizen-government relationships occur: an area focused on digital technologies, predominantly the Internet; an area focused on data in digital government relationships, including government data, big data research and citizen data and an area focused on digital government services.

The resulting gap analysis around digitally excluded population groups in digital government relationships is used in the final section of this chapter to explore citizens' rights in digital government relationships. Such citizens' rights could be used as input for the development of citizen-centric digital government intervention programmes, which, in light of increasing information asymmetries and power imbalances in digital government relationships with citizens as observed by scholars (e.g. Dutch Scientific Council, 2016; Pasquale, 2015; London School of Economics, 2005), would support the rebalancing of the unique relationship between digital government and citizens.

Multiple digital divides exist

Since the arrival of the Internet in the early 1990s, a dominant assumption has been that having access to Internet technology is better for people than not having it and, indeed, desirable to reduce social, economic and democratic inequalities in a society (Wyatt, 2003). Consequently, policy-makers around the world have been trying to close or at least narrow the gap of a digital divide that originally was acknowledged to exist between mainly young, more highly educated white males living in urban areas and other groups of the population (see, for instance, NTIA, 1995).

Nowadays, however, our understanding of the digital divide has changed substantially. For instance, for some time it was assumed that Internet use would automatically follow Internet access and that increasing and improving Internet access would be enough to close the digital divide (Wyatt, 2003; Bach, Shaffer & Wolfson, 2013). However, many studies have demonstrated that Internet use is not guaranteed by having Internet access and can be understood as a digital divide by itself with inequalities among various parts of the population (Hargittai, 2002; Thomas & Wyatt, 2000). Research variables that are often found significant in inequalities around Internet use are age, education, gender, income, race and geographical location (e.g. rural), with an acknowledgement that digital divides are not static but dynamic and have different social distributions of inequalities in countries around the world (Hargittai, 2002; van Dijk, 2005).

Many scholars have contributed to a better empirical understanding of these digital divides and identified different dimensions along which digital divides may exist, including technical or physical access to digital technologies, use, skills, (dis-)abilities, knowledge, motivation, the availability of social support networks

Digital citizenship 225

and trust (van Dijk, 2005; Hargittai, 2002; van Deursen & van Dijk, 2014). Also, Hargittai (2002) has found some empirical evidence of the existence of a second-level digital divide around the varying online knowledge and skills of Internet users, with age and experience with Internet technology showing significant variances amongst her US-based research population. Her findings point out that having access to or even being able to use an Internet-enabled device is not enough to use the Internet (more) effectively; in addition, training and education are needed for individuals to have the knowledge and skills to maximise the opportunities offered by the Internet (Hargittai, 2002, 2010).

These different dimensions of digital divides have ended up in broader, multi-dimensional conceptualisations of digital inclusion (Helsper, 2008). Many governments around the world have adopted such a broader understanding of digital inclusion and developed a digital inclusion strategy along these multiple dimensions to address specific digital inclusion issues for their respective jurisdictions. For example, in Australia, a digital inclusion index[1] has been developed by stakeholders from the private and public sectors in order to create a baseline for digital inclusion along those multiple dimensions and assess progress over time at local, regional and national levels. These progress assessments help public policy-makers to develop more effective programmes to enhance digital inclusion across Australia.

Digital inclusion issues require regular empirical research

Initiatives such as the Australian digital inclusion index show us not only that digital divides are multiple, multi-dimensional and more complex than we may have thought originally, but also that we should not assume that digital inclusion issues and their required solutions are similar for different regions or countries. Empirical research within each individual country and at various geographical levels is of critical importance to understanding the complex nature, diversity and depth of digital inclusion issues in a particular social, cultural, geographical or economic context. Furthermore, as digital inclusion issues are changing over time, they will need to be empirically revisited from time to time in order to monitor, measure and assess developments around these issues (Helsper, 2008). Many governments are investing in policies and programmes with the objective of narrowing or even closing the gaps in these multiple digital divides between different parts of the population. Regular empirical research will help to monitor developments around digital inclusion and exclusion, including the potential impact of government interventions or activities undertaken by others in order to narrow the gaps between different groups of the population.

Digital inclusion and exclusion

Digital inclusion is perceived by many as the norm: with that, many politicians and policy-makers consider digital inclusion as a social need to be fulfilled or, put differently, digital exclusion as a sign of deficiency to be remedied (Wyatt, 2003). Many governments around the world have put strategies in place

226 Emerging issues

in order to improve digital inclusion amongst various groups of the population and reduce forms of digital exclusion. Expected benefits of a more digitally inclusive society, including more digitally inclusive government, are the following:

- more vibrant and prosperous communities;
- increased social, economic and democratic participation;
- more productive use of digital technologies;
- increased digital literacy;
- increased uptake of digital government services;
- more equitable access to digital government services for all population groups; and
- better enabling digital citizenship.

However, the fact that full digital inclusion does not exist in countries around the world demonstrates that we will need to get a better empirical understanding about the phenomenon of digital exclusion, such as those people who do not use the Internet or have used it in the past. This phenomenon of digital exclusion seems much more complex and differentiated than being just the binary opposite of digital inclusion (Hargittai, 2002; Peter & Valkenburg, 2006). Wyatt (2003) points to the importance of considering digital technology users in relation to non-users; she warns of an exclusive emphasis on increasing digital inclusion and the number of users and of the misconception that, once a user, an individual will always be a user (Wyatt, 2003: 73). Although the availability of empirical research into digital exclusion is still limited, it is highly relevant as particular population groups seem to be substantially more affected by various forms of digital exclusion than others: significant factors raising the probability of being categorised as digitally excluded include age, gender, social class, income, education, ethnicity, disability, tenure, working status, the presence of young people in the household and geographical location (Bunyan & Collins, 2013; Yates, 2015; Lips et al, 2015).

Consequently, digital inclusion and digital exclusion are equally important areas that need to be considered as a continuum rather than as binary categorisations, taking into account that forms and gradations in frequency of digital use and non-use can be different for different groups of the population in different social, cultural and national contexts; may change over time and often depend on past personal experience or that of friends and family (Livingstone & Helsper, 2007; Wyatt, 2003; Anderson, 2012; Bach, Shaffer & Wolfson, 2013; Mubarak & Nycyk, 2017; Peter & Valkenburg, 2006)). This then also includes the possibility of change around a specific activity and within a certain context from use to non-use, low-use or ex-use, as well as a reversal from ex-use to using again. Furthermore, Helsper (2017) points out that even the personal characteristics of a digitally excluded individual, such as their socio-economic background, should not be assumed to consistently influence how they engage with digital technologies across different contexts over time. She sees the need to adopt a

Digital citizenship   227

relative, empirical non-linear approach to digital inequalities research in order to better understand and explain the critical impact of the social, geographical and temporal context of individual digital inclusion or exclusion behaviours.

This approach has found support with other scholars as well (e.g. Correa & Pavez, 2016). For example, Livingstone and Helsper (2007) have found that, since both the extent of Internet use and the reasons for low- and non-use vary by age, a different explanation for digital inclusion and exclusion is required for children than for adults. An example of the importance of using a continuum in order to understand digital inclusion and exclusion is the subtle differences in the online behaviours of people involved in digital government relationships, such as those using the Internet in order to search for government information but not using the Internet to follow up their information search efforts with a digital transaction (Lips *et al*, 2015). Based on comparative empirical research in two European countries – the UK and Sweden – another example of understanding digital inclusion and exclusion on a continuum points to the importance of taking into consideration national contexts, changing non-user characteristics and individual experience with the Internet in trying to find reasons, explanations and possible intervention solutions for digital exclusion: what worked a decade ago in a particular country might not work currently in a different or even the same country now (Helsper & Reisdorf, 2017). The same research also demonstrates that, between 2005 and 2013 and for different reasons, motivations for being online changed among non- and ex-users in the UK and Sweden and that non-user populations in these two European countries have become more concentrated in vulnerable groups (Helsper & Reisdorf, 2017).

Digital divides in digital government relationships

It is important to understand that, if we accept the scholarly view that the context of digital government has a major impact on digital inclusion and exclusion issues in relationships between citizens and government, we need to consider different dimensions of digital divides in those citizen-government relationships compared to digital divides existing in other contexts, such as commercial contexts and a social context with family and friends. This has everything to do with the unique nature of citizen-government relationships as discussed earlier.

For example, we have discussed that citizens usually do not have a choice regarding their use of digital government applications. Unlike the commercial or entertainment sector, for example, where people can shop around for their preferred goods or service, citizens are exclusively depending on a particular government agency to deliver them the service they need. Moreover, most governments have constitutionally arranged universal and equitable service obligations towards all citizens within their jurisdiction who meet the service provision criteria. Also, many governments around the world have adopted a digital-by-default policy in government service provision (see Chapter 4), which obliges citizens to use digital channels in their service relationships with government instead of paper-based or face-to-face interactions, for example.

228 *Emerging issues*

These are all examples of the unique institutional arrangements that determine the contextual settings of digital government relationships and, with that, citizens' digital inclusion and exclusion behaviours in the context of digital government. Consequently, if we consider a digital divide dimension that is often identified in scholarly literature as significant (van Dijk, 2005), namely motivation or voluntary use of digital technologies ("want" and "want-nots"), we need to come to the conclusion that this digital divide dimension often does not apply to the context of digital government relationships (see for instance Anderson, 2012). In this chapter, we explore and explain the following six dimensions of digital divides in order to identify digital inclusion and exclusion issues of relevance to digital government relationships:

- Have and have-nots (access issues);
- Can and cannots (abilities issues);
- Do and do-nots (skills issues);
- Know and know-nots (knowledge issues);
- Trust and trust-nots (trust issues); and
- Use and use-nots (use issues).

These dimensions are not binary categories but need to be seen as a continuum.

Another explanation for the need to treat digital inclusion and exclusion issues in the context of digital government relationships differently than in other social contexts is that a technology perspective, especially around the Internet, often influences both popular and scholarly debate on the digital divide. Indeed, scholarly technology acceptance models from the information systems literature, which do not factor in the relative, unique context of digital government relationships, are often applied when examining digital divide issues (Anderson, 2012).

As digital technologies, especially the Internet, are an important part of digital government but do not offer all the explanations for digital divides issues in the context of digital government relationships, we broaden our perspective by using two more focus areas where digital divides issues can be observed. In so doing, we further unpack the relevant context of "digital" in digital government relationships by focusing on digital divides issues around data collection, management and use in those relationships with citizens, and we further unpack "government" and its influence on digital government service relationships with citizens in order to identify further digital inclusion and exclusion issues. In summary, the following three different focus areas of digital divides are of critical relevance to the domain of digital government relationships with citizens:

1) Digital technology divides;
2) Digital divides around data; and
3) Digital government service divides.

We explore each of the digital divides' focus areas for digital government relationships with citizens, including the six relevant digital divides dimensions within each particular focus area, in more detail next.

1. Digital technology divides

Have and have-nots (access issues)

One of the first dimensions of digital divides has been for citizens to have Internet access or not in their relationships with government. Research shows that this digital technology divide turns out to be still relevant for digital government in many jurisdictions around the world for various reasons (Longley & Singleton, 2009; Philip, 2017; Rashid, 2016). Besides the issue of not having technical access or connectivity, access issues for citizens are caused by the cost involved in accessing the Internet, which is often a problem for people from low socio-economic backgrounds. Another digital divide issue is the geographic location of citizens: people or businesses based in rural or remote areas can experience Internet access problems, such as limited Internet speed, or may not have Internet access at all. Furthermore, for citizens in developing countries, cultural reasons can be an important explanation for digital exclusion on the access dimension of digital divides, such as in the case of women who prefer to access the Internet from home or another private location, instead of a public Internet access venue (Rashid, 2016).

Moreover, it is important to consider that digital technology access issues in digital government relationships can also emerge as a result of not having a suitable technical device. For example, in several countries around the world, primary schools have introduced mandatory policies for students to have a PC, laptop or tablet in order to do school work, which can be an affordability issue for parents. Furthermore, in many countries, citizens can afford the use of a mobile phone but do not have an Internet-enabled PC, laptop or tablet at home (see the discussion about m-government in Chapter 4).

Many governments around the world have put programmes or initiatives in place in order to solve the issue of access, including the following (NTIA, 1995; Lips & Frissen, 1997; Philip, 2017): improving connectivity by rolling out broadband, subsidizing the costs of Internet access, offering free WiFi in public spaces, establishing community hubs for Internet access in public places like schools or public libraries and installing Internet-enabled service kiosks in government service agencies. In 2016, the United Nations Human Rights Council adopted a non-binding resolution that condemns countries that intentionally take away or disrupt their citizens' Internet access: in other words, making a statement that Internet access needs to be considered as a basic human right for citizens.

Can and cannots (abilities issues)

Technological devices, the requirement to use a particular digital channel in digital government relationships, the configuration of web content and the technological configuration of hard- and software may cause major digital divide issues in digital government relationships for people with various disabilities, including people who are vision impaired, are deaf, or have autism spectrum disorders (Pacheco, 2016; Santarosa & Conforto, 2016). For example,

230　*Emerging issues*

based on their research into primary school students with autism spectrum disorders, Santarosa and Conforto (2016) found that, as laptops have complex operating systems with multiple configurations, they were not well suited for these students to undertake schoolwork; however, tablets and mobile phones turned out to be much better suited. Another example of disabilities issues in digital government relationships can be found in New Zealand, where deaf citizens had major problems with the need to phone up emergency services in case of an emergency. This digital divide issue was managed by enabling deaf people to send a text to emergency services, which has been an empowering experience for members of the New Zealand deaf community.

A particular digital divide issue around ability emerges amongst older senior citizens, such as people more than 80 years of age, who often experience issues around mental and/or physical deterioration which prevent them from using digital technologies (Mordini, 2009). Also, they may need assistive technologies in order to be able to access and use digital technologies (Mordini, 2009).

As government service provision is commonly based on a universal, equal access principle for all citizens, governments have an obligation to make sure that all citizens are able to use digital technologies in order to access digital government services. Consequently, besides offering digital government services through other digital channels or adjusting the required technological configurations for accessing digital government services, governments around the world have adopted web content accessibility standards and guidelines in order to manage digital divide issues around people's (dis-)abilities at various stages of their lives.

Do and do-nots (skills issues)

Digital skills are considered critically important for all citizens in order to more efficiently and effectively use digital technologies in various societal relationships, including in digital government (Eynon & Geniets, 2016; Hargittai, 2002; Mubarak & Nycyk, 2017). Research has identified substantial digital skills gaps between different groups of citizens, with gaps becoming even more profound beyond basic digital skill levels, such as online searching for information and when more complex and less generalised tasks need to be undertaken (Martínez-Cantos, 2017). Moreover, although a popular assumption is that young people, as digital natives, can simply learn digital skills by themselves, empirical research suggests that also they can experience digital exclusion in this area, especially as a result of the lack of access to and experience with digital technologies and the lack of social support networks (Eynon & Geniets, 2016).

Empirical research findings from New Zealand show that digital skills are not static but dynamic as people are learning about what to do and not to do with digital technologies, also based on their online experience (Lips *et al*, 2015). Significant inequalities in digital skills have been found amongst people of various age groups including among younger cohorts: between males and females, less and highly educated population groups, people with good access to digital technologies and those with poor access and experienced people and those with no or limited experience (Martínez-Cantos, 2017; Eynon & Geniets, 2016; Hargittai, 2002). Moreover, at a country level, living in a developed or a developing country, experiencing economic challenges and cultural beliefs also have an impact on digital divide issues and whether people, such as senior citizens, are able and willing to learn digital skills (Mubarak & Nycyk, 2017).

As digital technologies are increasingly used for a large variety of critical activities in societies around the world, including in varying forms of employment, governments are keen to reduce digital divide issues around digital skills. Governments around the world have put policy programmes and dedicated funding initiatives in place in order to close the digital skills gap, including training and education programmes tailored to different segments of the population (e.g. seniors, people with different education backgrounds) and to training needs for both basic and more advanced digital skill levels, the integration of digital skills into school curricula and programmes that put computers in homes in order to give people an opportunity to use Internet-enabled computers on a regular basis and, with that, get more digital confidence and experience.

Know and know-nots (knowledge issues)

Knowledge about how to use digital technologies efficiently, effectively and securely has been identified as an important digital divide dimension in digital government relationships (e.g. Seale & Dutton, 2012; Eynon & Geniets, 2016). Empowering citizens to become digitally included involves getting the knowledge to make informed choices about technology use in digital government relationships (Seale & Dutton, 2012).

Scholars have pointed to the importance of social support networks for digitally excluded citizens of varying age groups to get the knowledge to make these choices on how to use digital technologies (Courtois & Verdegem, 2016; Eynon & Geniets, 2016; Seale & Dutton, 2012). Also, governments are investing in education programmes to support digitally excluded citizens in this area. Moreover, in many countries, knowledge about how to use digital technologies has become part of primary and secondary school curricula.

Trust and trust-nots (trust issues)

Trust in digital technologies has been acknowledged as a critical digital divide dimension in digital government relationships, affecting all age groups of the population. For example, bad experiences with the Internet, such as a virus infecting a person's computer or other forms of cyber-enabled crime, can put people off using digital technologies (Lips *et al*, 2015). Media stories about cyber-enabled crime, cyber security problems or other bad digital experiences also have an impact on people's trust in digital technologies (Lips *et al*, 2015).

Research has demonstrated that citizens from different cultures, geographic regions and ethnic backgrounds place different levels of trust in digital

232   Emerging issues

technologies (Lips *et al*, 2015). For example, people from the Pacific Islands tend to trust digital technologies like the Internet much more than people with a European cultural background (Lips *et al*, 2015). Citizens from countries in Southeast Asia trust digital technologies more than public servants in their relationships with government and perceive them as important instruments to reduce corruption and establish good governance, as we discussed earlier. Similarly, for historical reasons, citizens from former East European states, such as Estonia, place high trust in digital technologies in their relationships with government.

Use and use-nots (usage issues)

Many scholars have argued that, as Internet access alone is not sufficient for people to use digital technologies, digital divide issues have shifted towards differences and inequalities in the use of digital technologies (van Deursen & van Dijk, 2014; van Dijk, 2005; Büchi, 2016; Borg & Smith, 2018). This also applies to the context of technology use in digital government relationships; we will need to empirically understand the full range of citizens' behaviours around digital technology use, non-use and ex-use in the particular social, cultural, geographical and temporal context in which digital government relationships unfold.

In general, although many research reports focus on (how to improve) digital technology use and inclusion, rather than reporting on non-use and digital exclusion issues, several scholars have found a large variety of digital technology use and non-use behaviours (Lips *et al*, 2015; Wyatt, Thomas & Terranova, 2002). Moreover, within specific segments of the population, such as elderly people, a large variety of digital inclusive and exclusive behaviours can be observed (van Deursen & Helsper, 2015). For example, Borg and Smith (2018) have identified the following five different types of Internet users in Australia on the continuum of digital exclusion and inclusion: non-users, sporadic users, social media and entertainment users, instrumental users and advanced users. Empirical research findings from New Zealand have found a variety of citizens' digital technology use, non-use and ex-use behaviours in their relationships with digital government (Lips *et al*, 2015). New Zealanders from different age groups, ethnic backgrounds and levels of education or Internet expertise demonstrated different online behaviours: for example, the large majority of senior citizens strongly preferred more trusted real-world non-digital channels in order to deal with government. Interestingly, although young people rely heavily on digital technologies for most of their daily life activities, they found digital channels in digital government relationships complex and hard to use and preferred more real-time interactive channels, such as the telephone, in their relationships with government in order to be able to ask questions about their individual cases (Lips *et al*, 2015).

Besides the importance of considering the usability and user-friendliness of digital technologies applied in digital government relationships, these empirical

Digital citizenship 233

research endeavours confirm the necessity for governments to get a better in-depth understanding of the full spectrum of different groups of citizens' digital technology use and non-use behaviours and what the implications are for designing and managing digital government relationships with citizens.

2. Digital divides around data

Have and have-nots (access issues)

As discussed in Chapter 5, the movement to open up government data has created new opportunities to publicly access a variety of non-personal and non-sensitive government datasets that used to be closed to the general public. In other words, citizens in many countries have become more digitally included around open government data. However, thus far, governments have not made all non-sensitive government datasets available in open format in the public domain, with some of the most relevant and often requested datasets from the general public point of view not being opened up (e.g. Helbig *et al*, 2012). Also, several countries have made non-sensitive data available in the public domain but for a cost, which raises a digital divide issue around affordability.

A variety of legal and institutional regimes exist around the world with regard to citizens' access to their personal data held by government agencies. In countries with data protection legislation based on the 1980 OECD data protection principles (which were slightly revised in 2013), citizens have a right to access their individual citizen data held by government agencies by means of a formal request. Several countries around the world, however, do not have privacy or data protection legislation and therefore commonly do not allow their citizens to make such a request. In countries like Estonia, Belgium and the Scandinavian countries, however, citizens are being offered full transparency through a personalised, secure government web portal into who in government is accessing and using their citizen data and for what purpose, with the possibility of checking and updating some citizen data for data accuracy reasons, such as their home address if it has changed.

Another digital divide issue exists between citizens who have access to national and local government databases or the digitised citizen identity management systems in which their citizen data is stored and those who do not, such as marginalised groups (e.g. homeless), migrants, refugees, citizens from other countries and people living in highly remote areas). A recent example of digital exclusion in the UK is the so-called Windrush generation, who do not have access to the British central government's databases or citizen identity management systems as their personal data is not represented in those databases and systems. As a result, people from the Windrush generation, who have lived and worked in the UK for many years and consider themselves British citizens, have been denied (digital) government service provision. Other examples of this digital divide issue can be found in countries like Indonesia, where the government does not have any citizen identity information for the groups of

234 *Emerging issues*

people living on remote islands, or Brazil, where Indians living remotely in the Amazon forests have not been identified through government identity management systems. An emerging problem around population groups that are not represented in government databases is that government big data analysis using those datasets may result in data bias as a result of underrepresentation.

Can and cannots (abilities issues)

New digitised citizen identification systems, such as biometric identification systems, cause a digital divide issue between those who can use those systems and those who cannot. A small group of the population will not be able to verify their individual citizen data in digital government relationships using biometric identification systems based on their personal characteristics: for example, people without fingerprints, fingers or thumbs will not be able to use digitised fingerprinting identification means and people who can't talk will not be able to use voice recognition.

Another digital divide issue can be observed between those who can access open data formats and portals and those who cannot, based on people's disabilities. Governments around the world are managing this issue by using dedicated web accessibility standards and guidelines in order to make open data accessible for citizens with disabilities, such as those with vision impairment.

Do and do-nots (skills issues)

Data skills, including data literacy or the ability to understand and translate data into information and knowledge in a particular context, have become critically important in an era where more and more data are being generated, processed, analysed and used in a large variety of societal activities, including in digital government relationships. Interdisciplinary and multidisciplinary data science skills applied to the public sector context, as well as basic statistical skills, are critical not just for people working in public sector jobs or politicians, but also increasingly for citizens in their data-enabled relationships with digital government. However, in many countries thus far, only an elite group of citizens, namely data science professionals, statisticians and others with professional training in data science and statistics, usually have the data skills needed for various data-enabled applications and service relationships in the public sector. However, as fast-moving smart technology and data use developments in the digital government context point to the increasing importance of having applied data skills in digital government relationships, more professional training and education is needed in the interdisciplinary area of applied data science in the public sector (see also the discussion in Chapter 6).

Governments around the world are aware of the digital divide gaps between those who have the data skills that apply to digital government and those who do not. In general, in addition to governments sponsoring professional data skills training and education, data skills are increasingly adopted in school curricula.

Digital citizenship 235

Moreover, as experimenting and other forms of experience with government data have had demonstrable success in developing (better) data skills, several governments around the world are hosting hackathons, where members of the general public and public servants come together and work and experiment with open government datasets to develop innovative solutions (see Chapter 5).

Know and know-nots (knowledge issues)

Knowledge on how to use data efficiently, effectively, safely and securely turns out to be a critical digital divide dimension in the data era, with the large majority of citizens being digitally excluded on this dimension; empowering citizens to become digitally included would involve their getting the knowledge to be able to make informed choices about citizen data collection and use in digital government relationships (cf Seale & Dutton, 2012).

However, thus far, several scholars point to the lack of knowledge around citizen data collection, processing, analysis and use in digital government relationships amongst various groups of the population (e.g. Lips *et al*, 2015). In particular, this applies to the collection of citizen data for data analytics and other "smart" research data (re)use in digital government relationships. In Chapter 6, we explored the lack of transparency around the application and use of algorithms in smart government relationships and their dependence on robust datasets, for example. We also discussed, in Chapter 5, how many citizens struggle with the supplier-led opening up of government data, instead of taking into account user needs, including around knowledge. As a result, knowledge about how to use open government data is particularly in the hands of data professionals and other data experts thus far (Zuiderwijk *et al*, 2012). Chapter 2 discussed the lack of statistical knowledge amongst many people, including public servants and politicians. Also, we discussed how easy it is to lie through the presentation of statistics and other data visualisations (Levitin, 2016).

Trust and trust-nots (trust issues)

Trust around both government and citizen data exchange in digital government relationships varies for population groups in different countries. Opening up government data can promote trust and, with that, improve digital inclusion amongst various groups of the population (see Chapter 5). Government data visualisation via government dashboards that are made publicly available can also help to promote trust amongst different groups of citizens (see Chapter 6).

Most groups of New Zealand citizens trust the collection, processing and use of their individual citizen data more in digital government relationships than in other relationships, such as those with commercial entities or in social media networks (Lips *et al*, 2015). However, for New Zealanders highly dependent on government services, such as those from low socio-economic backgrounds, the lack of transparency around the collection, use and processing of their citizen

236   *Emerging issues*

data in digital government relationships could also lead to an increased lack of trust (Lips *et al*, 2015).

Use and use-nots (usage issues)

Digital inclusion is often coerced around data use in digital government relationships: for instance, people highly dependent on social services provided by government have no choice but to share their individual citizen data in digital government relationships in order to be able to receive the services they need (Lips *et al*, 2015). However, we discussed in Chapter 5 the many barriers that exist for citizens to use open government data (Zuiderwijk *et al*, 2012).

3.   Digital government service divides

Have and have-nots (access issues)

Digital exclusion around the access of digital government services happens particularly amongst groups of citizens from low socio-economic backgrounds. For example, Lips *et al* (2017) found that New Zealand children from low socio-economic backgrounds can't do their school homework at home as they only have Internet access at school. Moreover, some children from low socio-economic backgrounds experience limited understanding and support from their parents and other family members around the necessity of having their own digital device for schoolwork (Lips *et al*, 2017). Another example from the education sector is the requirement for primary school and secondary school students in many countries to bring their own laptop to school in order to do their schoolwork, which, for parents from low socio-economic backgrounds, is difficult to afford.

In the USA, one of the core functions of public libraries nowadays is to provide vulnerable people from low socio-economic backgrounds Internet access to vital social services which are offered primarily or only online (Bertot, Jaeger & Greene, 2013). A further example of digital exclusion amongst population groups from low socio-economic backgrounds on this digital divide dimension is the New Zealand government expectation that all their social welfare customers have a mobile phone, which they need to use for online authentication in order to access the social welfare services they need; however, not all social welfare recipients turned out to have a mobile phone or had one they needed to share with other family members (Lips *et al*, 2015).

Also, citizens living in rural and remote communities often experience digital government access issues around downloading sizeable digital government forms with limited bandwidth (Lips, Barlow & Woods, 2016).

Can and can-nots (abilities issues)

The digital divide dimension of whether citizens can access digital government services or not shows several areas of digital exclusion for different groups of citizens. For instance, vulnerable groups of citizens who experience memory loss, including many senior citizens, are not able to access digital government services as they can't recall the critical personal data needed to do so, such as usernames, passwords and PINs. In several countries, people with disabilities continue to have problems with accessing critical digital government services.

Do and do-nots (skills issues)

Another digital divide dimension where vulnerable groups of citizens often experience digital exclusion is around the skills to navigate and consume digital government services, especially when people have complex service needs. Youth experience similar issues of digital exclusion as they may have digital skills, but not the skills relevant to navigating and consuming (digital) *government* services.

Know and know-nots (knowledge issues)

Vulnerable groups of citizens with complex government service needs often lack the knowledge of how to use digital government services. In the USA, a critically important social support network for getting the knowledge to use digital government services is public libraries, with more than 71 percent of public libraries in the USA helping unemployed job seekers to create resumes and apply for jobs online (Bertot, Jaeger & Greene, 2013: 38).

Trust and trust-nots (trust issues)

Many citizens of Southeast Asian countries, former Eastern European countries and African countries trust digital government services more than government services provided via traditional face-to-face or telephone channels as digital government services are more standardised and, with that, less amenable to potential corruption. However, digital exclusion on this digital divide dimension can be found amongst senior citizens in many countries, who usually place low levels of trust in digital government services and high levels of trust in government services provided through human interaction, which they perceive as superior in quality to digital interaction (Lips *et al*, 2015).

In an empirical study amongst New Zealand residents, many research participants expressed high levels of trust in digital government service provision by the New Zealand government specifically, as they saw New Zealand as more benign than governments in other countries, such as the USA or the UK (Lips *et al*, 2015). However, vulnerable population groups highly dependent on government services, such as people from low socio-economic backgrounds, did not trust digital government services in New Zealand that much.

Another way to promote trust in digital government service provision is for governments to offer more transparency in the consumption of these services,

238 *Emerging issues*

such as by using workflow management systems in which citizens can track the status of their government service application (e.g. building permit).

Use and use-nots (use issues)

The digital divide dimension of digital government services demonstrates mixed use and non-use amongst all segments of the population. For instance, those groups with integrated government service needs, such as vulnerable groups of citizens highly dependent on government services, commonly experience a mismatch between their individual complex needs and the ways in which digital government service offerings are structured and therefore usually prefer traditional service channels, such as face-to-face interactions, in order to be able to better navigate the administrative complexities of government service provision in general (Lips *et al*, 2010).

Research into digital government service consumption by small and medium business enterprise (SMEs) owners in New Zealand has demonstrated that, besides the popular use of digital government services to search for government information online, return a completed form or pay for a government service, citizens continue to use traditional channels for government service consumption, such as the telephone, regular mail and face to face (Lips, Barlow & Woods, 2016). Generally, in New Zealand, many citizens from different backgrounds demonstrate multi-channel behaviours in consuming an end-to-end government service: for example, they use the Internet to search for relevant government information online, phone up to ask questions about their individual case and conclude the government transaction offline via regular mail or face-to-face service channels (Lips *et al*, 2010; Lips *et al*, 2015; Lips, Barlow & Woods, 2016). Interestingly, although government agencies had expected citizens to use social media channels as part of their digital government service consumption, these channels were hardly used or not used at all (Lips, Barlow & Woods, 2016).

Although many research participants indicated their willingness to completely shift from traditional channels to digital channels for their government service consumption, they didn't find the digital government service channels currently available to them suitable to deal with the administrative complexities they experienced in their service interactions with government (Lips, Barlow & Woods, 2016). Research participants identified the following critical conditions to be met by government in order for them to prefer digital government service channels to traditional channels (Lips, Barlow & Woods, 2016):

- Government agencies need to design their digital government services strategy with the citizen-user in mind and, preferably, in close collaboration with members of the targeted population group;
- Digital government services need to have a user-centric design, including user-centric navigation, more user-friendly systems and functionalities, step-by-step user instructions and better and more user-friendly guidelines around changes in public policy and regulations;

- Digital government service offerings need to have functionalities that meet the needs of users, such as real-time digital access to an expert staff member (e.g. via online chat) and quick online response times, and provide more options for citizens to raise non-standard issues;
- Availability of end-to-end digital government services, including solutions around real-time or quick digital government responses, the use of digital signatures and other digital verification and authentication means and better Internet access in rural and remote areas; and
- Better integration of government services and increased data sharing across government to deliver more efficient (e.g. less duplication) and effective government services, including the re-use of non-sensitive information of individual citizens in integrated service provision.

Summary overview

In summary, as discussed earlier, the challenge that governments around the world face is to ensure that all citizens have equitable opportunities to engage, interact and transact with digital government. However, based on our research-based discussion thus far, we can observe that, across the three focus areas of digital government relationships, those who are most dependent on (digital) government services, such as citizens highly depending on social services and other vulnerable citizen groups, seem to experience the most digital exclusion in their relationships with government. This is further illustrated by a development in the USA, where support for vulnerable citizen groups with digital government service consumption issues, including access and use of vital social services, has become a core public library function (Bertot, Jaeger & Greene, 2013).

In general, the following groups of citizens experience forms of digital exclusion on the various digital divide dimensions within the three digital government focus areas: see Table 9.1. This overview clearly shows the large burdens in digital government relationships that are currently placed on citizens instead of government, in order to meet digital government service requirements. Vulnerable groups of citizens in particular are experiencing various forms of digital exclusion in these increasingly digitised government relationships. Moreover, popular assumptions that digital divides will disappear over time, with more people being so-called digital natives, are not supported by the empirical research findings presented earlier.

These empirical findings have major implications for government intervention programmes around digital divides. Although the findings presented earlier clearly suggest that exclusion in digital government relationships is not just a technology issue, governments around the world still predominantly implement digital divide intervention programmes that apply narrow technology-driven perspectives, especially focused on Internet technology, mainly to increase the

Table 9.1 Exclusion of population groups in digital government

	Digital technology divides	Digital divides around data	Digital government service divides
Have and have-nots (access issues)	- People in rural or remote areas; - People from low socio-economic backgrounds; - People with cultural reasons; - People who don't have a suitable device;	- All population groups; - Different personal data access regimes: EU, NZ; Estonia, Belgium; Countries without privacy legislation; - Marginalized groups; - migrants, refugees, citizens from other countries, people in remote areas;	- People from low socio-economic backgrounds; - People in rural or remote areas;
Can and cannots (abilities issues)	- People with disabilities; - Older people;	- People with personal characteristics not complying with biometric ID systems; - people with disabilities;	- Vulnerable groups with complex service needs;
Do and do-nots (skills issues)	- All population groups; - Developing countries; - People with cultural beliefs; - Significant inequalities: • All age groups; • Gender; • Education level; • Internet access; • Experience;	- All population groups except data science and statistics professionals;	- Vulnerable groups with complex service needs; - Youth;
Know and know-nots (knowledge issues)	- All age groups;	- All population groups; - Re open data, statistics: all population groups except data experts;	- Vulnerable groups with complex service needs;
Trust and trust-nots (trust issues)	- All age groups; - People with bad online experiences; - Different trust levels amongst people from different cultures, geographical regions, and ethnicities	- Varying trust in different countries; - in NZ: low trust by vulnerable groups highly dependent on government services (e.g. low socio-economic backgrounds);	- Older people; - Vulnerable groups highly dependent on government services (e.g. low socio-economic backgrounds);

	Digital technology divides	Digital divides around data	Digital government service divides
Use and use-nots (**use issues**)	- All age groups; - Different online use behaviour amongst: • Young people; • Senior citizens; • Different ethnicities; and • Low education.	- All population groups, except data experts; and - Mandatory personal data use for vulnerable groups highly dependent on government services.	- Multi-channel behaviours amongst all population groups; and - Vulnerable groups highly dependent on government services.

number of citizens included. In other words, instead of designing and implementing assisted digital intervention programmes to promote inclusion amongst citizens in digital government relationships, the empirical findings presented earlier suggest that governments should shift to developing citizen-centric assisted digital government intervention programmes to promote digital inclusion amongst government agencies, public servants and politicians involved in digital government relationships with citizens.

Citizens' rights in digital government relationships

What further guidance could be provided for the development of these citizen-centric, assisted digital government intervention programmes? Another way of looking at this would be to explore citizens' rights in digital government relationships. This would help governments to translate citizen-centric needs into actionable outcomes under these programmes.

However, as discussed earlier, it is critically important for governments to take the context of digital government relationships into account, including the social, cultural, historical, economical, legal, institutional and political contexts in which they operate. The revised ethical framework of contextual integrity presented in Chapter 6, especially the context-specific norms and values, will help governments to do so.

This implies that governments in different parts of the world, as they operate within different contexts, will need to meet different citizen-centric needs for their respective populations. This then means that each government will need to explore within its own jurisdictional context how context-specific norms and values would need to be translated into citizens' rights and actionable outcomes in order to meet citizen-centric needs. As indicated in Chapter 6, the general ethical and political principles that are commonly adopted in democratic societies can further contribute to the formulation of citizens' rights in the digital government context. In truly citizen-centric fashion, the draft formulation of citizens' rights in the digital government context will need to be conducted, tested, discussed and confirmed with citizens.

242 *Emerging issues*

If we apply the revised ethical framework of contextual integrity, including the general ethical and political principles defined for a democratic society, to the context of citizens' rights in digital government relationships, what would such (draft) rights look like? We'll further explore these citizens' rights in the context of digital government next. In so doing we make use of the relevant knowledge and insights presented in this book thus far.

Citizens' rights in digital government

As we saw in Table 9.1, citizens' digital exclusion in government relationships is rather complex in the sense that it is not the binary opposite of digital inclusion but has multiple dimensions within three different digital government focus areas. Its complexity can be further demonstrated by the fact that other general ethical and political principles are crosscutting these digital divide dimensions in digital government relationships, such as fairness, equality, social justice, privacy protection, openness and transparency, freedom, autonomy, dignity and welfare. Next, we'll explore in more detail citizens' digital inclusion rights within each of these digital government focus areas: citizens' digital technology- or Internet-related rights; their data rights, around both government data and big data research (i.e. government data integrated with other data) and their individual citizen data exchanged in digital government relationships (see Chapter 8) and the digital government service rights of citizens.

1. Internet-related citizens' rights

- *Right to Internet access and use*: all citizens need to have affordable and accessible Internet in order to be able to use and engage with Internet-enabled digital government;
- *Right to Internet knowledge and skills*: all citizens need to have basic Internet knowledge and skills to be able to confidently and appropriately use and engage with digital government;

2. Citizens' data rights

The following are citizens' general data rights applicable to government data, big data research and citizen data in digital government relationships:

- *Right to data knowledge and skills*: all citizens need to have basic data knowledge and skills to be able to analyse and interpret data and confidently and appropriately use data in digital government relationships;
- *Right to data (re-)use*: all citizens have the right to data (re-)use by government in those cases where data (re-)use enhances the quality of their lives;

Digital citizenship 243

2a Government data

- *Right to access government information in digital format*: all citizens need to be able to access government information in digital format;
- *Right to access public records*: all citizens need to be able to access public records available in digital format;
- *Right to open government data access and (re-)use*: all citizens need to be able to access and (re-)use open government data. Governments need to be committed to opening up government data of high utility for citizens;
- *Right to meaningful and actionable transparency*: all citizens need to be able to access, understand and act on open and transparent data use in digital government relationships. Only in this way will transparency be effective, leading to empowered citizens;

2b Big data research

- *Right to transparency of the public decision-making process*: all citizens need to be able to understand the whole data-enabled public decision-making process. Algorithm transparency is not enough;
- *Right to correct and challenge data-enabled public decision-making*: all citizens have the right to correct and challenge data, data analysis and algorithms used in public decision-making as well as the outcomes of data-enabled public decision-making;
- *Right to human expert–based decision-making*: all citizens need to be able to rely on human expert authority in data-enabled public decision-making. Data and algorithms are not driving public decision-making but are subject to public servant expert knowledge (e.g. frontline staff) in the decision-making process;
- *Right to meaningful human control*: all citizens have the right to meaningful human control in cases where autonomous machines, systems or technologies (e.g. drones, vehicles, care robots) make public decisions;

2c Citizen data

- *Right to citizen data integrity*: all citizens have the right to integrity of their citizen data in accordance with context-relative norms in digital government relationships (e.g. data privacy, data security, minimal use of identifiable citizen data) (see Chapters 6 and 8);
- *Right to access, correct and challenge citizen data held by government*: all citizens have the right to access, correct and challenge citizen data held by government. This may include deletion of data held in government databases that is not correct;
- *Right to use digital citizen identity management systems*: all citizens have the right to use digital citizen identity management systems applied in digital government relationships;

244 *Emerging issues*

3. Citizens' rights around digital government services

- *Right to have equitable access to digital government services*: all citizens have equal access rights to digital government services;
- *Right to citizen-centric understanding and use of digital government services*: all citizens have the right to understand and use digital government services based on their individual complex needs, not on a government-centric logic of service provision; and
- *Right to autonomy and dignity*: all citizens have the right to autonomy and dignity in machine-based public service provision. An example is unwanted paternalism by care robots (Van Est & Gerritsen, 2017).

Box 9.1 Exercise 9.1

1) Try and find statistical evidence for the use and non-use of digital government services by different groups of the population in your country. Who is digitally excluded from digital government services in your country?
2) Apply the draft citizen rights to the digitally excluded groups and make recommendations to your government about how these rights could be met.

Discussion questions

1 Try and find empirical evidence for the existence of multiple digital divides in digital government relationships in your country. What advice would you give to your government in order to close the gaps of these digital divides?
2 How would you assess progress around digital inclusion and exclusion issues in digital government relationships? Motivate your answer.
3 Which of the proposed draft citizens' rights would be of relevance to digital government relationships in your country and why? Motivate your answer.

Note

1 Australian Digital Inclusion Index, available from: https://digitalinclusionindex.org.au/ [accessed 11 February 2019].

References

Anderson, D. (2012) *A Phenomenographical Study of Voluntary Digital Exclusion*. R. Daniels, R. Snarski & L. Swopes, ProQuest Dissertations Publishing.

Digital citizenship 245

Bach, A., Shaffer, G. & Wolfson, T. (2013) Digital human capital: Developing a framework for understanding the economic impact of digital exclusion in low-income communities. *Journal of Information Policy*, 3, 247–266.

Bertot, J.C., Jaeger, P.T. & Greene, N.N. (2013) Transformative e-government and public service: Public libraries in times of economic hardship. In: Weerakkody, V. & Reddick, C.G. (eds.) *Public Sector Transformation Through E-Government. Experiences from Europe and North America*. New York, NY: Routledge, pp. 35–46.

Borg, K. & Smith, L. (2018) Digital inclusion and online behaviour: Five typologies of Australian internet users. *Behaviour & Information Technology*, 1–14.

Büchi, M. (2016) Modeling the second-level digital divide: A five-country study of social differences in Internet use. *New Media & Society*, 18 (11), 2703–2722.

Bunyan, S. & Collins, A. (2013) Digital exclusion despite digital accessibility: Empirical evidence from an English City. *Tijdschrift voor economische en sociale geografie*, 104 (5), 588–603.

Correa, T. & Pavez, I. (2016) Digital inclusion in rural areas: A qualitative exploration of challenges faced by people from isolated communities. *Journal of Computer-Mediated Communication*, 21 (3), 247–263.

Courtois, C. & Verdegem, P. (2016) With a little help from my friends: An analysis of the role of social support in digital inequalities. *New Media & Society*, 18 (8), 1508–1527.

Dutch Scientific Council. (2016) *Big Data in een vrije en veilige samenleving*. Wetenschappelijke Raad voor het Regeringsbeleid, 95, Den Haag: WRR.

Eynon, R. & Geniets, A. (2016) The digital skills paradox: How do digitally excluded youth develop skills to use the internet? *Learning, Media and Technology*, 41 (3), 463–479.

Hacker, K. & Mason, S. (2003) Ethical gaps in studies of the digital divide. *Ethics and Information Technology*, 5 (2), 99–115.

Hargittai, E. (2002) Second-level digital divide: Differences in people's online skills. *First Monday*, 7 (4). Available from: http://firstmonday.org/ojs/index.php/fm/article/view/942/864 [accessed 23 June 2018].

Hargittai, E. (2010) Digital na(t)ives? Variation in internet skills and uses among members of the 'Net Generation'. *Sociological Inquiry*, 80 (1), 92–113.

Helsper, E.J. (2008) *Digital Inclusion: An Analysis of Social Disadvantage and the Information Society*. London: London School of Economics Research Online.

Helsper, E.J. (2017) The social relativity of digital exclusion: Applying relative deprivation theory to digital inequalities. *Communication Theory*, 27 (3), 223–242.

Helsper, E.J. & Reisdorf, B.C. (2017) The emergence of a 'digital underclass' in Great Britain and Sweden: Changing reasons for digital exclusion. *New Media & Society*, 19 (8), 1253–1270.

Levitin, D.J. (2016) *A Field Guide to Lies and Statistics: A Neuroscientist on How to Make Sense of a Complex World*. London: Viking Penguin Random House.

Lips, A.M.B. & Frissen, P.H.A. (1997) *Wiring Government: Integrated Public Service Delivery Through ICT*. ITeR, Alphen aan den Rijn: Samsom BedrijfsInformatie bv, pp. 67–164.

Lips, M., Barlow, L. & Woods, L. (March 2016) *Conditions for Channel Shift Behaviours and Simplification in Business Individuals' and Small Businesses' Online Interactions with Government*. Survey Research Report. Wellington: Victoria University of Wellington.

Lips, M., Eppel, E., Barlow, L., Löfgren, B., Löfgren, K. & Sim, D. (February 2015) *Kiwis Managing Their Online Identity Information*. Final Research Report. Wellington: Victoria University of Wellington.

Lips, M., Eppel, E., Cunningham, A. & Hopkins-Burns, V. (August 2010) *Public Attitudes to the Sharing of Personal Information in the Course of Online Public Service Provision*. Final Research Report. Wellington: Victoria University of Wellington.

246   Emerging issues

Lips, M., Eppel, E., McRae, H., Starkey, L., Sylvester, A., Parore, P. & Barlow, L. (June 2017) *Understanding Children's Use and Experience with Digital Technologies*. Final Research Report. Wellington: Victoria University of Wellington.

Livingstone, S. & Helsper, E. (2007) Gradations in digital inclusion: Children, young people and the digital divide. *New Media & Society*, 9 (4), 671–696.

London School of Economics. (June 2005) *The Identity Project: An Assessment of the UK Identity Cards Bill and Its Implications*. London: The LSE Identity Project Final Report.

Longley, P.A. & Singleton, A.D. (2009) Linking social deprivation and digital exclusion in England. *Urban Studies*, 46 (7), 1275–1298.

Martínez-Cantos, J.L. (2017) Digital skills gaps: A pending subject for gender digital inclusion in the European Union. *European Journal of Communication*, 32 (5), 419–438.

Mordini, E. (2009) Senior citizens and the ethics of e-inclusion. *Ethics and Information Technology*, 11 (3), 203–220.

Mubarak, F. & Nycyk, M. (2017) Teaching older people internet skills to minimize grey digital divides. *Journal of Information, Communication & Ethics in Society*, 15 (2), 165–178.

NTIA. (12 July 1995) *Falling Through the Net: A Survey of the 'Have Nots' in Rural and Urban America*. Washington, DC: NTIA. Available from: https://www.ntia.doc.gov/report/1995/falling-through-net-survey-have-nots-rural-and-urban-america-html [accessed 23 June 2018].

Pacheco, E.B. (2016) *Vision Impairment and the Transition to University Education: The Role of ICTs*. PhD Thesis, Victoria University of Wellington. Available from: https://viewer.waireto.victoria.ac.nz/client/viewer/IE190189/rep/REP190208/FL190209?dps_dvs=1549586367708-538 [accessed 8 February 2019].

Pasquale, F. (2015) *The Black Box Society: The Secret Algorithms That Control Money and Information*. Cambridge, MA: Harvard University Press.

Peter, J. & Valkenburg, P.M. (2006) Adolescents' internet use: Testing the 'disappearing digital divide' versus the 'emerging digital differentiation' approach. *Poetics*, 34, 293–305.

Philip, L. (2017) The digital divide: Patterns, policy and scenarios for connecting the 'final few' in rural communities across Great Britain. *Journal of Rural Studies*, 54, 386–398.

Rashid, A.T. (2016) Digital inclusion and social inequality. *Gender, Technology and Development*, 20 (3), 306–332.

Santarosa, L.M.C. & Conforto, D. (2016) Educational and digital inclusion for subjects with autism spectrum disorders in 1:1 technological configuration. *Computers in Human Behavior*, 60, 293–300.

Seale, J. & Dutton, W.H. (2012) Empowering the digitally excluded: Learning initiatives for (in)visible groups. *Research in Learning Technology*, 20 (4).

Thomas, G. & Wyatt, S. (2000) Access is not the only problem: Using and controlling the Internet. In: Wyatt, S. (ed.) *Technology and In/Equality*. London: Routledge.

van Deursen, A.J.A.M. & Helsper, E.J. (2015) A nuanced understanding of Internet use and non-use among the elderly. *European Journal of Communication*, 30 (2), 171–187.

van Deursen, A.J.A.M. & van Dijk, J.A.G.M. (2014) The digital divide shifts to differences in usage. *New Media & Society*, 16 (3), 507–526.

van Dijk, J.A.G.M. (2005) *The Deepening Divide: Inequality in the Information Society*. London: Sage.

Van Est, R. & Gerritsen, J.B.A., with the assistance of L. Kool (2017) *Human Rights in the Robot Age: Challenges Arising from the Use of Robotics, Artificial Intelligence, and Virtual and Augmented Reality*. Expert report written for the Committee on Culture, Science, Education and Media of the Parliamentary Assembly of the Council of Europe (PACE). The Hague: Rathenau Instituut.

Wyatt, S. (2003) Non-users also matter: The construction of users and non-users of the Internet. In: Oudshoorn, N. & Pinch, T. (eds.) *How Users Matter: The Co-Construction of Users and Technology*. Cambridge, MA: Massachusetts Institute of Technology Press, pp. 67–79.

Wyatt, S., Thomas, G. & Terranova, T. (2002) They came, they surfed, they went back to the beach: Conceptualising use and non-use of the Internet. In: Woolgar, S. (ed.) *Virtual Society?* Oxford: Oxford University Press.

Yates, S. (2015) Digital media use: Differences and inequalities in relation to class and age. *Sociological Research Online*, 20 (4), 1–21.

Zuiderwijk, A., Janssen, M., Choenni, S., Meijer, R. & Alibaks, R.S. (2012) Socio-technical impediments of open data. *Electronic Journal of e-Government*, 10 (2), 156–172.

Further reading

Hargittai, E. (2002) Second-level digital divide: Differences in people's online skills. *First Monday*, 7 (4). Available from: http://firstmonday.org/ojs/index.php/fm/article/view/942/864 [accessed 23 June 2018].

Helbig, N., Cresswell, A.M., Burke, G.B. & Luna-Reyes, L. (2012) *The Dynamics of Opening Government Data: A White Paper*. Center for Technology in Government, State University of New York, Albany. Available from: https://www.ctg.albany.edu/publications/reports/opendata/opendata.pdf [accessed 23 June 2018].

Livingstone, S. & Helsper, E. (2007) Gradations in digital inclusion: Children, young people and the digital divide. *New Media & Society*, 9 (4), 671–696.

Oudshoorn, N. & Pinch, T. (eds.) (2003) *How Users Matter: The Co-Construction of Users and Technology*. Cambridge, MA: Massachusetts Institute of Technology Press.

van Deursen, A.J.A.M. & van Dijk, J.A.G.M. (2014) The digital divide shifts to differences in usage. *New Media & Society*, 16 (3), 507–526.

van Dijk, J.A.G.M. (2005) *The Deepening Divide: Inequality in the Information Society*. London: Sage.

10 Digital government strategy, leadership and governance

Learning objectives

By the end of this chapter you should be able to:

- Identify biases in digital government strategies around the world;
- Identify the required elements for a more comprehensive digital government strategy, taking a contextual approach;
- Understand the conditions, qualities and skills of successful digital government leadership;
- Identify the core elements of digital governance, similar to the new public governance (NPG); and
- Understand the integration of the vertical dimension, the horizontal dimension and the socio-technical construct dimension in digital governance and how this could be managed.

Key points of this chapter

- Digital government strategies around the world often display a bias towards technology, private sector approaches and solutions and digital government service provision;
- The unique digital government context requires a contextual approach to the development, management and implementation of a digital government strategy, with a critical emphasis on the socio-technical nature of digital government and governance;
- The most notable examples of government innovation through digital government programmes can be found in jurisdictions where those responsible for digital government occupy high positions in the government hierarchy and have managed to stay in office for more than one term;
- Digital government leaders need to have a strong background in the multidisciplinary area of complex public management;
- Successful public management of complex digital government initiatives requires two types of leaders: sponsors and champions;

Strategy, leadership and governance 249

- The core elements of the NPG model can be recognised in digital governance arrangements;
- Three types of conception-reality gaps make digital government reform failure more likely: rationality-public sector reality gaps, private sector-public sector gaps and country context gaps;
- The unique context of digital government requires a benefits realisation methodology which takes these contextual conditions into account, such as the unique requirement of creating public value in digital government initiatives and using a dynamic and cyclical benefits realisation management approach over a longer period of time; and
- Traditional vertical evaluation approaches of digital government performance and outcomes need to be reframed to suit increasingly horizontal governance arrangements around digital government initiatives. Moreover, a different normative evaluation framework is needed in order to move away from government organization-centric performance outcomes and allow for the assessment of the public value that is collaboratively produced by all shareholders involved in digital government initiatives.

Key terms

- *Digital government strategy:* a contextual digital government strategy, emphasising the socio-technical phenomenon of digital government.
- *Digital government leadership*: successful digital government leaders have a strong background in the multidisciplinary area of complex public management.
- *Digital government governance:* the governance landscape of digital government is multi-layered and complex and demonstrates the core elements of the NPG model.

Introduction

Digital government strategy, leadership and governance are three elements critical to successful digital government outcomes. As we have discussed throughout this book, digital government initiatives are highly complex, with chances of complete success being estimated around 20 percent to 40 percent (Heeks, 2003; Sandoval-Almazán *et al*, 2017). It may not be surprising, therefore, that many digital government projects end up being classified as "failures" (Sandoval-Almazán *et al*, 2017: 67); some studies demonstrate that 35 percent of all digital government projects can be classified as "complete failures," with 50 percent of these projects being classified as "partial failures" (Heeks, 2003).

Consequently, the strategic importance for digital government outcomes of a comprehensive digital government strategy, strong leadership and an appropriate governance arrangement cannot be underestimated. In most cases, before any digital government initiatives are taken, a digital government strategy is developed by a centralised government body close to those in power. Commonly,

250 *Emerging issues*

this digital government strategy is led by an executive officer with the primary responsibility for its development and implementation: a chief information officer (CIO), for example. Also, the digital government strategy is overseen by a governance board with member representation of various government programme stakeholders, including the CIO.

In this chapter, we further explore these three critically important digital government areas of digital government strategy, leadership and governance. Each of these three elements has the potential to shape digital government outcomes in a major way. We explore how digital government outcomes are, and can be, evaluated and assessed. In general, making use of the insights we have gained throughout this book thus far, we will discuss how some conceptualisations, interpretations and implementations of these critical roles and areas may be better suited for achieving the types of technology- and data-enabled public sector reform ambitions that governments have in the context of digital government relationships.

Digital government strategy

Digital technologies and data have become critical enablers of a wide variety of public sector functions, processes and activities to date. As we discussed earlier, the widespread application of digital technologies and data in the context of digital government and its relationships with citizens can be observed in different approaches to and forms of public service provision; in public sector reform activities to establish more open and transparent forms of government; more recently in governments' reform ambitions to become smart, or smarter, government and in more decentralised, participatory and collaborative forms of governance together with citizens.

These developments of increasing and widespread uptake of digital technologies and data in the public sector and their external relationships with stakeholders are happening throughout the world. Usually, we can observe differences in the locus and focus of technology- and data-enabled public sector reform. For instance, as we discussed earlier, many governments in developing countries have only recently started the introduction and use of digital government applications, in comparison with governments in countries that experienced early and widespread Internet adoption amongst their population. These governments are now investing in digital government initiatives in particular, not only to design, build and develop their basic digital government infrastructure, but also to enhance transparency in government and achieve more democratic forms of governance. As large parts of the citizen population of these countries usually do not have access to Internet broadband facilities but often do have a mobile phone, strategic efforts in the context of digital government in these countries usually focus on implementing mobile digital government solutions as well as digital government solutions that can be accessed by citizen-users via public Internet hubs or technology-enabled face-to-face government counters.

As we discussed earlier, it is within these different contexts and differences in socio-technical assemblages of digital government that we need to start

Strategy, leadership and governance 251

thinking about designing and developing an appropriate digital government strategy. And yet, many existing digital government strategies are not contextually oriented. Moreover, in many digital government strategies, we can often observe a certain bias, which then also has implications for leadership, accountability, budget allocation and governance of these digital government strategies. In general, there are three different sets of biases that can be observed in digital government strategies around the world:

1   A digital government strategy bias towards technology;
2   A digital government strategy bias towards private sector approaches and solutions; and
3   A digital government strategy bias towards digital government service provision.

We will briefly discuss each of these digital government strategy biases next.

A digital government strategy bias towards technology

By far the most common bias in digital government strategies is one that predominantly focuses on technology or the "digital" aspects of digital government (see Chapter 1). For instance, Sandoval-Almazán *et al* (2017) observe two distinct types of digital strategies being developed by governments in the broader digital government context: a national digital strategy which focuses on improving the social well-being aspects and economic development of a digital society and a digital government "enterprise strategy" which focuses on developing plans and implementing programmes to facilitate the creation of digital technology infrastructure and information systems that support the substantive work of government (Sandoval-Almazán *et al*, 2017: 7). Clearly, the latter is often considered the digital government strategy of a particular government.

As a result of this narrow technology perspective in digital government strategies (see also Chapter 3), we can observe strong similarities between a digital government strategy and a traditional information systems strategy in government (Sandoval-Almazán *et al*, 2017). Basically, there are three different approaches to such an information systems strategy, each of which can be recognised in digital government strategies across the world (Sandoval-Almazán *et al*, 2017: 15):

1   A master plan for digital technology infrastructure and information systems in government, including the basic operation of the digital technology function, systems maintenance, new digital technology initiatives and required budget;
2   Alignment of the digital technology function and its application to achieve the organizational mission. From this perspective, digital technologies and information systems are considered to be tools supporting key government goals, functions, processes, competencies and activities; and

252 *Emerging issues*

3   A government-wide vision of what it may achieve through the smart use
    of digital technologies and information systems. Such visions often include
    governments' adoption of the latest technology trends (e.g. the Internet in
    the early 1990s and more recently smart technologies, big data and AI), also
    as an attempt not to lag behind other sectors (see also Chapter 1).

Considering our discussion thus far, and particularly our emphasis on understanding digital government initiatives as socio-technical constructs or assemblages with context-relative outcomes, it is interesting to observe an almost
complete separation of the technical from the social in these digital government strategies. This then also leads to digital government strategies that are
more aspirational, in the sense that they focus on what the technology can do,
rather than on how the technology is, or will be, actually used in the context
of digital government. Especially in early digital government strategies, such as
those presented in the 1990s, we can observe the presence of a technological
deterministic perspective (see Chapter 2): a strong belief in the intrinsic technological capabilities of the Internet as a driving force of aspirational change in
government (Lips, 2012).

A digital government strategy bias towards private sector approaches and solutions

Quite a few digital government strategies demonstrate a bias towards private
sector approaches and solutions in their adoption (see Chapter 3). Examples can
be found in areas such as business process reengineering (BPR), business transformation, enterprise architecture, project management, agile methodologies
and methodologies to monitor and assess benefits realisation. One explanation
for the popularity of private sector approaches and solutions in digital government strategies is the fact that, in many governments, digital government functions, capabilities and projects have been contracted out to the private sector
(Heeks, 1999). As a result, there is often a lack of institutional knowledge and
skills in digital government areas, which creates for governments a dependency
on private sector contractors and consultants.

However, based on longitudinal empirical research in public service environments in the UK, Willcocks, Currie and Jackson (1997) demonstrate the
distinctive nature of public sector contexts, compared to private sector contexts, in the development and implementation of technology-enabled BPR
programmes. This then led to specific government barriers to the development
and implementation of BPR in UK public service environments, including
(Willcocks, Currie & Jackson, 1997: 105–132):

- A lack of cross-government control, coordination and collaboration;
- Separation of public policy-making from administration;
- Large complex bureaucratic organizations with constrained public budget
  rules;

Strategy, leadership and governance   253

- Problems of accountability;
- Organizational and individual resistance to change;
- Government operations based on a departmental or agency model rather than on a corporate enterprise model;
- Lack of technology and BPR understanding amongst senior management;
- Political barriers (e.g. political risk perceptions, including risk of digital government failure, job losses);
- Large number of stakeholders;
- Traditional organizational practices and procedures; and
- The importance of continuity as a basis for change.

These empirical findings reconfirm that the unique context of digital government and its relationships with external stakeholders need to be taken into account in designing and developing digital government strategies for change in government (see Chapter 1).

A digital government strategy bias towards digital government service provision

Many governments use a narrow focus on government service delivery improvements, such as enhanced efficiency and effectiveness, in their digital government strategy. One explanation for this can be found in governments' adoption of new public management (NPM) reform ideas in the 1990s, such as establishing modernised, efficient and customer-focused government services, which were in strategic alignment with governments' perceptions around digital technology capabilities at the time (Homburg, 2008; Bekkers & Homburg, 2005). Another explanation can be found in the global financial crisis, when governments were under enormous pressure to enhance their efficiency and achieve substantial cost savings. It was during this time period in particular that digital-by-default strategies became very popular amongst governments around the world (Lips, 2014).

Using empirical research findings from UK local government, Pratchett (1998) demonstrates that, although local governments could develop digital government strategies in areas of local democracy and public policy-making, there is a systemic bias which favours digital government service delivery reform to establish more efficient and effective government services; at the same time, it ignores technology-enabled reform in the other two local government areas. He explains this systemic bias by reference to a network of actors who determine digital technology policy in relative isolation from the other policy networks active at the local level (Pratchett, 1998).

Towards a contextual approach to digital government strategy

These three biases in digital government strategies reconfirm the importance of considering the unique nature of government and, with that, the unique context in which digital government strategies are being developed, managed

254 *Emerging issues*

and implemented (see also Chapter 1). Moreover, scholarly research has demonstrated that the unique institutional, social and democratic arrangements of governments are critical enablers of successful digital government initiatives, much more so than the digital technologies governments deploy (Gil-Garcia, 2012; McLoughlin & Wilson, 2013). This then also implies that it is critically important for governments to take into account their own unique digital government contexts, especially their own institutional arrangements, such as accountability and governance structures, and supportive legislation, in the design and implementation of a digital government strategy. In other words, a common practice amongst public servants to shop around the world for best practices of both digital government strategy design and digital government initiatives, "copy" these best practices and "paste" them into their own digital government strategy regardless of context is highly problematic.

As we discussed in Chapter 1, in an increasingly digital society, "digital" and "government" need to be treated as a combined, integrated and highly complex socio-technical phenomenon with a unique role, contribution and democratic relationships, all of which are different in different countries. This unique digital government context then requires not a technical, private sector or narrow public service provision approach, but a *contextual* approach to the development, management and implementation of a digital government strategy. This strategy should focus not only on the technical, but also, particularly, on the social, including the context-related actual use and non-use of the technical in the context of democratic governance (see also McLoughlin & Wilson, 2013). This then brings social, ethical and democratic issues, such as the ones we explored in Chapters 6 and 9 around a new digital government integrity framework, the existence of multiple digital divides and citizens' rights in digital government relationships, to the heart of digital government strategy formulation, together with other unique digital government contextual issues, such as using digital technologies and data to promote public value creation and enhance people's lives. Or, as President Obama put it in his opening statement of the 2012 US federal government's Digital Government Strategy: "I want us to ask ourselves every day, how are we using technology to make a real difference in people's lives?" (The White House, 2012: 1).

Digital government leadership

President Obama is a good example of strong leadership in the area of digital government; not only did he issue a Memorandum on Transparency and Open Government on his first day in office, as we discussed in Chapter 5, but he also used digital technologies in innovative ways during his presidential election campaign. Moreover, in 2012, in order for the US federal government to rapidly transition to being digital by default, he ordered government agencies to identify at least two major customer-facing systems containing high-value data and content, with the highest priority given to those systems that contained the most valuable data from a customer's perspective; expose this information

Strategy, leadership and governance   255

through web APIs to appropriate audiences; apply metadata tags in compliance with US federal guidelines and publish a plan to transition additional systems as practical (The White House, 2012).

In general, Obama's leadership was critically important for establishing technology- and data-enabled open and transparent government in the USA. This is confirmed by the research of Sandoval-Almazán *et al* (2017: 20), who point out that the most notable examples of government innovation through digital government programmes that they have observed occurred in jurisdictions where those responsible for digital government occupied high positions in the government hierarchy and managed to stay in office for more than one term. In other words, strong political leadership over longer periods of time is a critical enabler of successful digital government outcomes.

Many studies of technology-enabled public sector reform point to the critical importance of leadership at the most senior levels of government organizations (Eppel & Lips, 2016; Fountain, 2008; Institute for Government, 2010; Office of the Auditor-General, 2012). Strong leadership and support from senior government and political leaders, such as ministers, presidents or prime ministers, chief executives (CEs) of government organizations and other senior managers, are critical to not only effectively realising benefits in digital government initiatives, but also helping accelerate critical decisions for digital government projects, resolving resource blockages, setting and managing realistic expectations and adding impetus to a digital government project (Office of the Auditor-General, 2012; Eppel & Lips, 2016). Moreover, in those cases where a senior political leader makes a commitment to a digital government strategy, programme or project, just as we saw with US President Obama, this digital government initiative will be a priority for other senior government leaders and appropriate resourcing and budget allocation will be made available for this initiative (Office of the Auditor-General, 2012; Eppel & Lips, 2016).

Crosby, Bryson and Stone (2010) make a useful distinction between two main types of leaders which, according to their empirical research findings, seem to be necessary for carrying out successful collaborations in order to manage complex issues like digital government projects: sponsors and champions. They conceptualise sponsors as those having formal authority, financial resources and legitimacy to offer, whereas champions bring tireless commitment, networking skills and informal authority to a collaborative arrangement (Crosby, Bryson & Stone, 2010: 210). Moreover, champions are usually willing to take risks in the service of potential payoff, understand the complex change process required and take a long view (Crosby, Bryson & Stone, 2010: 210). Furthermore, their research shows that, in the longer term, champions also can become sponsors of the same government programme (Crosby, Bryson & Stone, 2010).

In order to be successful in managing a complex digital government initiative in a way that brings together relevant government actors, external stakeholders, processes, structures and resources from different sectors and governmental levels, "visionary leaders" as Crosby, Bryson and Stone (2010) call them, usually

256 *Emerging issues*

undertake the following activities within three main areas (Crosby, Bryson & Stone, 2010: 211–217):

1 *Seizing opportunities to provide interpretation and direction*: leaders help make complex issues real through a problem-definition process and give direction on how to respond to them. They do so through the following processes:

   a Making social needs or opportunities visible;
   b Detailing causes and consequences;
   c Framing the problem and solutions in ways that appeal to diverse stakeholders; and
   d Championing new ideas for dealing with the problem;

2 *Offering compelling visions of the future*: leaders engage in translation and social construction processes as they attempt to make an alternative, abstract future feasible and appealing in the minds of constituents; and
3 *Designing and using formal and informal discussion forums*: leaders design and use structures and processes for engaging internal and external government stakeholders in order to realise shared understandings of both the problem and possible solutions.

In addition, political leadership is critically important in order to build a sustainable coalition that can convince public decision-makers to approve proposed policies and protect them during implementation (Crosby, Bryson & Stone, 2010: 217).

These identified leadership activities and skills point to the necessity for digital government leaders to have a strong background in the multidisciplinary area of complex public management. And yet, many governments decide to put a leader with a technical background in charge of designing, managing, coordinating, implementing and overseeing digital government initiatives. Often, governments create a high-level CIO position to lead, coordinate and inspire internal and external stakeholders to appreciate the strategic value of digital government (Sandoval-Almazán *et al*, 2017: 108). For example, the US created the role of a CIO who is in charge of overseeing a digital government strategy across the federal government and reports directly to the president (Sandoval-Almazán *et al*, 2017: 14). Another related issue is that dedicated government units to support the CIO position and/or the management and implementation of the digital government strategy are usually digital technology–focused units separate from government programmes, processes and initiatives that are responsible for critically important digital government functional areas, such as public policy, government service provision, open and transparent government and participatory governance.

These issues and developments suggest that the right leadership for successful digital government outcomes may not be attained at the moment. There are a few more reasons that seem to point in that direction. For instance, in many countries, there is a general lack of understanding of the complex public

Strategy, leadership and governance 257

management aspects and implications of digital government amongst senior government leaders. Government business leaders, especially CEs of government departments, usually see digital government as a technology issue which does not belong to their own managerial portfolio and therefore do not understand the public management aspects of technology-enabled public sector reform initiatives (Lips, 2011; Lips, 2014).

Another reason we might not have the right leadership in place for digital government at the moment is that the majority of senior government leaders were born before the widespread societal adoption of digital technologies and are therefore "digital immigrants" (Palfrey & Gasser, 2008). Moreover, quite a few of these senior leaders do not actively use these digital technologies themselves (Dutton & Blank, 2011: 15). Similar observations can be made for quite a few political leaders around the world (Lips, 2014). Also, political leaders commonly want to stay away from perceived high-risk, complex and expensive digital government initiatives, which might attract negative media attention (Heeks, 2006). Moreover, political leaders usually like to see quick wins in terms of digital government efficiency gains, preferably during the time they are in office, and do not always understand the longer-term investments that are needed to realise benefits from digital government initiatives (Lips, 2014).

In other words, the fact that digital government strategies and initiatives need to be seen through the lens of complex public management in the public sector, rather than as issues for an IT department, has major consequences not only for the processes and outcomes of technology-enabled public sector reform, but also for digital government ownership, stewardship and leadership (Lips, 2011). However, ignoring and isolating digital technology and data in those public management activities, as is currently happening in many cases, are also not viable options (Heeks & Davies, 1999): instead, public sector leaders need not only to become digital technology- and data-literate in a way which integrates this knowledge with their public management knowledge and expertise, but also to recognise digital technology and data as key enablers of all government functions (Heeks & Davies, 1999; Lips, 2011). It is only through this integrated complex public management lens that public sector leaders will be able to successfully lead and manage the wide variety of socio-technical assemblages in the context of digital government. This is all the more important now that governments are increasingly adopting smart technologies and innovative data use solutions in their digital government relationships, which will require public sector leaders to open up, from a citizen's perspective, the black boxes of public decision-making around algorithms and merged datasets, which are affecting people's lives (see Chapter 6).

Governance of digital government

If we look through a technology lens to consider the domain of governance in the digital government context, we will likely see a more-or-less exclusive focus of government officials on digital technology or IT governance in

258 *Emerging issues*

government organizations. Similarly, if we utilise a data lens, we will find government officials predominantly occupied with data governance in a digital government initiative. Moreover, if we consider the domain of governance for a digital government project, we will likely find a dedicated governance board that has been set up to oversee that project and the benefits it aims to realise for the duration of the project. Another digital government governance body usually can be found to review and oversee a government's digital government strategy: commonly, members of this governance board include representatives from the IT departments and programme managers of different government agencies (Sandoval-Almazán *et al*, 2017: 16). And at the public management system level of digital government, there is another critical governance layer that needs to be considered for the oversight of digital government from a whole-of-government perspective.

As we can see, the governance landscape in the digital government context is multi-layered and complex; it involves not only a vertical dimension of governance layers, but also, as we saw in Chapter 7, a horizontal dimension. Moreover, increasingly, we can observe digital government developments where the horizontal dimension is an integral part of a governance system whole in which joined-up, horizontal digital government service networks operate alongside and in association with hierarchical processes within the government agencies involved to meet the requirements of their respective authorising environments (Eppel & Lips, 2016). In other words, within a digital governance system whole, we can increasingly observe the integration of the vertical, horizontal and socio-technical construct dimensions (Eppel & Lips, 2016).

Box 10.1 Integration of the vertical, horizontal and socio-technical construct dimensions

As an example of the integration of the vertical, horizontal and socio-technical construct dimensions and how this can be successfully managed, read Eppel and Lips (2016).

The governance landscape in the digital government context also involves different meanings for the term "governance" across those vertical and horizontal dimensions (Lynn, 2012; Hughes, 2010). On the one hand, we can observe the existence of the traditional conceptions of "IT governance" and "corporate governance" in order to run the (IT) organization well by providing strategic direction and setting up appropriate accountability structures, rules and procedures (Hughes, 2010: 88); on the other hand, so-called new governance conceptions can be identified as governance with government, in order to acknowledge that governments need to work collaboratively with citizens

Strategy, leadership and governance 259

to achieve their complex digital government goals (Lynn, 2012). For example, Christensen and Laegreid (2012: 256) use the term "governance" to describe changes in the nature and role of the government brought about by public sector reforms over the last two decades, whereby the previous focus on hierarchy has given way to a greater emphasis on networks and partnerships.

Importantly, under these latter "new governance" arrangements, direct participatory engagement of citizens in digital government relationships through co-production and co-creation reinforces the role of the citizen as the principal, in relationship to political decision-makers and public bureaucracies: in other words, citizens become part of government through these mechanisms, which confer authority on their inputs to digital government outcomes (Skelcher, 2010, in: Lynn, 2012: 51). At the same time, as a result of this active involvement of citizens, the exercise of power by government agencies can be better directed to enhance the effectiveness of public services, improve public policy- and decision-making and promote more open and transparent government, for example (Hughes, 2010). However, this shared, collaborative and decentralised governance conception doesn't sit well with traditional mental models of the state, such as NPM and traditional PA. For example, in an attempt to further conceptualise this new governance model, Osborne (2010a: 10) identifies a number of core elements of the so-called new public governance in contrast to PA and the NPM (see Table 10.1).

Table 10.1 Core elements of the NPG, in contrast to PA and the NPM

Paradigm / Key elements	Theoretical roots	Nature of the state	Focus	Emphasis	Resource allocation mechanism	Nature of the service system	Value base
PA	Political science and public policy	Unitary	The political system	Policy creation and implementation	Hierarchy	Closed	Public sector ethos
NPM	Rational / public choice theory and management studies	Regulatory	The organization	Management of organizational resources and performance	The market and classical or neo-classical contracts	Open rational	Efficacy of competition and the market-place
NPG	Institutional and network theory	Plural and pluralist	Organization in its environment	Negotiation of values, meaning and relationships	Networks and relational contracts	Open closed	Dispersed and contested

Source: Osborne (2010a: 10)

260　*Emerging issues*

In further support of the emergence of a NPG model in the context of digital government relationships, Moore and Hartley (2010) point to the following five unique, inter-related characteristics of public sector innovations in networked governance arrangements, such as digital government initiatives (Moore & Hartley, 2010: 64–68):

1. *Bursting the boundary of organizations and creating network-based production systems*: a particular organization stops being the sole locus of change and, with that, the sole focus of evaluation. Instead, the focus of attention shifts from the analysis of what happens inside an organization to an analysis of a production system that crosses organizational boundaries and sometimes reaches to the mobilisation of millions of decentralised, individual citizens. The innovation is evaluated on whether it succeeds in addressing the complex problem that has become the collective focus;

2. *Tapping new pools of financing, material resources and human energy*: regardless of the type or form of resources, one way in which these collaborative innovations seem to successfully address complex problems is by locating and mobilizing resources that were previously on the sideline or not fully exploited;

3. *Exploiting government's capacity to convene, exhort and redefine private rights and responsibilities*: government uses different instruments to achieve its results. For instance, government not only uses its money to direct the activity of its own employees or contractors, but also uses its direct regulatory authority and its public good–focused moral power to mobilise private actors to make contributions. It also allows individual citizens to make contributions to what were previously wholly government-controlled operations and, in doing so, allows the contributors to begin to make changes to the results of the public system;

4. *Redistributing the right to define and judge the value of what is being produced*: when government recruits private money, citizens and community organizations to its purposes, it seems to give up at least some of its power to define what should be produced, for whom and in what way. Because it seeks voluntary contributions, those who provide these contributions can negotiate the terms under which their contributions are offered. Because citizens have the power to exit, their voices become more powerful in shaping governmental policy and action. On the other hand, the locus of decision-making and judgments about value have shifted in emphasis away from the individual citizen to the state. Decision rights that used to be held by individuals in a private domain have been powerfully reconditioned by government authority; and

5. *Evaluating innovations in terms of justice, fairness and community building as well as of efficiency and effectiveness*: because these innovations use government authority as well as government money, and because they redistribute decision rights to the use of both publicly and privately owned assets, they invoke a different normative evaluation framework. Where innovations are

Strategy, leadership and governance 261

relocating either responsibilities for producing publicly valued results or rights to decide what constitutes publicly valued results, innovations need to be evaluated not only in terms of efficiency and cost-effectiveness, but also in terms of what might be considered right or ethical relationships in society, which includes notions like justice and fairness. Moreover, when a collective public-policy decision is taken to give private parties more power in shaping what were previously governmentally dominated operations, we will need to ask whether such a move is proper or not, and what the implications will be for the overall fairness and justice of a particular public production system.

As becomes clear, especially as a result of including horizontal dimensions of governance in digital government and its relationships with external stakeholders, these layered, multi-meaning and multi-dimensional conceptions of governance have critical implications for how we evaluate the outcomes of digital government. We discuss this important issue next.

Evaluating digital government outcomes

Digital government project failures, including not delivering the anticipated benefits, have had a lot of negative media attention over the years (Heeks & Davies, 1999). This may not be surprising, if we consider the extremely low success rates of digital government projects (Heeks, 2003; Heeks, 2006), as we discussed earlier. More or less every country in the world has its own (media) history of failed digital government projects; as these projects are usually also very costly, politicians perceive them as very risky as digital government project failure will not be seen favourably by voters. Interestingly, failure rates of technology projects in the private sector are not much different, according to Heeks and Bhatnagar (1999); it is just that the private sector has done a better job at keeping these failures quiet (Heeks & Bhatnagar, 1999: 58).

What explains these very low success rates of digital government projects in particular? According to Heeks (2006), digital government failure mainly has to do with poor project design and implementation and a lack of adequate project management of these highly complex initiatives. In addition, government organizations may lack a system for documenting the realisation of benefits and lessons learned in individual digital government projects, which then creates a situation where organizational learning for the benefit of future projects does not happen (Sylvester, 2010; Sandoval-Almazán *et al*, 2017). Another explanation for low digital government project success rates is a lack of attention to the unique governmental aspects of digital government projects, in particular complex institutional, organizational and managerial aspects (Gil-Garcia, 2012; Sandoval-Almazán *et al*, 2017).

In general, the conceptual models held and assumptions made by key stakeholders involved in technology-enabled public sector reform contribute significantly to whether a digital government project is seen as a success or a

262   *Emerging issues*

failure (Heeks & Bhatnagar, 1999). Heeks and Bhatnagar (1999: 59) point to the issue of so-called conception-reality gaps: namely, the gaps that exist between these conceptions and public sector realities that will determine success or failure. They observe three important conception-reality gap archetypes that make digital government reform failure more likely (Heeks & Bhatnagar, 1999: 62–71):

1   *Rationality-public sector reality gaps*: rational conceptual models assume that logic, objectivity and linearity underlie the workings of digital government reform initiatives and organizational change. This gap between the rational conceptions of technology-enabled public sector reform initiatives and non-linear political and institutionally driven public sector realities may occur because of a dominant emphasis on the rational technology aspects of digital government;
2   *Private sector-public sector gaps*: private sector conceptual models assume that the public sector could improve if it would adopt (better) private sector practices and solutions. Consequently, technology- or data-use solutions developed for private sector use can easily be based on conceptions that do not match public sector realities and will therefore be more prone to failure; and
3   *Country context gaps*: digital government initiatives designed and developed in the context of a particular country will incorporate common assumptions of that country context. This can cause problems if these digital government best practices or solutions are more or less directly transferred to other countries, regardless of context. Heeks and Bhatnagar (1999) point out that these problems are even greater if the direct transfer happens from an industrialised country to a developing country.

One particular conception-reality gap area, where private sector methodologies have been used and country contexts have been ignored, is in the area of benchmarking digital government progress across countries. For example, the United Nations has been publishing e-government and e-participation country rankings for many years,[1] the results of which have been widely publicly marketed by those countries that have come out at the top of the rankings. But other prominent international benchmarking activities of countries have also been undertaken in digital government domains, such as the Open Data Barometer.[2] The following main findings of the 2008 Gartner report "Be Aware of the Flaws in E-Government Surveys" are very insightful in this respect:

•   E-government surveys have been popular in the past to compare e-government progress. However, none of the surveys has been able to capture the relationship between functionality, quality, satisfaction and uptake;
•   Some jurisdictions around the world have invested resources with the explicit objective of improving their position in various e-government surveys; and

Strategy, leadership and governance 263

- The changing role of technology in government over time (e.g. use of social media) will make comparative surveys even more questionable.

Further problems with international benchmarking and other country-comparative efforts are research methodological inconsistencies around comparative data collection methods and measurements (i.e. what exactly is being measured in each country and when, what the criteria are, and how data are being compared) and different context-relative outcomes and implications of digital government for each country, leading to a situation of comparing apples to oranges: for example, an online student loan application service may not be available in each country for political reasons, and online individual tax returns (often an indicator of digital government success) are not always required (e.g. in New Zealand, most individual tax returns are automatically processed by government).

Another area where private sector methodologies have been used in digital government is in managing benefits realisation. In general, these private sector methodologies use linear models to identify two types of benefits in digital government: direct benefits, which are anticipated outcomes of value to the government organization, and indirect benefits, or anticipated outcomes of value to stakeholders. Moreover, managing benefits realisation is usually seen as being tied to a particular digital government project: put differently, when the project ends, the management and documenting of the benefits realised through that project also will be stopped. This then leads to relatively short-term, linear reporting of benefits realisation related to a digital government initiative (i.e. anticipated benefits realised or not, in accordance with the project plan).

However, as we discussed earlier, direct benefits or public value created in digital government initiatives can be done collaboratively and shared across all stakeholders concerned, instead of being attributed to a particular government organization; benefits resulting from a digital government project can be unplanned, unexpected and intangible (e.g. fairness in public decision-making) and benefits can be realised after the digital government project has ended. In other words, the unique context of digital government initiatives requires a benefits realisation methodology which takes these contextual conditions into account, such as using a dynamic and cyclical benefits realisation management approach over a longer period of time.

Osborne (2010b: 423) points out that this organizational performance management culture in government is one of the lasting legacies of the NPM: the use of government agency performance targets and indicators as a way to vertically control the agency's delivery of the outcomes. However, as digital government performance and outcomes are increasingly co-produced in horizontal governance arrangements, the existing vertical approach to performance evaluation is becoming problematic. This is all the more the case as the formal outcomes of this vertical approach to agency performance evaluation usually also determines the level of funding available for horizontal digital government projects owned by the vertical agency silo.

264   *Emerging issues*

Consequently, for various reasons, traditional vertical evaluation approaches to digital government performance and outcomes need to be reframed to suit increasingly horizontal governance arrangements around digital government initiatives. Moreover, we need a different normative evaluation framework in order to move away from government organization-centric performance outcomes, such as efficiency and cost-effectiveness, and to be able to assess the public value that is collaboratively produced by all shareholders involved in digital government initiatives (Moore, 1997). As an example of a different evaluation framework needed for horizontal governance arrangements, Gunton and Day (2003, in: Ansell, 2012: 507) use the following four criteria for evaluating success in collaborative governance arrangements:

1   Success in reaching agreement;
2   Efficiency of the collaborative process relative to alternative processes;
3   Satisfaction of stakeholders with the process and outcomes; and
4   Achievement of other social capital [or public value, ML] benefits, such as improved relationships among stakeholders and enhanced stakeholder skills and knowledge.

Box 10.2   Exercise 10.1

Choose a digital government project in operation and list the various benefits that can be realised from this project over time; besides direct benefits to government agencies, you should list the indirect benefits to stakeholders, unplanned or unexpected benefits, intangible benefits and benefits after the project has ended.

Discussion questions

1   Try and find a failed digital government initiative in your country. Why was this initiative considered a failure? What went wrong? For what reason? Motivate your answer.
2   Try and find a successful digital government initiative in your country. Why was this initiative considered successful? What went well? For what reason? Which benefits were realised through this initiative, and how have they been assessed?
3   What would you consider to be the vision and elements of a successful digital government strategy? Motivate your answer.
4   What makes a successful leader of a digital governance arrangement? And a successful manager? Motivate your answer.

Notes

1 UN E-Government Surveys, available from: https://publicadministration.un.org/en/research/un-e-government-surveys [accessed 25 June 2018].
2 The Open Data Barometer, available from: https://opendatabarometer.org/ [accessed 25 June 2018].

References

Ansell, C. (2012) Collaborative governance. In: Levi-Faur, D. (ed.) *The Oxford Handbook of Governance*. Oxford: Oxford University Press, pp. 498–511.

Bekkers, V.J.J.M. & Homburg, V. (eds.) (2005) *The Information Ecology of e-Government: E-Government as Institutional and Technological Innovation in Public Administration*. Amsterdam: IOS Press.

Christensen, T. & Laegreid, P. (2012) Governance and administrative reforms. In: Levi-Faur, D. (ed.) *The Oxford Handbook of Governance*. Oxford: Oxford University Press, pp. 255–267.

Crosby, B.C., Bryson, J.M. & Stone, M.M. (2010) Leading across frontiers: How visionary leaders integrate people, processes, structures and resources. In: Osborne, S.P. (ed.) *The New Public Governance? Emerging Perspectives on the Theory and Practice of Public Governance*. London: Routledge, pp. 200–222.

Dutton, W.H. & Blank, G. (2011) *Next Generation Users: The Internet in Britain*. Oxford Internet Survey 2011 Report. Oxford: Oxford Internet Institute.

Eppel, E.A. & Lips, A.M.B. (2016) Unpacking the black box of successful ICT-enabled service transformation: How to join up the vertical, the horizontal and the technical. *Public Money & Management*, 36 (1), 39–46.

Fountain, J.E. (2008) Bureaucratic reform and e-government in the United States: An institutional perspective. In: Chadwick, A. & Howard, P.N. (eds.) *The Routledge Handbook of Internet Politics*. London: Routledge, pp. 99–113.

Gil-Garcia, J.R. (2012) *Enacting Electronic Government Success*. Integrated Series in Information Systems, 31. New York, NY: Springer Science+Business Media, eBook, DOI: 10.1007/978-1-4614-2015-6_7

Heeks, R. (1999) Better information age reform: Reducing the risk of information systems failure. In: Heeks, R. (ed.) *Reinventing Government in the Information Age: International Practice in IT-Enabled Public Sector Reform*. London: Routledge, pp. 75–109.

Heeks, R. (2003) *eGovernment for Development: Success and Failure Rates of eGovernment in Developing/Transitional Countries: Overview*. Available from: https://www.egov4dev.org/success/sfrates.shtml [accessed 19 June 2018].

Heeks, R. (2006) *Implementing and Managing eGovernment: An International Text*. London: Sage.

Heeks, R. & Bhatnagar, S. (1999) Understanding success and failure in information age reform. In: Heeks, R. (ed.) *Reinventing Government in the Information Age: International Practice in IT-Enabled Public Sector Reform*. London: Routledge, pp. 49–74.

Heeks, R. & Davies, A. (1999) Different approaches to information age reform. In: Heeks, R. (ed.) *Reinventing Government in the Information Age: International Practice in IT-Enabled Public Sector Reform*. London: Routledge, pp. 22–48.

Homburg, V. (2008) *Understanding E-Government: Information Systems in Public Administration*. London: Routledge.

Hughes, O. (2010) Does governance exist? In: Osborne, S.P. (ed.) *The New Public Governance? Emerging Perspectives on the Theory and Practice of Public Governance*. London: Routledge, pp. 87–104.

266 Emerging issues

Institute for Government. (2010) *System Error: Fixing the Flaws in Government IT*. London: Institute for Government.

Lips, A.M.B. (2011) 'E-government is dead: Long live networked governance': Fixing system errors in the New Zealand public management system. In: Ryan, B. & Gill, D. (eds.) *Future State: Directions for Public Management in New Zealand*. Wellington: Victoria University Press, pp. 248–261.

Lips, A.M.B. (2012) E-Government is dead: Long live public administration 2.0. *Information Polity*, 17, 239–250.

Lips, A.M.B. (2014) Transforming government: By default? In: Graham, M. & Dutton, W.H. (eds.) *Society & the Internet: How Networks of Information and Communication Are Changing Our Lives*. Oxford: Oxford University Press, pp. 179–194.

Lynn, L.E. (2012) The many faces of governance: Adaptation? Transformation? Both? Neither? In: Levi-Faur, D. (ed.) *The Oxford Handbook of Governance*. Oxford: Oxford University Press, pp. 49–64.

McLoughlin, I. & Wilson, R., with Martin, M. (2013) *Digital Government @ Work: A Social Informatics Perspective*. Abingdon: Oxford University Press.

Moore, M. & Hartley, J. (2010) Innovations in governance. In: Osborne, S.P. (ed.) *The New Public Governance? Emerging Perspectives on the Theory and Practice of Public Governance*. London: Routledge, pp. 52–71.

Moore, M.H. (1997) *Creating Public Value: Strategic Management in Government*. Cambridge, MA: Harvard University Press.

Office of the Auditor-General. (June 2012) *Realising Benefits from Six Public Sector Technology Projects*. Discussion Paper, presented to the House of Representatives under section 20 of the Public Audit Act 2001. Wellington: Office of the Auditor-General.

Osborne, S.P. (2010a) Introduction: The (new) public governance: A suitable case for treatment? In: Osborne, S.P. (ed.) *The New Public Governance? Emerging Perspectives on the Theory and Practice of Public Governance*. London: Routledge, pp. 1–16.

Osborne, S.P. (2010b) Conclusions: Public governance and public services delivery: A research agenda for the future. In: Osborne, S.P. (ed.) *The New Public Governance? Emerging Perspectives on the Theory and Practice of Public Governance*. London: Routledge, pp. 413–428.

Palfrey, J. & Gasser, U. (2008) *Born Digital: Understanding the First Generation of Digital Natives*. New York, NY: Basic Books.

Pratchett, L. (1998) Technological bias in an information age: ICT policy making in local government. In: Snellen, I.Th.M. & van de Donk, W.B.H.J. (eds.) *Public Administration in an Information Age: A Handbook*. Amsterdam: IOS Press, pp. 207–221.

Sandoval-Almazán, R., Luna-Reyes, L.F., Luna-Reyes, D.E., Gil-Garcia, J.R., Puron-Cid, G. & Picazo-Vela, S. (2017) *Building Digital Government Strategies: Principles and Practices*. Public Administration and Information Technology Series, 16, Springer International Publishing, eBook, DOI: 10.1007/978-3-319-60348-3

Sylvester, A.J. (2010) *An Investigation into Organisational Learning by Public Officials Creating and Maintaining Multi-Channel Service Delivery Information Systems in the New Zealand Public Sector*. PhD Thesis. Wellington: Victoria University of Wellington. Available from: https://viewer.waireto.victoria.ac.nz/client/viewer/IE165554/details?dps_dvs=1549848431587-846 [accessed 11 February 2019].

The White House. (2012) *Digital Government: Building a 21st Century Platform to Better Service the American People*. Executive Office of the President of the United States, Washington, DC: The White House.

Willcocks, L.P., Currie, W.L. & Jackson, S. (1997) In pursuit of the reengineering agenda: Research evidence from U.K. Public Services. In: Taylor, J.A., Snellen, I.Th.M. & Zuurmond, A. (eds.) *Beyond BPR in Public Administration: Institutional Transformation in an Information Age*. Amsterdam: IOS Press, pp. 103–132.

Further reading

Gil-Garcia, J.R. (2012) *Enacting Electronic Government Success.* Integrated Series in Information Systems, 31, New York, NY: Springer Science+Business Media, eBook, DOI: 10.1007/978-1-4614-2015-6_7

Heeks, R. (2006) *Implementing and Managing eGovernment: An International Text.* London: Sage.

Levi-Faur, D. (ed.) (2012) *The Oxford Handbook of Governance.* Oxford: Oxford University Press.

McLoughlin, I. & Wilson, R., with Martin, M. (2013) *Digital Government @ Work: A Social Informatics Perspective.* Abingdon: Oxford University Press.

Moore, M.H. (1997) *Creating Public Value: Strategic Management in Government.* Cambridge, MA: Harvard University Press.

Osborne, S.P. (ed.) (2010) *The New Public Governance? Emerging Perspectives on the Theory and Practice of Public Governance.* London: Routledge.

Part V

Conclusions

11 Conclusions

Managing institutional innovation and digital governance

Learning objectives

By the end of this chapter you should be able to:

- Understand the complexity of the layering and adding of digital government reform waves to existing government systems;
- Identify the core elements of an effective institutional design for digital governance; and
- Identify the requirements for effectively managing digital governance in a particular context.

Key points of this chapter

- In order to understand digital government innovations in their particular context, and the impact and implications they are having for government and governance, we can use the empirical heuristic of the technology-enabled data polity to "X-ray" different contexts of digital government and governance. The empirical findings of this X-ray scan can be used as input for applying the revised contextual integrity framework;
- Hybrid government systems deinstitutionalise parts of the existing political-administrative systems and institutionalise new reform elements, such as new and adapted uses of digital technologies and data, in an ever more complex and layered government system where traditional elements from various past reform waves coexist with reform elements (Christensen & Laegreid, 2012: 255). Institutional enablement is required to do so;
- In the context of the emerging hybrid digital governance system, we are not just facing an adoption and layering of different government systems, but also, within the digital governance system itself, we are witnessing the processes of adopting, layering and managing new digital government reforms, often in parallel;
- Vertical and horizontal dimensions of digital governance should not be seen in competition but need to be married up as interrelated digital government innovation drivers under the emerging hybrid digital governance system;

272   *Conclusions*

- An institutional design for digital governance is required that rewards entrepreneurial behaviour by enhancing the bottom-up digital government innovation capacity of self-governing actors and supporting horizontal co-production and co-creation of digital government relationships with citizens;
- The complex public management lens uses a systemic approach in order to study digital government and governance;
- This digital governance system approach focuses attention not only on the institutional aspects and democratic relationships that enable and constrain digital government reform within a plural and pluralist system, but also on the critical involvement of both government organizations and citizens to co-produce context-relative, digital government phenomena;
- Empirical research is critical to better understand uses of digital technologies and data as part of socio-technical assemblages within the context of digital governance and their impact and implications; and
- Public managers responsible for digital government reform need to manage highly complex, interrelated nested digital government systems in multiple reform areas. Moreover, they will need to take a contextual approach for each of these nested digital government systems, appreciating that good digital government practice in one context may not be good practice in another.

Key terms

- *Digital governance system*: an integrated system of the vertical dimension, the horizontal dimension and the socio-technical construct dimension of digital government initiatives.
- *Hybrid government systems:* new reforms are added to existing government systems, such as the NPM was added to traditional PA, producing hybrid government systems.
- *Integrative leadership:* involves not only facilitating the exchange of perspectives and the exploration of mutual interests and concerns between the various stakeholders involved in digital governance initiatives, but also, in particular, establishing the contextual integrity of the technology- and data-enabled collaborative process by ensuring that all stakeholders involved abide by the contextual "rules of the game."

Introduction

In this final chapter, we reflect back on the insights from the previous chapters and especially consider the impact of using digital technologies and data in the context of digital government for contemporary government and governance. We particularly focused on the use of digital technologies and data in the context of digital government relationships with citizens in this book; this is not to say that other stakeholders of digital government are not important, but this chosen perspective has certainly narrowed some of the observations and

Conclusions 273

insights presented here. Empirical research into other digital government relationships and perhaps another book will need to provide some further insights into these other contexts of digital government.

In this chapter, we present the empirical heuristic of the emerging technology-enabled data polity in order to understand the digital government innovations in their particular context and the impact and implications they are having on government and governance, especially on digital government relationships with citizens. Governments could use the empirical findings of such an X-ray scan as input for the revised contextual integrity framework proposed in Chapter 6. We also discuss the increasing importance of the horizontal dimension, also compared to the vertical dimension, in these hybrid government systems and how these two dimensions can be married up as interrelated digital government innovation drivers under the emerging hybrid digital governance system.

Moreover, we discuss the similarities between managing digital governance and public management under the NPG regime. Based on this insight, our proposed complex public management lens as an alternative way to see and understand digital government more comprehensively and empirically turns out to be very useful. For instance, using this complex public management lens for understanding, explaining and managing digital governance also helps us to ask relevant empirical questions – questions that would not be raised if we had used one of the nine narrower perspectives discussed in Chapter 3. Furthermore, we discuss the fact that, even within the digital governance system itself, we are witnessing processes of adopting, layering and managing digital government reforms, often in parallel. This relatively fast, historical development of added layers of digital government reforms only adds to the complexity of managing digital governance and, with that, further shapes the digital governance context for public managers.

Institutional innovation of government

As we have seen in the various chapters of this book, digital technologies and data are becoming embedded in the fabrics of contemporary government and governance. Likely, in a decade or so, we will no longer talk distinctively about "digital government" or "digital governance," but only about "government": a development similar to those of other technological innovations in the past, where we do not talk in distinctive terms about "paper-based," "telephony-based" or "electricity-based" government anymore. These technologies have become an integral part of how governments are run today.

However, this is not to say that, in ten years' time, government will be the same as we know it today; the use of digital technologies and data in the context of digital government is having a major impact on the core functions, structures, processes and external relationships with citizens and other key stakeholders of governments around the world, creating digitised forms of government innovation. As Castells (1996) has forewarned us, in using digital technologies and data in the context of digital government, we are learning how to do things differently in government and governance.

274 *Conclusions*

In order to understand these digital government innovations in their particular context and the impact and implications they are having for government and governance, we only need to use the empirical heuristic of the emerging technology-enabled data polity to X-ray different contexts of government and governance and explore the following (cf Taylor, 1998; see Chapter 3): what new and traditional data flows are happening in different contexts of digital government and governance; how these data flows are used (e.g. to convert data into information and knowledge), for what reason and what the impacts and implications are; what current barriers there are to data flows in different contexts of digital government and governance and why are data not used and what the impacts and implications are.

However, in so doing, we should acknowledge the "social life of data and digital technologies" (cf Brown & Duguid, 2000) and empirically explore the socio-technical assemblages in the context of digital government relationships, of which data and digital technologies are integral parts (see Chapter 2). Moreover, the empirical findings of this X-ray scan can then be used as input for applying the revised contextual integrity framework, as proposed in Chapter 6, in the following way: which democratic government-related informational norms need to be considered in evaluating data use and data flows in socio-technical assemblages within the context of digital government relationships?

Empirical research findings from such an independently conducted X-ray are invaluable inputs in public sector reform efforts to reflect on and redesign existing democratic, institutional, organizational and operational arrangements in government so that traditional ways of governing are not standing in the way of using digital technologies and data to enhance public value and make a real difference in people's lives (cf The White House, 2012). Such efforts are highly complex as public sector reforms do not entail a replacement of one government system by another, transformed system, but involve processes of layering in the sense that new reforms are added to existing government systems, such as the NPM was added to traditional PA, producing hybrid government systems as it were (Christensen & Laegreid, 2012). These hybrid government systems then deinstitutionalise parts of the existing political-administrative systems and institutionalise new reform elements, such as new and adapted uses of digital technologies and data, in an ever more complex and layered government system where traditional elements from various past reform waves coexist with reform elements (Christensen & Laegreid, 2012: 255).

In our particular case of digital government reform efforts, the horizontal dimension is becoming increasingly important, compared to the vertical dimension, in this hybrid and ever more digitised government system. This means that traditional vertical rule-based PA elements and NPM elements of vertical top-down competition in developing, implementing and disseminating more and more digitised public policies and government services are increasingly challenged by technology- and data-enabled reform elements of horizontal collaboration with citizens and other stakeholders in co-producing public policies and services as part of the emerging hybrid government system

Conclusions 275

(Sørensen, 2012: 215). The way forward, however, is not to see these vertical and horizontal dimensions in competition, but to marry them up as interrelated digital government innovation drivers under the emerging hybrid digital governance system (Sørensen, 2012; Lips, 2011).

To do so requires an institutional design for digital governance that rewards entrepreneurial behaviour by enhancing the bottom-up digital government innovation capacity of self-governing actors (Sørensen, 2012: 218). Sørensen (2012: 223–224) provides us with the following strategic advice in that respect:

1   *Don't choose between top-down and bottom-up forms of governance, but make good use of both forms*: digital government innovation relies on the presence of autonomous spaces in which decentred entrepreneurs can develop and pursue innovative ideas. However, in order to be effective, this bottom-up interaction is in need of top-down governance that frames this interaction in ways that motivate the entrepreneurial actors to innovate and share ideas and knowledge through the institutional design of incentive structures that balance competitive and collaborative patterns of action;

2   *Use the strength of existing NPM elements to regulate and manage clear expectations of the involved actors*: NPM insists that public authorities send clear signals to the involved self-governing actors about what is expected of them in the shape of the overall public goal they are expected to achieve and clearly set out the conditions of the autonomy available to them; and

3   *Top-down governance and bottom-up decentred self-governance should not be institutionalised as separate processes*: institutional conditions are needed that promote feedback loops and dialogue between the vertical and horizontal governance dimensions. This is necessary to avoid decoupling the horizontal co-creation of innovative digital government ideas and solutions and the vertical implementation of these digital government innovations.

This then points at the necessity of "institutional enablement" of the emerging hybrid digital governance system (Lips, 2011): in other words, the necessity for the existing government system to accept, enable and embed digital government reform and innovations as part of existing institutional arrangements. One way to do so would be for governments to adopt new rules and regulations in order to institutionalise digital government reform and make it sustainable in the emerging hybrid system. As discussed in Chapter 6, this will also help governments to be transparent about the rules that govern data (re-)use and data flows in the digital government context, including the government-related informational norms and transmission principles.

Managing digital governance

As we discussed in Chapter 10, the emerging hybrid digital governance system features the core elements that Osborne (2010) has identified as part of the NPG regime. Moreover, he explains that the NPG regime should not be seen

276 *Conclusions*

as a normative alternative to the PA and NPM regimes, nor as the one best way by which to manage digital governance (Osborne, 2010: 413). In practice, these regimes will invariably coexist and interact rather than serially replace each other (Osborne, 2010: 414). However, this does imply that scholarly thinking about suitable ways of managing under the NPG regime also apply to managing digital governance. Moreover, an appreciation of the local digital governance context in which socio-technical assemblages are being constructed and managed is at the heart of the NPG regime.

This then brings us back to the usefulness of the alternative lens we proposed in Chapter 3 for seeing digital government: the perspective of complex public management. Applying the lens of complex public management helps us to both comprehensively and empirically observe, explore, understand and explain the complexity of managing the vertical, horizontal and socio-technical dimensions of digital government phenomena within their particular context: in other words, the complexity of managing the (nested) digital governance systems whole. Such rich empirical observations and deep understanding of the digital governance systems whole would not be available to us if we used any of the other nine lenses discussed in Chapter 3.

Furthermore, this complex public management lens is aligned with the systemic approach that Osborne (2010: 415) believes is required for the study of contemporary government and governance: a systemic approach that views digital government and governance from an open natural systems perspective. This digital governance system approach focuses attention not only on the institutional aspects and democratic relationships that enable and constrain digital government reform within a plural and pluralist system, but also on the critical involvement of both government organizations and citizens to co-produce context-relative, digital government phenomena. Also, using this complex public management lens for understanding, explaining and managing digital governance helps us to ask comprehensive and highly relevant empirical questions, such as the following:

- How are digital technologies and data used in context-relative, digital government co-production relationships between citizens and governments, and what are the implications? Under what conditions do uses of digital technologies and data make a real difference in people's lives?
- How are existing digital divides and citizens' digital inclusion rights being managed? Under what conditions could general ethical and political principles, such as fairness, equality, social justice, privacy protection and transparency, be met in the context of digital government relationships?
- Which stakeholders are involved in digital governance arrangements in a particular context, and how are they using digital technologies and data in collaborative ways to deliver enhanced public value?
- How are the vertical, horizontal and socio-technical dimensions within a particular digital governance context being integrated and managed in a way that public value is achieved?

Conclusions 277

- What conditions contribute to the effectiveness and efficiency of integrated vertical and horizontal digital governance arrangements? How could such arrangements be managed so that they are sustainable over longer periods of time?
- How is relational capital developed in digital governance arrangements in a particular context? Under what conditions could this relational capital be made sustainable and productive in other digital governance arrangements or contexts?
- How are digital governance arrangements in a particular context being held accountable for the delivery of outcomes? and
- How are outcomes of digital governance arrangements in a particular context being evaluated? What evaluation role and contribution could the revised contextual integrity framework perspective have in this respect?

Empirical research into questions such as these is critical to better understand how to manage uses of digital technologies and data as part of socio-technical assemblages within the context of digital governance and their impact and implications. Moreover, based on these empirical insights, we are able to make some further recommendations for effectively managing digital government reform.

In the context of the emerging hybrid digital governance system and the need to manage digital government phenomena, initiatives and collaborative arrangements, we should be aware that we are not just facing an adoption and layering of different government systems, but also that, within the digital governance system itself, we are witnessing processes of adopting, layering and managing new digital government reforms, often in parallel. In summarizing the digital government reform ambitions and developments we have been discussing in this book, the following short historical overview of these layered digital government reform processes can be provided.

Historical development of digital government reforms

As we noted in Chapter 1, digital government started to emerge with the arrival of computing in government organizations. The first computers were large centralised mainframes providing enhanced decision-making power to the top of government organizations. In the 1980s, we saw another digital government reform development emerging in government organizations through the introduction of decentralised PCs on the desks of individual government employees.

The 1990s saw the introduction of the public Internet in governments around the world as a new digital government reform effort. At first, governments used the Internet in electronic government reforms as an add-on to existing government structures and to "plug and play": a yellow pages approach was commonly used to provide the general public with new digital forms of access to government information.

278 *Conclusions*

Gradually, governments learned how to do different things enabled by digital technologies. Digital government reform efforts were aimed at achieving more customer-centricity in government service provision as well as integration of government silos. More and more, we saw that existing institutional arrangements in governments were challenged as a result of digital government reform: initial reform activities, focused on virtual front-office integration and leaving existing government structures intact, were followed by physical front-office integration enabled by digital technologies and technology-enabled back-office integration. Also, digital exchanges between front office and back office became critical for government operations. With the shift towards more transactional services in digital government service provision, we also witnessed that managing citizen identity, privacy and security became important issues for digital government reform.

A subsequent wave of digital government reform saw the adoption of mental models around citizen-centric government and the provision of more personalised services in digital government relationships with citizens. These reform ambitions put further pressure on existing institutional arrangements and traditional administrative values. Privacy legislation and a rules-based Weberian bureaucratic model underlying government operations turned out to be standing in the way of the delivery of individualised government services. Moreover, increasing tensions and lack of coordination between a government-wide view on digital government reform and the interests of individual government agencies also were barriers to progressing government reform ambitions around citizen-centric government.

In parallel, we could witness digital government reform efforts to open up government data, become more participatory and collaborative, enhance government transparency and deliver m-government services to citizens. Although government reform efforts to open up government data were often patchy from a cross-government perspective and supplied data which were not necessarily of high value to citizens, we gradually could see some more networked and participatory forms of governance emerging around the use of digital technologies and data. The adoption of social media by governments also contributed to government reform efforts to become more participatory and collaborative.

The global financial crisis in particular provided governments with a new digital reform incentive to become digital by default. These reform ambitions put further pressure on emerging multiple digital divides around digital technologies and digital government services, leading to multiple new social inequalities and further challenging traditional administrative equity principles in government. Also, laws created pre–digital age turned out to be barriers to digital-by-default reform progress.

More recently, the advent of smart technologies and innovative data uses leads to another digital government reform wave of governments wanting to become smart or smarter. This digital government reform wave sees large volumes of data being generated and integrated for innovative use by governments; the public sector becoming further loosely networked, collaborative and

Conclusions 279

participatory, including further opportunities for active forms of citizenship around innovative data use and technologies of expertise; blurring boundaries between public and private domains, especially around data and more digital divides emerging around data. We can witness that the traditional vertical Weberian model and administrative values are not appropriate any longer for the emerging new digital order; as a result, we propose a new contextual approach to digital government reform, where the horizontal meets the vertical, and a new ethical framework of contextual integrity. Also, new citizens' digital inclusion rights are needed, and are proposed in this book, in order to rebalance these fundamentally changing relationships between citizens and governments in the digital age.

This historical overview of added layers of digital government reforms within the digital governance system not only shows the relatively fast development of governments introducing and developing multiple ambitious reform efforts, often in parallel, but also points to the complexity of managing digital governance. This then sets some further requirements for effectively managing digital governance in a particular context.

As we discussed in Chapter 10, leadership is one of the most critical areas for success in digital governance. Public managers will not lose their jobs as a result of the increasing use of digital technologies and data in the context of digital government reform, but their managerial roles will involve managing highly complex, interrelated nested digital government systems in multiple reform areas. Moreover, they will need to take a contextual approach to each of these nested digital government systems, appreciating that good digital government practice in one context may not be good practice in another. They need to integrate and effectively manage the vertical, the horizontal and the socio-technical within a particular digital governance arrangement in order to realise public value; this will involve managing a number of emerging issues and barriers, as we discussed in various chapters. They will need to manage positive and negative feedback loops within a nested digital government system as well as adaptation and co-evolution within and between systems. Moreover, they are faced with multiple legacy systems within each nested digital government system, all influencing the starting point for system change.

But perhaps the most important requirement for effectively managing digital governance in a particular context is providing robust leadership to the increasing importance of the horizontal dimension, which includes technology- and data-enabled co-production relationships between citizens and government. It is in these co-production relationships in particular that digital governance arrangements can become learning eco-systems around developing effective solutions to particular public policy problems or the effective provision of public services.

Providing such "integrative" leadership, as Page (2010, in: Ansell, 2012: 506) calls it, involves not only facilitating the exchange of perspectives and the exploration of mutual interests and concerns between the various stakeholders involved, but also establishing, in particular, the contextual integrity

280 *Conclusions*

of the technology- and data-enabled collaborative process by ensuring that all stakeholders involved abide by the contextual "rules of the game" (Ansell, 2012: 506). These rules might require a trade-off between traditional values in government's relationships with citizens, such as universalism, equity and privacy, and values emerging in the specific context of digital government relationships, such as particularism, transparency and data sharing, for example. The contextual integrity framework proposed in Chapter 6 can be of further help to governments and public managers in this respect, to decide on appropriate contextual integrity norms and rules for a particular context of digital government relationships.

Discussion questions

1   Find a digital government or digital governance initiative and apply the empirical heuristic of the data polity in order to X-ray this initiative in its particular context. What impacts and implications does this digital government innovation arrangement have for government and governance?
2   Find a practical digital governance initiative and identify the requirements for an appropriate institutional design for this initiative. To what extent do your identified requirements match the actual institutional design of this initiative? Motivate your answer.
3   What would be the requirements for effectively managing a digital governance initiative in the context of your government? Motivate your answer.

References

Ansell, C. (2012) Collaborative governance. In: Levi-Faur, D. (ed.) *The Oxford Handbook of Governance*. Oxford: Oxford University Press, pp. 498–511.

Brown, J.S. & Duguid, P. (2000) *The Social Life of Information*. Boston, MA: Harvard Business School Press.

Castells, M. (1996) *The Rise of the Network Society: The Information Age: Economy, Society and Culture*. Vol. 1. Oxford: Blackwell Publishers.

Christensen, T. & Laegreid, P. (2012) Governance and administrative reforms. In: Levi-Faur, D. (ed.) *The Oxford Handbook of Governance*. Oxford: Oxford University Press, pp. 255–267.

Lips, A.M.B. (2011) 'E-government is dead: Long live networked governance': Fixing system errors in the New Zealand public management system. In: Ryan, B. & Gill, D. (eds.) *Future State: Directions for Public Management in New Zealand*. Wellington: Victoria University of Wellington, pp. 248–261.

Osborne, S.P. (2010) Introduction: The (new) public governance: A suitable case for treatment? In: Osborne, S.P. (ed.) *The New Public Governance? Emerging Perspectives on the Theory and Practice of Public Governance*. London/New York: Routledge, pp. 1–16.

Sørensen, E. (2012) Governance and innovation in the public sector. In: Levi-Faur, D. (ed.) *The Oxford Handbook of Governance*. Oxford: Oxford University Press, pp. 214–227.

Taylor, J.A. (1998) Informatization as X-ray: What is public administration for the information age? In: Snellen, I.Th.M. & van de Donk, W.B.H.J. (eds.) *Public Administration in an Information Age: A Handbook*. Amsterdam: IOS Press, pp. 21–32.

Conclusions 281

The White House. (2012) *Digital Government: Building a 21st Century Platform to Better Service the American People*. Executive Office of the President of the United States, Washington, DC: The White House.

Further reading

Christensen, T. & Laegreid, P. (2012) Governance and administrative reforms. In: Levi-Faur, D. (ed.) *The Oxford Handbook of Governance*. Oxford: Oxford University Press, pp. 255–267.

Levi-Faur, D. (ed.) (2012) *The Oxford Handbook of Governance*. Oxford: Oxford University Press.

Osborne, S.P. (ed.) (2010) *The New Public Governance? Emerging Perspectives on the Theory and Practice of Public Governance*. London/New York: Routledge.

Index

Note: Italicized page numbers indicate a figure on the corresponding page. Page numbers in bold indicate a table on the corresponding page.

Aadhaar register 200
accessibility of data 119, 120, 121, 156
access issues: benefits of Internet 224–225; to data 119, 120, 121, 156; digital divide 229, 233–234, 236; digital government services 97, 119, 243; rights to services 81
AccuWeather app 116
active citizenship 118
adaptation within systems 63
algorithms 45, 148–149
Allison, Graham 44
anonymisation strategies 217
ANZ Truckometer 117
application programming interfaces (APIs) 94
artificial intelligence (AI) 4, 12, 133, 146
automated public decision-making 45
automatic data processing (ADP) 8
automatic number plate recognition (ANPR) cameras 147

Better Reykjavik website 172
Big, Open and Linked Data (BOLD) 116
big data 133, 137–143, 160, 243
blockchain technologies 12, 214–215, 216
Bluetooth technology 145
bottom-up governance 275
bureaucratic perspective on government data 121
business as usual (BAU) 5
business logic 82
business process reengineering (BPR) 252–253

centralised database for child protection 26–27
channels of appeal 80
checks-and-balances point of view 109
child abuse case study 163
citizen activism 170
citizen-centric government 78, 89–93, 99
citizen-centricity 78, 89–93, 99, 153, 224, 278
citizen engagement 125, 154
citizen-government relationships 58, 81, 83, 198, 203
citizen identity attribution 198, 201, 203
citizen identity construction 198, 199–203
citizen identity fixation 198, 201, 203
citizen identity information 60, 137, 208, 210–211, 233–234
citizen identity integrity 198, 211–216
Citizens Foundation 172
citizens' rights in digital citizenship 241–244
civil liberties 43
clear transparency 109–110
closed-circuit television (CCTV) 30, 147
co-evolution within systems 63, 67–68
communication technologies (CT) 83
complex data 120, 139, 146
complexity of digital government services 14–15, 99
complex public management perspective 42
compression techniques, improvement 12
computer code and legislation 45

284 *Index*

computer processing power 12
conferences online 174
consultations online 173–174
ContactPoint system 26–27
contact services 88
contextual integrity in social contract 215–216
context-relative informational norms 157–160, 212–214
context-specific values 161–163
convergence of information technology 31
copyrights 9, 119, 120
corporate governance 61, 258
correlation *vs.* causation 35–36
country context gaps 262–263
creativity, defined 153–154
credit reputation importance 139
cross-government data sharing and integration 153, 207–211, 216
cross-government digital networks 46
crowdsourcing 178, 182–183
customer-centric thinking 78, 86–87, 89, 94, 98, 278

data: accessibility of 119, 120, 121, 156; accuracy of 155; as analysis method 140; availability and access 119, 120, 121, 156; big data 133, 137–143, 160, 243; citizens' rights to 242–243; complex data 120, 139, 146; contribution to societal change 32–36; defined 32–33; digital divide and 233–236; disclosure of government data 114, 119; easy-to-use data 121; ethics of personal data flow 212–214; forms of 33; government data access 97, 119, 243; health patient shared data 183–184; information perspective on 41, 47–49, 88; informed governments and 143–145; initiatives in 155–157; innovative use of 107; integrity of 198, 211–216; intensive use of 153; issues/barriers 125; knowledge pyramid and 34, *35*; legacy systems and 8, 100, 137, 144–145; primary data 34, 120; privacy concerns 210–211; producer of 34; quality of 155; re-use and redistribution 119, 155; service-oriented data management 126; as social construct 35–36; source of 33–34; statistics and 35–36; structure

of 33; transparency of 53, 155; types of 33–34; United Nations Global Pulse initiative 134–136; universal participation 120; unreasonable effectiveness of 148; visualisation of 155
data-enabled government 78, 95–97
datafication 133, 137–143
Data.gov 115–116
data integrity 198, 211–216
data mining 127
Data Science and Public Policy team (DSaPP) 152
data science applications 149–150
dataveillance 133, 202
deep institutions 56
demand-driven, joined-up government 53
desire for digital government services 98
deterritorialisation 42–43, 45
digital-by-default government 78, 93–95, 227
digital citizenship: citizens' rights 241–244; digital divide 223–225, 227–241, **240–241**; digital exclusion 223, 225–227; digital inclusion 223, 225–227; introduction to 223–224
digital collectivism 170
digital divide: abilities issues 229–230, 234, 236–237; access issues 229, 233–234, 236; data and 233–236; in digital government 227–241, **240–241**; government service and 236–239; introduction to 223–225; knowledge issues 231, 235, 237; skills issues 230–231, 234–235, 237; trust issues 231–232, 235–236, 237–238; usage issues 232–233, 236, 238–239
digital driver's licenses 200
digital economy 6, 9–11
Digital-Era Governance (DEG) model 61–62
digital exclusion 223, 225–227
digital forms of construction 199–203
digital governance system 272, 273, 275–280
digital government: adoption of Internet 78, 83, 90, 97, 250; alternative public management perspective 62–68; citizens' rights to services 244; complexity of 14–15, 99; data/information perspective

41, 47–49; defined 6–9; digital divides in 227–241, **240–241**; digital economy and digital society 6, 9–11; digital technologies and societal change 37; empirical and multidisciplinary understanding of 15–16; good governance perspective 42, 60–62, 109; historical development of reforms 277–280; institutional perspective 42, 55–57; before Internet 7–8; introduction to 4–6, 42–44; networked governance perspective 42, 57–58; overview of 11–14; private sector perspective 42, 51–52; revolutionary perspective 41, 49–50, *50*; short history 6–7; surveillance state perspective 30, 42, 43, 58–60; system whole 62–63; technology perspective 41, 44–47; transformational perspective 42, 52–55; working definition of 8–9; *see also* e-government

digital government strategies: bias toward private sector 252–253; bias toward service provisions 253; bias toward technology 251–252; contextual approach toward 253–254; evaluating outcomes 261–264; governance by 249, 257–264, **259**; introduction to 249–250; leadership 100, 249, 254–257; overview of 250–254

digital immigrants 257
digital inclusion 9, 14, 17, 223–228, 235–236, 241–244, 276, 279
digital natives 175, 230, 239
digital society 6, 9–11, 14, 251, 254
digital technologies and societal change: contribution of data to 32–36; digital government and 37; introduction to 24–25; mutual shaping of 28–32; social determinism 26–27; technological determinism 25–26; technology debate 24, 25–32
digitisation 12, 62, 99
direct democracy 7, 49, 58, 169–171, 174
driverless cars 133
Dutch Scientific Council 148, 149, 160

easy-to-use data 121
ecology of games 28–29
e-commerce applications 6–7, 51

Economic and Social Research Council (ESRC) 29
economic value 4, 118, 122, 133
eco-system shaping 28–29
e-democracy 4, 6–7, 171, 180
effectiveness, defined 154
efficiency, defined 154
electronic document interchange (EDI) 47–48
Electronic Numerical Integrator and Computer (ENIAC) 8
emergence of systems 63–64
empirical understanding of digital government 15–16
enacted technology 55–56
entrepreneurialism, defined 154
environment detecting sensors 148
equality, defined 154
ethics/ethical issues 100, 155, 157–163, 211, 212–214; *see also* citizen identity, privacy, ethics and security
European Union (EU) digital policy 9
evaluations online 174
evidence-based decision-making 153, 209
evolutionary perspective 41
ex ante disclosure of government data 114
experimentation barriers 127
ex post disclosure of government data 114

Facebook 175, 179
fallacies in data 35–36
farmlogs 116
Federal Government Open Data Policy (US) 115
Fifth Estate 58, 170, 181
financial transaction data 136
FIXiT app 92–93
FixMyStreet case study 92–93
flexibility in information technology 31
formal discussion forums 256
forms of data 33
"forward liability" data model 95
Freedom of Information Act (FOIA) 109
Freedom of the Press Act (*Tryckfrihetsforordningen* law) 109
fuzzy transparency 109–110

286 *Index*

Gartner Group 52
general office rules 80
General Services Administration
 (US) 115
GIS analysis 151–152
Global Pulse initiative (UN) 134–136
Going Digital Project 10–11
good governance perspective 42, 60–62,
 109
Google 142, 179
governance by digital governments 249,
 257–264, **259**
government data access 97, 119, 243
Government Digital Service (GDS) 87
Government 2.0 technology 169, 175
GOV.UK portal 87
GPS (Global Positioning Service) 183

hacker concerns 127
health patient shared data 183–184
horizontal integration 53, 86, 89, 145
horizontalisation 45
human expert–based decision-making 155
human resources management (HRM) 86
hybrid governance system 272

identity management systems 243
independent data 33
independent governance board 161
informal discussion forums 256
information and communication
 technologies (ICTs) 12, 83, 147
information and media ecology 176–177
information perspective on data 41, 47–49,
 88
information politics 185
information polity 49
information systems (IS) 13, 52, 145, 207,
 210, 228, 251–252
information technology (IT) 6, 31–32,
 47–48
initial conditions, defined 53
innovations, evaluation of 260–261
innovation support 118, 153
innovative data use 107
"inside-out" perspective 90
Instagram 175–176
institutional innovation: digital governance
 system 272, 273, 275–280; historical

development of reforms 277–280;
 integrative leadership 272, 279–280;
 introduction to 272–273; overview of
 273–275; perspective on 42, 55–57
institutional settings 80–81
instrumental transformation 54
integrated government organizations 53
integrating government 78, 85–89
integration, defined 12
integrative leadership 272, 279–280
intellectual property rights (IPR) 9,
 119–120
intensive use of data 153
interactive communication 26, 53
interactive mapping 135
interactivity 12
interdependent systems 63
International Open Data Charter 126
Internet: benefits of access 224–225;
 citizens' rights to 242; domain name
 policy 84; Fifth Estate and 58; frequency
 of use 14, 30; government adoption
 of 78, 83, 90, 97, 250; government
 organization on 52; inherent
 technological capabilities of 45; online
 privacy protection 157–159; political
 mechanisms on 173–174; socio-technical
 assemblages of 159
Internet of Things (IoT) 12, 133, 145, 148
inter-organizational portal 53
investment approach to welfare 96
issues and barriers 209–211

Jakarta Emergency Management Agency
 178

knowledge issues and digital divide 231,
 235, 237
knowledge pyramid 34, *35*

laboratories of democracy 184
Lapor! website 85
leadership: of digital government 100, 249,
 254–257; by example 127; integrative
 leadership 272, 279–280; political leaders
 5, 13, 37, 255–257; transparency and
 254–255; visionary leaders 255–256
learning by using/doing 50
legacy systems 8, 100, 137, 144–145, 210

legal entitlement 81
legislative barriers to digital government services 99
license-free data 120
logic in digital government services 99
lying with statistics 35–36

machine-processable data 120, 121
mass-listen *vs.* mass-talking 188
mass media 178
meta-data as personal data 210
m-government (mobile government) 78, 85, 278
minimum quality assurance standards for data 161
Ministry of Social Development (MSD), New Zealand 95–96
Ministry on Digital Economy and Society (Thailand) 9
Mobility Marketplace 117
moral power 260
multidisciplinary understanding of digital government 15–16
multiple interactive systems 63
mutual shaping perspective 50
myth of spectator citizenship 182

National Disaster Management System 148
National Science Foundation (US) 7
National Security Agency (US) 110
National Telecommunications and Information Administration (NTIA) 223
nation-state 42–43
nationwide portal 53
needs-based holism 62
nested systems 63–65, 272, 276, 279
network-based production systems 260
networked citizen 168–169, 177, 179–181, 186
networked governance perspective 42, 57–58
network technologies 86, 145
new public management (NPM) 6–7, 59, 86, 259, **259**, 263, 276
New Zealand Customs Service (Customs) 65–68
New Zealand Data Futures Forum 160
New Zealand Transport Agency (NZTA) 117

Nissenbaum, Helen 157, 204
non-discriminatory data 120
non-proprietary data 120
nowcasting *vs.* forecasting 140
NPG model **259**, 259–260, 273

Obama, Barack 114–115, 254–255
objective data 33
objective technology 55
office hierarchy 80
official jurisdictional areas 80
online privacy protection 157–159, 205–206
online provisional driver's licence application case study 212–213
open and transparent government: increase of 139; introduction to 107–109; issues and barriers 123–125; open government, defined 119–122; problems with 111–114; strategies for 125–127; working towards 109–111, 114–119; *see also* transparency
open collaboration 53–54
Open Database License 181
Open Government Declaration 108
Open Government Partnership 108
open participation 53, 182
OpenStreetMap 181
open systems 64, 127
optimisation modelling 137
organizational performance 118, 263
Organization for Economic Cooperation and Development (OECD) 9, 10–11
"outside-in" perspective 90

"panopticon" urban governance 152
participation designs 127
participation services 88
participatory democracy: active citizenship and 118; informational challenges 187–188; introduction to 169–171; issues and barriers 186–188; legal challenges 188; new forms of 179–186; organizational and cultural challenges 186–187; social media use 175–179; strategies for 189–190; systemic challenges 186; technological challenges 188
participatory governance 169–170, 174, 179–186, 188–190, 256
participatory lawmaking in Taiwan 173

288 *Index*

personal computers (PCs) 8, 83
policy proposals online 173
political leaders 5, 13, 37, 255–257
political mechanisms online 173–174
political perspective on government data
121–122
primary data 34, 120
privacy concerns: attitudes *vs.* behaviours
203–209, **209**; issues/barriers 124–125;
protection with digital government
services 98–99; rights of 9
privacy-enhancing technology (PET) 214,
217
privacy fatalist 206
privacy optimist 206
privacy pragmatist 206, 207
privacy victim 206
private sector perspective 42, 51–52
private sector-public sector gaps 262–263
procedure, defined 81
producer of data 34
professionalisation in government 80,
181
public accountability 118
public good 110, 134, 158, 168–170,
180–181, 183, 260
public management 5–6, 13–17, 62–68,
207, 248–249, 256–258, 273, 276
public sector reform 5, 42, 50, **50**, 55–57,
61, 78, 257; *see also* service state
public transport data 135–136
public trust 42, 118

QR code 200

radio-frequency identification 145
rationality-public sector reality gaps 262
raw material 31, 33
raw technology 55
real-time data 140, 146
Realtor.com app 116
re-identification strategies 210, 217
reinforcement thesis 42, 56–57, 69
reintegration in digital technologies 61–62
representative democracy 170, 177
retrospective analysis 140
revolutionary perspective 41, 49–50, *50*
robotics 4, 7, 12, 133, 198
rule-driven government 81–82, 186

security: of digital government services 98;
issues/barriers 124–125; of personal data
flow 214–215; *see also* citizen identity,
privacy, ethics and security
security-enhancing technology (SET) 214,
217
select committees 59, 174
self-organization 63–64
service-oriented data management 126
service state: digital forms of 82–97;
introduction to 59, 78–80; issues and
barriers to 97–100; reform implications
101; traditional to digital-era 80–82, **82**
Short Message Service (SMS) 85, 93, 111
simulation modelling 137
skills issues and digital divide 230–231,
234–235, 237
skills training with digital government
services 100
smarter governing 182
SmartGate case study 65–68
smart government: algorithms in 148–149;
benefits of 150–152; comprehensive
review needs 152–154; concept of 145–
148; context-specific values 161–163;
datafication 133, 137–143; data-informed
governments 143–145; data science
applications 149–150; digital government
and 145–154; ethical framework 155,
157–163, 211; initiatives 151–152;
introduction to 5, 133–137; issues
and barriers 155–157; online privacy
protection 157–159; strategy for 250
SmartStart case study 91
Snowden, Edward 110
social behaviour credit system 201
social determinism 24, 26–28, 49
social media: contextual integrity in
215–216; crowdsourcing 178, 182–183;
defined 169; participatory democracy
and 175–179; transparency in 111
social technologies 47–48, 149, 169, 175,
186–187
social welfare technology 47–48
societal change *see* digital technologies and
societal change
socio-economic background 226,
229, 236
socio-technical assemblages 64, 258, 274

soft accountability 110
Songdo, South Korea 147–148
source of data 33–34
stability *vs.* equilibrium 64
State Services Commission (SSC), New
Zealand 162
statistics and data 35–36
stovepipes, defined 53
Street Bump 183
street-level bureaucrat 81
structure of data 33
surveillance state perspective 30, 42, 43,
58–60, 204, 208–209, **209**
surveys 10, 262
systemic transformation 54
system influences 64–65

Taiwan, participatory lawmaking in 173
technological determinism 25–26
technological perspective on government
data 121
technology: blockchain technologies 12,
214–215, 216; debate over 24, 25–32;
digital government bias toward 251–252;
of expertise 184; Government 2.0
technology 169, 175; issues/barriers
125; issues with digital government
services 100; objective technology 55;
raw technology 55; robotics 4, 7, 12, 133,
198; savviness of 154; social technologies
47–48, 149, 169, 175, 186–187; socio-
technical assemblages 64, 258, 274;
wearable technologies 133; Web 2.0
technology 45, 169, 170, 175; wireless
technologies 145; World War II computer
technology 144
technology perspective, defined 41, 44–47
third-party contractors 124
top-down governance 182, 275
traffic fatality reductions 151
training with digital government services
100
transaction services 88
transformational perspective 42, 52–55
transparency: citizens' rights to 242–243;
clear transparency 109–110; of data 53,
155; by design 126; as event 110; fuzzy
transparency 109–110; leadership and
254–255; in retrospect 110; in social

media 111; *see also* open and transparent
government
transparency-enhancing technology (TET)
126, 217
transparency upwards 110
transparent government *see* open and
transparent government
trust: digital divide and 231–232, 235–236,
237–238; in digital government services
98; public trust 42, 118
Twitter 136, 175, 178
type of data 34

UK Driver and Vehicle Licensing Agency
(DVLA) 212–213
United Nations (UN) 9, 10
United Nations Development Programme
(UNDP) 116
United Nations Global Pulse initiative
134–136
United Nations Human Rights Council 229
universal participation of data 120
unreasonable effectiveness of data 148
uptake of digital government services 97
usage issues and digital divide 232–233,
236, 238–239
US Census Bureau 7

vertical integration 53
virtualisation 45
virtual public space 173
virtual public sphere 169
Virtual Society 28–32
visionary leaders 255–256
vulnerable individuals 151–152

Walzer, Michael 157
wearable technologies 133
Weberian bureaucratic structure 43, 182
Web 2.0 technology 45, 169, 170, 175
Wheelmap.org 181
Windrush generation 233
wireless technologies 145
World Bank 9
World War II computer technology 144
World Wide Web (WWW) 6, 45, 83
written files/records 80

YouTube 179